Bringing the World Home

Bringing the World Home
Appropriating the West in Late Qing and Early Republican China

Theodore Huters

University of Hawai'i Press
Honolulu

© 2005 University of Hawai'i Press
All rights reserved
Printed in the United States of America
05 06 07 08 09 10   6 5 4 3 2 1

LIBRARY OF CONGRESS CATALOGING-IN-PUBLICATION DATA
Huters, Theodore.
Bringing the world home : appropriating the West in late Qing and early Republican China / Theodore Huters.
p. cm.
Includes bibliographical references and index.
ISBN 0-8248-2838-0 (hardcover : alk. paper)
1. Chinese literature—20th century—History and criticism. 2. Chinese literature—20th century—Western influences. I. Title.
PL2302.H88   2005
895.1'09005—dc22   2004023334

University of Hawai'i Press books are printed on acid-free paper and meet the guidelines for permanence and durability of the Council on Library Resources.

Designed by University of Hawai'i Press production staff
Printed by Maple-Vail Book Manufacturing Group

Contents

Preface   vii

Introduction   1

Part I. Late Qing Ideas

CHAPTER 1. China as Origin   23

CHAPTER 2. Appropriations: Another Look at Yan Fu and Western Ideas   43

CHAPTER 3. New Ways of Writing   74

CHAPTER 4. New Theories of the Novel   100

Part II. Late Qing Novels

CHAPTER 5. Wu Jianren: Engaging the World   123

CHAPTER 6. Melding East and West: Wu Jianren's *New Story of the Stone*   151

CHAPTER 7. Impossible Representations: Visions of China and the West in *Flower in a Sea of Retribution*   173

Part III. The New Republic

CHAPTER 8. The Contest over Universal Values	203
CHAPTER 9. Swimming against the Tide: The Shanghai of Zhu Shouju	229
CHAPTER 10. Lu Xun and the Crisis of Figuration	252
Afterword	275
Notes	279
Glossary of Chinese and Japanese Terms	325
Works Cited	335
Index	363

Preface

This study had its genesis in a sudden realization in the early 1990s that modern Chinese literary critics, in castigating what they took as the manifold flaws of the Chinese literary tradition, were invariably more likely to place unique blame on that tradition for what turn out to be, after all is said and done, the universal problems of all literature. That this hypercritical disposition dovetailed with the general post-1919 intellectual denunciation of the Chinese past did not so much supply an answer to the question it raised as to deepen the mystery: what made the Chinese intellectuals of the twentieth century so determined to heap obloquy—far in excess of what any objective measure would demand—on their own social and intellectual traditions?

As I traced this problem, it quickly became evident that this negative perspective did not spring full-grown from the demonstrators in Beijing on May 4, 1919, but rather had begun more than twenty years earlier, in the period of introspection and crisis that followed China's devastating defeat by an upstart Japan in 1894–1895. Looking into the years between that fateful war and the late 1910s, I discovered a true world of difference, where the new and the old intertwined and jostled each other in ways that the later narratives of an exclusive modernity or the earlier discourse of a self-consistent tradition did not seem to allow for. In the interests of uncovering a vision of the intellectual life of a fascinating but indeterminate age, I explored this peculiar crossing of literature and history. The path I pursued was quirky and idiosyncratic to be sure, but no more so than were the times themselves.

The study also entailed looking back at the foundational Western work in modern Chinese intellectual history, once such a dominant presence in the sinological world but now generally seen as remote to the American scholarly community, both in time and historical significance. Partly because of this distance, it is not hard these days to find fault with the pioneering formulations of Joseph Levenson and Benjamin Schwartz for their generally pessimistic assessment of the possibility of a Chinese tradition that may still have signified even after China's realization of the need for fundamental reform. But their engagement with what I think are still essential questions of cross-cultural inquiry continues to compel attention, if only to attempt to come to grips with the faults that a later generation finds in their arguments, many of which have become basic postulates in our field. My inquiry here was also inspired by a large number of works of intellectual history produced after 1990 in China, where the academic world continues to be vitally interested in questions of how the accommodation between China and the West has worked itself out.

It remains to talk a bit about the role of literature in this study. When I use the word "literature," I am referring to a smaller subset of that august body consisting largely of *xiaoshuo*, or fictional narrative, and the prose essay. As Bonnie McDougall has recently argued, a well-justified debate continues about the quality and even the nature of modern Chinese literature. If even the evaluation of the post-1918 "New Literature" is still to be determined, then how is one to deal with the literature of this period in between, traditionally spurned by both students of the modern and students of the premodern? In other words, the novels I examined have never been secure in their relationship with the canon. This uncertainty has posed an interesting problem, but I have begun from the premise of discussing only work that I enjoyed reading. Coming up with standards of evaluation to justify my tastes, however, has been by far the more difficult task. Rather than trying to force these narratives into standard critical categories, I have taken this study as a challenge to the categories themselves, in the hope that works from radically different contexts and times can add to, rather than merely reify, our ordinary touchstones of judgment.

During the course of research and writing, I have incurred substantial intellectual debts, and I wish here to offer thanks to some of the many people who engaged in critical discussion of my ideas and/or gave me the chance to present earlier versions of the ideas set out here. A look at the list will go some way, I would hope, toward convincing readers that an international community of scholars has been forged over the last decade, a development that has rendered intellectual inquiry all the more worthwhile. I thank all of these people sincerely for their help and critiques but absolve them of all blame for whatever flaws the reader may detect in what I have written. I hereby express my gratitude to Cynthia Brokaw, Chen Jianhua, Chen Pingyuan, Chen Sihe, Kai-wing Chow, Milena Doleželová-Velingerová, Prasenjit Duara, Ben Elman, Josh Fogel, Fu Poshek, Ge Zhaoguang, Denise Gimpel, Bryna Goodman, Jonathan Hay,

Preface

Gail Hershatter, Michel Hockx, Hu Ying, Andrew Jones, Joan Judge, Lan Dizhi, Wendy Larson, Li Tuo, Lydia Liu, Meng Yue, Lisa Rofel, William Rowe, Haun Saussy, William Schaeffer, Shang Wei, Xiaobing Tang, Rudolf Wagner, Fred Wakeman, David Wang, Wang Hui, Wang Xiaoming, Wang Yuanhua, Bin Wong, Lawrence Wong, Xia Xiaohong, Xiong Yuezhi, Xu Baogeng, Yan Jiayan, Cathy Yeh, Michelle Yeh, Yeh Wen-hsin, Yuan Jin, Zhang Xudong, Zhou Wu, and John Zou.

I owe a separate debt of gratitude to the many graduate students who have participated in my seminars and especially the weekly Friday-afternoon discussions over the years. They have made the issues relevant and have lent both wisdom and intensity to the conversation about ideas. This group includes Eileen Cheng, Chi Ta-wei, Cong Xiaoping, Steven Day, Gao Jin, Roger Hart, Felicia Ho, Hu Ming-hui, Huang Yibing, Eugenia Lean, Li Li, Jeff Loree, Meng Yue, Makiko Mori, Wendy Schwartz, Vivian Shen, Andrew Stuckey, Mirana Szeto, Wang Chaohua, and Wu Shengqing.

I reserve particular thanks to Ming Feng-ying for both putting up with and encouraging the final stages of finishing this long labor.

Introduction

> China's actual transformation occurred under, if it was not exactly set in motion by, the Western impact (a hackneyed but still accurate description). It made a world of difference, both to the actual process of change and to the perception of its nature, that what might (or might not) have happened voluntarily happened under coercion, that what might (or might not) have occurred through the dynamic of domestic factors occurred under the overwhelming influence of foreign powers.
> Jiwei Ci, *Dialectic of the Chinese Revolution: From Utopianism to Hedonism*

> They [who] are accustomed to sailing on the "Pacific" Ocean can only live through "pacific" days *(taiping rizi)*.
> Harold Shadick (translator), *The Travels of Lao Ts'an*

As Mary Wright pointed out in a landmark essay written almost forty years ago,[1] many Western observers on the scene in the final years of the Qing dynasty were surprised and delighted by the new dynamism they sensed in the Chinese populace and zeitgeist in those years. As the by-then-venerable missionary-educator W. A. P. Martin wrote in the latter part of 1906, in the preface to a short book brightly entitled *The Awakening of China*, "Had the [Chinese] people continued to be as inert and immobile as they appeared to be half a century ago, I might have been tempted to despair of their future. But when I see them, as they are to-day, united in a firm resolve to break with the past, and to seek new life by adopting the essentials of Western civilization, I feel that my hopes as to their future are more than half realized."[2] Wright generally agrees with this assessment in her long essay's comprehensive description of the period, and the scholarly view that this was a period marked by a pervasive "air of optimism" has persisted as a strong minority opinion to this day.[3]

There can be no doubt as to the scope and scale of the changes that ranged over Chinese society and its polity in the final years of the Qing, but the matter of the Chinese participants' attitudes toward them is a question of much greater complexity. To cite but one instance, the initial chapter of Liu E's brilliant 1903 novel, *Lao Can youji* (The travels of Lao Can), introduces a telling parable of the Chinese empire as a foundering ship that has recently become unable to navigate outside *"taiping rizi,"* or the "pacific days," as the author characterized the period before the West arrived at China's doorstep.[4] Liu's perception that Chinese institutions were unable to meet the challenge posed by the coming of the West in the nineteenth century was widely shared by thinkers of Liu's generation and provided the motivation for efforts to deal with this newly perilous situation. With the closing words of his lachrymose preface to *The Travels of Lao Can*—"We of this age have our feelings stirred about ourselves and the world, about family and nation, about society, about the various races and religions. The deeper the emotions, the more bitter the weeping. That is why [I] have made this book, *The Travels of Lao [C]an*. The game of chess is finished. We are growing old. How can we not weep?"[5]—Liu suggests that an optimistic perspective on the late Qing transformation was far from universal, at least among the Chinese thinkers who contemplated the great sum of the problems with which they were now confronted.

In fact, many, if not most, of the ideas that were brought forward in response to the national crisis were accompanied by a pervasive sense of impasse. This sense reflected, among other things, the fear that adapting too easily to alien ways would result in irreparable damage to the very set of institutions that reform was designed to save—that is, a Chinese culture whose continuity as a unified whole could be traced back thousands of years. Given that China at all times held on to state sovereignty and maintained the use of the Chinese language in its institutions, the period in which it became suddenly insufficient to think only in terms of China is thus fraught with an anxiety growing out of a central paradox—a paradox that can usefully be thought of as the "semicolonial," as Mao Zedong put it.[6] The paradox is virtually unique to East Asia in the modern world and describes a situation wherein a nation was obliged, under an indigenous government, to so extensively modify its culture to save it that questions inevitably arose as to whether the resulting entity was that which was intended to be saved in the first place.[7]

In an elegant study of the historiographical ramifications of the 1900 Boxer Rebellion entitled *History in Three Keys,* Paul Cohen wrote that, "in China in the twentieth century, . . . the West has been *by turns* hated as an imperialist aggressor and admired for its mastery of the secrets of wealth and power . . ." (emphasis added).[8] Perhaps the fundamental problem with our understanding of the dynamics of modern China has been our failure to realize the difficult truth that "by turns" does not quite grasp the peculiar moment of Sino-Western relations: the West has, rather, been *at all times* and at the very same time in modern China "hated as an imperialist aggressor and admired for its mastery." The point of this book is to show a few of the ways in which this dialectic has worked, particularly in the crucial period between 1895 and 1919. This area had been a kind of scholarly marchland, which both students of tradition and students of the modern have sought either to claim as their own or, equally frequently, to abandon, deeming it as the exclusive jurisdiction of students of the other period, but it stands in urgent need of its own paradigm and research protocols.

In our own new century, in which the discourse of the transnational in academic cultural studies has become pervasive, it is too easy to think of problems like cultural translation, the questioning of universals, "postmodern" deconstructions of the tradition/modernity binary, and different positionalities vis-à-vis theory as being the unique products of late capitalism and neoliberalism. In fact, as I shall attempt to show in this study, contests of this sort have a long history. The many coincidences among the definitions of the semicolonial and what was later to be labeled as "neocolonial"—namely, the persistence of forms of colonial domination, primarily economic, even after the achievement of formal independence—are but a few indications of the extent of this history.[9] Recent sinological research has, however, most often been given to treating the late Qing gingerly, generally avoiding grasping the nettle of the trauma of accommodation that China underwent in these years.

The late Qing–early Republican period falls into what Chinese scholarly periodization has marked off as *jindai Zhongguo*. This period is, at least from the perspective of the traditional/modern binary that has tended to shape our thinking, located uneasily between "traditional" (*gudai*, literally "ancient"), or China before circa 1840, and "modern" (*xiandai*), a term ubiquitous in East Asian languages to signify the modern in most of its senses (i.e., *"xiandaihua"* = "modernization," *"xiandaizhuyi"* = "modernism"). In the domain of American sinology, at least, this tumultuous age between the First Opium War of 1840 and the May Fourth movement of 1919, has inspired more resistance to its very right to exist as a category of analysis than it has attempts at compelling narration of its characteristic features.[10] Could this uncharacteristic Western linguistic failure to find an adequate figure for translating *jindai* be related to an unacknowledged perception of the period's resistance to the traditional/modern binary, something related, in turn, to what Naoki Sakai has described as the West's preference for being "a supplier of recognition [rather] than a receiver thereof"?[11]

It must be confessed at the outset that the *jindai* demarcation makes no evident sense on its face, defined as it is on the one end by the clear political marker of China's first war with a European power and at the other by an act of cultural symbolism for which the precision of the specific date belies a much longer and more diffuse process.[12] More than that, it seems methodologically squeezed into an awkward zone between the end of the High Qing and the birth of what seems at first glance a fully conscious modernity; it is thus a period that few have ventured to define as a meaningful unit of time.[13] Nor, I hasten to make clear, will I try anything so grand here. Nonetheless, the crucial final third of this eighty-year period, from the mid-1890s until the New Culture movement, has attracted increased attention in recent years as constituting a pivotal epoch. There is general agreement that at the heart of this period lies the convulsive intellectual movement in which the means of understanding the world that had dominated Chinese thought since at least the late seventeenth century was subjected to an unprecedented test, a test that also far exceeded anything that emerged in the last trial of the ruling ideology in the late sixteenth and early seventeenth centuries. The upshot of this process—at least in the minds of those thinkers who have been best able to attract the attention of their successors—was that the old understandings were found, for really the first time, to be fundamentally inadequate.

Prior to Mary Wright's happy rediscovery in the early 1960s of the dynamism of the late Qing, the period had been generally regarded by sinologists as a locus of chaotic failure, even by those who studied it closely—the reason, perhaps, that many of Joseph Levenson's key ideas regarding the paralyzing conceptual impasses that beset modern China are based on insights gleaned during his examination of late Qing intellectual trends (i.e., the failure of the *ti/yong* idea, nationalism vs. culturalism, history vs. value).[14] Even after Wright ushered in an alternative view of the period, the positive assessments that followed were generally made in the name of the late Qing as a prelude to "modernity"—as a place, in other words, where much of the May Fourth agenda had actually been carried out, but which has been unjustly denied its rightful place in the sun. The phrase "repressed modernities" in the title of David Der-wei Wang's *Fin-de-siècle Splendor: Repressed Modernities of Late Qing Fiction, 1849–1911*, for instance, captures the essence of this sense of the late Qing as modernity manqué.[15] This perspective more than likely results from an inflexible notion of modernity itself, as being something essentially universal and invariable in its qualities, but even more fundamentally defined as the Other to that which preceded it. As Benjamin Schwartz noted some time ago: "[W]hile modernity is not contrasted to change—the acceptance of change as a value is one of the earmarks of modernity—the change always tends to be regarded as incremental change within the framework of an established modernity."[16]

Even the recent attention that has been lavished on the period has been conferred in the name of its being the key to the transition between traditional and modern China, or, in Douglas Reynolds's words, as "the first big step in China's sustained turn-of-the-century transformation 'from tradition to modernity.'"[17] Such a focus—notwithstanding its explanatory power over the rich array of events that mark the period—cannot help but contribute to a view of the period as "merely" transitional, as a zone conducive of either residual traces of the old or hopeful signs pointing toward the "modern." Even Wright, in summing up her essay recording the singular variety of the final dozen years of the Qing, remarks that "the roots not only of the post-1919 phases but of the post-1949 phases of the Chinese revolution lie in the first decade of the twentieth century."[18] And Schwartz, even as he seems to open up a new perspective on assessing the past in the passage quoted above, goes on the say that "some traditions, far from impeding certain aspects of modernization, may have actually facilitated them in some societies,"[19] thereby in effect reinscribing a Hegelian teleological perspective of a unilinear historical progression. In other words, the pull of historical teleology has proved relentless, particularly in light of the traditional/modern binary that just does not seem to go away as a characteristic of Chinese studies, whether inside or outside of China.[20]

This is not to say that the late Qing does not tell us much about what was to come (and what had just passed or was in the process of passing) and that the period between 1895 and 1919 cannot be regarded as the site of one of modern world history's most important transitions. It is to ask, rather, that we merely take a momentary step back from placing the age in the strict perspective of an ineluctably emerging and uniform modernity, a modernity "with fixed characteristics," to paraphrase the contemporary Chinese slogan. Ironically, it is only by thus looking closely at ideas that could not be implemented or at things that did not necessarily work out that modernity will reveal itself in its potential infinite variety and allow us to entertain alternative possibilities as to what might have come to into being.

As the Chinese government sought to insert its nation into the neoliberal world order in the 1980s and 1990s, a slogan came to the fore that recalled the attitudinal changes that began in the late nineteenth century and, indeed, served as the rubric under which research on and scholarly compilation of materials concerning that period of Chinese history were conducted. This slogan, "China moves toward the world, the world moves toward China" *(Zhongguo zouxiang shijie, shijie zouxiang Zhongguo)*[21] seems, at first glance, an adequate and appropriately upbeat summary of a salutary process. On reconsideration, however, the formulation increasingly takes on the qualities of Zeno's Racecourse, where each runner can complete only half the distance to the destination at any given time and thus can never actually reach the goal. There is no mention in the couplet of any meeting up or taking hold, thus indicating the question begged in the neat formulation and necessarily involved in reaching an accommodation: should China eventually reach the world (or the world reach China), what will be the range of possible results, or, more to the point, what will be the process by which any result is eventually reached? In not taking up these issues, the slogan seems simply to assume a predetermined end, thereby once again closing off inquiry into alternative possibilities.

Both Chinese scholarship and Western sinology, whether working from the paradigm of "modernization," "enlightenment," or even "socialist revolution," have over the years tended to take for granted the inevitability of the transformation of modern China into something that resembles the modern West more than it resembles China before, say, 1850. Given this teleology, the various sorts of Chinese resistance or alternatives set forth to this process have rarely been given the serious consideration they deserve, at best being regarded as noble rearguard efforts to stave off ineluctable and fundamental change. In recent years, some efforts have been made to derail this notion of preemptive inevitability—notably, Prasenjit Duara's landmark *Rescuing History from the Nation,* with its penetrating insights into the ways in which nationalism polices a Hegelian notion of necessary progress—but there remains a shortage of detailed studies of the process by which the thorny accommodation between China and the incoming rush of Western ideas and practices was actually effected.

How, then, to begin to define the period between 1895 and 1919 as something with its own unique character? It is an admittedly strange beast that starts with the end of the "Yangwu" (foreign matters) consensus in the period immediately following the catastrophic defeat by Japan in 1895. The Yangwu movement—which is the focus of chapter 1—began with real zeal in the 1860s and was marked by the borrowing of Western technology even as most Chinese institutions were deliberately left intact.[22] I contend that the rejection of the comfortable notions of easy grafting of foreign techniques onto indigenous ways after 1895 was largely built upon ideas set out in a series of iconoclastic essays published by Yan Fu in that year, something I take up in chapter 2. Yan Fu's furious search for an unprecedented foundation on which to base reform sparked a new and uncertain era of possibility, which was tempered by a kind of agoraphobic anxiety engendered by the very magnitude of the uncertainty implicit in such manifold potential. It was thus, by definition, a period marked by intellectual and political instability and suffused with blind spots, contradictory formulations, strange silences, frequent deferrals, and outright misjudgments. In many ways, it was a period that can best be defined negatively—as a long process of forestalling or deferring the resort to pat answers that had marked the preceding era, from which Yan Fu and those who followed him sought to differentiate themselves as they worked in this uncertain arena.

The real motivation in sloughing off the predetermined responses that had characterized the Yangwu era, however, was a hard-won and widely held conviction of the failure of the Yangwu movement itself. In fact, in summing up the post-1840 Chinese intellectual world, the prominent Chinese historian Xie Junmei wrote: "In reading [recent] history we discover that in the process of seeking genuine national salvation, progressive intellectuals are often transfixed by new ideas, but equally often become deeply pained by their swift failure, only to become excited anew by their yearning for the next new idea."[23] We can see the process Xie describes beginning to work itself out in 1895. In general terms, the process constitutes the framework on which this book is constructed—it represents an attempt to explain a repeating course of rejecting the old and then invoking the new, and the complicated and contradictory revisions and recantations that arose out of that process.

Much of the complexity that marks the period results from the paradox that these deferrals and rejections were quite the opposite of what anyone wanted; given the virtually universal perception of crisis, speed in coming up with solutions was of the essence for all players on the scene. The bewildering variety of response was also in part the result of an almost desperate new receptivity that brought in too many inputs at one time. The old classifying devices of grafting the new things onto indigenous roots, whether through creative readings of the historical record or assuming a stable Chinese essence underlying the use of any imported new things, had become suddenly discredited in the years after Yan Fu's powerful iconoclastic texts. The resulting taxonomic anarchy ushered in a new attitude toward the treatment of history, or, perhaps better to say, a skeptical distance toward history's possible meanings. In other words, the late Qing and early Republican period was like neither the Yangwu period before it nor the May Fourth period that followed, during both of which history was relentlessly leaned upon to produce both meaning and value.[24] The pressures of the teleology of history could never, however, just go away. It was just that in the years between 1895 and 1919, for a variety of reasons, they were not to be quite as insistent (or, at least, not insistent in quite the same ways) as they were in either the period immediately before or the period immediately following.

In contrast to this receptivity to variety, however, the period was also characterized by an agonism at the center of the whole process, resulting, I argue, in a countervailing tendency to shut off alternatives even as they were being advanced. This occurred because most of the new ideas that set in motion, suggested, or advanced revolutionary notions of political reform and cultural revitalization either did in fact come or were taken as having come to China from the modern West. If from no other source, this agonism was guaranteed by the central presence among these imported ideas of the concept of nationalism, that nineteenth-century European complex of notions that privileged the nation-state as the locus around which were arrayed all the various elements that made up the social order, not to mention cultural identity. Thus, the present study will focus on the ways in which the almost invariably foreign origin of these new ideas—or, equally significant, the perception of their origin as foreign—affected the nature of this intellectual process. This agonism also provided the motive power behind the pressures toward discursive closure that countervailed against the period's characteristic general curiosity and that, in the end, pulled to pieces the fragile intellectual regime that marked the period. In short, the Hegelian imperative to move ever onward was at least as powerful in post-1895 China as it has been in Western sinology.

I hope not to be misunderstood here. I am not saying that every intellectual initiative in late Qing and early Republican China was tinged by anxiety about how it would adapt itself to the new ideas coming from the West. Nor will I argue that Western ideas themselves, because of the vector of their entry into China, necessarily engendered anxiety. In fact, I argue, particularly in chapter 8, that there were many phenomena in Shanghai—to name only the place where the West made itself felt most palpably—in which things Chinese and things Western interacted in a model of productive hybridity. As I attempt to show, however, there was a particular discourse on the introduction of the West and its ideas that was so thoroughly suffused with this anxiety that to analyze it otherwise fails to do it justice. Furthermore, this discourse, I argue, became more rather than less dominant in the years leading up to the New Culture movement in the late 1910s, as new ideas rose ever higher on the horizon. The outpouring of iconoclasm that marked May Fourth, and the defensive moves to uphold Chinese culture that then issued forth in response from men like Liang Qichao and Liang Shuming (1893–1988), seem to offer incontrovertible evidence of this anxiety's substance and of its power to shape the intellectual arena in modern China.

The Era and Its Dynamic

In a recently published book, Yang Nianqun has dissected what has been universally regarded as the dominant paradigm in the Chinese academic historiography of the *jindai* period. According to this paradigm, the age can be divided into three distinct eras, each marked by a progressive realization of the true nature of the problems facing China. In this periodization the first early period before 1895 is marked by relatively superficial technological borrowing that was thought to be a sufficient solution to China's problems with the West. The second period between 1895 and circa 1917 is said to have focused on institutional reform, in which it was believed that China could straighten itself out by transformation of its political and economic institutions. Finally, the period after the New Culture movement in the late 1910s saw the realization that only the most thoroughgoing modification of traditional mentalities would suffice to salvage China and bring it into the realm of modernity. Yang notes, "[I]n fact, the power to explain the reform discourse of the earlier period has been in the hands of the creators of the reform discourse that followed. This circular process has brought about a discursive chain of negative explications."[25] The historicity of the period has, in other words, been shaped by a discourse of political necessity to show an unrelenting progress forward and to repudiate the recent past as having provided the motive force.

In *Rescuing History from the Nation*, Duara sets out what he labels as a theory of *"discent,"* within which a new national discourse at once claims both descent and dissent from prior cultural practices. He argues for the centrality of this concept to the process of "heightening the self-consciousness of this community in relation to those around it." The built-in paradox of at once identifying with and resisting the past thus challenges "the notion of a stable community that gradually develops a national self-awareness like the evolution of a species." At the same time, however, he grants this process an at-least-provisional capacity to facilitate "a deliberate mobilization within a network of cultural representations toward a particular object of identification," even if the "closure" that results will "unravel in time."[26] Although I think this formulation is a powerful analysis of the forces at work in late nineteenth- and early twentieth-century China, my focus here will be guided by the slightly different take that this collision between new and old in China was always already in the process of "unraveling" during any of the "deliberate [intellectual] mobilizations" that were undertaken in this period.

The issue I am seeking to examine here, then, is not primarily to establish whether there were alternative and at least potentially subversive discourses outside the dominant Enlightenment model. There certainly were these, and I hope that my account of a selection of some of the more memorable writings produced in this rich period shows some of the vibrant intensity of these alternatives. But in trying to somehow sum up the import of these various writings, it was impossible for me to escape the sense of a powerful force persistently pushing in another direction, which was a radical departure toward what was perceived as new. This direction was marked by a consolidation of a vision of how the new and the future were to be understood, the most important constituent of which was the ineluctable elimination of alternatives to itself. This vision—which could never quite separate itself from the need to somehow reconcile the demands of continuity with those of the break with the past, as signified by the modern—kept asserting itself largely through its persistent capacity to push alternative possibilities ever farther toward the margins. But in this process, the perception of the legacy of the past invariably turned up as a negative, and anything that became associated with the old came to be regarded as that which had to be left behind. The need to assert continuity was, however, so thoroughly imbedded in the discourses of the modern—mainly nationalism—that a central paradox became lodged in the process of reform itself, in which reform needed to present itself as an internally generated imperative even as it insisted upon rejecting the legitimacy of any possible content to anything marked with the stigma of the past. Thus, the process described by Xie Junmei and Yang Nianqun developed its own inexorable impetus of progress. At the core of this force was a continuous process of outmaneuvering anything that was seen as blunting its momentum, by working up strategies that made its own operation seem inevitable, and everything standing in its way numbingly obsolete.

What I attempt here is to look at various key moments, thinkers, and texts in the pre-1919 period to see how they deal with the question of the exigent need to incorporate Western ideas. What unifies these cultural artifacts is a particular pattern of anxiety that I attempt to trace out, in which the imperative to break radically with the past was precisely that which rendered the paradoxical and insistent need to maintain continuity with the past in some form. The need to establish a new nation, in other words, made the need to cherish that nation's history and traditions all the more insistent, even as they simultaneously needed to be denied. The end result, for all the variety of alternatives taken under consideration, was eventually pressure toward elimination of diversity of opinion, a tendency that ironically recalls the characteristic pattern of the periods both before and after.

Beginning with the work of Joseph Levenson in the 1950s, the agonism of Chinese accommodation has been recognized within American sinology, but it has been read as primarily a matter of deep psychological trauma, a species of acute homesickness over a vanished and irretrievable past. It has, moreover, been taken as an almost completely emotional response engendered by nationalism, something essentially lacking any intellectual content. As Levenson wrote: "[T]he fact that traditionalism had to be 'worked at' in Chinese nationalism, instead of exerting a natural charm, reminds us why nationalism swept into favor. The reason was that the tradition had lost its natural charm; Chinese thinkers, however reluctantly, had lost their faith in its continuing value. And nationalism justified emotionally the departure from tradition, which was already justified, only too well, by intellectual conviction."[27] Levenson here clearly assumes that traditional ideas and practices had somehow thoroughly demonstrated their intellectual inadequacy, and he thereby shows himself to be faithful to the teleological reasoning that Duara questioned. Another of the goals of my study, in fact, is to show that, pace Levenson, these old ideas showed remarkable staying power, and that in many, if not most, ways the intellectual activity of the *jindai* period was characterized by conflicts engendered precisely by the immense intellectual "charm" of traditional notions of social and personal morality.

This study therefore undertakes the examination—and sometimes reexamination—of a number of important Chinese writers active in that liminal period between the war with Japan of 1894–1895, when real accommodation with the West first seemed incumbent upon a solid majority of educated power-holders, and the culmination of the "New Culture movement" on May 4, 1919, when a small group of the highly educated was able to set a new intellectual agenda for China based on an essential rejection of key elements of the national tradition. The rapidity of this discursive transformation is astonishing enough in itself, and it should thus come as no surprise that it contained a deeply fraught set of intellectual initiatives, hesitations, reconsiderations, disputes, and plain contradictions. This study will look at some of these intellectual struggles, focusing on the realm of literature. For a number of reasons, which I attempt to explain below, the field of literature was regarded as a privileged locus of intellectual activity throughout the period, and the various intellectual moves that characterize the era are either implicitly or explicitly set forth within it.

One entirely sensible way to characterize the period between 1860 and 1919 would be to focus on the sense of transformation that permeates almost every significant utterance on the state of China emanating from that era, and particularly to focus on the sense that this transformation was unprecedented in Chinese history. In chapter 1, I rehearse the process by which leading reform thinkers in China attempted to claim ultimately indigenous origins for the ideas they were trying to implement. The peculiar shape their arguments took was necessitated by the fierce resistance from the majority conservative faction at court, who objected to reform precisely on the grounds that it was based on harmful, "alien" ideas. Beyond this dispute, however, the various ideas bruited about during this time share the traits of modernity as set out by Marshall Berman in *All That Is Solid Melts into Air: The Experience of Modernity*. These traits include

> the contradictory forces and needs that inspire and torment us: our desire to be rooted in a stable and coherent personal and social past, and our insatiable desire for growth . . . , growth that destroys both the physical and social landscapes of our past, and our emotional links with those lost worlds; our desperate allegiances to ethnic, national, class and sexual groups which we hope will give us a firm "identity," and the internationalization of everyday life—of our clothes and household goods, our books and music, our ideas and fantasies—that spreads all our identities all over the map.[28]

In China, however, the perception that it would be impossible to exercise indigenous agency over these changes was also a concomitant and constant undercurrent. All these upsets were understood as being the result of momentous movements inspired—or, even worse, enforced—by others, the movers and shakers in the metropolitan centers who, together with their local lieutenants, were seen as exercising a vast and amorphous power over this whole range of bewildering developments within China. As overwhelming as "modernity" appears in the West in Berman's characterization, it was that much more so in the Chinese case when it manifested itself with the added complication of being what Lydia Liu has felicitously called "translated modernity."[29]

I do not mean by any of this to assert a strict genealogy of ideas in which some are essentially Western and others essentially Chinese. I take for granted Liu's powerful notion of "translingual practice," which holds that the complex historical process of the last 150 years has brought about a sea change to all ideas that have been deployed in the Chinese discursive sphere, denaturalizing all of them and making them thus "new" in the new contexts in which they now appeared. The result was a process in which "intellectual resources from the West and from China's past [were] cited, translated, appropriated, or claimed in moments of perceived historical contingency so that something called *change* [might] be produced," as Liu describes it, adding, "In my view, this change [was] always already different from China's own past and from the West, but [had] profound linkages with both."[30]

Although it may have become impossible for us retrospectively to positively identify the national origin or ideas that circulated in China by the late nineteenth century, those who engaged these ideas at the time constantly assumed diverging national origins to be self-evident, and they attempted to build structures of intellectual significance on such assumptions. As is clear in the case of Yan Fu, as set out in chapter 2, these notional attributions are often, at best, highly problematic. This did not, however, prevent them from being extremely effective in galvanizing public opinion and becoming the basis for wide-ranging policy recommendations. In the case of the Chinese intellectuals under discussion here, the impetus to identify which of the ideas they were forced to work with were "Chinese" and which were "foreign" developed into a kind of obsession, which added greatly to the complexity of building an intellectual foundation for proceeding in the new era in which they had come to reside. Ironically, because ideas of Western and Chinese origin so often could not in any sensible way be sharply distinguished, traditional Chinese concepts kept demonstrating their "charm." For if "new" ideas were looked at hard enough, linkages or points in common with the "old" were bound to surface.

Given my assumption of a basic fungibility for most of the ideas that were circulating in this period, it follows that this study is frankly more oriented toward process—or, to be more fashionable, discourse—than toward substance. In other words, I am less interested, for instance, in the question of whether Yan Fu is authentically liberal or not than in why that question itself is problematic and might not be the best one to ask about him and his intellectual trajectory. In this, I assume that whether there is any ultimate convertibility among ideas Western and Chinese is a question that needs to remain in play while we examine the various historical factors, political contexts, and assumptions that provided the dynamism for underlying ideas that may seem on the surface virtually identical. This is not to deny that fundamental commonalities may eventually prove to be the norm, but rather to stress the power that assessments of national dissimilarity had over the writers of the period. It was these perceptions of difference of national origin and their highly complicated configurations within the context of the times that caused the various terms and ideas at issue to be invested with the extraordinary power they often possessed.

In answer to the objection that China had it own "China-centered" modernity that early on was fully capable of charting a consistent course through the difficult waters of constructing the modern, I can offer only overwhelmingly empirical evidence that the most historically significant thinkers in the period between 1895 and 1919 were driven by a constant anxiety that such a modernity was, in fact, not possible.[31] This book is largely the story of the various reflections of that anxiety and its movement over time. There were, unquestionably, "surpluses of meaning," which opened up new possibilities, but, again, this is the story of the alarming extent to which these surpluses were turned into agonized rejections that blocked rather than facilitated the imagination of new possibilities. This is not to deny the possibility of "Occidentalism," or the process by which the ideas of the West were amenable to free appropriation for indigenous Chinese purposes,[32] but just to show how much more difficult it was to manipulate Western ideas in places that had to cope with the reality of Western imperialism. Occidentalism was, then, a significantly more problematic notion than the vastly more pervasive Orientalism, an idea expressing the way in which the overwhelming might of the West enabled it to imagine and formulate the non-West for its own imperial purposes.[33]

This anxiety created a double bind—in which recourse to the West was at the same time mandatory and highly distasteful—that has caused a number of characteristic distortions to the historical record, thereby complicating clean documentation and a straightforward narrative. In a number of cases, for instance, the nature of an argument precluded explicit recognition of the sources on which it was based. A conspicuous example of this is set out in chapter 4, in the discussion of Liang Qichao's silence vis-à-vis the contest for novels on reform topics sponsored by the missionary John Fryer in 1895. Although Liang was almost certainly aware of Fryer's contest, it can only be assumed that the exigencies of nationalism kept him from referring to it in his remarks on the novel that date from 1898 and that at several points virtually echo the missionary's words. A similar lack of acknowledgment is seen in Du Yaquan's failure to mention the possible influence of Chen Duxiu and his new radical journal, *New Youth*, in Du's 1916 about-face on the question of differences between China and the West, as described in chapter 8. When the circumstantial evidence for influence in such cases is so overwhelming, however, the silence itself becomes an important part of the data.

The Centrality of Literature

We now return to the conviction of the centrality of literature expressed by those who worked in that field in the years under discussion. Although it is probably true that every newly reformed field of intellectual endeavor in the years after 1895 saw itself as the key to national renewal,[34] it still remains to account fully for literature's taking upon itself the powerful sense that it occupied a uniquely privileged position. Literature was both the medium that sold itself as being most opportune for spreading the message of cultural reform, and at the same time something that could not be denied its long history within the old dispensation. It thereby embodies the paradox of semicolonial nationalism in its most acute form. As many have argued, Hegelian notions of the progress of world history dominated the Western discourse on the concept of progress in the world for much of the modern period.[35] Central to the Hegelian perspective was the idea that there were certain areas (and, as Hegel specifically mandates, all of Asia is included in this stipulation)[36] whose time had come and gone and that were therefore "out of history." Did it not thus become incumbent upon any zones implicitly or explicitly excluded from the ongoing march of history to somehow demonstrate the ways in which their own histories, if not alive at present, could be brought into being and fused with the universal history that Hegel theorized? The very plasticity of literature made it seem to be the ideal locus of such attempts at historical fusion.

The bulk of this study is devoted to tracing out how China's crisis of accommodation worked itself out in the realm of literature—in particular, in narrative fiction and the critical work that accompanied the very self-conscious transformation of the genre of the novel after 1895. The role of literature in the ongoing project of modernization in Europe has been widely recognized, beginning as early as the late eighteenth century. As Raymond Williams showed in *Culture and Society* and *The Long Revolution*, his seminal pair of early works analyzing the complicated history of the development of modern Great Britain, literature and the arts were a crucial nexus of the social necessity both of communication and of working toward visions of new social possibilities.[37] This function of literature was equally evidently a key concern in China, where public writing occupied a central position in theorizing about the transformation of society and the organization of a new type of state. Beyond its role in communication and creating visions of new possibilities, however, literature served a key role in conceiving of the new nation as such. As Bill Readings has explained, "Of course, the role of the literary had been clearly acknowledged by Schlegel, who claims in his *Lectures on the History of Literature* that it is literature rather than philosophy that binds together a people into a nation." Readings goes on to quote Schlegel: "There is nothing so necessary . . . to the whole intellectual existence of a nation, as the possession of a plentiful store of those national recollections and associations . . . which it forms the great object of poetical art to perpetuate and adorn. . . . [I]n a word, . . . they have a *national poetry* of their own."[38]

The way in which literature in fact provides the most attractive packaging to that sense of history required by nationalism is fairly clear here, but literature also presents itself as the keenest example of the paradox of modern Chinese nationalism. If after 1895 those intellectuals in China who were very self-consciously trying to bring China into the modern world regarded their most important task to be finding some way for their old country to cast itself off from the burden of its own history, how, then, could literature, this core paladin of the nation-state, fulfill its role of affirming identity? How could it fashion itself from the "plentiful store of . . . national recollections and associations" if at the same time reformers had come to regard the denial of the critical weight of this heavy legacy as central to their modernizing project? The late Qing witnessed an outpouring of attempts to finesse this issue, from notions of how literature should be divided generically to the question of how to write the "new novel" that was so widely seen as the key to national mobilization. Chapters 3 and 4 take a detailed look at the world of literary theory, while chapters 5, 6, 7, and 9 examine individual novels to see the uphill struggle of balancing the demands of affirming national identity with those of thoroughgoing reform on the Western model.

Chapter 6 looks in some detail at the problematics of the "semicolonial" and at the ways in which both its practice and its theory are actually more complicated than our ordinary conceptions of coloniality. It should not come as much of a surprise that it was far easier to phrase the need for accommodation than to actually write it out in well-wrought narratives. This core problem is one that would seem to impinge acutely on all colonized and "semicolonized" zones, where everything attached to the old ways had been at least implicitly implicated in the failure of these regions to resist the incursions of foreign powers. Partha Chatterjee's important book on this issue, *Nationalist Thought and the Colonial World,* is significantly subtitled *A Derivative Discourse?* One his central theses, however, is that a successful way around this impasse of finding a satisfactory national identity was the positing of an indigenous spirituality in opposition to the overwhelming material power of the Western aggressor. This solution, as set out in chapter 8, was voiced from time to time in China but just as often was shouted down as an inadequate sham.

There is a further problem here: to what extent were literature itself and its modern manifestations regarded as part of the very problem of foreign origins that national forms were meant to overcome? In a recent article, Franco Moretti has presented the issue quite bluntly, in delimiting what he calls "[Frederic] Jameson's law of literary evolution": "in cultures that belong to the periphery of the literary system (which means: almost all cultures, inside and outside Europe), the modern novel first arises not as an autonomous development but as a compromise between a Western formal influence (usually French or English) and local materials."[39] As chapter 4 explores in some detail, nationalism would have, in other words, special and obvious problems in incorporating the new narrative forms that were so hopefully regarded as the future locus of national identity.

Behind the issue of origins is a larger and even more fundamental question: is it actually possible to represent this process of crushing transformation adequately, including a satisfactory sense of Chinese thought and society in the years before circa 1920, after which Western ideas arguably shaped Chinese discourse decisively? Is the project at hand, in other words, really feasible? The matter of the very possibility of the representation of otherness has proved to be the focus of an inordinate amount of Euro-American critical inquiry over the past several decades. One of the most influential critics in assaying this question has been Luce Irigaray, the title of whose most recognizable essay, "This Sex Which Is Not One," conveys the difficulty of asserting a genuine female otherness in the face of the relentless domination of a male (or "phallocratic") epistemic order. Irigaray sees the need for differentiation to be able to express this otherness extending even to language—"Woman's desire would not be expected to speak the same language as man's; woman's desire has doubtless been submerged by the logic that has dominated the West since the time of the Greeks."[40]

The mechanics of finding different verbal registers, however, pose great difficulties in themselves. One cannot, for instance, simply seek to overturn the ruling discourse, because any such effort would inevitably replicate the monist, male-based discourse that constitutes the order being interrogated in the first place. As Irigaray puts it, "[I]f [woman's] aim were simply to reverse the order of things, even supposing this to be possible, history would repeat itself in the long run, would revert to sameness, to phallocratism."[41] In taking up this problem, with the assumed impossibility of ignoring the ruling order, Judith Butler stresses the power of "subversive repetition" to enable the possibility of "effective inversion, subversion, or displacement *within* the terms of the constructed identity" (emphasis added).[42] According to Butler, the point of this repetition is to disclose the fundamental facticity of basic power relations, something that bears a clear relationship to postcolonial critic Homi Bhabha's notion of subversive mimicry, in which the creation of crises "in the positionality and propositionality of colonialist authority destabilizes the sign of authority."[43] It is important to point out, however, that all of these theories of undermining a dominant discourse point to the fundamental incontestability of the regime they are ostensibly contesting. In the case of the non-Western culture in its moments of becoming subject to the discursive power of the West, the question of the inevitability of the new order is much more contingent, but in ways that, as Irigaray and Butler suggest, have no ready-made mode of expression. I would hope to show here one case of how this process worked out, thereby adding to the inventory of examples of cultural interaction and opening up space for new ways of thinking about it. The example of Lu Xun discussed in chapter 10 is a particularly poignant case of awareness of the fundamentally linguistic nature of the crisis of cultural accommodation. In his chronic doubts about his own status as a speaking subject, Lu Xun embodies the depths of that crisis. This study can only hope, then, to point to alternative possibilities without foreclosing the questions and problems that they raise.

One example of how the contingency of new possibilities keeps getting buried in the trajectory of the modern is the notion of nationalism versus "culturalism," with the latter defined as "the significant unit [that] was really the whole civilization rather than the narrower political unit of a nation within a larger cultural whole."[44] The problem with this thesis, long accepted as the norm in Chinese studies in the West, is that there was never the theoretical possibility of a "narrower political unit" within the "larger cultural whole" of Chinese civilization, for the two had always been, and continued to be, coterminous (to which the continuing obsession over the status of Taiwan offers eloquent demonstration). It is therefore natural that Chinese thinkers could not think of the life or death of one without the automatic inclusion of the other, since Chinese "nationalism's" "larger cultural whole" after the coming of the West was still the one Chinese nation, something that had never been the case with any single nation in the West. Given that the Chinese were faced with an overwhelming binary fact—that is, themselves versus the "West"—Chinese nationalism as it evolved after the 1890s by definition included important elements of "culturalism." This should remind us that, at a fundamental level, even the vocabulary used to describe changes in China needs to be carefully examined so as not to import conclusions based on European usage and historical trajectories.

The impossibility of separating nationalism and culturalism can be best illustrated by considering the discourse having to do with Japan in this period. As Reynolds has pointed out, "[l]ittle of the Xinzheng [1898–1912] achievement could have been attained without Japan, the story's missing key." In fact, one of the major concerns of Reynolds' book is to supply this missing story, the proper understanding of which he maintains has been "retarded severely by academic taboos that bar from consideration the element of Japan, which alone can explain what happened and how."[45] In elucidating why this story has been ignored, Reynolds is in agreement with other scholars in assuming that Japan's long history of aggression and imperialism toward China after 1915 is accountable.[46] What is striking, however, is that even in what Reynolds labels the "Golden Decade" of the late Qing, when Sino-Japanese amity and cooperation were at their height, there is little serious analysis in China—as opposed to exhortations to emulate the political institutions—of the root causes of Japanese success. This paucity of analysis certainly contrasts with the intense scrutiny of Western society and history that we shall see illustrated in Yan Fu's writings, the focus of chapter 2.

Writing toward the beginning of the period, for instance, the great late-Qing moderate reformer Zhang Zhidong (1837–1909) adduces a number of reasons in urging Chinese students to study in Japan: "[The Japanese language] is close to Chinese, making for ease of comprehension; there are vast numbers of Western books, and whatever is trivial in Western learning has already been sifted through [in Japan]. The situations and customs of China and Japan are similar, and [Japan] is thus easy to imitate."[47] The view of Japan here is little more than as the most convenient path to Western learning. Even more striking is that, as we shall see in chapter 10, Lu Xun, writing in Tokyo in 1907–1908 at the height of the "Golden Decade," has virtually nothing to say about the Japanese cultural matrix that is the source of his new, Western ideas. One would think that the example of Japan's easy modernization, its rapid accommodation with the West, the ideas that arose as part of that process, and/or the underlying causes that enabled the Japanese renewal after 1868 would have inspired much comment and emulation in China. There was emulation enough, to be sure,[48] but there is all along a curious silence on Japan as an intellectual model or even as a potential source of original ideas.

Given that Japan had suddenly emerged on China's borders as the most tangible threat to national sovereignty, if nationalism were in fact divisible from culturalism, the newly powerful eastern neighbor would surely have attracted the kind of Chinese attention to and anxiety about the roots of its national success in the period after 1895 that the West did. Instead, Japan seems to figure as nothing more than a transparent window on the West, incapable of adding anything of its own to the complex of new ideas that needed to be dealt with. Japan's presumptive identity in China as a subsidiary part of the Chinese sphere of civilization rendered it invisible to the sort of cultural/national inquiry that marked the final decade of Qing rule, even as the newly powerful neighbor was posing the most serious sort of challenge to China's national existence.

Finally, with regard to conditions in which the Western discursive order had not yet come to dominate, the generational configuration of the thinkers discussed here is significant in itself. Virtually everyone who figures on these pages was born between 1850 and 1881. The accident of birth thus placed these men in a peculiar position; growing up in a world of Chinese learning, they generally became acquainted with Western ideas while quite young and intellectually receptive. The resulting struggle to reconcile the two worlds was thus characterized by an awareness not accessible to their forebears and by a lived-in sense of the tradition that was to become rare in the generation(s) to come—they were in a privileged position to look both ways in full seriousness. In this context, it would be worth comparing intellectuals like both Yan Fu (b. 1853) and Lu Xun (b. 1881) with the young radical politicians that the emissary from Bloomsbury, G. Lowes Dickinson (1862–1932), encountered on a journey he made to China in 1912–1913:

> I met in Canton some of the chief officials of the revolutionary government, the chief justice, the foreign secretary, and others. I was astonished. They were exactly like American undergraduates. Their whole mentality, so far as I could see, was American. . . . This conversion may, of course, be superficial. There may be underlying it an unchanged basis of Chinese character. It is these young men that have made the revolution and established the Republic; they are doing all they can to sweep away the old China, root and branch, and build up there a reproduction

> of America. There is nothing, I think, which they would not alter if they could, from the streets of Canton to the family system, and the costume of a policeman to the national religion.[49]

Even allowing for Dickinson's wariness of things American, this is still a revealing observation and would apply equally well in many respects to Beijing university students in 1919. Although it is no doubt safe to say that in later life most of the men that Dickinson met would reveal a good deal more of "an unchanged basis of Chinese character" than the British visitor could discern at the time, it remains the case that their fathers' generation could never have so serenely and at such tender ages expressed themselves in a way that would have struck any observer as being so Western in outlook and behavior.

All in all, such transformations of character and changes in intellectual disposition as Dickinson describes must be seen as the denouement of a long and complex series of developments rather than simply a sudden "awakening" as to the inadequacy of Chinese intellectual life in the years around 1919. In fact, the extraordinary currency of the notion of a sudden enlightenment originating among the *New Youth* group on the campus of the reorganized Peking University in the years after 1916 was, as Wang Xiaoming has argued, the result of a particularly successful propaganda campaign launched by the group itself,[50] as well as yet another manifestation of the process by which the past needed to be suppressed in the interests of forward motion. One result is that, as Bonnie McDougall has acerbically pointed out, "modern Chinese literature is in most instances a product created by a small number of self-identified intellectuals for an audience only slightly broader than itself."[51] Because of the institutionalization that followed May Fourth, in other words, the culture that was produced and vetted after that time can seem monochromatic at times. The period of intense cultural contestation and diversity of the years immediately before stands in sharp contrast. As the world drew ever closer to China in the late 1910s, however, the struggles over identity and direction were eventually to offer themselves as symptoms of an incapacity to adapt rather than as the profusion of riches they now seem in retrospect. Perhaps the revival of interest in the late Qing over the past two decades both in China and in foreign sinology bespeaks a belated attempt to place in the foreground once again the extraordinary dynamism of a period whose hallmark may be its contradictory stance toward its own diversity.

PART I
Late Qing Ideas

CHAPTER 1

China as Origin

> For domination today is rarely justified through oracles, ritual superiority, or claims to birth rights; domination is now more frequently justified in terms of better acquaintance with universal knowledge and better access to universal modes of acquiring knowledge.
> Ashis Nandy, "Shamans, Savages, and the Wilderness:
> On the Audibility of Dissent and the Future of Civilizations"

> Even in submitting to the dominance of a world order it is powerless to change, nationalism remains reluctant, complaining, demanding, sometimes angry, at other times shamefaced.
> Partha Chatterjee, *Nationalist Thought and the
> Colonial World: A Derivative Discourse?*

The relationship between domestic and foreign learning has been one of the most enduring issues in determining the intellectual direction of modern China. The contention implicit in discussions of the issue as to the degree to which each mode of learning could claim universal value has overdetermined the discourse since at least as early as the mid-nineteenth century. For all the debate, however, until the very last years of the past century the majority of Chinese scholars rarely conceded that China had any real intellectual lessons to learn from the West.[1] This disinclination to take the West seriously persisted in spite of a long history of the use of Western technical knowledge prior to the end of the Qing dynasty, but the pattern by which this use was justified always insisted upon ultimate cognitive superiority for China. Nevertheless, as the nineteenth century drew on and the Western presence became ever more ineluctable, claims for Chinese intellectual precedence became more highly fraught. In commercial, diplomatic, and military interactions with foreigners during these years, China was continually being reminded, literally at gunpoint, that its ways of doing things were not the only ways. And in most matters having to do with the state and its survival (or, perhaps more accurately, its reconstruction), this demonstration invariably seemed to point to the conclusion that the Chinese way was the wrong way.

After China's painful defeat at the hands of the United Kingdom and France in Tianjin and Beijing in 1860, an influential minority among China's leaders became convinced of the need to adopt at least some elements of Western technology in order to counter the ever greater threat from across the ocean. The importation of Western ideas was justified, by a curious discourse, on the grounds that the ideas behind them had originally been Chinese and had moved West to be fully developed in Europe. As I shall demonstrate in this chapter, this notion of indigenous origins of foreign technology was shared by virtually all those who advocated technological borrowing in the period between 1860 and 1895. The ideology of this group of men, now known as the Yangwu movement, has generally been given short shrift within Western sinology. Paul Cohen's summary is characteristic: "This exercise in intellectual gymnastics [i.e., claiming Chinese origins] had the political virtue of disarming the opposition. It had the psychological merit of enabling Chinese to assimilate 'Western' learning without any attendant feelings of cultural inferiority or national shame. Finally, by encouraging a revival of antiquity, it harmonized with one of the most deepseated of Chinese cultural predispositions."[2] Though accurate in itself, this rather curt synopsis has the net effect of dismissing any possible significance to a mode of thought that was pivotal to the period in which it flourished.

The effect of such discussion has been to reduce this thesis of Chinese origins to a simple compensatory device—which it certainly in some part was—and thus to overlook the importance of the complex series of political negotiations of which it was a key feature. Although it will probably never be possible to gauge the sincerity of the belief in this idea on the part of those who advocated it, it is clear enough that it played an indispensable rhetorical role in enabling the always embattled Yangwu minority to further its reform schemes in the teeth of entrenched conservative opposition. Thus it is difficult to ascertain with any precision the degree to which the notion of indigenous origins offered not so much a matter of genuine intellectual conviction or psychological comfort but rather a necessary political instrumentality in the fierce policy debates of the late nineteenth century. One suggestive clue that political considerations dominated in this context, however, is that once the notion of adopting Western ideas became the mainstream intellectual position in China after the defeat by Japan in 1894–1895, the whole discourse of Chinese origins had virtually disappeared from serious intellectual consideration by 1900.³ Probably the most telling indicator here is Zhang Zhidong's 1898 *Quanxue pian* (Exhortation to learning), an extremely influential reform document that in most ways is a continuation of Yangwu ideas and a deliberate riposte to the more radical ideas that began to appear in the 1890s, particularly after 1895. Throughout the first half of the document, Zhang is at pains to make claims for the wisdom of tradition; he eventually comes around in the second half to deny explicitly the thesis on ultimate Chinese origins.⁴

Jesuits Bearing Gifts

Although the pressure to come to grips with Western science and technology reached unprecedented proportions after 1860, circulation of Western ideas within China had a history several centuries old by the late Qing. The Jesuit missionary Matteo Ricci (1552–1610) at the turn of the sixteenth century had brought with him to China a considerable portion of Renaissance science, and it had received a good deal of attention and dissemination. Through much of the Qing dynasty, in fact, Jesuit scientists has been charged with the custody of the official calendar—and the mathematical calculations that made it possible. According to contemporary Jesuit reports, the Kangxi emperor (1622–1722) maintained an intense interest in science and mathematics, studying it assiduously with Jesuit instructors. He encouraged the study of science and even brought the young Mei Gucheng (1681–1763), the scion of a mathematical family, to court to study mathematics under imperial supervision.⁵

Mei was eventually to speculate upon the similarities between the Western techniques brought by the Jesuits and indigenous traditions of calculation, which led him to theorize an account of the relationship that he believed these similarities implied. Upon receiving an imperial notification of the existence of algebra, along with the comment that "Westerners call this the book of *a er re ba da,* which is the translation of 'Method from the East,'" Mei concluded:

> I respectfully received it and read it. Its method is marvelous and can in fact be called the key *(zhinan)* to mathematics, but I privately wondered at its similarity to the technique of *tian yuan yi.*⁶ When I took up the calendar and glanced at it, things became instantly clear: in fact, the names differ but the substance is the same; it is not that they "resemble" one another. So when scholars of the Yuan wrote books, and the astronomical officials regulated the calendar, this is the method they used, and I don't know why it was not passed down to us. We are fortunate that people from afar were drawn to [our] civilization *(mu hua)* and that this ancient thing was

thus restored to us. But via the name "from the east," they will not be able to forget its origin.⁷

Mei's puzzlement as to why earlier traditions of Chinese science had apparently not been passed on was to be shared by many later scholars speculating on the origins of China's need to borrow ideas from the West. By the late nineteenth century, in fact, this idea was to underlie efforts to justify borrowing from the West, on the grounds that such moves merely brought back to China things that had originated there but had been lost in transmission.

Mei's rather subtle affirmation that an underlying similarity signified Sinitic origins was given official status by a pronouncement of the Kangxi emperor himself in regard to the origins of the calendar: "Those who discuss [the calendrical system] and assume that the new [i.e., Western] and the old [i.e., Chinese] systems are different are profoundly ignorant of the source of the calendar. It originated in China and was transmitted to the Far West. Westerners attended to it and did not neglect it, continued to make calculations with it, and improved it year by year. It was in this way that they refined its measurements—no other technique was involved."⁸ For the purposes at hand, what these statements have in common both with one another and with other analyses of the relationship between Western and Chinese ideas that were to follow is their stress on the ultimate Chinese origins of the borrowed ideas and on the notion that the Westerners had been able to keep alive what had "failed to be transmitted" *(shi chuan)* within China itself. The school of evidentiary learning *(kaozheng)*, the most vibrant intellectual movement in the early and mid-Qing, also stressed the failure of textual traditions to be transmitted through the complacent intellectual atmosphere of the Ming, reaching back as far as the Han dynasty to find what the school took to be appropriate textual evidence. Speculation on the atrophy of indigenous scientific ideas, then, demonstrates just how congruent these reflections on Western ideas were with the most important scholarly movement of the Qing era.⁹

The *Siku quanshu zongmu tiyao* (Annotated general catalog of the Complete Library of the Four Treasuries)—written during the 1770s—contains a number of entries on calendrical books that follow this pattern, further demonstrating the consonance of this idea to the most influential thinking of the time. A generation later the prominent evidential scholar Ruan Yuan (1764–1849) expanded the scope of the sorts of knowledge claimed as having its origin in China and thereafter developing more extensively in the West. He added trigonometry and the idea of the rotation of the earth and threw in the notion that the self-striking clock imported into China after the sixteenth century was based on the concept of the

Chinese water clock.[10] More than anything else, perhaps, this pattern can be seen as a response to increased Chinese awareness of the existence and importance of an ever growing body of Western scientific knowledge. Ruan's efforts also mark the extension of the claims for Chinese origins from those things, such as algebra and calendrical calculations, that have a reasonably clear record of indigenous development (at least through the Ming dynasty) to reliance upon the less easily demonstrated (or falsified) terrain of cryptic remarks from poorly understood works of high antiquity that were read as evidence of the existence of advanced technology in ancient China. It was just such claims that were to anchor the discourse on Western theoretical indebtedness to China that developed at the end of the nineteenth century.[11]

Ruan Yuan's taking up of this idea is significant for another reason. From his sponsorship of evidential scholarship through establishing the Gujing jingshe Academy at Hangzhou in 1801,[12] through his years as governor of Zhejiang (1799–1807, 1808–1809) and on to his more eclectic patronage of the Tongcheng figure Fang Dongshu (1772–1851)[13] at the Xuehai tang Academy in Guangzhou during the 1820s, Ruan seemed to have an unerring eye for figures and ideas that either had gained or soon were to gain currency throughout the empire. He was by far the greatest scholarly patron of his age, with a vast appetite for ideas. By writing on and extending the purviews of the discourse on the relationship between Western ideas and their ostensible Chinese origins, Ruan both considerably expanded the range of the discussion and graced it with an intellectual respectability that it might otherwise have lacked. It should be kept in mind, however, that the issues at stake in these years before the war with Britain and France were not of great significance for the Chinese thinkers of the time. For all the increased presence of the West after 1800, Europe was still far from pounding at the gates in the years before 1830, nor did anyone in China imagine that it was or, indeed, ever would. Nor were the great changes to the intellectual order that would eventually be entailed in the effort to build a modern military, and the industry needed to support it, contemplated in these years. The question of where scientific ideas originated, then, was still almost entirely an academic exercise, without the intense political overtones it would take in the years after 1860.

The Advent of Yangwu

In the years that followed Ruan's argument, it is no real surprise that a number of writers echoed it, if for no other reason than that issues of such little import could safely be based merely on such a prominent authority, however untested they were. After China's second defeat at the hands of France and Britain in 1858–1860, however, a prescient minority became aware of the need to come to an accommodation to Western technology, and the shape and weight of the thesis concerning ultimate Chinese origins were abruptly transformed. To the extent that the unprecedented might of Western arms had undermined Chinese amour propre in these years, the notion of the ultimately Chinese origins of the ideas that fostered this technology became an indispensable rhetorical adjunct to the arguments for bringing these ideas to China. For instance, Feng Guifen (1809–1874) in "Zhi yangqi yi" (On the manufacture of foreign implements)—one of the famous treatises collected in his 1861 *Jiaobinlu kangyi* (Words of remonstrance from the hut of examination of the refined)—argues forcefully for fundamental equality between China and the West. On the way to nominating the reasons he believes that China has sacrificed its natural advantages in size, population, and resources, he mentions the following: ". . . China (Zhonghua) [always] had soaring talents accumulated in vast measure; the inventions of the [now assumed to be mythical] assorted worthies of the golden age like Youchao shi, Suiren shi, Xihe, and Xuanyuan were all employed by our people in former times. The various barbarians emerged later, so how could they not have stolen our leftovers? How can [our] people not be equal to theirs?"[14] It is worth noting the hints of anxiety that suddenly appear at the end of Feng's utterance: after asserting with apparent conviction the firm preeminence of China's ancient culture heroes over the Western latecomers, he suddenly shifts to an almost plaintive appeal for mere equality between the two peoples. Someone as forward-thinking as Feng could not, in other words, bring himself simply to dismiss the cognitive might inhering in Western technological superiority.

It should also be noted, however, that this tendency to see all culture as having only a single origin was hardly peculiar to Chinese thinkers of this period. Among the Christian missionaries to China who were considered serious scholars, there was a parallel predisposition to regard the crucial elements of Chinese culture as having originated in the West or, more accurately, the ancient Near East. The Reverend Mr. Joseph Edkins (1823–1905), of a sufficiently scientific turn of mind to have served as a collaborator with Li Shanlan (1810–1882) in translating Western mathematical treatises, was moved by his piety to try to demonstrate the thesis that "[i]t was reserved for Christianity to make known the true commencement of history and language in the narrative of the creation of Adam." In this attempt, he wrote, "To suppose that the Chinese originated independently the arts and usages to which allusion has now been made is to assign two beginnings to a many-branched civilization."[15] Beginning in 1880, the sinologist Terrien de Lacouperie (1844–1894), by origin French but based in London, began to produce a series of writings attempting to adduce philological proof for the Babylonian origin of the

Chinese race. Among his claims was that the Chinese had come to their new land only relatively recently and, in fact, had "only occupied it, slowly and gradually," and that "their progressive occupation was only achieved nominally during the last [i.e., the eighteenth] century."[16]

If anything, the Westerners' claims for common origins were even more sweeping than those among the Chinese: whereas the latter were concerned simply with finding the traces of technological migration, the Westerners were convinced that even such cultural basics as language and religion migrated to China from points to the west. This faith-based assertion of universality had two possible influences on Chinese thinkers contemplating the nature of the relationship between Western and Chinese thought. First, it invariably marginalized China in the great sweep of world development: China in this system could be, at best, a minor offshoot of a more powerful stream, something highly problematic in an environment where Western notions of nationalism were joining rather easily with Chinese ethnocentrism and thereby rendering the need to assert indigenous roots that much stronger. Second, the notion that European civilization itself had an Eastern origin—the ancient Middle East—made it that much easier to push that origin even farther to the east, to China, an approach clearly apparent in the theories of Wang Tao (1828–1897) on the subject.[17]

Perhaps in response to Feng Guifen's lead, the notion that all Western technology was rooted in ideas of Chinese origin first appears as a matter of official policy in a lengthy and closely argued political document that dates from January 28, 1867, and was submitted under the name of Prince Gong (Yixin, 1833–1898), a younger son of the Daoguang emperor (r. 1821–1850) and thus a younger brother of the Xianfeng emperor (r. 1851–1861). Prince Gong had up until the battles of 1858–1860 been uncompromisingly and narrowly antiforeign in his advocacy at court. The influential prince had, however, while still in his twenties, been the ranking member of the imperial family remaining in Beijing after the emperor fled during the allied invasion of 1860, and he had thus been placed in the harrowing position of being in charge of the Chinese military forces that were so catastrophically defeated, as well as of the subsequent peace negotiations with the invaders.[18] It was probably the trauma of seeing the war from the losing side and at first hand that caused Yixin to begin to move beyond his earlier rejectionist position at this time, and through the diplomatic expertise and increased tolerance he gained during the negotiations with the foreigners, he secured an immense fund of political capital that lasted throughout the 1860s. Following the death of the Xianfeng emperor in August of 1861, Yixin allied himself with the imperial regents—the empress dowagers Cixi (1835–1908) and Cian (1837–1881)—to gain decisive power at court.[19] The ambitious Cixi soon recognized

Yixin as her main rival for power and succeeded in having him demoted in 1865. Nevertheless, he still maintained substantial power from his base at the Zongli yamen (Office of Foreign Affairs), a new and unprecedented agency devoted exclusively to the conduct of foreign affairs and founded at Yixin's behest in early 1861.

By the time Yixin submitted his momentous memorial to the throne in January on behalf of the Zongli yamen, he had become the leader of the progressives who sought greater knowledge of foreign techniques, something he explained in detail as he outlined the reasoning behind a briefer memorial of December 11, 1866. The earlier piece had advocated the teaching of mathematics and astronomy (following contemporary Chinese practice, these two subjects stand in for science in general) to young, degree-holding Chinese students. He argued that these scientific subjects be taught by Western instructors as part of the curriculum of the Tongwen guan, an institution founded in 1862 to train translators under the auspices of the Zongli yamen.

By 1866 Yixin did not even feel the need to argue in his memorial on the need for technology—rather he seemed able simply to assume it as being self-evident. He also took for granted that Westerners were more advanced in the mastery of scientific knowledge, which lay at the heart of the technical applications he saw as so vital to China's defense. Only in advocating that such knowledge be included in the Tongwen guan curriculum, and that Westerners be commissioned to teach it, did his case start to become an argument. He began his representation by stressing how commonplace it had become to entrust technological education to foreigners, citing the experience of Li Hongzhang (1823–1901) in Shanghai and Zuo Zongtang (1812–1885) in Fujian in setting up bureaus in which Westerners taught technology as well as the foreign languages. Yixin concluded: "From this, one can see that Western learning is something urgently in need of study, and this is not merely the private opinion of your minister and his fellows."[20]

From this point, the prince moved on directly to an explanation that, by his time, already had a long history. In doing this, he incidentally shaped the argument into the form that it was to have for the next thirty years:

> The Western technique of [mathematics] came originally from the Chinese *tian yuan*, which the West regards as an Eastern technique. Owing to the punctiliousness of their natures and their skill at implementation, [Westerners] are able to innovate, and so they get credit overseas [as the originators of scientific learning]. But in fact it was a Chinese method all along. If astronomy and mathematics are like this, then everything else is like this as well. China created the method and the Westerners imitated it.

> If China is to be able to harness [these powers], it will be because we have realized their [indigenous] roots. [Then], when we encounter problems, we will not need to seek [answers] abroad, and the benefits will be highly significant.[21]

Prince Gong closed his text with two more arguments, the first being that technical knowledge is one of the six arts *(liu yi)* of antiquity, and the second a general appeal to the universality of knowledge, based on the notion that the true scholar will be shamed by any deficiency in his general erudition. This shame of ignorance should take precedence over the shame entailed in confessing a lack of knowledge, and it should be remedied by inviting Westerners in to serve as teachers. "Nowadays," Yixin wrote, "rather than taking our inferiority *(buru ren)* as a matter for shame and, based on this [recognition], to seek [assistance] from others, thus perhaps to overtake them at some future time, we instead simply take the fact that we must learn from others as a matter for shame, thus being content to rest inferior and finally not to learn [from them]. Will this enable us [ever] to clear away our shame?"[22]

At no point in the memorial did Yixin and his Zongli yamen colleagues actually argue that the fruits of Western technology in the form of steamships and weapons were needed to deal with China's new predicament in the world. It would seem that the need even then was too obvious to require reiteration. Instead, the document was concerned strictly with implementing what it took as a basic, if new, requirement of policy. It was, therefore, a piece of political rhetoric designed to persuade more conservative members of the Beijing political community to overcome their instinctive objections to what they would regard as compromise with the foreign enemy. The first and most famous response to Prince Gong's proposal—subsequently much cited and even translated in full into English[23]—was a memorial to the throne presented on March 20, 1867, and composed by Woren (1804–1871), the Mongolian Bannerman grand secretary whose claims to be the guardian of Confucian orthodoxy were widely accepted.[24] The Zongli yamen's careful argument had no effect on Woren's response, for the simple reason that he rejected its unargued premise—that is, the need to accommodate Western technology in the first place. In his memorial, which sounds eerily prescient of some of Mao Zedong's more extreme statements on relying on the national spirit that were to issue forth almost exactly a century later, Woren affirms:

> I have heard that establishing a country rests on valuing propriety and righteousness, not on schemes and stratagems. Efforts toward the fundamental lie in people's hearts and minds, not in skills and crafts. Now, for the sake of trivial crafts, we will honor barbarians as our teachers.

> Even if the cunning barbarians—who may very well not transmit their most essential proficiencies—do teach sincerely, and even if the students also study sincerely, the net gain will merely be some technicians. From ancient times until now, I have never heard that reliance upon technical skills can raise [a country] out of weakness.[25]

For all the passion of Woren's rejoinder, a much longer and more careful rebuttal submitted some months later represents the full flower of the conservative majority's objections to the Zongli yamen's proposals. In it, a very junior official, Yang Tingxi, elaborates on ten points having to do with Prince Gong's case that Yang professes not to understand *(bujie)*. Most of his issues center around the need to cope satisfactorily with the humiliations the West had imposed upon China in the years after 1842. The first point, for instance, a purely rhetorical one, consists of Yang's objection to the prince's contention that the source of shame should be that China contains "scholars who do not know the geography of the heavens," for in Yang's opinion the true source of shame is China's humiliations at the hands of the perfidious West.

In his second point, however, Yang agrees with Prince Gong on the indigenous origins of science, taking issue with the Zongli yamen memorial only on the notion that the Westerners have been more skillful of late in developing scientific knowledge into practical applications. Yang elaborates on the idea already conceded by Yixin that China originated scientific knowledge, and then Yang draws what for him are the appropriate conclusions:

> Of those countries that have discussed astronomy, China's work has been the finest. Of those that have discussed mathematics, China has been superior, and in the discussion of technical matters, China has been the most complete. I am afraid, then, that steamships and machines are not so mysterious and wonderful. Moreover, China contains a vast amount of talent, and there has been a concentration of skill in the principles of mathematics in our dynasty. There can be no derision that our calendar has missed any internal calculations[26] during the past two hundred years, and no ridicule that we have become confused about celestial phenomena. This is because the study of mathematics and astronomy in our time is so superior to what it ever was in the past.[27]

Several things about this statement are striking. First is the startling modesty of Yang's demands upon mathematics and astronomy—there is no hint of the practical demands for technology occasioned by modern warfare that so worry the reform group. Aside from this, however, the memorial's chauvinism is the most remarkable thing about it. It fails to mention any of the widely acknowledged foreign assistance in calibrating the very Qing calendar in which Yang takes so much pride, and, beyond this, generally assumes that China has nothing to learn from the West in this field.

The conservative insistence upon maintaining strict intellectual separation from the West manifests itself even more stridently in a diary entry from Liu Xihong, an official sent as part of the first Chinese diplomatic mission abroad, which left Shanghai for England in December of 1876. The mission was led by Guo Songtao (1818–1891), a man distrusted by conservatives for his open attitude toward things foreign, and Liu had been included in it as a check on Guo's liberal leanings. The chauvinist obscurantism of Liu's response to seeing England is immediately evident in his writing:

> Everything in England is the opposite of China. In politics, the commoners are above the king; in family regulations, the wife lords it over the husband. (At home, the wife makes all the decisions and the husband follows her. At dinner table, the wife takes the seat of honor while the husband sits in a humble position. In all matters of daily life, the husband serves his wife much as the most filial son in China serves his parents. Otherwise, people would laugh at him.) At birth, girls are esteemed but not boys. . . . This is because their country is located under the axis of the earth, so that heaven and earth are in reverse order.[28]

Perhaps more than anything else, the determination to resist the foreign by making them seem as different from China as possible comes through here.

Given the unreflective nativism evident in Yang's polemic and Liu's diary, it is easy to see why Prince Gong and the Zongli yamen felt obliged to base their argument concerning the desirability of adopting Western science into their curriculum on a theory of its ultimate Chinese origins. Although there is no evidence that would cause one to question Yixin's sincerity in framing his exposition the way he did, it nevertheless smacks of rhetorical compromise with the fundamentalist ideology of the conservatives. Given the makeup of the metropolitan bureaucracy of the day[29] and the general climate of opinion,[30] however, this compromise argument most likely represented the only way by which the case could have been made at all. In any event, the ubiquity of this particular formulation of the case does not seem to have done any material damage to the cause for reform in the years in which it dominated debate about the desirability of importing science and technology into China. After 1895, however, a new group of thinkers took Chinese inadequacy in science and technology as emblematic of the need for a more thoroughgoing reform of thought, education, and the indigenous intellectual system in general.

It was only at this point that the theory of Chinese origins came to be regarded as a hindrance to the radical reform this new group of thinkers felt that the country so urgently required.

In this particular struggle, official sponsorship of scientific education did win the day, for repeated protests by Woren and his sympathizers eventually met with curt dismissal from the imperial institution, with Woren even being deliberately humiliated personally. This is particularly noteworthy in that the aging Bannerman had been one of the officials who had come to the loyal assistance of the already powerful Cixi in her only partially successful efforts to limit Yixin's power in 1864–1865.[31] If nothing else, this harsh treatment meted out to Woren demonstrates how powerfully seated were the voices advocating the teaching of Western science during these years, if even the bitter opponents Cixi and Yixin were united in favor of the proposal. Ultimately, the effort to attract a new cadre of highly educated young officials to science studies failed, partly out of personal loyalty to Woren, who had been in charge of the Hanlin Academy between 1862 and 1867 and was thus regarded by many in the eligible pool as their teacher.[32] Another part of the problem lay in the strict limitations placed on the nature of the pool of eligibility itself, but perhaps the decisive factor was that, given the conservative atmosphere that pervaded the bureaucracy, few ambitious young men saw any chance of making a successful career for themselves in this newly sanctioned field.[33]

In looking over the episode as a whole, however, it is clear that success for both sides depended upon gaining political advantage at court. Because the stakes were so high, both at court and in terms of the actual policy outcome, the temptation to pursue the most politically expedient argument would have been difficult to resist. In other words, it would seem inevitable that rhetorical "spin" at some point would take precedence over intellectual conviction. This would be particularly true for the proponents of Yangwu, who had to tread the difficult path of simultaneously demonstrating the steadfastness of their opposition to the Western aggressor even as they advocated learning from him. Given that the conservatives always had the easier task of the local equivalent of wrapping themselves in the flag, the need to meet the patriotic argument at least halfway by insisting on ultimate Chinese origins is evident. In tracking this line of argument in the years following 1867, the highly fraught rhetorical arena must always be taken as a predominant factor. What sort of factions deploy which tropes, and for what strategic purposes, are perhaps the best indicators of the actual potential for change in the years before 1895, after which *xixue,* or Western learning, was to become an insistent and exacting taskmaster.

There is a further, and ultimately more enduring, point to be made about the nature of the argument between the two factions. As the modern scholars Ding Weizhi and Chen Song point out:

> The conservatives were more sensitive to the question of dealing with the relationship of Chinese and Western learning than were the "enlightened" faction *(kaiming pai)*. The enlightened faction never saw beyond the utility of Western learning, nor did they ever consider in any depth what sort of conflicts it would create with Chinese learning. [For their part], the conservatives took the fact that they regarded Western learning as heterodox as the direct explanation of the reason that traditional Chinese learning could never accommodate it.[34]

In other words, the political position the reformers found themselves in made it impossible for them to consider the ultimate consequences of their advocacy, something the conservatives were always aware of, even to the point of obsession. As we shall see in later chapters, the failure to recognize that reform would eventually and necessarily entail sweeping changes to the Chinese system was something that would come back to haunt later reformers like Yan Fu, Du Yaquan, and Lu Xun, as well as a number of prominent novelists. For all their sense of the need for change, the most serious of the post-1895 thinkers found themselves obliged to share some of the concerns over the metaphysics of change that had once been the exclusive province of the late Qing reactionaries.

The most extensive elaboration of the notion of the indigenous origins of scientific ideas occurred during the 1880s and early 1890s, when it was located at the heart of the Yangwu movement's augmented efforts to theorize a place in China for the importation of Western technology.[35] By this time the claims made on behalf of Chinese origins vastly exceeded the scope of anything described by Ruan Yuan or Prince Gong, including as they did most of the major categories of Western science then known in China. The list of scholars who at one time or another came to propagate theories of Chinese origins for Western ideas included Chen Chi (1855–1900), Chen Li (1810–1882), Feng Guifen, Huang Zunxian (1848–1905), Jiang Biao (1860–1899), Liang Qichao (1872–1929, at least until 1896),[36] Tang Caichang (1867–1900), Tang Zhen, Wang Kaiyun (1833–1916), Wang Tao, Wang Zhichun, Xue Fucheng (1838–1894), Ye Dehui (1864–1927), Yu Yue (1821–1907), and Zheng Guanying (1842–1922). This group includes most of the important thinkers of the Yangwu movement, itself the consortium most heartily concerned with reforming China by adapting imported technologies to local needs.[37] What they all shared was the advocacy that the roots of all or some of the most important of the Western sciences, or even the most fundamental organizing precepts of "Western" culture (such as certain religious ideas), could be demonstrably found in the writings of Chinese antiquity. Going far beyond the prior realms of mathematics and astronomy, the group of scientific fields that were classified this way included chemistry *(huaxue),* electricity *(dianxue),* optics *(guang-xue),* and physics *(zhongxue),* not to mention the finding that the fundamentals of Christianity were based on the Mohist concept of *jian'ai* (concern for everyone).³⁸ The list of things borrowed from the West and the citations of the texts demonstrating this are remarkably consistent from one writer to another, both being remarkably widespread and even, as we shall see in chapter 6, being listed in the "science fiction" novels of the period.³⁹

What is more interesting, however, is the elaborate rhetoric employed to explain both how and why China failed to develop its own theoretical insights. Central to this rhetoric were assertive arguments against those who did not realize that turning to technological insights developed in the West was but an extension of indigenous learning rather than the adoption of alien ways of thought. These arguments were knitted together with discursive threads from many of the most important domestic cognitive issues of the times. In his 1893 preface to Zheng Guanying's *Shengshi weiyan* (Blunt words of warning in a time of prosperity), for instance, Chen Chi followed the antiquarian mood of the late Qing by blaming the Qin dynasty for the failure of China to develop the rich lode of theoretical notions contained in ancient texts:⁴⁰

> The realm⁴¹ originated long ago, and order and chaos have alternated ever since. Chaos reached an extreme during the Warring States period [403–221 B.C.E.]; this was carried on by the Qin [221–207 B.C.E.] and heaven was at a loss as to what to do. So, in order to pattern people's minds and achieve the heavenly *dao,* it gave birth to Confucius. But preserving the *dao* requires implementation *(qi),* and these means of implementation cannot be so dispersed such that there becomes no place to maintain [the *dao*].⁴² The Qin administration was fiercely cruel, so China had no place for [the implementations], and the people and rulers of the Roman Empire thereupon arose to fill the gap. Their declarations about the cultural artifacts *(wenwu)* that inspired them always [have it] that they came from East to West. They thus had [only] the implementations to model themselves upon, so that although all their techniques had become highly refined, they had no *dao* to hold them all together. There was, therefore, no century [in the West] that did not witness chaos. [These implementations], which an alien regime⁴³ caused us to be separated from for over two thousand years, are now about to be brought back to China.⁴⁴

In other words, Chen claims that the split between Chinese and Western knowledge was really a gap between theory and practice, and that the long history of Western warfare was due to the failure of the Europeans to realize the *dao* that undergirded the practical ideas they had been so adept at developing. In claiming that the reunion of the long-split *dao* and *qi* will bring harmony to the West, along with technological advance to China, Chen also gives voice to a prevailing utopianism that can also be found in such contemporary thinkers as Kang Youwei (1858–1927).[45]

For his part, Chen's contemporary Wang Zhichun, as part of his explanation for China's failure to live up to its own past, casts aspersions upon contemporary learning in a manner also characteristic of the times:

> Today, those who consider themselves complete scholars *(tong ru)* disdain Western matters *(yangwu)* and consider Western learning shameful. Those who study Western languages and their scripts are held in silent contempt, and then abused, even to the extent of casting them out as criminals against the teachings of the sages *(mingjiao zuiren)*. This is laughable in the extreme, for what is esteemed among scholars is wide knowledge of the past and thorough familiarity with the present. May I inquire whether or not contemporary scholars are masters of the languages of all nations? Or of the scripts of all nations? Even if people inquire about the facts of the nations, can they be assumed to have a comprehensive knowledge? If one is vainly stuck in the triviality of examination-style prose *(zhiyi)*, then one's learning and knowledge of statecraft *(jingji)* will not extend beyond this. But more than that, Western learning is not just the learning of Westerners. In calling it Western learning, scholars take its alienness as a matter for shame. But if they realized that its roots lay in Chinese learning, then scholars would not assume it to be something shameful.[46]

Wang follows this statement with the familiar catalog of ideas originating in China but developed in the West, leading the reader to conclude that the frivolities of the examination system have contributed to the decline in Chinese learning such that it cannot even recognize its own historically documented strengths.[47]

Elsewhere in his preface to Zheng Guanying's book, Chen Chi makes it more than clear that for him the only way by which it is permissible to borrow techniques from the West is to recognize their true Chinese origins. After allowing that time and distance have created certain differences between China and the West, Chen goes on to affirm:

> There is not one fine idea or worthwhile method that has not migrated [from China] and taken root in the West. Therefore, to respect China and to have contempt for foreign barbarians is all right. But to respect China

and to have contempt for the ancients is not permissible. To take Western methods as Western methods and to thus keep one's distance from them is all right. But to realize that Western methods are none other than China's ancient methods, and then to despise them and discard them is impermissible. . . . Nowadays everyone wishes to restore the past *(fugu)*, but out of fear and distaste they shut out and refuse to countenance those ancient ideas that still endure in the West. It is as if we had had a luminous pearl in our household and had lost it on the road. The person who found it behaves unselfishly and returns it to us, but we grasp our sword and glare at him, refuse it, and do not accept it. Is this intelligent or not? . . . I hate the Westerners and I contemplate the old ways; now that the rituals have been lost, we must seek them on the outside *(shi li qiu ye)*;[48] we choose the best and pursue it so as to gradually restore the flourishing pattern of our [ancient] Yu, Xia, Shang, and Zhou [dynasties]. It is only a matter of time before investigation makes this clear. Thus one can say that the Westerners opened *(tong)* China as ordained by heaven, and that heaven is affording us an opportunity to restore the past, to reform our institutions, and to begin the great unity *(da yitong)*.[49]

Remarks like this are striking both in their passion and in the depth of their historical and canonical resonance. The invocation of the phrase "to begin the great unity" evokes once again the fervent dream for a universal utopia that had begun to be developed as early as the 1880s by Kang Youwei. But for all their absorption in the grand narratives of the day, such declamatory statements invariably frame a set of concrete recommendations at once more substantial and more pedestrian in their urgent recommendations for the virtual reconfiguration of Chinese material and institutional life along Western models. A key theme running through these accounts is that China really has not proved itself adequate to the task of keeping up with the world. As Zheng Guanying wrote in his own introduction to his book:

> For a number of years now, those in power have been advocating foreign studies, and the creation of armories, the stringing of telegraph lines, the building of railroads, and the opening of mines and textile mills have been the response. The only [problem] with this is that all the machines used and all the engineers hired have come from overseas. So both those in charge and their subordinates simply follow the old ways and have no idea how to comprehend the [concomitant] changes. The German chancellor Bismarck has said that we know only how to purchase armaments and that we neither emphasize technology nor encourage commerce, thus demonstrating a lack of comprehension of the roots of wealth and power. These are not empty words.[50]

It is, therefore, tempting to read statements asserting ultimate Chinese origins for Western-developed technology not only as mere rhetorical window dressing for advocacy of radical reform but also as a way of dealing with the trauma occasioned by the sudden realization of China's inadequacy vis-à-vis a vastly more competent West. In fact, the young, progressive provincial director of education in Hunan in the late 1890s, Xu Renzhu (1863–1900), gave expression to just such a view (which we will see again in chapter 2 as a fundamental motivation for Yan Fu) in *Youxuan jinyu* (Words for the present from a light carriage), his famous reformist pamphlet of that time: "In recent years, our researches on Western studies have become quite detailed, even if there is still scant discussion of Western political systems in China. In the past, however, Chinese were in awe of Western learning, feeling that it represented the highest ingenuity and that we could not match it, thereby negating ourselves. So some of our contemporaries fabricated a series of forced interpretations to show how all of Western learning had its origins in China. This is simply our habit of pumping up our self-esteem, and it is nonsense."[51]

The awe of the West and the sense that these writings may in fact be compensating for the deficiency implicitly expressed in the writings advocating foreign studies occasionally become overt even in the writings of those Xu is taking to task. For example, Tang Zhen argues against those who would be disheartened by the contrast between China and the West in an essay that was part of his 1890 *Weiyan* (Blunt words): "In general, the greater portion of Western policies and teachings are based on the *Zhou guan,* while the greater portion of their technology comes from the Hundred Schools [of pre-Qin thought]. If you consult the appropriate categories in the *Guanzi, Mozi, Yinzi, Liezi,* and *Huai Nanzi,* all the roots [of Western learning] can be found. Thus to say that present-day China is inferior to ancient China is all right, but how can one thereby recklessly conclude that China is inferior to the West?"[52] Zheng Guanying combines a number of these concerns in the chapter of his *Shengshi weiyan* devoted to the issues raised by the need to accommodate Western learning. After claiming once again that the roots of science and technology were fully developed by the sages of Chinese antiquity, he goes on to lament:

> Since scholars began to devote themselves to empty forms and avoid the substantial, they have swamped their native sensibilities *(xingling)* in the composition of shallow, insubstantial examination-style essays *(bagu)* and in the details of fine calligraphy and regulated verse. They thus led the whole realm toward inutility, and Chinese learning became ever more bereft, while we could not see the richness of Western learning. We did not know that Westerners followed in the footsteps of what we had originally had, and employed it with care and strength; their accomplishment was

so profound as to be unfathomable. It is now the time for "seeking ritual on the outside when it has been lost." . . . Who could say that the skills of the Chinese are inferior to those of Westerners? To take learning that we originally had and return it to China is like taking something from the outer stable and presenting it to the inner stable.[53] If we still timidly hold that the learning of Westerners is something that China has never had, that is to return all credit to the Westerners. If Westerners could read Chinese books, would they not find this ridiculous?[54]

In this passage Zheng neatly sums up the architecture of Yangwu theory: he insists upon ultimate Chinese superiority even as he confesses that China has gone astray for a long, although unspecified, period of time. But at its heart, Zheng's claim for Chinese equality seems filled with a gnawing doubt that could not be more eloquently expressed than by the ironic invocation of foreign opinion to arbitrate the matter of cultural precedence. In fact, as the next chapter will show, those foreigners most familiar with nineteenth-century China would also have been the least likely to grant Chinese claims even to indigenous epistemological equality, much less historical superiority.

It will probably never be possible to ascertain with any precision the extent to which considerations of political tactics make up the impetus for this discourse, although it is a good deal easier to trace the retreat of later generations of writers and thinkers from such hypertrophied claims of absolute intellectual originality.[55] But the Yangwu persuasion does bring to light the basic difficulty in negotiating the advent within China of a powerful new set of ideas and techniques that even then was enabling not just Western material domination of the world but also the capacity for the West to define the rest of the world on its own terms. These Western ideas claimed universality for themselves as a condition of their existence, a claim that would have been hard to deny for anyone who looked very hard at how history had developed in the nineteenth century. To be part of that universal history, China had to find some way to take part in it, and the Yangwu thinkers did have an instinct for claiming the most advantageous position they could justify, however far they attenuated the evidence. But the compromise they developed with earlier theories of outright Chinese superiority seemed, to those who came later, to share far too much with those that flatly rejected any settlement with the West or with its ideas.[56]

But I do think it is important to realize the extent to which the Yangwu compromise symbolizes the problematic involved in the collision between two bodies of knowledge that both claim universality, but only one of which is in an ever escalating superior material position to back up its claims. As Naoki Sakai has pointed out, the very claim to universality is predicated upon subordinating the other of the entity claiming universality,[57] underlining the extent to which late Qing thinkers were on the losing end of a zero-sum game. True as this may be, however, whatever else it did, the Yangwu ideology rejected subordination and insisted upon equality of access to and the transparency of the methods of Western learning. But even as it did this, it had at the same time to accept and reposition the powerful new notions of universality that Western ideas brought along with them. Xiong Yuezhi has analyzed this response:

> Those who advocated learning from the West used the notion of the origins of Western learning being in China to mediate the conflict between Chinese and Western learning and to bridge the gap between them. By transforming the study of Western learning into the restoration of [Chinese] things of old, they reduced the resistance to the introduction of Western learning. This is also the response of China, with its glorious history of civilization, manifesting its backwardness in the face of Western incursion and comparison, but at the same time not being content with being behind. It is a complex cultural psychology that is ashamed to admit it is learning from the West even as it embarks on an effort to do so.[58]

The underlying instability of this notion of Chinese historical primacy became evident even as the ascendancy of the theory of ultimate Chinese origins began to fade. After 1900 a new generation of radical Chinese intellectuals like Zhang Binglin (Taiyan, 1869–1936) and Liu Shipei (1884–1919) began to advocate a diametrically opposite theory—namely, that the Chinese people had originated in the Tigris-Euphrates region and had migrated east, eventually conquering the aboriginal Sanmiao and Jiuli peoples. Based on the theories of Terrien de Lacouperie, which had been translated into Japanese at about this time, the thesis of exotic origins of the Han race represented a complete switch in the notion of beginnings, reflecting the new urgency that marked the period after 1895.[59] If a sweeping concept of Chinese centrality had marked a period dominated by conservative confidence, the sudden advent of a new theory that absolutely denied this centrality proclaimed the coming of a new era of uncertainty. Although the assumption of unified human origins remained the same in this new idea, the complete dislocation of the site of that origin undermined the foundation of previous notions of the seamlessness of piecemeal reform.

Given that this claim of ultimate Chinese origin eased the pain of recognizing Western claims to intellectual superiority, it was ironic that the argument against this Yangwu thinking that welled up after 1895 was based on the idea that it had blunted the urgency and magnitude of the task of adapting Western learning. In other words, the new reform generation saw in the minimizing of difference between China and the West a concomitant danger of minimizing the difficult transformation implicit in these differences. As we shall see in the next chapter, a sense that relativizing the difference between China and the West dampened the urgency for change was to inspire a more radical group of thinkers who emerged on the scene after 1895. Led by Yan Fu, they saw this mode of thinking as fostering a dangerous complacency. What the post-1895 radicals wanted was an idea that would provide leverage for change—change drastic enough to enable China to transform itself sufficiently to hold off ever more exigent Western incursions. And what could be more insurgent than the denunciation of the dominant intellectual formulation of the times, in favor of an assertion of basic intellectual difference that permitted a brutally frank discussion of the advantages of the West? Always lurking in the background of this radical new discourse, however, was a real concern that it might ultimately efface the intellectual autonomy it was ostensibly designed to salvage.

CHAPTER 2

Appropriations
Another Look at Yan Fu and Western Ideas

He who unconsciously designates himself as a native-place writer has, in fact, been driven into exile by his native place before he even begins to take up his pen to write native-place literature. Life having driven him to an alien location, all the writer can do is recall his "father's garden," although it is a garden that no longer exists. He recalls the things of his native place that no longer exist, because they are more comforting to him than those things that clearly do exist, but to which he can no longer have access.
  Lu Xun, "Dao yan" (Introduction) to "Xiaoshuo erji"
  (The second anthology of fiction)

It isn't easy to turn your back on the past. It isn't something you can decide to do just like that. It is something you have to arm yourself for, or grief will ambush and destroy you. That is why I hold on to the image of the garden trampled until it becomes ground—it is a small thing, but it helps.
  Indar in V. S. Naipaul's *A Bend in the River*

Writing in the period between 1902 and 1904, Jin Songcen (1873–1947) and Zeng Pu (1871–1935) began the third chapter of *Niehai hua* (Flower in a sea of retribution), which is populated throughout with transparently disguised historical figures, with this piece of bitter self-reflection about the relative status of Chinese and Western learning:

> Those gathered at the table talked of many things, most of which concerned politics and learning in the West. Wenqing sat to one side and listened silently, with no clue whatsoever as to how to enter the conversation. He was inwardly ashamed, and thought to himself: "Although I

attained the very top degree in the imperial examination and would have thought that my fame would resound through the realm, who could have predicted that I would come here [to Shanghai] and be surrounded by talk of foreign learning? I really never even dreamt such a thing could happen! If I look at things from this new perspective, I can't count on my official degree at all, so I'd better learn something about the West and get involved with foreign learning. . . ."[1]

Thus the authors introduce their highly educated protagonist, Jin Wenqing, to what they claim to be the Shanghai of 1868. That is the year in which, Hong Jun (1840–1893), on whom the character Jin is based, placed first in the palace examination, gaining the coveted title of *zhuangyuan* (*optimus,* or first place in the triennial metropolitan examinations). Because of his new celebrity, Jin is invited by a reform official (a thinly disguised Xue Fucheng) to dinner at the famous Shanghai restaurant Yipin xiang. There Jin is introduced to the other diners, who include such eminent Yangwu personages as Li Shuchang (1837–1897) and Ma Jianzhong (1844–1900). Jin quickly realizes, *zhuangyuan* notwithstanding, that he is out of his depth in this company. The astringent tone of Jin's meditation on his inadequacies, however, no doubt more closely reflects the period in which the novel was actually written, more than thirty years after the events depicted were supposed to have taken place. By the time of this later period, even those who had received the most careful instruction in the orthodox tradition had increasingly come to call into question the authority of Chinese learning. The contrasting, yet oddly consonant, epigraphs above from Lu Xun and V. S. Naipaul together provide a vivid sense of the resulting tension. It is a tension between the ultimately futile wish to restore one's old situation, on the one hand, and the equally powerful need to snuff out its very memory, precisely because of the pain entailed in imagining that which can never be restored.

Jin's feelings of inadequacy, essentially an anxiety about the extent of the range of new possibilities, reflects a persisting paradox about the status of Western learning within China. Certainly by the period after 1895 there was widespread recognition that Western learning would somehow have to be incorporated into the repertoire of knowledge available to every educated person. The generation of Yangwu thinkers prior to 1895 had been content to claim Chinese origins as a kind of import license for Western ideas. Wang Tao's change of heart on the legitimacy of these claims in his late years (mentioned in chapter 1), however, indicates just how threadbare the whole thesis of ultimate Chinese origins had become by the 1890s, although any number of important thinkers still tried to argue its legitimacy. As we shall see, probably the single most important argument underlying the essays Yan Fu (1853–1921) wrote in

1894–1895 that established his reputation as the major theoretician of thoroughgoing change in those years was the denunciation of the claims for Chinese origins to Western ideas that had been the ideological foundation of the Yangwu school since the 1860s. If nothing else, he seems to have regarded these claims as fostering a dangerous intellectual complacency that was a serious impediment to the sweeping rethinking that China needed for developing practical solutions suited to the gravity of to its crisis.

With the discrediting of this rationale, however, came new problems. If Western learning was no longer to be declared a descendent of the Chinese tradition, just what would its new relationship be with indigenous learning, in which the educated classes had invested vast amounts of time and energy, not to mention basic intellectual conviction? Could common elements between the two bodies of knowledge be found and built upon? Or was Chinese learning simply irrelevant to the new regime, as Jin's melancholy ruminations seem to imply? I wish to suggest that the question of the position of Western knowledge became an important—if not the most important—leitmotif within late Qing thought, with overtones reaching throughout the twentieth century. A larger and more vexatious question underlay what on the surface seemed an issue that could at least be framed with considerable clarity. This underlying matter was not so amenable to conscious formulation and was for that reason the occasion for greater anxiety. What seems to come up again and again is a question regarding the genesis of ideas considered fundamental to organizing human society, such as issues concerning the canons of morality or the prerequisites for scientific thinking. How could one go about determining whether such ideas were of foreign origin or instead had a long domestic history? This problem consistently lurked behind and complicated what seemed to be more insistent and more pragmatic questions that were discussed to a much greater extent and with much greater ostensible certainty, such as how technology was to be implemented.

This chapter will set out the basic argument that, at least in the case of Yan Fu—by common agreement the key mediator between Chinese and Western ideas in the period immediately after 1895[2]—no ultimately satisfactory method could be found to balance these conflicting demands. There seemed, in other words, no way to ensure a smooth reception for the inevitable foreign ideas by neatly fitting them into a domestic context. Too great an insistence upon difference—with its clear implication of absolute Western superiority—led to nationalistic backlash, more often than not (as with Yan Fu) a response stemming from further reflection by those who had posited the radical difference in the first place. Claims for universality, however, led to even shriller denunciation of provinciality and downright failure to understand Western knowledge on the part of those who claimed it by ever more radical voices. The denunciation was even harsher of those who attempted to argue with the premises or conclusions of Western ideas.

In this period, then, the question of accommodation became pivotal, in that all other issues kept being pulled into the orbit of the essential insolubility of this core problem. A partial list of the matters that were overdetermined by this central question would include almost everything that constituted the intellectual agenda of the time: How was the new concept of nation to be defined? How were this nation and its people to be renewed? How was a new set of values to be generated that would be appropriate both to new, more perilous times and to time-honored ways of doing things? How were old convictions to be renegotiated in a transitional period? What was damaging and what was good about the old ways? What was damaging and what was good about the new Western scheme of things? And, perhaps most highly fraught of all, how was loyalty to the nation to be balanced against the need to import ideas from precisely those countries that were perceived as posing the greatest threat to China's continued existence as a sovereign entity, both politically and culturally?

It was not as if the issue of how to incorporate Western learning into China sprang full-blown into intellectual debate only in the late 1890s. As outlined in chapter 1, extensive discussion of the issues involved dated back at least to the early 1860s. With China's defeat at the hands of Japan in 1894–1895, however, came a general sense that more-radical measures were needed to cope with the challenge that the West had long posed.[3] In retrospect Yan Fu seems the obvious candidate to have sounded the general alarm. He was a man of Fuzhou who had tested into the newly opened Fuzhou Shipyard School of Navigation (Fuzhou mawei chuanchang chuanzheng xuetang) in 1866, when he was but fourteen *sui*, graduating five years later.[4] He had taken the entrance exam the same year his father died. As we saw in chapter 1 regarding the Tongwen guan's inability to recruit competent students, in those early days of Western learning in China the new institutions offering such training had a very difficult time recruiting anyone of real talent, in spite of the full stipends offered to successful candidates. One may safely assume, then, that for a young man of Yan's educational ambition to have taken this exam was more than anything else an indication of difficult family finances. During his course of study, built upon an English-based curriculum, Yan gained a considerable knowledge of basic science and, after graduation, served tours of duties on two Chinese naval vessels. In 1877 he was sent to England for almost three years of advanced training, time he devoted primarily to the general study of England's strength above and beyond his own technical studies. The extracurricular knowledge he gained thereby was eventually put to good use when he began translating in earnest in the 1890s.

Upon his return from Europe in 1879, Yan took up a series of administrative appointments in Chinese naval schools. He always felt, however, that his lack of a degree from the Chinese examination system hampered his utility as an officer, rendering him voiceless in governmental deliberations. He thus tried his hand at taking the imperial examinations four times—in 1885, 1888, 1889, and 1893—each time failing to pass. As a consequence, he often voiced feelings of inadequacy concerning not just his career pattern but also the quality of his traditional Chinese learning. For instance, as he wrote to Liang Qichao, most likely in 1902,[5] concerning the latter's critique of his translation of Adam Smith's *Wealth of Nations:*

> As for the superficiality of my Chinese learning, it is something my friends have all observed, so I am not simply being modest [when I mention its inadequacy]. I am not proficient at both ways *(dao)* [i.e., Chinese and Western learning], having abandoned one and later taken up the other. Add to this that I took up learning late and had no teacher. Thus, in regard to the classics of the sages and the traditions of the worthies *(shengjing xianzhuan),* I have never "gained admittance through the gate . . . to see the sumptuousness of the palaces or the magnificence of the official buildings."[6] All I have for my pains is some facility at letters *(wenci),* and I don't even have much flexibility at this.[7]

It is worth noting Yan's sense that his most serious claim on Chinese learning lies in the realm of letters, a claim, as we shall see in chapter 3, that was widely shared among the educated men of the late Qing.

The Four Early Essays

Yan's career as a social commentator begins with a series of closely argued essays he contributed to the Tianjin newspaper *Zhibao* even before the Sino-Japanese War was officially ended by the Treaty of Shimonoseki on April 17, 1895. Zhou Zhenfu, Yan's most important biographer and the editor of Yan's work published in the 1940s and 1950s, calls these essays Yan's most significant writings. The first is a piece entitled "Lun shi bian zhi ji" (On the urgency of change in the world), published on February 4–5, 1895. This opening shot was followed in quick succession by "Yuan qiang" (On the origins of [national] strength) between March 4 and 9;[8] "Pi Han" (Refuting Han [Yu]) on March 13–14; and "Jiuwang juelun" (Decisive words on our salvation) between May 1 and May 9. In a letter to Liang Qichao probably written in October 1896, Yan expressed both the urgency and the inadequacy he felt in undertaking the immense burden of reform that motivated the writing of these articles: "Toward the end of the *jiawu* year (i.e., in late 1894–early 1895),[9] just when affairs in the east were tottering *(niewu)*, I suddenly felt that a number of things came to mind to which I simply had to give voice. At that point, the set of essays that included 'Yuan qiang' and 'Jiuwang juelun' were published in the *Zhibao*. But my talents were so straitened and my spirits so weary that I could not measure up to my original intention and the [four essays] that resulted are thus far from being adequate to the task at hand."[10]

In carefully examining "On the Urgency of Change," it is easy to detect—if not so easy to comprehend fully—the basic qualities on which Yan predicates his sense of the need for urgent reform. These consist of a set of complicated distinctions he himself generates concerning social qualities he determines to be definitively Chinese as opposed to those he categorizes as characteristically Western. One of his primary concerns is to hold up to critical scrutiny the complacent assumption of an underlying unity between the West and China, thereby opening new and implicitly perilous cognitive terrain that Yangwu thinkers had always tried to paper over.[11] As will become clear, however, even as he insists upon making radical distinctions, Yan also seems gripped by a parallel—if considerably less manifest—urge to seek an underlying identity related to that which had animated the ideas of the Yangwu reformers on the relationship between China and the West. The oscillation between these two antithetical modes of perception—seeing China and the West as completely distinct on the one hand, or marked by an ultimate identity on the other—creates a tension in Yan's thinking in the final half of the 1890s. This tension explains much of what some other scholars have taken as evidence of either an imperfect commitment to or an imperfect understanding of the values of the new ideas Yan is introducing from the West.

Perhaps the most striking thing about Yan's initial essay is the way in which he begins. He starts off by sharply delineating different conceptual realms for China and the West, a scheme that breaks, as pointedly as possible, with comfortable Yangwu presumptions concerning the ultimate convergence of Chinese and Western ways of thought: "It has been said that of things in the West and in China that are most unlike and, in fact, cannot even be harmonized, nothing is more different from the Chinese love of the past and neglect of the present than Westerners' determination to have the present overcome the past."[12] Yan explains this difference further by linking it to the idea of progress in the West, which he characterizes as the linearity of history that has allowed the transcendence of certain historical problems through time. This approach to history stands in contrast to that of China, where he sees all things involved in a process of perpetually recurring cycles. Yan goes on to trace the origin of this distinction to the motives of the ancient Chinese culture heroes, who, in the face of material shortage, sought to diminish competition rather than encourage ways of overcoming the shortage. In raising the issue of a material basis for the difference and the contention associated with it, Yan hints at the social Darwinian motivation behind his theory. He also effectively preempts the continuing sense of underlying identity that was to make it possible for thinkers to demarcate a Chinese essence *(ti)* that could have a Western function *(yong)* grafted onto it—a fusion credited both at the time and after to the progressive official Zhang Zhidong and his 1898 *Quanxue pian*.[13] A few years later, after it had become popularized, Yan was, in fact, to attack this distinction sharply and explicitly.[14]

In pursuing the effects of this historical difference, Yan narrows them down to a few that have profound resonance within Chinese thought. Two of these are the Western determination "in learning to dismiss the false and value the true, and in politics to curb the private *(qusi)* in favor of the public *(gong)*." That he uses the venerable Chinese concept of *gong* to define the essence of Western morality is perhaps the surest indication of the conclusion he is reaching for here: "There is [however] no fundamental divergence between these two and basic Chinese principles *(lidao)*. They [i.e., Westerners], however, have generally been able to implement them, whereas our attempts at implementation have generally been flawed. This is the difference between freedom and lack of freedom *(ziyou)*."[15] From stressing the differences between China and the West in the passage quoted in the preceding paragraph, Yan has temporized here and allowed himself to come close to finding common roots. What he says, it will be recalled, is congruent with what the Yangwu scholar Chen Chi had written in 1893.[16]

For all their apparent agreement on the basics, however, Yan's differences with Chen are even clearer. For one thing, Yan's momentary flirtation with the idea of consonance between China and the West is not undergirded by the notion that all useful things in the West have Chinese origins. Beyond that, and more to the point, Yan almost immediately oscillates back to a notion of definitive difference by invoking what he regards as the particularly Western idea of freedom.

Yan goes on from this point to catalog some of the contrasts between China and the West that ensue from the absence or presence of freedom, which by now has become the key variable in his argument:

> China values the Three [family] Bonds *(san gang)* most highly, while the Westerners give precedence to equality.[17] China cherishes relatives, while Westerners esteem the worthy. China governs the realm through filial piety, while Westerners govern the realm with impartiality *(gong)*. China values the sovereign, while Westerners esteem the people. China prizes the one Way, while Westerners prefer diversity. . . . In learning, Chinese

praise breadth of wisdom, while Westerners respect new knowledge. In respect to disasters, Chinese trust to fate, while Westerners rely on human strength.[18]

In all, it is a long list that sounds remarkably familiar even a hundred years later. In retrospect we can thus see this to have been a profoundly influential formulation.

What is most striking about Yan's interpretation, however, is something that is deceptively easy to overlook—namely, his redeployment of such binary terms as *"gong"* (public) and *"si"* (private). These terms had always been used to describe the range of experience purely within the realm of Chinese intellectual discourse and, in fact, had often been regarded "as complementary rather than opposing values."[19] And within the moral economy of these complementary terms, *"gong"* had almost invariably been regarded as the valorized member of the pair, a usage that was to continue, as can be seen clearly in Liu E's 1903 masterpiece, *Lao Can youji:* "What [Confucianism, Buddhism, and Daoism] have in common is that in enticing people toward the good they lead them to dwell in public-spiritedness *(dagong)*."[20] Yan, in his essay, however, redistributes these virtues differentially between China and the West, in effect to remap onto separate cultural terrains the qualities that canonical neo-Confucian texts like the *Da xue* (The great learning) had always linked on a continuum.[21] Within this new scheme, the terms assigned to China generally fall in the realm of private or even domestic virtues, whereas those assigned to the West occupy the space allotted to public practice and the virtues of the state. In this redefinition of the concepts of public and private, one can even see here the origins of the gender coding of values and nationality that were to become such a prominent feature of intellectual life during this period and continuing well into the May Fourth era.[22]

Such constructions of diametrical opposition between China and the West had a momentous effect on Yan's early thought as a whole. We would do well here to digress a bit from consideration of this particular essay in order to explore some of the ramifications of such an extreme notion of difference. For one thing, the invidiousness of the sort of distinction Yan is making here between China and the West pervades all four of the 1895 essays. It stands out with special force in a particularly sharply worded—but not atypical—passage from the essay written right after "On the Urgency of Change," entitled "Yuan qiang" (On the origins of [national] strength):

> In the West, equality is the teaching, so the people are ruled with fairness *(gong)* and freedom is valued. Because of this freedom, keeping one's

word *(xin guo)* is also valued. In the East, the teaching establishes fixed principles *(gang)*, so filiality is used to rule the realm *(tianxia)*, and relatives are most valued. Because relatives are valued, one's word is taken lightly. But the defects [of this latter system] run to the extremes of deceit and fraudulence, affecting all levels of society. So [those countries] who live by loyalty and filiality do not survive as well as those that live by relying on one's word. There is thus a reason behind the fact that Western countries are able to have their people love their countries and rulers as if they were of their own [families] and to treat a general *(gong)* war as if it were a private grievance.[23]

Based on his rigid essentialization of China and the West, Yan proceeds to find quite dreadful consequences following upon this finding that the notion of public spirit is the exclusive property of the West. As part of the process of creating such a dichotomy, Yan seems to require himself to disallow the possibility of any sort of purposeful communal activity under the traditional system of Chinese values. And the crux of the issue is that he regards just such communal activity as being essential to the running of a viable modern state. The extent to which this sort of negative evaluation of Chinese thought and its relationship to politics and society dominates Yan's 1895 writings cannot, by the way, be overstressed.

The ways in which Yan's denial of the possibility of a public arena within China either influenced or struck a chord with late Qing opinion can be seen in Liang Qichao's important essay of 1902, "Xin min shuo" (On renewing the people). In commenting on the question of morality, Liang wrote: "It cannot be said that our nation was not early in developing morality. Although this is true, we have developed private morality *(si de)* and lacked in public morality *(gong de)*. If one looks at works such as the Confucian *Analects (Lunyu)* and *Mencius (Mengzi)*—all tocsins to our people and the sources of morality—nine out of ten moral teachings are private morality, with fewer than one in ten devoted to public morality." After citing a number of examples of how this is true, Liang goes on to specify the loci of private and public:

> Because of [these teachings represented in the examples], *one cannot compare the old Chinese ethics with the new Western ethics.* The categories of the old ethics are ruler-minister, father-son, older brother–younger brother, husband-wife, and friend-friend. The categories of the new ethics are family ethics, social ethics, and national ethics. What the old ethics emphasize are matters between one private person and another, but the new ethics emphasize matters between one private person and the group.[24] (Emphasis added)

Liang focuses in here on the *si/gong* binary posited with such finality by Yan Fu. Following Yan, Liang assigns *"gong"*—a term with the deepest of resonances within Chinese history and almost invariably marked as superior to its partner, *"si"*—as being virtually the exclusive property of a Western social and moral order.[25]

Ironically, in positing such dramatic differences between China and the West, Yan ends up emphasizing the centrality of the need for moral revival in a manner quite similar to that of the conservative thinkers to whom he was most opposed. In discussing the Yangwu platform of incremental reform, for instance, Yan criticizes it thus:

> The policies [they] espouse now are simply concerned with wealth and power. Since the Western countries are truly rich and powerful, [they] think that there is no other way than to learn from the policies of the West. In terms of government *(yu chao)*, they wish to establish democracy and a true prime minister; in terms of society *(yu ye)*, they advocate building railroads, opening mines, training a national army, and constructing numerous fleets of naval ships. Such policies all seem correct, and more or less in line with what we need. If, however, we carry them out based on our current way of doing things, and don't change our current customs, then I am afraid that ten years from now the effects will not be limited to just [a continuation] of our weakness and poverty.[26]

In other words, Yan is saying here that a general moral and intellectual revival takes precedence over an incremental adoption of foreign techniques. He is contending that without such a revival, the consequences of merely carrying out a policy of incrementalism actually threaten the survival of the country.

A comparison of Yan Fu's views with some of the statements of the late Qing anti-Western conservatives reveals certain points they have in common, despite the obvious differences in their respective visions of the constituent elements of the moral revival. They both are written in opposition to what they see as an ultimately barren policy of incremental reform, and, as a logical consequence, they both give priority to intellectual and moral agency in the cause of national renewal. A case in point is Woren's famous memorial of March 20, 1867, in which he rejects Yixin's suggestions for hiring Western instructors for the Tongwen Guan (quoted in full in chapter 1).

Although Woren demonstrably differs from Yan Fu and Liang Qichao in his complete rejection of any compromise with the West, he does share in common with them an important element: the uncompromising conservative insists upon a seamless web between the moral order and any political or technical means, even as Yan and Liang base their advocacy on a notion of the irreducible importance of a consistent framework of ideas behind any practical implementations. Yan and the obstinate Bannerman (and, as we shall see, the young Lu Xun) share a contempt for efforts to install piecemeal reform without considering its broader implications, however opposed their respective differences on what that moral order should be and where it originates. It is easy to discern just behind this emphasis on consistency the moral focus that had always resided at the heart of the Confucian political economy.

In returning to the course of Yan's argument as he sets it out in "On the Urgency of Change in the World," however, his conclusion at the end of his list of differences comes as a real surprise. Given his apparent determination in constructing as many differences between China and the West as possible in his list, not to mention his clear implication that the Western ways are superior, it is difficult to know what to make of the following statement: "Since both [sets of things] exist in the world, I really would not dare to hastily declare one superior to the other."[27] On a strictly literal level, this makes sense, for in reality most of the attributes he set out have long histories in Chinese thought. But assertion of fundamental equality has plainly not been his intention here. Given the rhetoric of the rest of the essay, however, with its manifest intent to valorize what he seeks to define as the "Western" qualities, this evaluation reads as if it might be a sop to conservative notions of Chinese superiority. Or, and perhaps more likely, it represents a belated attempt to recuperate equality within a newly constructed bilateral arena after he had just assigned all the positive instrumental values to one side. The net effect of the passage is at once to construct and to undermine a notion of a Chinese "tradition" that diverges from the uses of the modern West at all important junctures. The sudden access of what seems to be nationalistic sentiment that marks his final statement of equality complicates this by adding an apparent ideologically imperative declaration of equality. As Yan seems to frame it here, however, it is an equality without any real conviction to it and, more important, almost deliberately devoid of any positive local instantiation, whether actual or potential.

Nevertheless, we should not dismiss out of hand the sincerity either of his desire or of his conviction that some common denominator could be found between China and the West. The reasons behind his need to differentiate between the two are clear enough. He had long been frustrated by what he regarded as the half measures of the Yangwu movement. He looked with evident disfavor on that enterprise's characteristically piecemeal efforts to develop military or infrastructural strength on the Western model, without any serious examination of the conditions enabling the Western science that had been the basis for the West's development in the technical sphere. And what had made the Yangwu position so unsatisfactory to Yan was that it had so plainly failed: the need to address the long, downward course of China's position vis-à-vis the Western powers was suddenly rendered even more urgent by the recent defeat at the hands of upstart Japan. If nothing else, Yan's accentuation of difference represents an effort to obtain new leverage over an intractable situation. Whatever his deepest convictions were concerning the relative merits or ultimate values of China and the West, the long string of political failures China had endured had persuaded him of the need to differentiate his ideas from the current mind-set, which had so evidently not yielded practical solutions. To a certain extent, then, his denigration of the Chinese element of the binaries he establishes represents a rhetoric of alarm calculated to awaken policy makers to what Yan regarded as their failure to commit to the radical measures that the situation demanded. There is, in other words, a profound and unabashedly instrumental motivation in Yan's turn to the West for political and sociological inspiration.[28]

The three essays that follow "On the Urgency of Change in the World" are, on the whole, even more devastating in their critiques of China and their advocacy of Westernization. But even as they body forth their criticisms, Yan periodically reminds his readers of the validity of a set of ideas that seems to transcend the twin goals of wealth and power that he seeks from the West:

> [N]ational prosperity and decline, weakness and strength, are only relative matters. It is true that from the perspective of present-day China the West is powerful and rich, but to conclude from this that [the West] has achieved perfect governance and maximum prosperity *(zhi zhi ji sheng)* would be completely foolish. What we called in ancient times perfect governance and maximum prosperity was self-sufficiency for every person and family, each household containing people worthy of commendation, and the elimination of punishments.[29] None of the Western nations has been able to reach this condition. In fact, it is not just that they cannot attain it, but, according to what sociologists say, it seems as if they are leaving [this goal] ever farther behind. For an era to achieve perfect peace *(zhi taiping)* the people must have extremes neither of wealth nor of poverty, nor may there be huge distinctions of status.[30]

The reader would be well served to keep in mind the important distinction between power and social good that Yan makes here, something that more often than not becomes obscured by the urgency of his advocacy. In other words, his instrumental need to prescribe the gospel of wealth and power does not necessarily mean that they have supplanted all other notions of morality or visions of how to order the world. As Wang Hui has so compelling observed, Yan seems to have remained committed at some basic level to the ideal—common to both Confucianism and Daoism—of a noncontentious world uninfected by schemes of personal gain.[31]

This underlying set of values may explain why Yan often demonstrates an impulse to pull back from the brink of what would later be described variously as "wholesale Westernization" or "totalistic iconoclasm,"[32] even as he seems at the point of expressing the utmost contempt for what he defines as the Chinese tradition. For instance, in "Jiuwang juelun" (Decisive words on our salvation), he begins by brutally dismissing—as inconducive to a new and absolutely essential scientific outlook—not only the examination system but also the whole body of more substantial learning that constituted the canon of Chinese writing. But at this point Yan suddenly pulls his argument in a different direction:

> After you gentlemen immerse yourself in Western learning and seriously consider it, you will realize that politics and doctrine *(jiao)* in China have more shortcomings than points that are correct. Even the subtleties of our own sages can be established permanently only after undergoing scrutiny in the light of Western learning. In China the point of learning is to reattain one's basic good nature, whereas in the West, learning is for cultivating the self and serving God; *the basic idea is the same.* It is just that in the West the notion is based on improving human life, whereas in China, whenever we encounter a natural disaster, we assume it have been caused by heaven and that it has nothing to do with us. From their [i.e., the Westerners'] point of view, however, we have not planned well, and they assess our guilt such that they even think we should be attacked [for these transgressions against common sense]. . . .[33] (Emphasis added)

Beginning this passage with a denunciation of Chinese inadequacy that is consistent with the overall tone of the essay, Yan suddenly shifts in the third sentence to a surprising confirmation of basic equality between the two traditions. This underlying commonality was one of the "subtleties" hidden by centuries of misrule by tyrants ("from the Qin on, those who have ruled China have been those particularly violent and aggressive and particularly adept at robbery"[34]). As soon as he announces his idea of a fundamental likeness between Chinese and the West, however, he just as suddenly returns to a focus on the differences in implementation of the ideal. His concern with this point seems to originate in an evident anxiety concerning the harsh judgment of Western onlookers regarding China's failure to live up to the norms of the modern (Western) state. Yan seems, in other words, uncomfortable with both positions on the extremes, but he cannot appear to find any way to mediate between them.

Perhaps Yan's final word in his 1895 essays on the question of difference between China and the West comes toward the end of "Decisive

Words on Our Salvation," where he excoriates those he sees as worshipping the past so much as to read all Western ideas as being ultimately of Chinese origin:

> Recently there has been a group of those who consider themselves to be persons of distinction *(mingliu)* who take up merely the idle talk about the various branches of Western science *(gezhi)* without ever delving into the substance. In an effort to promote themselves and put down others and to boast of their learning and discernment, they hunt around for what amount to clichés in our ancient books, claiming that Western learning is something that China already had and that there is simply nothing new about it.

After listing a number of examples of what he regards as tendentious claims of Chinese ancestry (for other instances of the sort of thing he lists, see chapter 1 above) for Western science, Yan concludes:

> In other words, [these statements as a whole constitute] a boasting so endless that it would be almost impossible to enumerate it all. I won't go into the question of whether the instances they are referring to actually work or not, but even if what they say turns out to be factual, is this not the same as to arrogantly praise a rough-hewn chunk of wood as superior to a great warship, or to disesteem an elaborate chariot in favor of the crudest of wheels? In what way could this possibly serve to open people's eyes? It is simply a matter for the greatest shame.[35]

Yan's frustration at those who complacently claimed and boasted of Chinese origins for Western technology is more than evident here. For all his invidious comparisons, however, he in fact seems to suspend judgment on the important question as to whether the extravagant claims of ultimate Chinese origin advanced by the Yangwu school are empirically demonstrable or not. Instead, his animus is directed at the utility of the arguments in furthering the greater cause of reform. In other words, he meets the Yangwu thinkers on their own turf, on the very matter of decisions about relative utility that are arguably their original point of departure. Yan's ultimate position seems to be that if resting on one's laurels militates against "opening people's eyes," one has no choice but to castigate complacency in the harshest terms.

Second Thoughts

In spite of revealing moments of temporizing on the key question of cultural difference, Yan in these early essays was clearly driven more by a need to establish the difference between the West and China than by a need to seek an equation. In the preface to his translation of Thomas Huxley's *Evolution and Ethics*—which dates from the end of 1896, only a year and a half after his *Zhibao* essays were published—Yan seems suddenly determined to reverse course and to emphasize just how much Chinese and Western thinkers have in common. While protesting several times that he is not trying to ally with the discredited sinocentrism of the Yangwu reformers or to "make forced interpretations of our [own role],"[36] Yan does insist that the roots of a number of important scientific ideas can be found in the Chinese classics. In fact, he goes a bit further: "In the past two hundred years European academic knowledge has far surpassed anything in the ancient period. In establishing principles and rules, they [the Europeans] have reached the utmost and are not subject to challenge. But the insights of our own ancients always preceded theirs, and this is no forced interpretation or self-promotion on my part."[37] At this point, Yan seems to consider that gaining knowledge of how Western learning developed these ideas not only reveals the rich germ contained within indigenous thinking but also shows how later thinkers failed to expand upon profound ideas that would have led to science, had anyone been furnished with the requisite empirical curiosity:

> In China now the Six Classics [guide us] as the sun and moon do heaven and as the rivers and streams frame the earth. Among the Six, Confucius most respected the *Changes (Yi jing)* and the *Spring and Autumn Annals (Chunqiu)*. Sima Qian said that "the *Changes* are based in the hidden and arrive at the manifest, while the *Spring and Autumn Annals* push from the obvious back to the hidden."[38] These are the most exquisite words ever uttered in our realm *(tianxia)*. Originally, I thought that "based in the hidden and arriving at the manifest" was merely a reading of the trigrams used in augury, and that "pushing from the obvious back to the hidden" referred only to moral judgments on human activity. When, however, I read about the Western study of logic, I saw that in regard to the investigation of things and the extension of knowledge, [these two ideas] contained the techniques of induction and deduction. . . . [When I read this,] I pushed the book away, stood up, and said: "This is it! This is none other than the learning of the *Changes* and the *Spring and Autumn Annals*." What Sima Qian called "based in the hidden and arriving at the manifest" is deduction, and what he called "pushing from the obvious back to the hidden" is induction. His words as much as proclaim it. These are the two most important techniques in the investigation of physical matter, and the failure of later scholars to expand upon and use these [insights] is simply a result of their failure to inquire further into these techniques.[39]

Having established this discovery, however, Yan immediately becomes embittered at the failure of later Chinese to develop these ideas:

"The ancients originated [the ideas], but later men could not continue them. The ancients set out the great principles, but later men could not refine them. [We] are thus the equivalent of an unlearned, untempered, and unskilled people. Our ancestors may be sages, but what good does this do their ignorant descendants?" Yan also seems to realize how close how he had come to Yangwu theorizing about ultimate Chinese origins. He thus takes special care to deny that interpretation: "Although this [i.e., that certain ideas can be found in China earlier than they can be found in the West] is the case, to develop from this fact the idea that all their [Westerners'] discoveries were things we had already, or even that their learning all came from the East, is simply not in accord with reality. In fact, it is simply something we can use to deceive ourselves."[40] Again, even when Yan is in a mood to grant the Chinese tradition more validity in its invention of important ideas, he hedges himself in with his own brusque qualifications.

Yan thus seems to trap himself by an apparent inability either to imagine a situation in which the Western ideas he is so eager to introduce lack underlying similarities to indigenous ideas on the one hand, or to accept that the ideas are indeed similar on the other. In so doing, Yan in effect becomes the first enunciator of a new discourse of anxiety that was to become widespread in the twentieth century. The dominant premise in this discourse has been that certain key Western ideas were superior and that China could not do without importing them. At the same time, however, there has always been an equally steady undercurrent insisting on reciprocity—that there must be some sort of equality between the intellectual traditions of China and the West if Western ideas are to be able to flourish there. If this issue is, in fact, as important as I claim it to be, it is equally significant to be able to trace the dynamics of how it has worked itself out. Those who have studied this issue, both in China and the West, have tended—as Yan does when he makes policy recommendations—to frame their arguments within an unquestioned assumption of the simple superiority of Western ideas. This has been true whether consciously enunciated or not, or whether the matter at hand is the metaphysics of religion or an analysis of the modern enlightenment. And it must be said that if the conversation is premised on the needs of the modern state, that assumption is perhaps inescapable. But, as was the case with Yan, an underlying discomfort has always accompanied the very universality of the assumption in China, awareness of which has produced a variety of explanations for why this assumption of Western superiority seems at once so irresistible and so hard to digest.

Joseph Levenson, for instance, in the course of his meditations on Chinese history posited a series of dualisms that he took as the master tropes of Chinese intellectual and political life. Perhaps the most important of these for the modern period was the universal/particular binary. In the spirit of the times in which he wrote, Levenson built his argument on the unquestioned assumption that the Western discourse had always been the universal one. Thus, the Chinese share in ideas raised by various thinkers as compelling universals could be nothing more than simply the psychological fallout of an intellectual system that had lost its integrity and fundamental intellectual appeal. As Levenson wrote of Cai Yuanpei (1868–1940), an educator and the builder of the modern Beijing University:

> [Cai's] theory, then—"best in East and West"—with its surface commitment to general validity alone, but its inner, perhaps defeatist commitment to a share in validity for the historically Chinese, was an incantation which some nationalists used to stave off suspicion that traditional Chinese civilization was petering out, and in no condition to set the terms of its modification. As such, it hastened the day when the tradition's ruin could no longer be concealed.[41]

The assumption here—that traditional ideas and practices had somehow simply lost what Levenson, in the passage quoted in the introduction to the present book, referred to as their "charm"—begs the question of why this situation came about in the first place. Was it, as Levenson implies when he uses the phrase "Chinese civilization was petering out," merely that the marketplace of ideas had guaranteed the transcendent allure of the Western, the "new"? If this is the case, then Levenson's conclusion—that the invocation of Chinese ideas was invariably a kind of psychological compensation brought about by what was at base a sentimental attachment to a notion of national identity—becomes the only explanation that makes any real sense.

But before we too readily concede this, we would do well to consider another point or two. First, it is always important to remind ourselves that imperialism, rather than some abstract coming to awareness of which set of ideas was superior, provided the real motive force behind the reconsideration of "tradition." Even "On the Urgency of Change in the World," the 1895 essay in which Yan Fu insists upon cleanly dividing up ideas between China and the West in a way that always seems to advantage the West, contains a passage that provides a powerful insight into his underlying motives:

> When the Westerners first came, bringing with them immoral things that did harm to people [i.e., opium], and took up arms against us, this was not only a source of pain to those of us who were informed; it was then and remains even today a source of shame to the residents of their capital

cities. At the time, China, which had enjoyed the protection of a series of sagacious rulers, and with its vast expanse of territory, was enjoying a regime of unprecedented political and cultural prosperity. And when we looked about the world, we thought there were none nobler among the human race than we. Then suddenly one day a group of island barbarians wearing wild clothes, with a birdlike language and animal-like faces, sailed to our shores from thousands of miles away and knocked at our gates, requesting access. When they failed to attain their aims, they breached our coastal defenses, imprisoned the officials of our land, and even burned the palaces of our emperor. At the time the only reason we did not devour their flesh and sleep upon their hides was that our power was insufficient.[42]

If this passage is contrasted with the praise of Western things that constitutes the overwhelming majority of these first four essays, it would be possible to dismiss it as simply a rhetorical summary of mid-nineteenth-century educated opinion, even one that is offered with a certain amount of irony. But if we place it beside Yan's almost ecstatic account of his discovery of a protoscientific method while reading the *Shiji*, another interpretation suggests itself. Perhaps the old—whether conceived of as a set of ideas, a set of social practices, or some combination of the two—does exert a real "charm," so great as to require (as Naipaul's Indar suggests) conscious and painful suppression in the interests of immanent demands of utility and the construction of a viable nation-state.

Yan Fu in Retrospect

As Yan Fu's rather modest invocation of his "facility at letters" suggests, he was greatly concerned with the elements of Chinese prose style, something immediately evident in his elaborate use of allusion, his arguments built from textual precedent, and his exploration of the full range of Chinese history precedent. In fact, his deep attachment to the tradition of Chinese writing represents the intensity of his involvement with Chinese history as a whole and evokes some of the contemporary pressures to keep Chinese history alive or, perhaps better said, to revivify it. The question of attitudes toward Chinese history in China past and present has been a vexatious one for scholars. The general Western sense in the age of imperialism that no real history existed outside the European orbit has been pithily summed up by Hegel ("The Far East is outside the course of world history"[43]) and Marx ("Indian society has no history at all, at least no known history"[44]). Moreover, this supposed lack was often invoked by the British to explain and/or justify their dominion over India.[45] The domain of historiography, in other words, provided one of the most powerful links between the notion of the strong nation-state and the existence of a strong and articulated national history, at least in the context of the comparison of Europe's strength with that of the various countries of Asia.

Writing in a book that was published in 1901, W. A. P. Martin, an American missionary-educator and the longtime head of the Tongwen guan in Beijing, made a number of comments about the Chinese sense of history—as he perceived it—that very much grew out of this European contempt for Asian historical traditions. At the beginning of a long section entitled "The Study of Chinese History," Martin allows that the writing of history was important in China, citing Hegel to the effect that "the Chinese hav[e] a historical literature more voluminous than that of any other nation on earth, and the Hindus none at all."[46] It is the very bulk of this tradition that irritates Martin, however, for he can find no principles of order within the vast corpus, only simple chronicle. This finding causes him to pose the instrumental question: "But are these venerable remains of any value to us?" Beginning his answer, he sets the basic terms of his inquiry in a most invidious fashion: "In forming an estimate, we must not forget that our standard of value in the criticism of such work differs as widely from that of the Chinese as a golden sovereign does from the cheap productions of the native mint." He follows with his explanation for this difference: "[T]he whole range of their literature contains nothing that can be called a Philosophy of History. They have no Hegel, who, after reconstructing the universe, applies his principles to explain the laws of human progress; no Gibbon or Montesquieu to trace the decay of an old civilization; no Guizot or Lecky to sketch the rise of a new one."[47] All this from a scholar who professes great sympathy to the Chinese predicament and who writes in his introductory chapter that the Chinese "have passed through many and profound changes in the course of their history."[48] What most seems to bother Martin, in other words, is that he can find no theoretical principles underlying the Chinese writing of history, and as his choice of examples indicates, historical theorization to him necessarily implies a teleology that would narrate a trajectory of historical progress.

In a book published a decade later, J. O. P. Bland offers a rather less erudite version of Martin's evaluation: "[T]he Chinese, like the Hindoos, have ever been peculiarly lacking in historic consciousness. The annals and records of successive dynasties provide little or no material for critical or scientific study of the evolution of the nation's laws, institutions and culture."[49] Of all the negative evaluations of China's fitness to survive in the modern world contained in Bland's book, this is among the harshest. Although he crudely lumps the Chinese and Indian historical records together, his conclusion is of a piece with that of Martin. What

Bland seems to be asserting here is the uselessness of the past, as it was conceived in premodern China, for the purpose of building a modern state: "The scientific interpretation of sociological phenomena, by the accumulation and critical comparison of groups of facts, and by tracing back of proximate causes to those more remote, presupposes continuous and fairly trustworthy historical records."[50] The negative consequences of the parlous state of the Chinese historical record are implied when Bland invidiously compares China with Japan, the latter landmarked implicitly by a more careful nurturing of its historical traditions and thus possessed of "[h]er centuries of discipline, of loyalty, civic virtues and social cohesion," in other words, of a "good" history apparently defined by its utility in creating the preconditions for modern statehood.[51]

Martin and Bland each represent contemporary Western discourse on China and are part of a powerful and ineluctable Western demand that China, if it were to survive, must reconstitute itself in accordance with the world system. In light of the concept of the nation they embody in their writings, we should be able to understand Yan Fu's sense of the imperative to include a uniquely national history within his purview. This imperative is rooted in neither simple psychological need for compensation nor even necessarily part of an abstract intellectual conviction of a Chinese "essence" of some sort. It was, rather, very practically a necessary condition for attaining status within the community of nations. As Peter Munz has written: "Since the doctrine of nationalism required people to believe that every nation had existed for many centuries even when its existence was not socially and politically noticeable, the proof for its existence depended on the continuity of its linguistic and cultural coherence."[52] In writing the introduction to his "Xin min shuo" (On renewing the people) in 1902, Liang Qichao expressed a keen awareness of this imperative. After making it clear that nationalism *(minzu zhuyi)* was the reason for the development and expansion of the European powers in the most recent four hundred years, he goes on to enumerate the requisite building blocks for nationalism:

> For a nation to be able to stand in this world, it requires particular characteristics on the part of its citizens. From morals and laws on down to customs, habits, literature and the fine arts, all have an independent spirit that has been passed down from father to son. In this way, society *(qun)* is formed and the nation is created; these are the real roots and sources of nationalism. For our people to have established a nation on the Asian continent for several thousand years, we must have some characteristics that are grand, noble and perfect, as well as being distinct from those of other races *(qunzu)*. We need to preserve these and not allow them to become lost.[53]

In the strongest sense, as Partha Chatterjee maintains, the call to preserve—or to create—a national history "implied in effect an exhortation to launch the struggle for power [against Western hegemony], because in th[e] mode of recalling the past, the power to represent oneself is nothing other than political power itself."[54]

Another source of Yan's characteristic oscillation thus comes into focus: with every reason to be fearful that China was in danger of demise, his turn toward a utilitarian perspective on complete Westernization is understandable. But the ideologies he was so intent upon importing carried within themselves contradictory terms. Even as the theory of the modern nation seemed to demand a ruthless desire for wealth and power and extirpation of any traditional notions that militated against this, the demand for a native pedigree that was part of modern nationalism made this extirpation intellectually and politically impossible. Jia Baoyu—the protagonist of the eighteenth-century epic novel *Shitou ji* (The story of the Stone), brought back to life in turn-of-the-century Shanghai by Wu Jianren in his 1905 novel, *Xin shitou ji* (The new story of the Stone)—sums up the contradictory situation embodied by the comprador Bai Yaolian: "In other words, just because he understands a few foreign words, everything foreign becomes good, and he would just love to discover that his parents were actually foreigners. But yesterday I sat up reading the whole night through, and I learned that the thing foreigners value most is patriotism. So I'm afraid patriotic foreigners wouldn't recognize such an unworthy descendant as he."[55]

A complete accounting of Yan's contradictions on this issue requires some delving into the question of the extent to which politically alert Chinese were conscious of Western judgments of contemporary China. Previous scholarship has been largely silent on this point, which is one reason it is difficult to come up with a clear answer, although it is plain that the deluge of translations of Western material in post-1895 China signaled a greatly augmented awareness of Western opinion in general. There is considerable evidence that Yan Fu paid close attention to contemporary Western writings about China and was concerned about the negative tenor of the evaluations. Perhaps the most convincing single piece of evidence is that between October 26, 1897, and October 14, 1898 —the first year Yan was editing the *Guowen bao* in Tianjin with Xia Zengyou (1863–1924)—72 of 212, or fully one-third, of the articles in the editorial section of that newspaper were translations from the foreign press, the coastal and metropolitan papers of China.[56] Internal evidence from Yan Fu's own writings is also plentiful. Aside from the two instances cited above ("From their point of view, however, we have not planned well . . ." and ". . . it was then and remains even today a source of shame to the residents of their capital cities"), in "On the Origins of [National] Strength"

Yan cites the response of the Western press to Chinese behavior during the war with Japan: "They said that our people sold out our nation and our military for the merest of pecuniary advantage and thus lost our land and our troops.[57] And if the result is our present defeat and future destruction, it cannot really be labeled unfortunate. It goes without saying that this is enough to make one's hair stand on end."[58]

Given that Yan Fu did not leave China during these years, it is probable that the Western press he is referring to is the press on the China coast, an assumption substantiated by the fact that at least one letter written by Yan in English to the *North China Daily News* was published in that paper, in December 1911.[59] In addition, in an 1898 essay critical of contemporary defenders of Confucianism, Yan acknowledges the force of a characteristic Western appraisal of China: "Foreigners have said that from the standpoint of the mentality and actions of the contemporary Chinese gentry *(shi dafu)*, if the results of three thousand years of education are no more than this, then the teaching itself must contain the roots of its own corruption. It is because of this that things came to be the way they are today."[60]

That Yan's first extended translation from English was *Missionaries in China*, an 1892 tract by Alexander Michie (1830–1901)—something the scholarship on Yan is largely silent about—is perhaps the best indication of how sensitive the Chinese scholar was to foreign opinion and the Western gaze. Michie, who was an old China hand, a sometime editor of an English newspaper in Tianjin, the author of several books, and a correspondent for the *London Times*, wrote the work as a sharp-edged and sarcastic attack on missionary work as it had been practiced in China.[61] It takes particular aim at the intolerance the majority of Christian fundamentalist practitioners manifested toward the canons of Chinese morality and the Chinese way of life, and their tendency to conflate conversion to Christianity with the embrace of a Western style of life.[62] Yan complained later that he had been frustrated by his considerable difficulty in finding a publisher for the piece; he eventually wrote a brief summary of the work that apparently served as an introduction when the translation was eventually published via the assistance of Zhang Yuanji (1867–1959), but only after Zhang had become head of the Translation Bureau at the Shanghai Nanyang gongxue (forerunner of Jiaotong University) in 1899.[63] In this introduction Yan reveals again the extent to which his chagrin over domestic squabbles originates from an awareness of the possibility of judgments that would be part of a Western standard of evaluation: "If [scholars] are bickering about the defense of China from the barbarians, and arguing about what is orthodox and what is heterodox, this is not something I really wish to know about. I am afraid, however, that the author of this book [i.e., Michie] is laughing up his sleeve about it."[64]

Behind all the circumstantial issues surrounding the appropriation of Western ideas, however, lies a larger and more substantial question. This question is not so much the extent to which Yan borrows the ideas he is so entranced with, but rather the extent to which these ideas are being filtered through concerns generated out of his own intellectual experience within China. On the surface, Benjamin Schwartz assumes that Yan has been able to find real correspondences between Chinese and Western ideas, if only because Schwartz does not seem to believe that Yan made substantial categorical distinctions: "'Chinese tradition' as an all-inclusive abstract category does not become a target of his attack, because it is doubtful whether the tradition presents itself to him as an integrated synthetic whole."[65] This statement seems quite curious in light of Yan's constant determination to make just such distinctions in his key writings of the mid-1890s. Schwartz' formulation does, however, at least account for—if not very precisely—those moments in Yan's writing when he suddenly claims identity for the basic ideas of China and the West.

Just underneath Schwartz' surface optimism concerning Yan's ability to smoothly amalgamate Chinese and Western ideas, however, lie doubts that the faithful student of Herbert Spencer was really able to grasp the concept that Schwartz seems to value most highly—namely, the genius of Western liberalism:

> If Yen Fu thus escapes the dogmatic features of Spencer's individualism, the real question which confronts us is, How profoundly rooted is his variety of liberalism? In the final analysis one may assert that what has *not* come through in Yen Fu's perception is precisely that which is often considered to be the ultimate spiritual core of liberalism—the concept of the worth of persons within society as an end in itself, joined to the determination to shape social and political institutions to promote this value. Yen Fu's concept of liberalism as a means to an end of state power is mortally vulnerable to the demonstration that there are shorter roads to that end.[66] (Emphasis in original)

For all the precision with which this passage retroactively adumbrates the unhappy history of modern Chinese liberalism, there seems to me to be something not quite fair about it in respect to Yan Fu and his intentions in turning to the West. Yan never fails to be frank about his motives: he simply assumes that his country is in the gravest danger of disintegration and thereupon takes national survival as his overriding premise. He makes no real pretense of describing liberalism as anything other than the key feature that makes the Western nations more viable than China. In fact, Schwartz' critique of Yan Fu's utilitarian approach to Western ideas had been anticipated in a more historically specific fashion by Qian

Zhixiu, a key editorial writer at *Dongfang zazhi* (The Eastern miscellany) during the late 1910s, in an influential essay published in that journal in 1918 and entitled "Gongli zhuyi yu xueshu" (Utilitarianism and scholarship). In claiming that utilitarianism was the major premise under which all Western ideas came to China, Qian says:

> When [the concepts of] popular sovereignty and freedom, constitutionalism, and republicanism are employed by Europeans and Americans to eradicate the old systems of feudalism and the power of the church or to implement the ideals of humanism, they cannot simply be encompassed by the notion of utilitarianism. But this is not true for us [in China]. In taking these ideas, we are basing ourselves on the notion that the European and American powers now so prominent in the world have passed through these stages, and since we wish to emulate their wealth and power, we cannot but follow in their tracks. . . . [This attitude] evolves out of utilitarianism . . . [and] anything from foreign cultures that has no direct utility is also thrown away in disgust *(tuoqi)*.[67]

Thus, according to Qian, the very perception of historical difference and the Chinese deficiency that it implies to those engaged in the modern state-building project render utilitarianism the only actual means by which Western ideas can be implemented in China.

Moreover, Schwartz, like Levenson, will not really entertain the idea that there might be a legitimate competing value system to which Yan owed serious allegiance and which thereby seriously overdetermined his commitment to those Western ideas that Schwartz holds most dear. The presumption that liberalism transcends all other values in the end renders Yan something of an imaginative failure in Schwartz' eyes. In other words, rather than treating Yan Fu as someone torn by intellectual demands that could not possibly be reconciled, Schwartz treats him more as someone who cannot quite grasp the nobler ideas he ought to be reaching for. The contemporary Chinese thinker Wang Hui has turned the tables here, supplying a historical context for Schwartz' conclusions: "In the atmosphere of the cold war, Schwartz, by means of Yan Fu's observation that the 'Western spirit' was suffused with nationalism and the worship of power, sought to emphasize the absolute, autonomous, and nonutilitarian value position of liberalism, in order to overcome the excess of the notion of collective strength in the 'Western spirit.'"[68]

In another article, Wang Hui sheds further light on the question of Yan Fu's ultimate intellectual convictions. Wang analyzes Yan's various statements about science *(gezhi)* and finds them to be heavily influenced by traditional Chinese ideas on "the investigation of things." The key concept here is that celestial, terrestrial, and human *(tian, di, ren)* activities are linked on one continuum of causality rather than being the result of independent processes, as is posited by Western science. As Wang put it:

> Nature, psychology, and society possess an objective "principle" *(li);* however, they are not independent of one another but collectively implicated; they differ only in their level of articulation and not in their qualities. This difference in level of articulation is determined by their distance from the ultimate goal of "cultivating [the person], ordering [the family], governing [the country], and pacifying [the realm]."[69]

In other words, for all Yan's passion in invoking the need to pursue the spirit of Western science, behind it lay an enduring neo-Confucian motivation to have it serve the even more basic cause of bringing order to the realm and peace to the world. It was in the end just another aspect of Yan's utilitarian pursuit of the elements necessary to allow China to cope with an ever more threatening world.

The point of convergence between Yan's thinking and the Chinese ideas he vacillated about was not lost on later commentators on Yan's work. These commentators, however, rarely regarded his intellectual link to the past in a favorable light. Writing around 1920, even Liang Qichao—someone who, as we have seen, had been much in Yan's intellectual debt early in his career—saw fit to damn Yan with faint praise: "[T]here was at that time the unique Yen Fu . . . who translated a number of books . . . , all of them famous works, although half were old and rather out-of-date [lit., 'removed from the trends of the time']." Liang goes on, however, to acknowledge the importance of Yan's work in translation: "Nonetheless, among the students who had returned from the West, Yen Fu was the first to make connections with the intellectual world of China."[70] Liang's approbation lies strictly in his gratitude toward Yan for introducing Western ideas into the Chinese discourse of the time, and he is quick to judge Yan by the social Darwinist standard that Yan himself had introduced: Yan was "removed from the trends of the time" in a rapidly changing world that demanded swift adaptation. It is particularly noteworthy that Liang does not see fit to mention any of Yan's own intellectual contributions to late Qing thought, in spite of Liang's own evident debt to them. In fact, this focus on Yan's translations and the concomitant silence about Yan's original work is something most later commentators have in common.

For all the general inattention to Yan's own ideas, many scholars of the next generation gratefully acknowledged their gratitude for Yan's pioneering translation work. Lu Xun (1881–1936), for instance, was ungrudging in his praise for Yan's work.[71] But a larger number of voices of the May Fourth generation criticized Yan even here, and in highly revealing ways. This May Fourth critique eventually came to dominate the response to Yan Fu, resonating within the English-language scholarship as well. Much like Liang Qichao, Hu Shi (1891–1962) displayed a mixed feelings toward Yan's translations. On the one hand, writing in the early 1930s, he acknowledged their tremendous influence: "Within a few years of its publication *Evolution and Ethics* gained widespread popularity throughout the country, and even became reading matter for middle-school students. . . . Within a few years these ideas spread like a prairie fire, setting ablaze the hearts and blood of many young people."[72] On the other hand, that Yan Fu wrote in what Hu thought of as the elitist "Tongcheng style" of classical prose caused Hu to pass harsh judgment on Yan's efforts overall. In an essay written in 1935, Hu first quotes Yan's own conclusions as to why his translations were so difficult: "Those within China who read my translations always find that they cannot immediately understand them, and criticize their complexity. Do they not realize that the original works actually surpass them in difficulty? The ideas within are subtle and profound, and thus cannot be mixed with words that are not eloquent in themselves." After this declaration by Yan, Hu concludes: "This is ironclad proof of his failure at translation. Today there are still people who copy Yan Fu's method of translation, like Mr. Zhang Shizhao [1882–1973], but their translations will have no readers."[73] Thus, by the 1930s Hu, like Liang Qichao before him, seems to hold Yan to the same standard of social Darwinist obsolescence that Yan himself introduced into modern Chinese thought.

A younger generation delivered even harsher judgment. Fu Sinian (1896–1950), then a student activist at Beijing University and already a major player in the New Culture movement, would write in early 1919: "Of the books translated by Yan Fu, *Evolution and Ethics* and [Montesquieu's] *The Spirit of Laws* are the worst. . . . This is because he did not take any responsibility toward the original authors, but only toward himself; [in fact] he took responsibility only toward his own fame and position."[74] Fu pays inadvertent homage to Yan's early writings even as he passes this harsh judgment: Fu in effect consigns Yan to the "Chinese" half of the binary that Yan himself had established in his seminal essay of 1895. That is to say, in castigating Yan with the words "he took responsibility only toward his own fame and position," Fu seems to relegate Yan to the realm of strictly private *(si)* motivation. And as Yan had defined it, *si* lay at the other end of spectrum from the public-spiritedness that both he and Liang Qichao had praised so highly, even as they marked it as being characteristic of the more dynamic West. By 1919, in other words, Yan had come to be condemned by a younger generation in almost precisely the same terms with which he had rebuked his elders in 1895.

Writing a few years later, the philosopher Zhang Zhunmai (1886–

1969) would maintain: "[Yan] uses ordinary ideas from the present and the past to translate the meaning of Western science. Therefore, though the words are beautiful, the meaning diverges. . . . In sum, when Yan translates, he likes to use old Chinese concepts to translate new Western thought, thereby losing the spirit of precision of Western science."[75] For Zhang, even Yan's translations have been infected and thereby vitiated by traditional ways of thought. In a commentary on Yan's 1959 preface to Huxley's *Evolution and Ethics,* Zhou Zhenfu remarks in a similar vein: "The pains Yan takes to spread Western learning are admirable, but the sort of forced interpretations [he makes] are unworthy of emulation. Moreover, they are not in accord with fact."[76] Harsh criticism of Yan Fu's intellectual range is by no means restricted to Chinese commentators. In fact, perhaps the most extreme example of this dismissal of Yan Fu's intellectual legacy can be found in James Pusey's jejune rejection of even the possibility of finding any rigor in Yan Fu's thought as a whole. After failing to find consistency in Yan's attempts to characterize the role of the Chinese sages in history, Pusey concludes: "There is no logical way out of these contradictions in Yen Fu's early essays. But never mind. Confusion was a deeply important part of Yen Fu's influence."[77]

Perhaps the problem here is best represented by Benjamin Schwartz' sympathetic and insightful treatment of the relationship between Yan and his Western sources. Schwartz makes note of the following passage from Yan's "On the Origins of [National] Strength," in which the Chinese scholar sums up the contribution of Herbert Spencer's sociology:

> Spencer was also English and was a contemporary of Darwin's. His book was published earlier than *Origin of Species* and based itself on the ways of evolution to explain human relations and ordering society. It was called *Sociology (Qunxue),* and his [motivation] was similar to that of Xunzi when he said that the reason humans were superior to beasts was that they could group *(qun).* [Spencer says] that whatever humans do to help one another survive, to cause change so as to bring about merit, even to the extent of [the installation] of punishments, government, ritual, and music, are all based on this capacity to group. He also uses the most recent principles of science to illuminate matters concerned with [self-cultivation], regulating [the family], governing [the country], and bringing peace [to the world].[78]

In analyzing this statement, Schwartz offers a minatory remark: "It will be immediately noted that all these traditional Chinese phrases give a somewhat odd twist to Spencer's prosy tract. This terminology, in fact, imposes a prescriptive, programmatic interpretation which would have scandalized the master. Spencer is not providing prescriptions for social action by an intellectual elite."[79]

Schwartz was the first to point out that what fascinated Yan about the West was his discovery of the link between group custom and the individual dynamism that gives the latter a practical arena in which to operate.[80] Yan duly explicates Spencer in terms of this fundamental insight about the nature of modern English society, but it is an interpretation that Schwartz is quick to label as a mistake. In so doing, Schwartz' reading of Yan as being idiosyncratic in his rendition of Spencer in effect sums up the relationship between the Chinese scholar and the ideas he is trying to introduce. The way Schwartz phrases his comment implies that Spencer is the independent variable and that anything Yan has to add is merely supplementary (the very obliqueness of which needs to be explained) rather than something that might change our perception of Spencer's basic ideas. As a result, in regard to their respective positions of authority, Spencer's text and Yan's commentary could not be more different. Not just the later commentators but also Yan himself assume Spencer to be the universal case and Yan's remarks to be particular to the occasion. For Yan, Spencer both resonates with his own Chinese education—hence the allusion to Xunzi—and to the new universal order represented by ideas from the West. In fact, Spencer comes with the dual imprimatur of describing the West and having a high degree of prestige there (at least as far as Yan understood at the time he was initially attracted to Spencer). Yan's appropriation of Spencer, however, does not share the same privilege. Although Yan can read and appreciate Spencer, Yan's own reading could never attach itself to Spencer's text in any but the most contingent and marginal ways.

Levenson has commented upon this difference of enunciating position, although in a rather different context:

> Translating and expounding Montesquieu, Mill, Huxley, [and] Spencer, [Yan] felt himself to be dealing with intellectual actors, men who had changed history. But Yen was a reactor. The fact that he had to go to them to find his affirmations—even though he changed them in the process—meant that anyone translating and expounding Yen would be explaining Chinese history, not going to Yen for *his* affirmations. Darwin and even his epigones were intrinsically, supra-historically, interesting. Yen was interesting for what he made of them. What was weak about modern China was not simply what Yen detected with his Darwinist vision; it was what he reflected, too, in depending on that vision. What China lacked—and what drove Yen to an intellectual life that exemplified that lack—was more than wealth and power, conventionally understood. It was power to launch a Yen Fu into universal significance, instead of holding him down,

just historically significant, while he made a particular, Chinese record by reacting to what he considered universal.[81] (Emphasis in original)

Although I think it a bit unfair to hold Yan up to some standard of seeking universal relevance that he himself never claimed, Levenson's remarks certainly shed light on the underlying predisposition that later scholars, Chinese and Western alike, held toward Yan.

Thus, future Chinese adepts of the philosophy of social Darwinism might be attracted to it for exactly the same reasons that Yan was, but they were free, even encouraged, to reject Yan's interpretation as being marred by the admix of "traditional" ideas. The ideology of social evolution itself led in that direction, as witnessed by Liang Qichao's dismissive attitude toward Yan's choice of texts to translate. In general, such rejection is precisely what happens: later Chinese scholars analyzing Yan's work tend to focus strictly on the fidelity of the translations rather than upon his commentaries and essays.[82] This limitation of the discussion to issues of Yan's fidelity to the original texts (something that neither Schwartz nor Zhou Zhenfu is guilty of, by the way) assumes from the start that Yan can have nothing of value to offer on his own and thus painfully constricts his range. By contrast, one has only to recall Qian Zhongshu's recognition that Lin Shu in fact made a creative transformation of Dickens and other English novelists in his classical Chinese renderings of the foreign texts.[83] It is of particular interest that Fu Sinian and Zhang Junmai accuse Yan of exactly the same sort of parochialism and narrow self-interest that Yan himself had used to characterize the essential differences between China and the West in early 1895.

But for later writers, the appeal of social Darwinism lay, after all, specifically beyond what Yan was able to reach—the foreign text's apparent authenticity as a discourse from a broader world, with the capacity to speak clearly about the keys to success in that world. From that perspective, Yan's take on these works becomes, at least potentially, a source of pollution; the Spencerian text's aura of authenticity is easily seen as vitiated by what those who came later would tend to regard as Yan's parochial remarks. I think we can even see here the seeds of the propensity of later modern Chinese thinkers to undercut the positions of their intellectual predecessors as part of the endless process of reinventing discursive structures every few years. In other words, while certain Western ideas—social Darwinism in particular—would endure from intellectual generation to generation, the association of such ideas with indigenous notions in hybrid constructs required their constant reconfiguration in purer, more consciously cosmopolitan form.

The source of the problem that Yan left for his successors is most evident in his oscillation between sometimes needing to argue that China and the West were completely distinct from one another and at other times finding them to share a number of fundamental ideas. One could try to periodize this wavering by concluding that his disposition for finding cultural difference was more radical in his first four essays and had already become tempered in his preface to Huxley, written some eighteen months later. Such a scheme would not, however, explain his many references to the common origins of ideas between the West and China even in the early essays themselves. Zhou Zhenfu, in a book published in 1940, found his own way of dealing with the problem: Yan's writing on this issue becomes much more consistent once Zhou finds that Yan saw post-Qin Chinese history as betraying the early promise of Chinese thought.[84] Although it is certainly true that Yan, like most scholars of the time, makes a dramatic distinction between the political and intellectual conditions in pre- and post-Qin China, this formulation brings along problems of its own. If he finds that pre-Qin China and the West share common ideas, is he now denying the foundational cultural differences he had built upon in "On the Urgency of Change in the World," such as the notion that freedom is what had given the West its momentum? If so, is he thus also denying a concept of radical difference that can be used as leverage in what he continues to insist is a dangerously static situation? After all, for all his temporizing, Yan continues to proclaim his contempt for those who "deceive themselves" with the idea that China had every important idea first, however close he comes to advocating this point himself.

Lurking unstated in the background, however, is another, even greater, blind spot. For all the acuity Yan brings to the discussion of ultimate origins, he seems almost willfully unaware of the basic architecture of his argument, invidiously comparing the wisdom of the ancients with the failure of those who come later to live up to it. It is unmistakably the pattern that characterized the very intellectual life of post-Tang China that Yan is so intent upon denouncing. As we have seen in chapter 1, the Yangwu thinkers of the late Qing—implicitly denounced by Yan for seeking a Chinese origin for every Western idea or invention of merit—were particularly given to this form of argument. In attempting to trace the origins of these things, they find outlines of them in early Chinese books but must then note that later dynasties "failed to hand them down" *(shi chuan)*.[85] The epistemological links between Yan's sense of pre-Qin possibility and the basic orientation of the school of evidentiary learning *(kaozheng)* of the mid-Qing are also obvious, particularly so if one calls *kaozheng* by its less precise but more popular label of Hanxue (school of Han dynasty learning). Its perception of a post-Han decadence that blinded later generations to earlier insights is echoed throughout Yan's introduction to his translation of Huxley.[86] And even if Yan is careful to say only that the ideas are the same rather than to specify a necessary Chinese source, from the perspective of the radical voices that follow him he still seems a prisoner of the late Qing rhetoric of Chinese origins.

The intensely overdetermined nature of each strand of the argument that Yan chooses for constructing a coherent narrative has a number of consequences for the new regime of ideas he is so intent upon establishing. For one thing, a dramatic disproportion exists between the fragility of his attempts to declare points in common between Chinese and Western intellectual history and his tactical inability to recognize the more evident points his own argument has in common with the voices he is ostensibly arguing against. This lends a profound instability to Yan's stance: the close attention he pays to avoiding or qualifying manifest declarations of filiation to the past contrasts with a curious lack of awareness of the shared elements between the underlying pattern of his arguments and certain paradigmatic forms that had been shared earlier by both neo-Confucian and Han learning discourse. Given the resulting tension, the easiest resolution to it becomes a line of retreat to a conservative position that advocates a return to tradition. Such a move would represent, after all, only an increased self-awareness of the unacknowledged terms of his own discourse.

Another problem inheres in Yan's cutting himself off completely from the recent past in favor of a valorization of remote antiquity. The result is an attitude of "always jam yesterday, never jam today," or a permanent regression of useful precedents into the past. This renders problematic any efforts to locate proximate roots to contemporary practice, something any theory embracing a teleology of progress needs for justifying its course of action. The upshot of these complications is that Yan's discourse moves on two opposed tracks at the same time. If finding a base in the remote past moves in the direction of conservatism, the denial of the validity of more recent precedent leads to the most uncompromising iconoclasm: because they are denied any substantial justification, existing institutions can put up no strong arguments toward coping with calls for their own rejection. This paradoxical combination of archaism and iconoclasm, however, makes the search for specific and indigenous local instances of universal truths almost an impossibility: by the very terms on which Yan bases his own arguments, everything within reach must be found wanting. In this way Yan Fu's early writings of 1895–1896 already adumbrate what was to develop into a pervasive instability within modern Chinese cultural discourse, in which local application of cosmopolitan ideas became at the same time both ideological imperative and practical impossibility.

CHAPTER 3

New Ways of Writing

> The imagination developed in Europe and expressions found there are rich and extraordinary. Once in possession of them, one will be able to triumph over all ages and encompass everything.
> Liang Qichao, "Travels to Hawaii," quoted in Xiaobing Tang's "Poetic Revolution"

> We cannot say that we know a particular form or period of society, and that we will see how its art and theory relate to it, for until we know these, we cannot really claim to know the society.
> Raymond Williams, *The Long Revolution*

The question of the role that the West and its vigorous ideas was to play in modern intellectual life, which so preoccupied Yan Fu, also manifested itself powerfully in the realm of letters. The issue played itself out across the whole spectrum of literary genres, sometimes posed explicitly and at other times visible only by reading carefully between the lines. At virtually all points in the various critical discourses on renewing or reforming literature, however, the catalytic power of Western theories of writing is plainly evident. There was a particular complication in this field: because literature's long tradition was unalterably rooted in indigenous modes of writing, any transformations would ultimately have to make their peace with the intricacies of literary history. Given that writing was so clearly marked as indigenous, the contradictions between preservation of the national tradition and the need for thoroughgoing reform were to prove particularly vexing in this area. This chapter will pursue the development of this story by examining the work of a number of different writers and thinkers who discussed how to create that most basic of literary media, written prose. It will begin, however, with a short reminder of just how significant the coming of Western books was to one particularly important late Qing thinker.

New Sources of Inspiration

In late June of 1906, Zhang Binglin was released from prison in the international settlement in Shanghai. He had served a three-year term for anti-Manchu activities while he wrote for the *Subao,* a radical Shanghai newspaper shut down by the Qing government in 1903.[1] Zhang was immediately escorted to Tokyo, where on July 15 he gave a speech to a welcoming meeting of Chinese students studying in Japan. Characteristically for the time and place, the speech concerns itself almost exclusively with the question of how to increase China's wealth and power in the world. Considering that the speaker was a man whose dense and highly erudite scholarship was built on his conviction of the enduring unity of Chinese culture, the beginning of the address comes as a bit of a surprise:

> When I was young, I read the *Donghua lu* (Records from within the Eastern flowery gate) of Mr. Jiang [Liangqi, 1722–1789],[2] which contained accounts of the cases of Dai Mingshi [1653–1713], Zeng Jing [1679–1736], and Zha Siting [1664–1727].[3] I was moved to anger, thinking that an alien people had brought disorder upon China, something that became our greatest source of resentment. I later read books by Zheng Suonan and Wang Chuanshan [Fuzhi, 1619–1692],[4] which are full of nothing but words [advocating] the protection of the Han race, and my nationalistic thought *(minzu sixiang)* gradually developed. None of the words of the two gentlemen, however, was animated by any theory *(xueli)*. After 1895, however, I got hold of some books from countries both East and West, and it was only then that I picked up any theory. When I told my friends at the time of my notions of expelling the Manchus, they always shook their heads: some said that I was mad, some said that I was a rebel, and some said that I was setting myself up for the executioner.[5]

A powerful anti-Manchu xenophobia suffuses the entirety of this brief autobiographical snippet. Given that Westerners and the Japanese had lately posed the most serious threat to China's status in the world, there is something just a trifle odd in his directing the entirety of his animus at the Manchus and his sense of their past crimes against Han scholars. As Marie-Claire Bergère has said in regard to this issue: "Although foreign imperialists were identified as the most dangerous enemies, the Manchus were the ones who were attacked because they represented an easier target. Anti-Manchu struggle could thus be seen as an escape, a non-rational solution to the fundamental contradiction between the violent anti-imperialist feelings and an impossible anti-imperialist struggle."[6] I would argue that it is not just the "impossibility" of the anti-imperialist struggle that caused Zhang to displace his rage onto the Manchus, but also his awareness that the only model that China could pursue to escape its precarious situation was the one provided by the very Western powers that were hammering at the gates. Zhang was aware, in other words, that intellectual anti-Westernism would at this point in history run a real risk of occluding the possibility of needed reform.

For all the conflicting feelings under the surface in this speech, the openness with which Zhang admits to his audience that the theoretical insights necessary to galvanize his theretofore only latent nationalistic thought were gained only by reading Western books is still striking. It is true that Zhang makes a halfhearted attempt to diminish the force of this utterance by saying that he had read books "from countries both East and West." This claim follows, however, a quite unambiguous statement that prior to 1895 he seems to have read every available indigenous work concerned with Chinese nationalism and that they had all lacked the power to synthesize experience the way that the new books had. Moreover, the term he uses to signify "theory," *"xueli"* (now obsolete), is one of the many neologisms invented in Meiji Japan to express ideas that were regarded as being within the province of the new and the Western and thus not capable of being voiced in the lexicon as it had previously existed.[7] Zhang's conceptualization of the issue of nationalism, then, has become possible only through new ideas and terms imported either directly from the West or, more frequently, from the West via Japan. Zhang's statement of inspiration from imported ideas is hardly unique in this period. Yan Fu, for instance, in the preface to his 1903 translation of Spencer's *Study of Sociology,* muses: "I read this book in 1881 or 1882, and was immediately sorry that I had not seen it earlier, for up until that time I had favored extreme and one-sided statements. It was only at this point that I realized my error."[8]

Wenxue and Its Complexities

As the examples given above suggest, the initial intellectual encounters between Chinese thinkers and the West in this period were heavily bookish. As a result, in taking the measure of the interplay between Chinese and Western theories of culture after 1895, it is clear that the questions of what to write and how to express one's insights quickly came to occupy key positions in the intellectual life of the time. Even the word used to signify the general field of literature registers the complexity of the transformation that China was beginning to undergo. In China the term *"wen-*

xue," which can now be appropriately translated only as "literature," originally had a range of meaning that is, paradoxically, at once both broader and more limited than that denoted by the latter word's modern English usage. The traditional meaning of *"wenxue"* was humane letters in general, one of the four categories of learning, according to Confucius.⁹ Beginning in the 1890s, however, the term was borrowed back from a new usage popularized in Japan, where it had come to be used as a translation for the English term "literature." Of all the terms imported from Japan in these years to stand in for Western concepts, it is perhaps *"wenxue"* that continued to be most fraught with the legacy of its earlier meaning, giving rise to a term that could never quite comfortably be taken for granted. Its broader connotation lingered on, and the ambiguities of the term inevitably added to its rhetorical charge, with the older and more extended meaning hanging over the more restricted, purely literary sense and increasing its resonance. One of the possible consequences is that *"wenxue"* was throughout the twentieth century called into service in a remarkably wide variety of social and political situations—its position as the locus of the intellectual purges that constituted the proximate cause of the Cultural Revolution in 1965–1966 is only the most spectacular example.

Part of the reason for this enduring aura surrounding *"wenxue"* was the continuing use of the term in its old sense in the period of intense reflection that began in the 1890s. The following instance of the way the term was used in these years may be taken as emblematic. The American missionary educator-journalist Young J. Allen (1836–1907; Chinese name, Lin Lezhi) was the editor of the influential weekly Chinese paper *Wanguo gongbao* (A review of the times), published in those years by the new Society for the Diffusion of Christian and General Knowledge among the Chinese ("Guangxue hui" in Chinese; the English title was later simplified to "Christian Literature Society"). After Japan's defeat of China in 1895, Allen collaborated with his aide, the *jinshi* (metropolitan degree holder) Ren Tingxu, to translate into Chinese a book entitled *Education in Japan: A Series of Letters Addressed by Prominent Americans to Arinori Mori,* originally published in New York in 1873.¹⁰

Mori Arinori (1847–1889) had been an important Japanese diplomat and reformer who eventually became Japan's first minister of education *(mombu daijin)* in 1885. During the time of his posting to the United States between 1870 and 1873 he had taken it upon himself to send a number of letters to prominent American educators, inquiring about the links between education and national strength. According to Allen's preface to the translation, Mori translated the collected responses into Japanese, entitled them *Bungaku kōkoku saku* (Stratagems to revive the country through education), and dispatched them back to Japan, where they became blueprints for educational reform in that country.¹¹ In his preface

Allen also expressed the wish that China could learn from recent Japanese success in renewing itself. The collected letters were attached to a compendium of *Wanguo gongbao* articles concerned with the recent war with Japan, entitled *Zhong-dong zhanji benmo* (The full story of the Sino-Japanese War). With its publication date of 1896, the prominence of the translators as sources of information, and the relevance of both the recent war and the newly invigorated demands for reform, this book became highly influential in its day.

What stands out from our contemporary perspective is that Allen and Ren use the term *"wenxue"* throughout to translate what had invariably been "education" in the English original. Given that education, in its sense of an organized and dynamic social enterprise, had no real equivalents in China at the time—the term *"jiaoyu,"* pioneered in Japan to translate "education," had yet to arrive in China—it is not surprising that the translators had a difficult time finding the mot juste. *"Wen,"* or "writing," had long been associated with moral endeavor in China, and with increased force after 1820 or so,[12] so the translators' adoption of this term had the advantage of suggesting the Confucian sense of education as personal cultivation, a personal cultivation that had always had profound social and statecraft implications. By the time the translation appeared, however, the term *"bungaku"* had for some time been used as the equivalent of "literature" in Japan, a usage that began to catch on in China during the 1890s but was not completely naturalized until the first decade of the twentieth century.[13] As the new definition of *"wenxue"* became popularized in China as part of the general reform effort, it almost invariably brought along with it a didactic connotation, something that Allen and Ren's use of the term to translate "education" could only have reinforced.[14]

To fully understand the vicissitudes of the term in the last century, we must first look into some of the influential cultural theorizing that surrounded it in the years after 1895. The related notions of *wen* and *wenxue* came to be an indispensable part of the response to the attack on tradition so sharply set forward by Yan Fu, as a key portion of the process of cultural recuperation—recall that even Yan Fu had almost immediately engaged himself in such recuperation after his initial iconoclasm. A variety of notions was put forward to counter directly the shattering effect of the new currents of thought that followed upon Yan's iconoclastic essays of 1895. Many of these notions attempted to reestablish a unified conceptual order. The most spectacular attempt at holding the center of a rapidly dispersing intellectual horizon was no doubt Kang Youwei's effort to put state Confucianism on a religious footing.[15] What Laurence Schneider has identified as "the discovery of culture," however, was perhaps more significant in the long run.[16] The new theory of "national essence" *(guo-*

cui) that eventually crystallized in the first decade of the new century represented an effort both to guarantee continuity with the past and to separate culture from an earlier and demonstrably unsuccessful political realm.

Probably the most important vehicle for this envisioned essence came to be a more unified concept of belletristic writing than had ever existed before, encapsulated within the old term *"wenxue."* The tension inhering in the *guocui* ideal of trying to separate historical context from transhistorical significance is nowhere more apparent than in this "new" and highly ideological field of *wenxue*. Literature became, above all, an arena of tension between utopianism, along with the hopes for real departure from old concerns projected onto it, and the enduring influence of traditional patterns of thought that resided in the intellectual environment out of which the newly defined category had grown. In other words, *wenxue* offered everyone who cared to think about it a realm of potential in which traditional preoccupations could be resituated and—at least such was the hope—transfigured, more or less, depending upon the individual viewpoint. The almost bewildering variety of views set forth on the subject in the years after 1895 is at once emblematic of its importance to the overall cultural enterprise and of the tremendous frustrations involved in trying to construct that enterprise itself.

Prior to 1895 the category of embellished written expression was simply *"wen,"* a term that represented a palimpsest of related meanings ranging from simple prose to decorated prose and decoration itself in combination with the traditional idea of personal and social cultivation in the broadest sense. *"Wen"* was thus a heavily fraught word even before it was weighted with an array of new tasks in the reform period, for use of the term in any of its senses tended to carry along with it overtones of the other meanings. The ubiquity of the moral overtones that had long attached itself to the term helps explain why advocacy of a particular type of *wen, guwen* (archaic prose), became one of the principal intellectual vehicles of the court faction that had sought to strengthen a weakening political order with a moral revival along orthodox neo-Confucian lines in the 1820s–1840s.[17] Zeng Guofan (1811–1872) had seized upon this idea of prose in the 1850s–1860s and further developed it as part of his effort to galvanize the morale of the intellectual elite against the social erosion brought about by the Taiping rebellion. For the purposes at hand, it is sufficient to note that the melding of aesthetics with moral concern provided the occasion for a revival of *guwen* in particular and *wen* in general during the course of the nineteenth century. This was in the end to be the one constant among the various justifications for *wen* and *wenxue* that crowded the discursive field in the final decade of the dynasty.

After 1895 the process of elevating the role of writing continued even as that role was transformed by the flood of doubts assailing the intellectual assumptions that had provided the context for the earlier emphasis on *wen*. The practical demands made on the new idea of literature were a response to the need to use *wenxue* to fill a variety of needs, including coming to terms with the challenges that Western ideas, now regarded as ineluctable, had presented to the old order. The newly conceptualized literary field had to provide a theory powerful enough both to unify and to continue the focus on theretofore disparate genres of writing,[18] as well as to validate old ideas concerning the utility of writing that needed continued recognition and, above all, to underwrite the authority necessary for providing cultural significance to writing in difficult times. The literary discourse that followed in the years after 1895 took a number of distinct directions, some of which tried hard to stay within traditional patterns of significance and others that tried quite self-consciously to set out in new directions. Each trend, however, was eventually moved in directions its principal advocates could not foresee, by unpredictable combinations of new theories and residual influences from preexisting modes of thought that no one ever seemed quite able to take the measure of. In a sense, the legacy of the earlier nineteenth century, with its tendency to conflate utility and aesthetics (or, perhaps more accurately, a particular notion of "moral aesthetics") provided a hidden gravitational pull that no one seemed able to escape. Beyond this central issue of utility and aesthetics, however, the situation was complicated by other theoretical axes, such as faithfulness to traditional forms versus willingness to experiment, and fidelity to the established literary languages versus a new determination to experiment with the vernacular. That none of the main theoretical groupings ran quite parallel to what at least some of them claimed as traditional antecedents again testifies to the monumental transformation of literary discourse in these times.

Prose Schools

I divide the literary discussion of the 1895–1908 period into four distinct areas, primarily on the basis of shared intellectual affinities within each division (a fifth category — *xiaoshuo*, or fiction — is so crucial that it merits its own chapter). There is some overlap, and the final category admittedly comprises everything that fails to fit into the first three. The primary defense of this categorization is that this is how writers grouped themselves at the time, a time when both preexisting and self-consciously new genres were engaged in complicated conversation with early practices of writing. The first two of these intellectual groupings represent explicit continuations of traditional schools of prose. The first of these, the Tongcheng school of archaic prose, was by far the most influential voice concerning prose theory through most of the nineteenth century (at least after c. 1820), but its position eroded quickly after 1900. The second category, the so-called Wenxuan school, based itself on the theories concerning the aesthetic preeminence of parallel prose as promulgated by the eminent scholar and official Ruan Yuan in the 1820s.[19] Because Ruan's ideas were conducive both to the aesthetic elevation of parallel prose and to the abstraction of that prose from quotidian concerns, it fit the newly exalted idea of *wenxue* better than did the more plainly didactic and less embellished Tongcheng *guwen* style. In addition, the Wenxuan school's sense that parallel prose partook directly of the essence of Confucian thought was even better suited to the needs of those searching for a national essence. Ruan Yuan's "heirs" thus became considerably more influential than did those of Tongcheng's Yao Nai (1732–1815) in the waning years of the Qing, a dramatic reversal in the relative positions of these two dominant prose genres.

The third group, which sought to open a less mediated path of expression, was led by Liang Qichao and his New Prose Style *(xin wenti)*. Liang's effort to create an accessible style more in accord with the ostensible transparency of the vernacular was arguably not much different from the dominant classical language ubiquitous in official documents. It was, however, eventually to create reverberations that would shock Liang himself to the core, and his expressed willingness to write a prose that was meant to break decisively with precedent was perhaps its most important feature in the long run. Liang was also a pioneer among the large and varied company who advocated the novel as a vital medium of social and political reform (and who are the subject of the next chapter), something evidently related to his willingness to experiment with new styles of prose.

Finally, there were a number of prominent individual scholars who, on first glance, hardly seem to constitute a coherent group at all—they seem only to share a mood of dissent from or resistance to more dominant trends. They are represented at one extreme by Zhang Binglin, with his resolute denials that prose could have any special aesthetic properties, and on the other extreme by Wang Guowei (1877–1927), who by 1906–1907 had come to see aesthetics as the defining feature of human behavior. These two had in common, however, a conscious denial of any strictly utilitarian view of *wenxue*, perhaps the surest indication of the overt Western influence on their views of writing. The younger Zhou Shuren (1881–1936), later to become famous as Lu Xun, was influenced by both men and combined elements from each in such a way as to demonstrate the strengths, the weaknesses, and the limits of the traditional Chinese view of the capacities of literature. His writing is the subject of chapter 10.

Guwen

A primary concern of the so-called Tongcheng theory of prose was to maintain a uniform, archaic style that was also evocative and relatively accessible to all educated men. The moral qualities held to be the immanent core of *guwen* were seen as the key to both the uniformity and the accessibility of proper composition. The moral authority of prose thus to some degree required that no form of writing become so specialized that it risked losing the general qualities that all *guwen* was supposed to share. Indeed, many of the late Qing calls for archaic prose rest specifically on a faith in the clarity of diction that ostensibly guaranteed accuracy of expression. As Yan Fu wrote concerning the style he had chosen for his translation of Huxley's *Evolution and Ethics:*

> Confucius said: "The purpose of words is only to communicate" and "language without embellishment will not carry far."[20] . . . [But my] wish is not simply to carry the words far; in fact the essentials and subtlety [of the text] are most readily conveyed by using pre-Han style and syntax. *If one uses the vulgar language current today, it is difficult to get the point across: one always suppresses the idea in favor of the expression,* and a tiny initial error leads to an infinite error in the end.[21] (Emphasis added)

In light of the May Fourth–inspired and subsequently widely held view that *guwen* is perversely elitist and obscurantist,[22] it is important to recall that one of the principal Tongcheng claims for itself was the precision of archaic prose in conveying complex ideas. On the other hand, Tongcheng theorists always acknowledged a stylistic density to *guwen* that was an equally important characteristic. The later Tongcheng master Wu Rulun's musings on translation, written in the late 1890s, bring out the contradictions between these two views. In his 1898 preface to Yan Fu's *Tianyan lun,* Wu dealt extensively, if finally indecisively, with the relationship between content and form. After briefly summarizing Huxley's argument in the first third of his preface, Wu devoted the rest of his discussion to analysis of the stylistic elements of the Chinese translation. In the tripartite taxonomy of writing that he then set forth, Wu also demonstrated the extent to which orthodox neo-Confucian moral philosophy depended upon careful cultivation of written expression. His first category consists of prose in which both the *dao* and the style are superior; prose of this sort will certainly last through the ages. In the second, the *dao* is inferior but the prose is good enough to survive on its own, while the third type consists of inferior prose that will be soon forgotten regardless of the quality of the moral philosophy that the author is seeking to express. The weight Wu apportions to each segment of his argument—

two-thirds being on matters of style—tellingly indicates the real locus of his concern. As if to underline this, Wu noted that his understanding of Huxley was made possible primarily by Yan's strengths as a *guwen* stylist.[23]

Wu blamed the deficient literary climate in China for the difficulties that had been encountered in successfully bringing Western ideas to China, denouncing such forms as examination prose *(shiwen),* better known as the "eight-legged essay" *(bagu wen);* the plain style used in document composition *(gongdu);* and the mixed style used in anything from fiction to diary jottings *(shuobu).* Pragmatically, Wu was concerned that foreign works translated into inferior Chinese would earn only the contempt of "knowledgeable men." He believed that writing as competent as that of Yan Fu is guaranteed to endure if—and this seems to Wu to be a large if—the current trend of debased prose can be overcome and people can recognize that Yan's writing aspires to be on a par with that of Sima Qian in the *Shiji* and the great prose work of the eight masters of the Tang and Song. Along with Wu's magnified concern with style, however, lies a certain ambivalence about a potential disharmony between form and content, something that the early advocates of the post-1800 *guwen* revival had been quite certain they would be able to obliterate. Wu says that Yan Fu makes Huxley's message all the clearer, but he admits to a certain wariness about the ultimate utility of the message itself. For, after implicitly ranking Yan's prose with that of the traditional masters of archaic prose, Wu goes on to say:

> I don't know that the *dao* of Huxley compares with that of Buddhism, but I do know that to rank it with that of [Sima Qian] and Yang [Xiong, 53 B.C.E.–18 C.E.] would be difficult. I also know that it would be difficult to rank it with even the writers of the Tang and Song. But with the embellishment of Master Yan *(Yanzi yiwen zhi),* the book can run neck and neck with the thinkers of the late Zhou dynasty *(wan Zhou zhuzi).* Can writing style, then, be unimportant?[24]

In the rather more private form of a letter written in response to Yan Fu, Wu is more open about his misgivings concerning the general currency of translation. Much more explicitly than in the preface, Wu wonders in the letter whether the vast differences between the Western languages and Chinese do not require that a wholly new form of Chinese be created to do justice to the ideas of the West, much as a new style was required to translate the Buddhist canon from Sanskrit. But Wu is also concerned lest the newly ascendant Western learning begin to supplant the Chinese learning upon which the indigenous culture is based. Because he views writing as the key to that culture, the use of vernacular Chinese as the medium of translation is unacceptable, for its widespread adoption would only hasten the demise of a tradition based upon a carefully cultivated writing style. Wu, then, quite tentatively confers his approval upon Yan's transformation of Western texts into elegant *guwen*, evidently, however, feeling a good deal of discomfort in so doing. His misgivings ultimately oblige him to come down firmly on the side of loyalty to style over consonance with the meaning of the original text, advising Yan that it is better to "sacrifice fidelity [in your translations] than to do harm to the purity [of their style]." Wu elaborates: "What harm is there in not noting minor matters of little consequence? To call something *wen*, yet to include therein the vulgar, base, and shallow, that which men of title refrain from speaking of, is something that men of knowledge have never failed to abstain from; it is what Mr. Zeng [Guofan] referred to as 'avoiding the vulgar in one's diction' *(ciqi yuan bi)*."[25]

Wu's determination to grant primacy to style over content was by no means the only position advanced on this important question in the late Qing and was, in fact, in sharp contrast to a number of other scholars' views on the proper way to translate. For instance, Hua Hengfang (1833–1902), writing perhaps two decades before Wu, mused about the problems involved in translating abstruse mathematical treatises into proper Chinese. Hua, a scientist and co-translator of Western technical books at the Jiangnan Arsenal (Jiangnan Zhizaoju), participated in a two-man team in which one member orally translated the foreign work while the other concentrated on rendering it into good Chinese. Hua was the latter member of the team, and he wrote a number of essays on the difficulties he faced in such projects. In his discussion of the issues involved, he came to the following conclusion:

> In producing the written text, one must by all means write out every single word of the oral translation. There can be no omissions at all, and neither may one augment or reduce or offer any changes at all. When it comes to making the fair copy, then one must consider making corrections for grammar and style *(wenli ziju)*, but any changes must be as close to the intention of the oral translation as possible. *It is impermissible to create departures from the original in pursuit of the elegance of the archaic (guya)* . . . and also impermissible to insert your personal opinions. If there are errors in the original and you have an opinion on them, you can insert a note to clear them up; you may not change the original.[26] (Emphasis added)

It is hardly surprising that a man as dedicated to science and its diffusion in China as Hua was would have such strict views on fidelity in translation, but Hua's views do show how problematic Wu's opinions were even in the period of cultural turmoil in which they were set forth.

The injunction to hew to the path of utmost cultivation in written expression still does not satisfy Wu that the gap between the Chinese tradition and the newly imported ideas of the West has been closed, so he adds the somewhat anticlimactic suggestion that a curriculum of sanctioned Chinese prose texts be added to the Western-style education to be offered at the new schools. Following the practice of the post-1820 Tongcheng school, Wu places the writings of Yao Nai at the core of this body of work, basing himself now on a wish for clarity. He notes that any older —and, by implication, more profound—books would simply be over the heads of novice learners. The extraordinary vacillation with which Wu approaches the whole question of the flexibility of *wen* demonstrates, I think, how much more is as stake here than can be accommodated by any notions we might consider to be "mere" style. When Wu thinks of *wen* here, he evidently has in mind at all times the overtones of the word having to do with the essence of the cultural tradition itself and the means by which one gains access to it. His insistence on a punctilious observation of formal detail is thus only natural. The adamant refusal to recognize the possibility of any stylistic variations among different registers of writing, however, isolates Wu and his cohort on one horn of a dilemma. While he does evince an awareness of the need to reconcile the new ideas being introduced in response to the great social changes in the burgeoning cities of maritime China, at the same time he determines himself to hold steadfast to the purity and integrity of the old forms of expression.

In a new environment in which practical links between past and present became ever more difficult to maintain, the problems inhering in the Tongcheng literal adhesion to *guwen* norms, with its concomitant emphasis on a direct line of succession from the Tang and Song, became increasingly evident. That the most significant prose produced after 1900 within the school is archaic prose translations of Western works—including, ironically enough, *guwen* translations of novels—demonstrates just how untenable were Tongcheng theories of maintaining intellectual unity in their own time by upholding a direct link with the sages. The Tongcheng writers did take great pains to put their own notions of style ahead of generic distinctions whenever they ventured into an unfamiliar mode of writing. Their audiences, however, inevitably seemed to focus on the surface message rather than on the intricate cultural code so sedulously inscribed within the careful texture of the writing itself.

The greatest translator of foreign works into *guwen* other than Yan Fu was Lin Shu (1852–1924), whose choice of genres presents something of a taxonomic problem. Lin was a remarkable scholar who knew no English but wrote classical Chinese adaptations of Western novels as he listened to an assistant proficient in a European language orally translate into colloquial Chinese.[27] Even more remarkable, perhaps, are Lin's endeavors to colonize the previously tabooed territory of the novel for archaic prose. The irony of his rendering the most vernacular of genres into the most formal linguistic mode is best illustrated by the fact that the net result of his efforts to translate foreign novels into *guwen* was to augment the prestige of the novel rather than to produce any long-term gain in the audience for archaic prose.[28] Thus the question arises of whether to discuss his work under the rubric of classical prose—which almost certainly would have been his choice—or in the next chapter, which is devoted to the novel and its late Qing critics. There is no real answer here—the choice itself mirrors the difficulty of the question, but in the end I have decided to follow Lin's own visions of himself as a promoter of archaic prose.

If Lin's prefatory remarks to his translations are to be believed, however, he was anything but condescending in his approach to the Western novel. On the contrary, he appears deeply impressed with what he finds there, particularly the elements of formal composition, which he compares favorably with the *guwen* style of the *Shiji*.[29] But what Lin seems to find most remarkable about the Western novel is the sustained interest in the commonplace that Dickens is able to maintain throughout the recounting of a long chain of events. In his introduction to his translation of *David Copperfield,* for instance, Lin admits to being unable to find any Chinese equivalent to Dickens' skill at narrative. After first dismissing the Ming novel *Shuihu zhuan* (The water margin) for sensationalism, not to mention its inability to sustain character individuality over the full course of the story, Lin says of *David Copperfield:* "This book narrates only the most scattered events of everyday life; if someone with skillful pen were not writing it, then of course it would be so placid as to put one right to sleep. But Dickens is able to transform the worn-out into the wonderful, to take the dispersed and organize it, to take the five animals and myriad oddities and fuse them through his spirit—his is truly a unique style."[30]

Style and plot structure were not, however, the only things that attracted Lin Shu to Dickens. The translator was equally interested in what he perceived to be the Western novel's profound capacity to inspire social reform. In his preface to his adaptation of *Oliver Twist*, for instance, Lin goes so far as to imply that England owed much of its position in the world to its novels, which had engendered prodigious governmental and social reform:

> Without Dickens describing the situation, how would people know about this nest of thieves persisting in their midst? England's ability to be strong, therefore, lies in its capacity to reform and follow the good. If we in China attend to this [example] and transform ourselves, we will also easily be able to change. I regret only that we have no Dickens capable of revealing accumulated social wrongs by writing [such] a novel and thus reporting these wrongs to the authorities, perhaps with similar results.[31]

Although Lin's ability to move so easily from considerations of the aesthetic to the utilitarian may strike the Western reader as odd, fluidity between the two in fact reflects the common moral basis expressed in Tongcheng ideology in particular, and in late Qing theorizing about *wen* in general. But in a time when specialization at all levels of society was proceeding apace (including in the system of imperial examinations, where tests on specialized topics were the norm after 1901),[32] Lin's attempts to embrace all facets of social organization and expression within the confines of an archaic prose style seem foredoomed to failure. That he settled on the novel as the perfect genre for his instinct for synthesis is perhaps only natural, for despite the novel's traditionally low status, there was a widespread belief at the time (as is illustrated in the next chapter) that *xiaoshuo* was seemingly the only form loose and capacious enough to hold all the elements he sees as required. But embracing the novel meant admitting the heterogeneity of the form into orthodox literary discourse and thereby running the risk of allowing the notoriously imprecise criteria for *xiaoshuo* to dramatically reshape established boundaries. The eventual supremacy of the novel in modern Chinese literature and the almost complete disappearance of *guwen* illustrate the nature of the risk that Lin was running. The compromises involved in trying to maintain an ancient prose style that could be all things to all people contributed to the growth of prose genres that increasingly marginalized the archaistic style that the late Tongcheng writers had labored so hard to infuse within such forms as the novel and the policy essay. It is a mark of the eclipse of style by content that the late Qing writer Li Xiang (1858–1931), in his 1908 account of the Tongcheng persuasion, could completely overlook Yan Fu's and Lin Shu's achievements by holding that the school had been unable to generate any writers of ability following the death of Wu Rulun in 1903.[33]

Wenxuan

The Wenxuan school was named after the Six Dynasties anthology that contained a significant portion of writing composed in the parallel style.[34] Its organizing theory followed Ruan Yuan's definition of *wen* as only that mode of writing composed of parallel couplets. *Wen* could thus easily be distinguished from purely utilitarian writing, which was classified as *bi*. In a sense this distinction offered a ready solution to the Tongcheng difficulty in absorbing new forms of writing. By setting apart a body of writing said at once to contain the direct spirit of the ancients and to be quite separate from utilitarian concern, the Wenxuan theory allowed for different writing styles, not to mention accommodating more readily to ideas about literary autonomy that became increasingly implicit in the new definition of *wenxue*. As long as one style could be set aside as the abode of the essence of the Chinese tradition, various other modes could be freely employed to account for the most recent historical contingency. This ability to be abstracted from the daily grind, indeed from all recent history, no doubt accounts for the popularity and vitality of parallel prose in the final years of the Qing. In addition, Ruan Yuan had claimed that Confucius himself had initiated the parallel style, but that this fact had been obscured for hundreds of years until Ruan rediscovered it.[35] These intimations of mystical significance, with Confucius at the center, accorded perfectly with the post-1895 temper. *Wen* as Ruan Yuan had defined it many years earlier thus became a likely resting place for a new concept of "national essence," abstract and defiantly transhistorical as the idea was.

At the center of the national essence movement was Liu Shipei (1884–1919), a scholarly prodigy who, along with Zhang Binglin, was one of the twin pillars of anti-Manchu revolutionary anarchism in the period between 1903 and 1908.[36] Born to an illustrious family of scholars that had resided in Yangzhou for several generations, Liu gained the *juren* (provincial level) degree at the tender age of nineteen *sui* but was unsuccessful in the metropolitan examinations the next year, 1903. After failing the exams, he went to Shanghai, where he met anti-Manchu activists like Zhang and Cai Yuanpei and quickly became involved in radical politics himself. Returning home, he soon came back to Shanghai, bringing his fiancée, He Ban, back with him; they married in that city soon thereafter. She entered the Patriotic Girls' School (Aiguo nüxue), changing her given name to Zhen ("shock, shake") in the process, a sign of her entry into radical politics.[37] Liu was involved in a number of publishing ventures in Shanghai, notably the *Jingzhong ribao* (Alarm bell daily news). When the newspaper was closed by the authorities in 1905, Liu fled, first to Zhejiang and eventually to Anhui, a center of radical activism, before ending up in Japan in February 1907.

Zhang Binglin had been appointed editor of the *Minbao* (People's journal)[38] — the organ of Sun Yat-sen's revolutionary political organization, the Tongmeng hui — after his release from prison in Shanghai and removal to Tokyo in the summer of 1906. Zhang invited Liu Shipei to participate in the magazine, which was apparently extremely popular and influential at the time,[39] and Liu became a principal contributor to it, joining the Tongmeng hui soon after his arrival in Tokyo. For the remainder of 1907 and much of 1908 Zhang and Liu managed to transform the tenor of the journal from one devoted to practical politics to one that focused on abstruse matters of political and cultural theory. During their time in Tokyo, Liu and He Zhen also published the *Tianyi bao* (Natural justice journal), which was devoted to the promotion of radical anarchism. Both journals were shut down by the Japanese government in 1908, not long after Liu and He had a falling out with Zhang;[40] Liu then returned to China. In general the Tongmeng hui was having a hard time of it in this period, with a good deal of dissension, internal strife, and questioning of Sun's leadership, but Liu's suddenly turning up in the personal secretariat of Duanfang (1861–1911), the Manchu governor-general at Nanjing, right after Liu's departure from Japan must still be counted as a remarkable turn of events.[41] Even though Duanfang was an enlightened modernizer and a generous patron of talent, for someone of Liu Shipei's extreme views to move suddenly toward accommodation with the regime he had bitterly opposed for so many years came as a real shock to his erstwhile compatriots. Liu remained in Duanfang's entourage until the distinguished official was killed in Sichuan in the revolutionary violence of 1911. Liu himself eventually ended up in Beijing in 1914, became a professor of Chinese at Beijing University in 1917, and died prematurely of consumption in 1919, at the age of thirty-six *sui*.

For all the mutability and even caprice apparent in Liu's strange political career, his thinking about culture remained consistent. In fact, his most important legacy from these years, certainly in terms of scholarly influence, was his co-founding of the Society for the Protection of National Studies (Guocui baocun hui) in January 1905 and his continuing participation in the society, along with Deng Shi and Huang Jie. Within a month of its founding, the society began publishing the *Guocui xuebao* (National essence journal).[42] The term *"guocui"* had been borrowed from Japan, where, as *"kokusui,"* it had been a concept developed in the late 1880s to assert a sense of national singularity in the face of pressing demands for Westernization.[43] As cosmopolitan as he may have been in his role of revolutionary at the time, Liu clearly felt the need to anchor himself with a firm sense of Chinese cultural identity. As part of his cultural explorations, he wrote a treatise on the idea of *wen*, wherein one of his central concerns was to verify Ruan Yuan's understanding of the term and its history. He gathered elaborate amounts of historical evidence to support what he regarded as the vital distinction between belletristic *wen* and the utilitarian *bi*. Much of this treatise is devoted to strictly textual questions, where he does not go into the reasons he considers *wen* to be so important.

Occasionally, however, Liu offers impassioned explanations of the source of his commitment, as in this passage analyzing the various meanings of *wen:*

> In China during the Three Ancient Dynasties [Xia, Shang, and Zhou], cultural works were taken as *wen,* elegance was taken as *wen,* rites, music, law, etiquette, and letters were all taken as belles lettres *(wenzhang).* From this the classics came to be called *wen,* as did writing *(wenzi),* as well as the spoken language *(yanci).* The use of *"wen"* in the belletristic sense began

with the "Wenyan" [commentary on the *Book of Changes*] of Confucius. So *"wen"* is to be glossed as "ornament," that is to say, as a beautiful and ordered display. Therefore, *wen* is the external manifestation of the *dao* as well as the sequential ordering of events.[44]

While Liu rigorously sets out the various meanings of *wen* through most of this passage, he ends in a display of historical faith by gathering all the overtones of *wen* into a definition that is much greater than the sum of its parts. As with the theorists of *guwen*, for Liu *wen* turns out to be not only the "external manifestation of the *dao* as well as the sequential ordering of events" but at the same time a specific literary style. In other words, the conflation of a particular writing style with the cultural legacy as a whole urges Liu to the judgment that cultural continuity depends upon certain clear rules of rhetoric as difficult to deploy successfully as they were easy to describe. It is hard not to see this move as marking off the territory where the national essence will reside. Liu's definition also clearly seems to be a justification for the incipient promotion in status of a newly defined conception of what was even then coming to be thought of as *wenxue*. Liu's choice to focus upon restoring Ruan Yuan's notion of *wen* implied a consequential reduction in value of other forms of writing to a position of mere utility, necessary for a host of general purposes but without the links to the *dao*, or cultural essence, that Liu saw as the sum and substance of *wen*. This division among the functions of various literary styles, however, was not available to the heirs of the Tongcheng school. For Liu, as for many of the English romantics analyzed by Raymond Williams in *Culture and Society*, the "reach for control" over society, which Williams takes as the core function of culture in an unstable period, required that literature retreat to more rarefied precincts, even as those engaged in its creation asserted the mystical preeminence and theoretical omnipotence of literary writing.[45]

The ability of parallel prose to split practice and essence and to sanction a realm of purely literary expression perhaps accounts for its resurgence during the last years of the Qing. This impression is fortified by the fact that many of the new adherents to the *pianti* style were converts away from archaic prose. The young political activist and victim of the September 1898 reaction, Tan Sitong (1865–1898), for instance, wrote in his "Sanshi ziji" (Personal account at thirty) — in tones that perhaps influenced Liang Qichao when he came to write his own memoirs at thirty a few years later — that he had recently made just such a conversion:

> When I was young, I was very much in awe of the Tongcheng school, and for a number of years I made a point of basing my writing on theirs. Eventually I thought my writing had come to resemble theirs, and other

people thought so too. By the time, however, that I had happened to read a good number of books and had come to know many of the learned men of our age, I began to feel a bit ashamed of having no real way to express myself. Someone showed me the [parallel prose] of the Wei and Jin dynasties, which made me happy; I frequently read it and became ever more fond of it.⁴⁶

Tan's sense that *guwen* is neither fine enough to allow nuanced expression nor broad enough to accommodate a wide range of learning evinces itself here.

Comparison between the two schools of prose that had dominated intellectual discourse in the nineteenth century in their final, late Qing manifestations reveals how the intellectual crisis that precipitated the "discovery of culture" undermined the hopes for a unified field of learned discourse that at least the Tongcheng definition of *wenxue* had taken as its goal. Those devoted to archaic prose—with their ideal of learning, moral cultivation, and expression all conducted within the same stylistic frame of reference—concentrated their intellectual efforts into holding to the carefully developed and deliberately austere *guwen* style, even when they ventured out into experiments with new genres. In an age of increasing specialization on the one hand, and increasingly strident demands to expand the potential audience for written texts on the other, however, advocates of the ancient style were probably doomed to fighting a rearguard action to hold on to a steadily diminishing middle ground of discourse.

For their part, the Wenxuan school writers were freer to develop writing for practical application in other directions, as long they left a place atop their literary hierarchy for a prose based on the parallel prose that had flourished during the Six Dynasties. In the highly allusive, elaborately complex prose employed by leading Chinese thinkers like Liu and Huang Ren after 1895, we can see the influence of these efforts to place prose style on the highest possible cultural plane. Because the Wenxuan notion of *bi* in effect mandated legitimate distinctions among different levels of discourse, however, more vulgar forms became permissible, providing they recognized their lower position. Those who could not comprehend the most refined level of writing could thus always tune in some lower register. As a result, the Wenxuan theory shows much less of the intolerance toward what had often been seen in the past as unorthodox and hence somewhat dangerous "lower" forms of prose. If the Wenxuan writers were able to accept such unembellished forms, however, the Tongcheng school and its followers continued to express a quite rigid intolerance toward any writing that did not demonstrate a fine attention to style, manifested in Wu Rulun's difficulties with finding appropriate ways to fit Chinese and Western together in his ideal school curriculum.

The following argument from Liu Shipei demonstrates just how much easier it was to find justification for working with unorthodox styles within Wenxuan theory than from within Tongcheng notions of the sanctity of a unified, archaic style. Given his exalted notion of what *wen* should be, it would seem counterintuitive that Liu could accept what he would inevitably regard as the debased form of the vernacular, no matter how much attention was devoted to its composition. He in fact prefigures what would eventually become the mainstream position on the vernacular by claiming its advent to be part of the general process of evolution. With this justification, he not only found his way to accepting it, however, but also actually embraced certain uses of the vernacular as a matter of some urgency, the refinement of language in this case being furthest from his mind. The following discussion of *baihua* from his work *Lun wen zaji* (Miscellaneous notes on literature) has often been cited as evidence that Liu supported the general use of the colloquial language,[47] but his argument is more complex than it may seem at first glance.

After first establishing that the Chinese language has been in a long process of decline, Liu allows that use of the vernacular is but the next logical step in the process:

> Speaking of writing in terms of the general theory of evolution, China upon entering into the modern age must reach the stage of allowing the common language to penetrate literature *(wen)*. . . . Uniting speech and writing will lead to an increase in literacy, while using the vernacular to promote books and periodicals will allow those who are even slightly literate to place [these publications] in their homes, thereby aiding in the awakening of the people. This is indeed a pressing task in today's China.[48]

But after allowing the colloquial a generous space with one hand, he sets it firmly in its place with the other:

> How can we, however, then rush to discard the ancient language? Contemporary writing should thus be divided into two schools: one devoted to the common language and used to enlighten the mass of people, and another using the ancient language and used to preserve the national learning in order to carry on the norms of the venerable sages. If, however, one boastfully ranges too widely in pursuit of the strange and takes Japanese as a model, I have never been able to see how this can become *wen*.[49]

Liu thus always believed there to be a higher mission for superior prose that allowed for the simultaneous existence of a utilitarian and stylistically crude vernacular, a division of literary labor evidently quite common in societies with both expanding rates of readership and uneven distribution of educational opportunity and attainment.[50] Nevertheless, as the final sentence of the passage indicates (one can safely assume that it is an attack on Liang Qichao's "new style"[51]), Liu is determined to resist any broadening or hybridization of the discrete prose styles he has taken such care in identifying.

The Wenxuan tolerance of unorthodox styles played an important part in bringing to late Qing letters in general a sense of freedom of manipulation that often had utopian overtones—particularly in regard to those who advocated the novel, as chapter 4 will demonstrate. The consequent loss of a unified field of intellectual discourse, such a vital focus of scholarly attention throughout the Qing dynasty, was, however, to have a number of unforeseen results. One of the most important is hinted at by Yan Fu's lament quoted above: "If one uses the vulgar language current today, it is difficult to get the point across: one always suppresses the idea in favor of the expression." In other words, Yan feared that the move away from a uniform writing style would be a Tower of Babel and the source of pollution for Chinese written expression. If *guwen* (for all its ostensible lack of flourish) demanded years of practice before a satisfactory result was in reach of the individual writer, it also promised to deliver standard meanings within standard contexts. Any trifling with this order of expression, then, threatened the onset of a terrible opacity within the realm of letters.

The New Style

Toward the end of his life, Liang Qichao wrote a brief account of Qing intellectual history, in which he included a fairly substantial third-person narrative of his own position. One paragraph describes his mature prose style and how he developed it:

> Liang never liked the ancient-style writing of the Tongcheng school. His own early writing had been modeled after that of the late Han, Wei, and Jin [i.e., parallel prose], and it particularly attended to dignity and refinement. Once he had attained this, he liberated himself from it and made it a rule to be plain and fluently expressive. He would often interlard his writing with colloquialisms, rhyme, and foreign expressions, letting his pen flow freely and without restraint. Scholars vied to imitate it, labeling it the "new style of prose" *(xin wenti)*. The older generation, however, resented it and slandered it as heretical. Nevertheless, his style had a clear structure, and his pen was often full of feeling, with a special charm over the reader.[52]

At first blush, the reader might be inclined to take this as simple self-promotion. Hu Shi, however, writing in 1923, noted that "over the past twenty years, there have been almost no scholars who have not been influenced by [Liang's] style."[53] The literary scholar Qian Jibo (1887–1955), writing in 1930, also offered evidence that Liang was not idly boasting: "Even now, when scholars under sixty and over forty [i.e., those born between 1870 and 1890] write of politics or academic matters, they never fail to display the hidden influence of Liang."[54]

Liang Qichao left an even more detailed account of his own educational experiences and the literary influences he was subject to in a brief memoir he published in 1901. Entitled "Sanshi zishu" (Personal account at thirty), Liang's narrative of his own Bildung, or experience of intellectual development, provides eloquent testimony to the anxieties occasioned by the unsettled intellectual environment in China during the final years of the nineteenth century. Liang begins this short saga by recounting his experiences when he entered a preparatory academy near his home at age twelve *sui:*

> [There I] daily worked at examination prose *(tiegua)*, and although I was not satisfied with it, I did not realize that there was anything on earth other than examination prose that could be called learning. So I immersed myself in it. But I still loved belles lettres *(cizhang)*, and my grandfather and my parents gave me Tang poetry from time to time, which delighted me far more than did *bagu* [essays in the examination style]. Because our family was poor, we owned few books, and we had only a copy of the *Shiji* and the *Gangjian yizhi lu* (Primer of historical events). My father and grandfather taught me from these books, and to this day I can still recite eighty or ninety percent of the *Shiji*. Among my father's close friends was one who cherished intelligence, and he presented us with a copy of the *Hanshu* and Yao Nai's [anthology], the *Guwenci leizuan*.[55] . . . At thirteen *sui*, I first learned of the philology of Duan [Yucai, 1735–1815] and Wang [Niansun, 1744–1832]. I liked it very much and gradually developed the ambition to cast aside examination-style prose. . . . [At age fifteen *sui*], I took up my studies at the Xuehai tang in the provincial capital, an institution founded by former viceroy Ruan Yuan in the Jiaqing period [1796–1820] in order to train the Cantonese in philology and belles lettres. At this time, I decided to give up examination prose in favor of these pursuits, and I came to the realization that aside from philology and belles lettres there was nothing on earth that could be called learning.[56]

In other words, Liang had begun with a fairly standard education in examination prose and *guwen*. He had, however, quickly moved beyond these two genres once he discovered the appeal of the combination of scholarship and embellished prose that became the trend in the final years of the dynasty.

After an unsuccessful attempt at the *jinshi* degree in Beijing, Liang (by now a prodigious *juren*) returned to Canton in the autumn of 1890. There his classmate at the Xuehai tang, Chen Qianqiu, told him of the political activity and of the novel ideas of the activist scholar Kang Youwei. Upon first going to see Kang, the two younger men stayed the whole day. Liang described the experience:

> [It was like] cold water poured on my back or like a direct blow to the head: in one moment the entire structure of my old [learning] *(gulei)* was gone, and I was at a loss as to what I was doing. I was in shock, but happy; resentful, but composed *(yi)*; full of doubt, yet fearful. [That night] I shared a room with [Chen Qianqiu], and neither of us could sleep the whole night through. We went again to visit the next day and asked for scholarly guidance, and the teacher [Kang] taught us of the *xinxue* (learning of the heart-mind) of Lu [Jiuyuan, 1139–1193] and Wang [Yangming, 1472–1529], as well as touching upon the basics of history and Western learning. From this time on, I determined to cast aside the old learning, so of course I withdrew from the Xuehai tang and every other day sought to continue my studies with Mr. Nanhai [Kang Youwei]. What I know of learning in my life began from that moment.⁵⁷

As the example of Yan Fu makes clear, it was not particularly remarkable in the volatile period of the 1890s in China for such oscillations of scholarly orientation to be registered. On the other hand, it is of interest that in this account of intellectual peregrination, Liang presents the new learning from the West only as a small part of the knowledge that he eventually came to take as definitive and as much subsidiary to Lu-Wang *xinxue*. Although one suspects that the advent of Western learning actually represents a much larger part of this transformation than Liang allows here, his ability to portray an almost purely domestic intellectual world marked by substantial variety and scope is significant. On the other hand, the very Kang Youwei who figures so largely in Liang's narrative "is said to have told a reporter in 1898 that he owed his conversion to reform chiefly to the writings of [the missionaries Timothy] Richard and [Young J.] Allen."⁵⁸ Liang himself in his autobiography has a brief account of a visit to Shanghai in 1890, where he "bought a copy of *Yinghuan zhilue* (Treatise on the world), by Xu Jiyu [1795–1873],⁵⁹ in a bookstore." Liang continued, "Upon reading it, [I] realized for the first time the existence of the five continents and the assorted countries on them. [I] also noticed that the Jiangnan Arsenal (Jiangnan zhizao ju) had translated a number of Western books, and I was drawn to them; unfortunately, I was unable to buy any [because of a shortage of funds]."[60] In other words, however casual he pretends to be about it, the above reference to his discovery of the world only through Western books discloses the extent that Liang's encounters with Western books were a crucial part of the mix in his educational progress in his formative period.

As Liu Shipei pointed out, the literary sources Liang claims as instrumental to his liberation—colloquialisms, rhyme, and foreign (principally Japanese) expressions—are precisely those elements that both of the dominant schools of late Qing prose would have ruled out as unorthodox and thus detrimental to the purity of either form. In a sense, then, Liang stresses the types of literary expression proscribed by the major theories, but he is aware that the usage of them was so widespread that any comprehensive notion of writing or literature would somehow need to account for them. Moreover, Hu Shi suggests that every stage that Liang went through left its trace on the style he had developed by the late 1890s, specifically including the *bagu* form that was such a bête noir to modern Chinese men of letters.[61] Both Hu and Qian Jibo stress the innovative qualities to Liang's style—for instance, its liveliness and capacity to expound at length.[62] Hu, however, is critical of what he seems to regard as a kind of rhythmic verbosity embedded in the style, something he sees as especially noticeable—and unfortunate—in attempts by others to imitate Liang's style in later years. For his own part Liang gives no indication that any higher order of writing anchors his eclectic New Prose Style, although the mode in which "Personal Account at Thirty" is composed is notably denser than what we take as the norm for his prose.[63]

The general late Qing conviction that literature was obliged to be hortatory concorded perfectly with the dictum of Zhou Dunyi (1017–1073) that "writing should convey the way" *(wen yi zai dao)*, a phrase that had been enthusiastically adopted by Zhu Xi (1130–1200) and had thus become the key neo-Confucian guide to prose composition in the Ming and Qing. The various theories of how to write prose generated under this general guideline, however, invariably also took great care to stress the authority of earlier writing thought to embody the right combination of moral rectitude and practical direction that constituted the *dao*. Although this guideline may have muted creativity, as many modern critics were to claim, it did guarantee a continuity and a gravity to language by limiting abuse of the accepted conventions of meaning and usage. This was something on which the Tongcheng tradition put the greatest of stress. The Wenxuan school and Liang Qichao were now calling, each in his own way, for an equally (if not more) didactic writing, but without the built-in limits mandated by the need to appeal to precedent. It was also true, though, that for Liang and Liu Shipei alike, unprecedented events called for new means of expression, however much they were to be controlled by careful taxonomies of writing. These new means quickly found their own paths, much to the surprise and chagrin of those who had sanctioned the departures in the first place.

Two Nonconformists

Difficult as it was to swim against this strong pragmatic tide, there were a few nonconformists, each of whom was quite aware of how outside the mainstream he was. In fact, the rarity of attempts to deny the hold of didacticism or a special role in political discourse for various genres of writing ironically highlights just how difficult it was to separate any concept of *wenxue* from the global practical concerns of the post-1895 reform movement. Perhaps most influential of those who swam against the tide was the brilliant Zhang Binglin, a major figure in the national essence movement and a profound influence on the young intellectuals of the time. Zhang's conception of *wen* could not have differed more dramatically from that of Liu Shipei, a young man otherwise very much an intellectual collaborator of Zhang's. As we have seen, Liu had exalted *wen*, held it up as the key to the maintenance of the national essence, and even spoken of its incommensurability with learning *(xue)*.[64] Zhang, on the other hand, rejected any notion of special status for writing of any sort, seeing it instead as a historical storehouse that provided evidence of common national origins.[65] A self-conscious adherent of the philological rigor of the great days of the Han learning in the late eighteenth century, Zhang devoted himself to arguing against what he regarded as the pernicious effects of dehistoricizing the written tradition by indulging in overembellished letters based on misperception of the true meanings of the terms *"wen"* and *"wenzhang."*[66]

That belles lettres should not be a primary vehicle for political issues was virtually the only idea about writing that Zhang held in common with Wang Guowei. But where Zhang attempted to push literary expression aside, Wang sought to place it on a completely different plane from ordinary written discourse. This separation of literature into a rarefied realm might seem to share something with Liu Shipei, but Wang moves the distinction into quite a different direction. Wang had become familiar with the ideas of Arthur Schopenhauer before he entered the realm of literary criticism with his well-known 1904 essay on *Hong lou meng* (The dream of the red chamber; hereafter referred to as *The Story of the Stone*). Soon after he completed his critique of the famous novel by Cao Xueqin (1715–1763), Wang moved away from the metaphysical Sturm und Drang of Schopenhauer toward a Kantian definition of art as that which was characterized by "purposiveness without purpose" and marked also by a pure "disinterestedness."[67] If the import of Liu Shipei's various theories added up to a call for raising the status of aesthetic writing, Wang upon entering his Kantian phase sounded a new note in Chinese criticism: he raised the cognitive position of literature even as he promoted it to a separate ontological level. The result was a perspective that allowed more attention to the features needed to generate art and less anxiety about addressing the national agenda. The principal idea to emerge out of Wang's writings during the next several years aimed at creating a separate realm for art, as he had described it in his article on *The Story of the Stone*. This idea led to a radical new theory of the autonomy of aesthetics from social and political concerns, which he outlined in 1906 in "Wenxue xiaoyan" (Remarks on literature). He holds here that literature and philosophy must be concerned with truth rather than utility and are therefore above the conflicts of interest that inhere in any social or political analysis of phenomena. He concludes his argument rather starkly, with "literature produced for the sake of filling one's stomach simply cannot be literature."[68]

On the surface, Wang's Kantian aesthetic offers Chinese artists a freedom from political involvement rare indeed within the tradition of post-Song-dynasty Chinese letters. Closer examination, however, reveals that, rather than having severed for good the relationship between literature and politics, Wang's theory of writing seems based instead on a perception of an inevitable relationship of opposition. The idea that the pursuit of truth inherent in his concept of literature demands that literature take a critical stance toward the society it describes can easily be read into both Wang's critique of *The Story of the Stone* and his later 1906 definition. Moreover, his classification of literature as being a member of the same category as philosophy would seem to be a direct threat to maintaining aesthetics as a value transcendent in itself.

Indeed, Wang almost in spite of himself often admits of the close relationship between literature and society. In discussing Schopenhauer and Nietzsche, for instance, he avers that the two "were alike in using their unparalleled literary talent to propagate their thought."[69] Much as the thought would probably have horrified Wang at the time, this statement of the link between the world of ideas, even political ideas, and that of literary style sounds more as if it belongs to Wu Rulun writing to Yan Fu than to someone who thought of himself as the apostle of literary autonomy. As if to demonstrate his affinity to Wu, Wang made perhaps one of the more utilitarian arguments for literature on record in 1906–1907 when he, in Joey Bonner's words, declared: "There is no pastime in all of China . . . that is more sinister than opium smoking, and it is as an alternative to that repellent habit that he proposes the lower classes turn to religion and the upper classes to art."[70] Wang's eventual abandonment of literary criticism to pursue a more specifically cultural-nationalist agenda should thus not be regarded as a complete about-face. Certain clear but unspoken aspects of his ardent pursuit of a distinct literary realm between 1904 and 1906 reveal the unconscious hold on him of certain key patterns of traditional Chinese notions about writing, even as he ostensibly distances himself from them in pursuit of an admittedly Western-inspired agenda.

Looking at these theoretical writings as a whole, one cannot but be struck by the extent of their ambitions for literature, even as that new category is being articulated for the first time. Elements perceived as indigenous are in constant negotiation with those regarded as being new imports, with the results almost always being other than what the advocates of various ideas had in mind to start with. From one perspective it would be easy to dismiss these struggles over writing as merely desperate attempts to salvage cultural meaning that never succeeded in making substantial links to literary practice. Indeed, the one thread that seems to link all the theories—namely, that literature could serve as a vital center for cultural renewal—now looks more like a revelation of the depths of the cultural crisis of the time than a realistic expectation for its solution. Nonetheless, the uncertainties brought to the fore by these struggles marked the signal importance of the literary arena, and this critical ferment brought a new vitality to literature. The primary locus of this activity, however, was to be the novel, a genre rarely taken seriously before that time. And as we shall see in chapter 4, it was, paradoxically, precisely this low esteem and scant attention that allowed fiction to be at once the repository of hopes for the future and the site wherein could be heaped much of the intellectual discontent with the legacy of the Chinese past.

CHAPTER 4

New Theories of the Novel

> People these days are reluctant to read the canonical texts, but they love fiction. Not all fiction, mind you, for they are sick of exemplary themes and far prefer the obscene and the fantastic. How low contemporary morals have sunk!
> Li Yu, in Patrick Hanan (translator), *The Carnal Prayer Mat (Rou putuan)* (1657)

> We speak of a cultural revolution, and we must certainly see the aspiration to extend the active process of learning, with the skills of literacy and other advanced communication, to all people rather than to limited groups, as comparable in importance to the growth of democracy and the rise of scientific industry.
> Raymond Williams, *The Long Revolution*

Even after discounting the heavy irony in Li Yu's assessment of literary taste in seventeenth-century China, his words still serve to underline the suspect position of the novel in premodern Chinese letters. That even Lin Shu, however, representing the most conservative literary force in the China of his time, was enticed by the possibilities he saw in fictional narrative illustrates both the appeal that some sort of renewed *xiaoshuo* held for post-1895 intellectuals and the transformation in ideas concerning literature that began to ferment during this era. The novel was eventually to become so important in this period that it is virtually the only form about which theorists from each of the literary schools outlined in chapter 3 had something to say. Undergirding this critical attention was an explosion in the number of novels written and published in the last fifteen years of the Qing, including the unprecedented phenomenon of large numbers of translations into Chinese of European, American, and Japanese fiction. This activity centered on Shanghai, where remarkable economic and population growth was creating a new type of urban society that in many ways resembled modern cities in Europe and America more than anything ever seen previously in China.[1]

In fact, the general effort to raise the social and intellectual status of the novel is probably the best-remembered literary event in the final decade of Manchu rule. The plasticity and popular appeal of the genre itself accounted for most of this enthusiasm, offering the prospect of vastly increasing the audience for the messages that writers hoped to get across. This sense of potential—combined with a lack of any firm or, at least, positive notion of what the *xiaoshuo* actually had been in prior Chinese literary thought—brought forth a wide variety of hopes for and definitions of the novel, most of them centering on the educational function of the genre. But this combination of a sparse critical tradition, plus the sense that there were few specific indigenous models to provide guidance, raised basic questions regarding the relationship of the events it narrated to events that had actually taken place. It also brought considerable anxiety and confusion, in regard not only to what the *xiaoshuo* could and could not do, but also to what it should and should not do.[2] The efflorescence of the late Qing novel, then, was built on a highly unstable substratum.

Probably the clearest justification for the new focus on the novel was the idea that the form could accommodate two urgent requirements: a larger audience for writing, and a form that could effectively represent to this larger audience the full dimensions of the crisis that China was facing. The social demands on writing extended well beyond the advocacy of a new importance to be conferred upon the novel. The summing up of recent changes in methods of poetic composition as a "revolution in the realm of poetry" *(shijie geming)*, for instance, was announced in 1901 by Liang Qichao even before his call for the New Novel.[3] Huang Zunxian (1848–1904), the best-known advocate and practitioner of a new sort of poetry, had clearly been intent upon both meeting the twin demands of increasing readership for his chosen vehicle of expression and investing it with new social content.[4] In his determination to broach issues related to politics and technology, Huang quite self-consciously sought to broaden both the scope and the reach of the lyric genre that had previously been regarded as the avenue for the self-expression of only a narrow group of the highly educated.

The novel, however, was soon to be regarded as the obvious candidate for appropriation as a tool to reach a broader audience. As Yuan Jin characterizes the situation, "poetry seems to have been the first to use the term 'revolution' to boast of changes to literary genres, but fiction eventually dominated in this."[5] The dominance of fiction came about not only because of the historical view that it was the genre that spoke to the elite about popular concerns but also because it had, in fact, enjoyed widespread popularity throughout the nineteenth century.[6] For all its evident suitability for the task of popularization, the *xiaoshuo* took some time to catch on as a medium of political reform, perhaps because of lingering prejudice about the vulgarity of the form. For instance, Huang Zunxian in his discussion of literature in *Ribenguo zhi* (Treatises on Japan), a popular series of observations composed in the late 1880s and published in China in 1890, launches one of the first comprehensive appeals for the use of the vernacular in Chinese writing, based on the notion that a closer link between the spoken and written languages will render the latter easier to learn. Even though he mentions the novel as being close to the spoken language, he makes no attempt to advocate either its widespread use or its reform.[7] The early reform activist Qiu Tingliang (1857–1943) was even more militant on the matter of the utility of the vernacular, as is evident in the title of his most famous surviving piece of writing, the 1898 "Lun baihua wei weixin zhi ben" (On the vernacular being the basis for reform). In a long text that goes into any number of reasons for and historical references to the vernacular, he mentions fiction but once, and then only in passing, as something that Japanese schoolchildren can read because of the closer links between writing and speech that had become the norm in that country.[8]

One practical consequence of the eventual adoption of the novel as a device to further reform was a new pressure for relevance, with the direct result that fiction written after 1895 took a much more direct interest in current issues than had fiction written before that time. The semi-journalistic tone of much of the new writing perhaps inevitably represented a coarsening of the refined argumentation that had characterized earlier "literati novels" such as *The Story of the Stone* and *The Scholars.* As part of a general sense that the scope of civic discourse needed to be widened, the presumed simplicity of *xiaoshuo* (a term roughly synonymous with "fictional narrative") vernacular was reevaluated in these years. This simplicity was seen no longer as a mark of cultural inadequacy but as the genre's great advantage—its ostensible legibility was transformed suddenly into its great virtue.

The concomitant augmentation of *xiaoshuo*'s responsibilities was made possible by a more fluid environment in which previously stable hierarchies of literary genres were suddenly seen as being contingent upon particular historical circumstances and thus open to wide-ranging change. One of the principal justifications of the need for a wider readership, for instance, arose out of a particular Chinese reading of Japanese and Western modernization as having been the result of increased civic participation, facilitated in large part by popular consumption of socially progressive novels.[9] Of course, such a drastic recasting of interpretive mode also implied a more or less desperate search for a new intellectual order to replace the old one. But this new enthusiasm for the novel contained an important caveat, in the pattern first introduced by Yan Fu: the discussion of the genre often made explicitly invidious distinctions between the desirable novel in its foreign (i.e., Western and Japanese) setting and the traditional Chinese narrative, a form considered rife with corruption. This same distinction was to be mirrored almost precisely in the May Fourth discourse on the realistic novel some twenty years later.[10] Critics thus discriminated within the genre of the novel itself. The traditional (i.e., Chinese) *xiaoshuo* was retrograde, and a new ideal form based on Western and Japanese models was explicitly called for and established as a new object of emulation. As with Yan Fu's new ideas on the advantages of Western statecraft, it was the external origins of the new novel that provided it with the leverage it required for its new mission of effecting social communication and reform.

A Critical Discourse Begins

The principal justification offered by critics for their enthusiasm for fiction was the link between the popular appeal of the novel and the prospects for mass education that the novel thus represented. A focus on the possibilities for mass education dominated fiction criticism in the period of the "New Novel" *(xin xiaoshuo)* after Liang Qichao popularized that term in 1902. The resulting ferment has been often been subsumed under the general category of "revolution in the realm of fiction" *(xiaoshuo geming)*, Liang Qichao's 1902 term that was a back-formation on his characterization of the new poetry.[11] The first straightforward summons to unite fiction and education, however, can be traced back to none other than John Fryer (1839–1928; Chinese name, Fu Lanya), the would-be Anglican missionary who had come to be almost by default the major translator of primarily secular Western ideas into Chinese in the 1870s and 1880s. Fryer, an impecunious 1860 graduate of a government normal school in London, had come to China in 1861 to teach at an Anglican school in Hong Kong, moving on to Beijing in September 1863. After studying Beijing Mandarin for barely two months, he was obliged by the illness of his predecessor to take over as the English professor at the Tongwen Guan in November of that year. After its creation in 1862, this was a post appointed by the Chinese government, but evidently via the recommendation of the Church Missionary Society (CMS). An Anglican body existing to promote the church's missionary effort in China, the CMS duly "accepted [Fryer] as one of their agents" shortly thereafter.[12] Although Fryer often expressed strong reservations about both his enthusiasm for and the good of teaching English, this appointment must at least have caused him to think that he had been brought closer than ever to his "desire to be engaged in more direct missionary work,"[13] which had motivated his journey to China in the first place. Moreover, having now secured a stable position in Beijing, Fryer proceeded in 1864 to send for his fiancée from England, and she duly arrived in Beijing in the fall of that year.

A terrible—and fateful—scandal ensued. Fryer's intended had apparently had an extended affair with the captain of the ship on which she was traveling, and she seems to have arrived in China pregnant. Fryer married her soon thereafter in a hasty wedding ceremony in November in Beijing, after which he arranged immediately for her to return to England from Shanghai early the following year, along with "her child."[14] Word was out within the small foreign community in the Chinese capital, however, and the resulting brouhaha caused the CMS to make a quick decision: "The only course open, in respect of the Society, is that you [i.e., Fryer] should close your connexion with us. It is quite impossible that we should retain as an accredited Agent of the Society one whose wife is under such a cloud."[15] Fryer's protestations that his wife "was during the great part of the voyage kept, by the captain, under the influence of some drug of strong aphrodisiacal properties, and thus became an easy prey to him, when he had insinuated himself into her confidence"[16] were of no avail. Upon severing its ties with him, the CMS caused Fryer to lose his position at the Tongwen guan, where he was replaced by the redoubtable American W. A. P. Martin. Because of his lack of funds, he had no choice but to stay on in Shanghai after his wife's departure from the port.[17]

Even as the CMS ended its relationship with Fryer, it made possible an appointment at a new institution, the Anglo-Chinese school for Chinese boys at Shanghai, similar to his old post at St. Paul's College in Hong Kong. Although he predictably expressed little enthusiasm for this project, Fryer was obliged by bare necessity to accept the position, which he took up in the autumn of 1865. The school was a financial success and Fryer reported being pleasantly surprised by the quality of the students he had to work with. He worked out his frustrations with this meager employment not only by continuing his study of Chinese but also by taking on the editorship in November 1866 of the *Shanghai xin bao,* a Chinese newspaper founded in 1864 by the British-owned English-language weekly *North China Herald*.[18] While serving as editor of this sheet, Fryer inaugurated the first of what would become a series of contests for essays written in Chinese. This first contest, probably held in 1867 and for which three prizes were offered, required a disquisition on the "advantages and disadvantages of Chinese intercourse with Western nations,—how to increase the one and diminish the other." Fryer noted that the entries were to be "in no way flattering to Foreign Governments in their relations to China," adding, "This is especially the case in reference to the remarks on our own country."[19]

After applying to the "American Mission" for membership and being rejected "for the same reason I had to leave the C.M. Society,"[20] Fryer in 1868 finally managed to secure employment with the Chinese government at the impressive salary of eight hundred British pounds a year. Owing to his reputation for skill at Chinese, he was hired at the new Jiangnan Arsenal (Jiangnan zhizaoju), the impressive shipbuilding and armaments factory set up at the behest of first Zeng Guofan and then Li Hongzhang in the southern suburbs of Shanghai in 1865.[21] In line with the broad mandate characteristic of the so-called Tongzhi restoration of the 1860s, the enterprise extended into numerous fields, including a translation bureau that was eventually headed by Fryer. Although Fryer was delighted to leave teaching, he was also required by his employer to give up his editing job at the Shanghai Chinese paper, for the government did not wish to be affected by anything negative that might happen to be reported on its pages.

Once at the arsenal, Fryer settled in for almost thirty years, bringing his wife out from England once again and starting a family. He was ultimately to be responsible for more than half of the translations actually published at the bureau (92 out of 162), translations he first worked orally into Chinese, with a collaborator then rendering them into acceptable literary form.[22] He continued to take part in the general diffusion of scientific knowledge, primarily by acting as one of the principals behind the founding of the Chinese Polytechnic Institution and Reading Room (Gezhi shuyuan), and its attendant publication, the *Gezhi huibian* (eventually called *The Chinese Scientific and Industrial Magazine* in English) in 1875.[23] In the mid-1880s, as part of an effort to revivify the institution, Fryer inaugurated another essay contest, in this case a series of works on public affairs. The topics were set by high government officials (i.e., *daotai* [circuit intendant] and above), and each contest in the series was advertised in both the *Shen bao* and the *Hu bao*, the most important Chinese newspapers of the time (the old *Xin bao* had folded in 1872, apparently unable to compete successfully with *Shen bao*). According to a long report issued by Fryer in 1887, these contests were highly elaborate, with a new topic chosen each quarter and with three prizes awarded each time. At the end of the year, the twelve winning essays were published together as a book, and Fryer announced that he was pleased with the quality of the winning efforts.[24]

Thus, when Fryer announced his call for a "new trend in the novel" (*qiuzhe shixin xiaoshuo qi*) in the June 1895 issue of the *Wanguo gongbao*, it came as the culmination of almost thirty years of efforts to elicit written work from his Chinese reading audience, part of his long-standing general interest in popular education. The notice he posted was quite long and went into some detail as to the advantages of writing in the theretofore suspect form, now suddenly valued for its capacity to reach a large readership:

> In my opinion, nothing is more capable of moving people and changing social custom than novels, which circulate quickly and widely. After they have been in circulation for only a short time, everyone knows about them and they can thus easily transform popular habits. The three greatest evils afflicting China today are opium, the examination essay, and foot binding. Failure to make efforts to reform them would surely be a sign of a lack of wealth and power. I hereby would like to request Chinese who want their nation to flourish to write novels with a new appeal *(xin qu)* that would illuminate the harm caused by these three things and present ingenious ways to extirpate them. [Writers] should present their case, structure it as a whole, explicate it, and render it into a penetrating work, such that people who read it are powerfully moved to engage in the reform effort. It is vital that the language and syntax be clear and that the implications be graceful and compelling, such that even women and children will be able to understand it. In choosing which events to depict, take those that are contemporary and most likely to occur; above all avoid using stale formulae and do not indulge in creating strange and grotesque events that will startle the readership.[25]

As Yuan Jin has noted, "this was modern China's first explicit advocacy of the novel as a device to eliminate old abuses and to usher in the new, to enlighten the popular mentality and to transform the populace."[26] Given that Liang Qichao in these years "recommended . . . *[Wanguo gongbao]* as required reading for those who were interested in foreign affairs"[27] and that he also closely tracked Fryer's scientific translations,[28] it is almost certain that he was prominent among those who read Fryer's call for a new sort of fiction.

Although Fryer had publicly noted how pleased he had been by the writings submitted in his earlier contests, he was conspicuously disappointed by the fiction entries. His harsh assessment was published—in English—in the missionary organ *Chinese Recorder* in March 1896:

> On the whole these stories are quite up to the standard one might expect. There is a great paucity of new ideas among the Chinese, and hence many of these attempts are merely old literary rubbish and poetry worked up in a new form under a new name with but little attempt at disguise. It is a common remark that the inventive powers of the Chinese are of a low order, and this fact is abundantly manifested in these stories. There is but very little originality in them.[29]

Even if one sets aside the casual slights on the Chinese national character that were standard practice in the missionary writing of the time,[30] this is a particularly negative evaluation of the practice of Chinese fiction. This criticism was to be echoed in quite similar admonitions regarding fiction writing that were issued by Kang Youwei and Liang Qichao not long thereafter.

The idea of the novel as a serious avenue for reform was also given a major boost in the 1890s by Timothy Richard ("Li Timotai" in Chinese). He produced an abbreviated rendering in classical Chinese of *Looking Backward 2000–1887*, a 1888 novel about a future socialist utopia written by an American, Edward Bellamy. First serialized in the *Wanguo gongbao* between late 1891 and April 1892 as *Huitou kan jilue* (A short account of looking backward), it was published as a single volume in 1894 by the Guangxue hui under the title *Bainian yijiao* (A hundred-year sleep) and in a vernacular edition in 1898. The work was popular and influential, receiving notice from such important figures as Kang Youwei, Liang Qichao, and Tan Sitong; clearly influencing Liang in his unfinished 1902 venture into writing fiction, *Xin Zhongguo weilai ji* (The future of new China); and being one of the sources of inspiration for a much more important novel, Wu Jianren's 1905–1906 *Xin shitou ji* (The new story of the Stone), which is the focus of chapter 6.[31]

The mixing of advocacy of the novel into the discourse of the indigenous reform movement followed shortly. In early 1897, Liang Qichao, as part of a much longer work advocating total educational reform, included a series of recommendations on the sort of texts that should be used to educate children in a new, more vibrant fashion. He proceeded from his observation that there are far more readers of fiction than of the classics to his final recommendation of the five he issued regarding the use of fiction *(shuobu)*. Liang advocated the novel as an educational device for its ease of comprehension, noting that a general disdain for the form in the past had caused it to fall into the hands of the "modestly talented" *(xiao you cai zhi ren)*, who had merely indulged themselves in work that "incites robbery and lust *(hui yin hui dao)*." His ultimate justification for creating novels, however, contains a number of clear echoes of Fryer's formulation of two years before:

> It would now be appropriate to use solely the vernacular *(liyu)* in creating a wide range of [novels]. At their best we can use them to propagate the teachings of the sages, and at the least they dispense miscellaneous historical knowledge. In the short term they can arouse awareness of our national humiliation, and in the long term they can even tell us about the foreign mentality. As for the buffoonery of the officials, the various evils of the examination system, the stubbornness of opium addiction, and the

cruelties of foot binding, [the novel] can depict them all in great detail and can shake up the hoi polloi. Is there thus any limit to the good they can do?³²

Although Liang plainly shares a number of assumptions with John Fryer, including the conviction that the educational novel must be something new, any debt he may owe the British translator goes unacknowledged here. This failure to recognize a text he must have read probably reflects a reluctance to admit the foreign origins of ideas needed for China's form, something consonant with the Yangwu ideology described in chapter 1. It was around this time, after all, when Liang was still making the characteristic Yangwu claim, in Hao Chang's words, "that the Chinese cultural tradition had anticipated many of the modern Western values and institutions and had also developed some of them to a higher degree than had yet been attained in the West."³³

Toward the end of the same year that Liang was writing his views on reform, the Tianjin *Guowen bao* published over three days a long, anonymous leading article entitled "Guowen baoguan fuyin shuobu yuanqi" (The reasons behind our decision to publish a fiction supplement). Because the article was not signed, it was assumed to have been written by the editors, Yan Fu and Xia Zengyou, and most scholars concluded that because of the many references to Western history and literature in the piece, it was mainly the work of Yan Fu. The editor of *Collected Works of Yan Fu*, however, considers Xia to have been the essay's primary author,³⁴ so I will assume it to have been a collaboration, at least in general conception. Be that as it may, the leaders' argument centers, as had Liang's, on the popularity of the novel, perceived to be a result of the form's vividness of description, which ensures the endurance of the events it narrates. But even as the essay goes on to presuppose the extravagant proposition that "[w]e have heard that . . . Europe, America, and Japan invariably relied on the assistance of the novel at the time of their enlightenment *(kaihua),*"³⁵ it contains an undercurrent of disapproval of the moral improprieties and untruths the genre allows.

The authors attempt to reconcile themselves to these moral problems by making the following assertions: "[W]hen the ancients composed novels, they may well have included subtle implications that they lodged between the lines of their texts. These were, however, well hidden and difficult to uncover. People of shallow learning, lost as they were [in the surface meanings], were thus unable to overcome the damaging features of fiction [by unearthing these implications], and it is difficult to identify the advantages to be gained [from reading it]."³⁶ By maintaining that the novel can ultimately be justified only by investing it with subtleties that have, almost by definition, eluded the very readers who created its popularity (the only real reason Yan and Xia take it seriously in the first place), the authors have gravely complicated their case. If they have at one stroke cleared the way for a more positive critical evaluation of the form, they have also rendered the argument for popular education through fiction problematic. And they have raised the stakes for novels of the future: if they cannot be found to contain the subtleties so carefully imbedded by the ancients in their fictional works, novels will be found wanting. The grounds for which they will be found wanting, however, must remain ultimately ambiguous: will it be a matter of imperfectly placed political messages or imperfect composition?

Kang Youwei entered into this discussion at about the same time, also noting the popularity of novels and their consequent suitability as texts to teach children. His advocacy, however, sacrifices the complex reservations registered by Liang, Xia, and Yan, resulting in a utilitarian exhortation that seems little more than a pastiche of pedagogical slogans:

> Among those who are barely literate, there are those who do not read the classics, but none who do not read novels. So if you cannot teach them the Six Classics, you should use novels to teach them. If the standard histories make no impact, novels should be used. If law cannot control people, then novels should be used for control. People of complete knowledge are scarce in this world, while the ignorant are many. People with a thorough grounding in the humanities *(wenxue)* are few, while those with a crude knowledge are many.... There are few literate people in China today, and even fewer who thoroughly comprehend the humanities *(wenxue)*, so fiction is the perfect vehicle to communicate the intentions of the classics and a knowledge of history. How the study of the novel is valued in the West![37]

While the educational benefit of the (right kind of) novel is trumpeted here, Kang also is at pains to draw attention to the immense gap in learning between the highly educated (i.e., those few who can actually purchase and read the classics) and the broader mass of the barely literate. In this passage it is impossible to determine whether by *"wenxue"* he intends the broader meaning of the humanities in general or its new, restricted sense as a translation for the English word "literature." In any event, the suitability of the novel as a component of high culture seems thoroughly compromised here, although the utilitarian tagline of its contributions to Western success in the world does paper this over.

When Liang Qichao returned to commenting on fiction—one of the first things he did after narrowly escaping with his life to Japan after the failure of the "Hundred Days Reform" in September 1898—the reservations he had expressed the year before were amplified. In "Yi yin zhengzhi xiaoshu xu" (Preface to publishing translations of political novels), a work that was to become extremely influential, Liang announced the need for the importation of a new category of fiction from the West, the political novel. Even as he made extravagant claims for its social role, however, he contrasted it invidiously with the Chinese novel as it existed at the time. In fact, according to this essay, about the only thing the traditional Chinese novel was good for was to reveal that only the vulgar avenue of fiction could reach out beyond the small band of men who defined themselves as dedicated to high cultural seriousness:[38]

> *Xiaoshuo* in China, although listed in the traditional bibliographic categories [of the *Hanshu*], has produced few good works since the *Yu chu* [the work conventionally regarded as having initiated the category].[39] When [a writer] wished to write of heroism, he took *Shuihu zhuan* [The water margin] as his model; when he spoke of relationships between men and women, he followed *The Dream of the Red Chamber*. In general there was nothing that did not fit into the two categories of inciting robbery and inciting debauchery *(hui yin hui dao)*. All these [works] followed one another and stuck with one another [in their perpetuation of the harmful]. Therefore, presentable writers disdained [the genre].
>
> Although this is so, the fact is that human nature hates the serious and likes frivolity . . . . So there is nothing to be done about it when scholars take time from their learning and take up *Dream of the Red Chamber* and *The Water Margin*. Therefore, to try to forbid [fiction] is not as good as trying to make it better. What Mr. Nanhai [Kang Youwei] said [in the passage quoted above] is correct.[40]

This total condemnation of the Chinese novel as it existed up to Liang's time is striking, and his choice of the two most prominent works in the fictional canon as implicit negative influences would seem to allow for no exceptions. That he ends the piece with a ringing affirmation of the powers of a specifically political novel in the West—"It often happened that upon the appearance of a book a whole nation would change its views on current affairs. The political novel has been instrumental in making the governments of [the West and Japan] daily more progressive or enlightened"[41]—does nothing to close the gap between his hopes for the form in general and the low regard he has for every novel ever written in Chinese. By thus cutting off any practical appeal to native precedent, Liang's call puts up a huge barrier between what he advocated and the fictional languages available to writers at the time, even as he agrees with his mentor Kang about the necessity of turning fiction into a medium for education. In addition, by focusing exclusively on the presumed flaws in the indigenous fictional texts, Liang is able to displace any traces of Fryer's influence onto praise and blame for specific novels, rather than having to acknowledge the embarrassing presence of the Western intellectual initiative that suggested fiction as a device for national reform in the first place. Fiction's potential as a formative influence on the new nation is thus kept that much closer to a discourse of national history, however fraught with ambiguity as to the extent of foreign inspiration and influence involved in the turn to the form.

This thoroughgoing rejection of the indigenous narrative tradition was to become an intellectual commonplace in the twentieth century, from the May Fourth period in the late 1910s to the critiques by Qu Qiubai (1899–1935) in the early 1930s and on to the Chinese critical arena as it sprang back to life in the 1980s, forty or so years after Mao Zedong's proclamations on literature at Yan'an in 1942.[42] But Liang's steadfast vision of a novel that can, after it has been thoroughly reformed, serve as the most powerful instrument of change is probably the most remarkable thing about this essay. To cite only one of the problems with this formulation, however, the contrast between Liang's positivism about the ability of the novel to deliver a straightforward political and social message and the tentative and ironic representations found in such novels as Cao Xueqin's *Story of the Stone* could not be more striking. Clearly, only by positing radically other, external origins for the new novel is Liang able to indulge his extreme notions of the instrumentality of fiction.

Critics have long wondered exactly where within the European or Japanese discourse on the novel Liang Qichao, Xia Zengyou, and their contemporaries found the idea of the novel as the key to successful reform.[43] Although, as is discussed below, a compelling case can be made for the importance of the political novel in Japan, it is hard to see it as a serious precedent for the extravagant claims made by the reform critics. It is more likely that Liang is basing his influential genealogy of the power of the novel on a simple strategic reversal of the traditional literati view of the harms lurking in fiction, with which, after all, he begins his essay. In other words, Liang's censure of the traditional Chinese *xiaoshuo* is founded upon a highly traditional view of its capacity to produce certain undesirable sorts of human behavior. In the new era of possibility, however, narrative retains its old power over behavior, but it is now and only now suddenly reinscribed as capable of being transposed into a positive key. In other words, the core assumption of the old conception of the relationship between the novel and its influence on behavior has not changed, merely the direction and nature of that influence. But there was a high cost to this reformulation—the rejection of any extant Chinese novel and a concomitant need to theorize fiction as a category transcending any prior practice.

The New Novel

During the early years of his exile in Japan, Liang took action on his conviction of the importance of the novel, founding the new journal *Xin xiaoshuo* in 1902. It almost instantly became the most important literary journal of its time and spawned a host of imitators, both in Japan and at home in China, principally Shanghai.[44] As a number of scholars have demonstrated, the publication rate both of novels originally written in Chinese and of translations from other languages expanded exponentially after 1902. For instance, according to statistics adduced by Ouyang Jian, only 3 original novels were published in 1900, and 9 each in 1901 and 1902, whereas the figures are 39, 19, and 33 for 1903, 1904, and 1905, respectively, and reached a height of 104 in 1909.[45] The figures for translations are even more dramatic: from a total of 16 published between 1900 and 1902 to 110 and 126 published in 1906 and 1907, respectively.[46] Although debate about the absolute precision of these figures has been considerable, there has been no debate whatsoever about the relative numbers. This phenomenon can in good measure plausibly be credited to Liang's efforts to popularize the genre.

In the inaugural issue of his new journal, Liang published a long theoretical essay explaining the power of the novel and its links to political activity, thereby setting the tone for the frenzied pace of the creation of both fiction and fiction criticism that followed. The piece, "Lun xiaoshuo yu qunzhi zhi guanxi" (On the relationship between fiction and public governance), is where the term "revolution in the realm of fiction" first appeared. Capturing as it does the messianic spirit of its times, the essay has remained a key document of modern Chinese literary criticism ever since. In its use of parallel structures and Buddhist lexicon, it is also an exemplary piece of prose in Liang's "new style." The essay begins in an incantatory fashion reminiscent of Kang Youwei's remarks on the efficacy of the novel published five years earlier:

> If one wants to renew a nation's people, one must first renew that nation's novels. Therefore, should one want to renew morality, one must first renew the novel; should one want to renew religion, one must renew the novel; should one want to renew politics, one must renew the novel; if one wants to renew popular custom, one must renew the novel; if one wants to renew the arts, one must renew the novel; and even if one wants to re-

new the popular mentality *(xin)* and people's characters, one must renew the novel. Why? Because the novel has an unimaginable power to govern *(zhipei)* the ways of human beings.⁴⁷

Traces of previous remarks of various critics on the need for fiction are in plain evidence here, even though Liang has moved far beyond them in his claims for the utility of the novel. More than that, however, he moves from this assertion of utility on to an unprecedented declaration of superior quality, calling the novel the "Great Conveyance for literature" *(wenxue zhi zui shangcheng)*—"Great Conveyance" is a Buddhist term signifying the most powerful means of conveying ultimate truths. Such rich praise is quite absent from the condescension accorded the novel in the earlier essays that were based almost exclusively on the social efficacy of the form. Even as Liang tenders his extravagant claims for the high quality of fiction and for the enormous power of fiction to move people, however, a troubling element haunts his new equation. Toward the end of the essay, Liang affirms that all the customs of the Chinese people of which he disapproves—such as the tendency for people to wish to "place first place in the exams and become prime minister," the concept of "the talented man meeting the beautiful woman *(caizi jiaren),*" and fantasies about "bandits and the brotherhood of rivers and lakes"—are all the result of the pernicious effects of reading earlier novels that had glorified these things.⁴⁸ In other words, the problem inhering in the earlier comments of a theoretical high quality and function running up against a dismal, if not actively harmful, set of practical results remains, but now, ironically, with redoubled force.

The question of the intellectual basis for this dramatic promotion in the theoretical status of fiction has posed a problem for scholars ever since. Xia Xiaohong, for instance, claims that it could have come only from Liang's new familiarity with the Meiji tradition of political novels in Japan, where a number of these were written by reform politicians. This possibility calls into question Liang's claims for "pure" literary quality as the basis for his reassessment.⁴⁹ Xia's identification of an ultimately utilitarian motive behind Liang's claims is undeniable, as is the influence of the Japanese political novel. Another factor, however, would seem to be at work here, for in the same year that Liang published his landmark work on the novel, he published another essay with virtually the same title, namely, "On the Relationship between Buddhism and Public Governance" ("Lun fojiao yu qunzhi zhi guanxi"). In this latter essay as well, the social utility of the religion is stressed. As Hao Chang has written: "It seems obvious that what Liang prized in religion was not any specific religious faith or doctrine but the motivational function of religious faith. . . .

Liang now found such a religious faith in Buddhism. . . . [and] he went so far as to claim that the new sociopolitical order that he envisioned in his *New Citizen* could find a cultural function in Buddhism."[50]

The links between the two essays extend beyond the titles. "Fiction and Public Governance" is suffused with Buddhist terminology—"Great Conveyance" is but the most conspicuous example—which provides vivid imagery as to how fictional writing works its way into the individual mind. The move to center the intellectual justification for the New Novel in Buddhist thought does displace the locus of the conversation away from the appeal to Western and Japanese texts, which had been at the heart of Liang's essay in 1898, back to what might seem at first glance to be home ground. Although Buddhism was enjoying a conspicuous revival among late Qing intellectuals in general,[51] it was still exotic in respect to mainstream intellectual discourse as it had been conducted before the 1890s. Moreover, there is a question as to whether Buddhist philosophy and terminology can legitimately serve as appropriate conveyances for a message of social mobilization. Hao Chang concludes, for instance, with a certain amount of understatement, that Liang's "unqualified depiction of Buddhism as worldly activism is patently an exaggeration."[52] By moving Buddhism in to fill gaps now visible in an increasingly vulnerable Confucian-based ideology, Liang is working in an ostensibly national idiom, but it just as surely represents a newly uncertain arena from which to pursue the understanding, the representation, and the transformation of the outer world.

The problems intrinsic to Liang's inflated and contradictory assumptions about and expectations for the novel ultimately became apparent nowhere more clearly than in his own writings. He recognized, for instance, that his single, uninspired attempt at writing original fiction —the five-chapter fragment of *Xin Zhongguo weilai ji* (The future of new China) that he began serializing in the first issue of *Xin xiaoshuo* in the fall of 1902—was not able to achieve formal consistency: "In this issue of the journal, I am publishing the first two or three chapters [of my novel]. In reading it over, it seems to be both fiction *(shuobu)* and not fiction, both anecdotal *(baishi)* and not anecdotal, both treatise *(lunzhu)* and not treatise; I don't actually know what sort of form it ends up being, and I can't help laughing at myself as a result."[53]

In 1915, at a much later point in his life, after his early hopes for reform had been dashed, Liang published his "Gao xiaoshuo jia" (An indictment of the novelists), in effect a valedictory essay on fiction. In it, he expresses attitudes that are mirror images of his remarks in "Fiction and Public Governance" and in fact resemble even more the remarks of Li Yu quoted at the beginning of this chapter. Liang continues to adhere to his idea that fiction has immense power to move people, but he now sees only the negative side. After first declaring once again that the behavior of Chinese people in the past had been molded by novels, he goes on to affirm: "Over the last ten or so years, the social climate has declined precipitously. In what way can this not be said to be a calamity brought about by the so-called new novelists? If we continue along this course for a few more years, China faces limitless peril."[54] If in earlier years his utopian hopes had become lodged in a hyperbolic faith in the novel, by now Liang blamed the same instrument for the disappointment of those hopes. In both cases, however, the novel becomes the site where displaced desires to gain control over an intractable social process are given voice.

Whatever Liang's final perspective on the novel was to be, the immediate response to his essay of 1902 was extraordinary, in terms of additional critical essays and a significant outburst of creative work, both original and translated. Writing toward the end of 1906, for instance, the novelist Wu Jianren unhesitatingly credited the explosion in the production of novels to Liang's seminal essay.[55] Because Liang's essay contained such a multiplicity of ideas, this new work was able to go in many, often contradictory, directions. For instance, Di Baoxian (b. 1873), an influential advocate of fiction who became one of the founders of the important Shanghai newspaper *Shibao* in 1904,[56] further complicated the issue of how fiction was to be created. In his 1903 essay on the genre, which was published in *Xin xiaoshuo*, Di called for an end to the frivolity he saw as endemic to all writing in the classical language and for a general turn to the utilitarianism that he saw as endemic to the vernacular:[57]

> If literature *(wen)* is to be taken as having a function, it must be taken not as a plaything but as a staple *(shusu)*. Once, an epigrapher *(jinshi jia)* gave a banquet and brought out his Shang[-dynasty] *yi*, Xia *ding*, Zhou *dui*, and Han *jue* to use as containers for food and wine. The result was that both host and guests ended up with diarrhea for the week. Beauty is beauty, but what if it is not appropriate? Therefore, the accession of the vernacular style is really an unavoidable consequence of the selection of the superior.

Liang's implicit call to transcend prior practice is left intact here, much as the equally insistent instrumentality of the earlier text is also reinforced. Di adds to this mix an explicit social Darwinism, demonstrating just how fast the influence of Yan Fu's translation of Huxley had spread. This call for stripping language of its refinement in the writing of *xiaoshuo* must have left the would-be novel writer in a quandary. One the one hand, there was a persisting note expressed in fairly withering terms that fiction as it had been written in China was of a markedly lower order than other writing and that it would have to improve. On the other hand, there was an equally forceful stress on the idea that this very lack of aesthetic polish was the essence of the genre, not to mention that which made the genre mandatory as a stimulus to change in these perilous times. How was an author to respond to these conflicting demands?

One of the ways these two guidelines were mediated was by establishing a genealogy of fiction that stressed hidden meaning as the core of the traditional form, an avenue opened by Xia Zengyou and Yan Fu in their long editorial of 1897.[58] Thus, the perception of the low quality of premodern fiction and its irrelevance to contemporary times could be ascribed to the need for earlier authors to protect themselves against persecution by the state, with political dissidence assumed to be an inherent part of the novel form. Although this idea allowed the novel theoretically to fit the new activist profile that reformist critics demanded after 1897, it had little to offer writers who no longer had to obscure the called-for political side to their work. By mystifying the origins of the form and creating a notion of a secret power inaccessible to those living in more open times, this conjuring of a hidden force within the traditional novel ultimately heightened anxiety among contemporary authors regarding the present potential of the novel.

On the other hand, the utopian side of this discourse lodged itself in a series of wildly optimistic pronouncements about the potential of fiction to bring about a brave new world. The general tenor of these utterances fall into two distinct categories: those, like Liu Shipei, who saw the novel as uniquely suited to communicate with the semi-educated, and those who accepted fiction as having a universal audience. An anonymous essay entitled "On the Educational Value of Fiction" ("Lun xiaoshuo zhi jiaoyu"), published in 1906, is a good example of the first group. After first reciting the standard litany of charges against the bad influences of novels, the text goes on to explain how these negative influences can be transformed: "Should we begin one day to tell beneficial things to the masses, we will not have to reform the popular habit of listening to storytellers. What has been told up until now has all been baseless chatter, but were we to change that to things that people really need to know about life, then not only will it penetrate the streets and teahouses, but it also will work, in effect, to establish innumerable schools in these places. Will there be any who do not come to listen and then go on to exhort one another to the good?"[59]

The didactic portion of this declaration is, of course, anything but new. The sense that the pedagogical effort is ultimately directed at an entirely different group from the elite readers of the document itself, however, marks a radical difference from past apologies for the novel, which, hortatory though they often were, still acknowledged the appeal of fiction to the writer's own peers. To realize the extent to which this represents an amplification of the instrumental approach to the novel, one need only recall Lin Shu's prefaces to his translations, with their complete lack of condescension to the form, and their determination to judge the novel by a presumptively universal *guwen* aesthetic. As Hu Shi pointed out long ago, this post-1895 shift from talking about *us* to talking about *them* was to become pervasive in discussions of vernacular literature in the years to come.[60] If traditional discussions of writing had been inextricably linked to notions of self-cultivation, then moving the burden toward taking responsibility for others who were explicitly defined as being quite different from oneself had a major impact on the development of modern Chinese letters. Literature moved decisively into a more public arena, thereby inevitably taking an ever greater role in the molding of public opinion. This new publicity for literature augmented its position in cultural discourse even as it rendered it less personally compelling. The new stress on its social role served to put it at a greater distance from the personal feelings of reader and writer alike than anything that had ever been part of Chinese literary discourse in the past.

There were those, on the other hand, who posited a universal appeal for the novel. The confluence of national essence ideas and imported, more democratic conceptions of literature created a heady mixture that seemed irresistible to those with a less refined palate than the likes of Liu Shipei. If Liu had maintained a strict distinction between what he thought of as *wen* and the new vernacular forms he suffered to exist, many of his contemporaries were far less discriminate. In 1906–1907, for instance, the critic Tao Zengyou contributed a series of articles with titles like "On the Power and Significance of Literature" ("Lun wenxue zhi shili jiqi guanxi") to the Shanghai entertainment press. Tao's rich prose requires only a small sampling to show the powerful mélange of ideas that had coalesced into a notion of literature that held out to writer, reader, and nation alike the promise of a tool to control their fates:

> I have heard that to establish a country on this globe requires a particular spirit. . . . And for it to be strong for eternity, it requires a natural endowment for strength. . . . Ah! What is this particular spirit? What is this natural endowment? It is literature! "When letters receive their proper treatment, the world will know a wave of reform." Countrymen! Countrymen! Do you not know that this literature is superior to other branches of learning? That it truly possesses the greatest of power? That it should enjoy the most beautiful of names? That it contains limitless significance? And that it alone should occupy the highest position in the world?[61]

While a finely educated *wenren* (man of letters) like Liu Shipei would no doubt have been horrified by the crudity of Tao's expostulations, there can be little doubt that Liu's own statements about the power of *wen* contributed to the ambience that encouraged such effusion. If Liu could at least have recognized the sentiments behind Tao's notion of the power of writing, he would have had to resolutely oppose in its entirety another essay of Tao's,[62] in which the latter placed fiction squarely at the top of the hierarchy of literature:

> Oh! There is great monster at the heart of the twentieth century. It walks without legs, flies without wings, sounds without speaking; it stimulates the mind, surprises the eye, opens one's mental horizons, and increases the intelligence; it can by turns be solemn, facetious, lyrical, lachrymose, angry, hortatory, satirical, or mocking. . . . It has immense strength and attraction as well as unimaginable force; in the realm of literature it casts a particular brilliance and indicates a special quality. What is this thing? It is the novel. . . . The novel! It truly is the most noble vehicle in world literature.

If Liang Qichao had begun the discourse on the potential of the novel with his 1902 essay, Tao amplified and popularized it even as he drastically simplified and vulgarized the message.

A few critics in this period were able to avoid the hyperbole and contradiction of the general discourse and to engage, instead, in a more disinterested appreciation of the novel. Preeminent among these was Huang Ren (1866–1913), an erudite man of letters who participated in a variety of literary and publishing venues. A member of the important literary society Nanshe (Southern Society), Huang in 1907 was also a founder of *Xiaoshuo lin,* one of the three important successor fiction journals to *Xin xiaoshuo*. His "Zhongguo wenxue shi" (History of Chinese literature), generally taken to be the first history of Chinese literature, is based on the notes for the lectures he gave at Soochow University (Dongwu daxue) in the years after 1900.[63] These lectures, filled with astute commentary on the work of foreign critics, were apparently quite popular with the students, even though the odor resulting from Huang's habitual failure to bathe (a predilection he shared with Zhang Taiyan, by the way) made it exceedingly unpleasant for any of them to sit in the first three rows of the classroom.[64]

In his *History*, Huang makes an eloquent and well-documented case for the autonomy of literature, based as much on the work of foreign critics like Matthew Arnold as on Chinese example,[65] and he later argues in a similar vein for the literary status of fiction in his "Xiaoshuo xiao hua," a series of articles he published in *Xiaoshuo lin*. This series is notable for, among other things, his taking the Chinese narrative tradition as a serious resource: all his examples are drawn from Chinese novels. As Huang carefully anatomizes his texts, however, he too becomes drawn into the discourse on the novel as a source of utopian possibilities, at least in the sense of opening new avenues for Chinese writing. For example, in comparing fiction with the *bagu* essay required for the imperial examinations, he says: "Thus, those who write examination prose *(shiwen)* and those who study it know almost nothing, whereas those who write novels and those who read them know almost everything—the difference between the two is that great."[66] Although it is easy to agree with Huang's proposition that the novel is obliged to be wide-ranging in its selection of topics, it is another matter to see the novel as the symbol of a new, more scientific approach to perceiving the world and to agree that this quality was quite absent from all the literary forms that had enjoyed higher status in pre-1900 China.

In sum, the mixture of enthusiasm, disdain, and condescension that critics of the time directed toward the novel at the very least presents a vivid case study of the upheaval in the world of Chinese letters that took place after 1895. Even more important, placing fiction at the heart of a sweeping transvaluation of ideas about the form and function of writing provides a suitably complex representation of the tensions facing the Chinese intellectual world as a whole in this pivotal period. Fiction, for all the attention lavished on it by twentieth-century scholars, had, in general, before this time never been taken as a serious contender for preeminence among the many genres of Chinese writing. Thus, it could be welcomed as something new and, above all, as something saturated with the prestige and authority of the modern West, a matter almost invariably alluded to in the critical texts that marked the period. At the same time, fiction undeniably had a long indigenous history, which was at once a source of embarrassment and denial and the source of a firm footing for fiction as an indigenous product, something ultimately indispensable in the new age of nationalism. The volatile mix of indigenous and exogenous features provided the energy for fiction's sudden rise to eminence in these years, as well as for its equally rapid collapse as a genre of high seriousness after 1908.

To the extent that Liang Qichao validates the novel, we can take it as an opaque figure for the superiority of the foreign, a matter about which he is quite explicit in 1898.[67] On the other hand, many of the other major voices discussing the novel at this time make it clear that it is primarily an instrumental form of writing (Liu Shipei is explicit on this, and we can see traces of it almost everywhere else). So although we might seem to have, in the novel, a carefully coded endorsement of the foreign as the salvation for China's problems, behind it lies the shadow of the other, more basic forms of writing that have a longer history of elite participation and critical acceptance. It was the same with Yan Fu's call for complete appropriation of the foreign: behind it lay a solid discourse of morality and fundamental value, which was solidly Chinese and emerged from time to time regardless of Yan's best efforts to suppress it. Things Western remain the site of utility, or *yong*, in spite of the recognition by the most astute critics of the time that a purely instrumental approach will not be enough to allow the magnitude of transformation they see is needed.

For all the celebration and utopian hopes invested in the writings of New Fiction advocates, the narrative work produced either in response to these calls or simultaneous with them presented a far bleaker sense of the actual possibilities, as Leo Lee and Andrew Nathan have pointed out.[68] Given the contradictory elements that contributed to the various voices advocating a new fiction, it is not surprising that the gap between theory and practice worked itself out into this particular division of labor. Using their foreign sources of inspiration as a basis, the critics found it easier to position themselves outside the social maelstrom and to transcend the inescapable contradictions that a purely local genealogy would present. As we shall see in the chapters that follow, the novels themselves could do little to avoid becoming caught up in those contradictory details. For our purposes, what is most significant about this discrepancy between theory and practice is the manifold pressures it exerted on authors. They ended up writing in a genre sponsored by a group of reformers who set contradictory demands that by definition could never be reconciled. Given that the only thing that all of these demands had in common was a predisposition to accord to the novel enormous influence in the abstract, the tensions surrounding the composition of actual texts became that much more acute.

PART II
Late Qing Novels

CHAPTER 5

Wu Jianren

Engaging the World

> The only authentic artworks produced today are those that in their inner organization measure themselves by the fullest experience of horror.
> Theodor Adorno

> In all other genres ... affirmation of a dissonance precedes the act of form giving, whereas in the novel it is the form itself.
> Georg Lukács, *The Theory of the Novel*

Wu Jianren was the most prolific of the numerous writers who answered Liang Qichao's call and began writing and publishing their fiction in the "short" final decade of the Qing dynasty—roughly between 1902 and 1910. In November 1906, Wu wrote of Liang's influence in his introductory words to a new journal of fiction:

> When I took up my pen to create fiction, I thought it would be permissible to talk of the novel in terms of the novel itself. Why would it first be necessary to raise all the evils of society and expose them? I had been influenced here, influenced by Liang Qichao's "On the Relationship between Fiction and Public Governance" and its advocacy of the reform of fiction, within a few years of which new original and translated novels filled the shelves *(han wanniu chong wandong)*, with no sign of surcease.[1]

Although Wu registers a note of disapproval at the massive response to Liang's call, as well as a certain resentment about the pressures it exerted for thematic unity, and although Wu himself wrote in a number of different novelistic genres, the bulk of his work gravitated toward attempting to represent the cultural and political crises facing China during his rather brief life span. In thus devoting himself primarily to what he called the "social novel" *(shehui xiaoshuo)*, Wu very much adhered to the mainstream of his time, following the general trend set by Liang in his calls for the "New Novel," which we examined in the previous chapter. And whatever else concerned Wu, he was certainly much given to "rais[ing] the evils of society and expos[ing] them" in most of his fictional work. What sets Wu Jianren apart from most of his cohort, however, are his narrative innovations, along with the rich complexity of his characters and situations, in which the various constituents of the general crisis facing China are set out in agonizing and compelling detail. One may even regard his rich oeuvre as the most intricate and profound depiction of the age, especially, perhaps, in those places where the situation he sets out to represent proves itself to be beyond representation. In fact, one of the remarkable features of Wu's writing is its ability to set out the full extent of the paradoxes and contradictions of the difficult period in which he lived and worked.

Compared with most of the figures we have examined in earlier chapters—men of either high birth, extraordinary educational achievement, or both—the more pedestrian Wu Jianren seems at first an unlikely person to have played such a prominent role in the social and intellectual turmoil of the late Qing. Unlike most men of even modest educational attainment, Wu never prepared himself for the governmental examinations, and in fact he supported himself by writing for the new print culture market in Shanghai for most of the final dozen years of his life. It is just this career track, however, that offers a revealing picture of the new opportunities and career options in the sphere of cultural production that were opening up in China—and preeminently in Shanghai—in the final years of the dynasty. It is also his deep involvement with these new career tracks that throws into high relief his engagement with the foreign ideas and institutions becoming pervasive in his adopted home. Before we dig into his narrative work, therefore, his life is worth a detailed look.

Wu was born in Beijing on May 19, 1866. His highly educated family was from Nanhai in Guangdong Province (which was also the ancestral home of Kang Youwei) and had had governmental affiliations for several generations. His original given name was Baozhen, which was soon changed to Woyao. His first *hao*, or cognomen, was Jianren, the first character of which was changed to another character of the same sound and meaning, Jianren, the name by which he is now best known. Another of his more famous style-names was Wo foshan ren (I, a man of Foshan), taken from Foshan (Fatshan), the prosperous city in Guangdong that his family had come from and in which he had spent most of his childhood. The family fortunes seem to have been on the wane over the several generations preceding Jianren's birth. His grandfather, Wu Xinshe (1804–1863), who was serving as a minor official in Beijing at the time of his death, was assisted in his duties there by Jianren's father, Wu Yunji (1841–1882). With the death of Wu Xinshe, the family's fortunes went into even steeper decline, and the family returned to their ancestral home in Foshan in 1867. Jianren began his schooling in 1874, at the age of eight *sui*, eventually enrolling in the Foshan Academy (Foshan shuyuan) in 1878. Wu Yunji had been obliged to seek his fortune in Ningbo after the family's departure from Beijing, where he died unexpectedly in 1882.

After Wu Yinji's death, the financial position of Jianren's family took yet another turn for the worse, and the young man was forced to seek work in Shanghai, probably in the fall of 1883, or at least before he reached the age of eighteen *sui*. In traveling to Shanghai to seek his fortune, Wu joined a long line of Cantonese who had done the same, including Zheng Guanying, who had arrived there in 1858.[2] Once in Shanghai, Wu found work at the Jiangnan Arsenal, the employer of John Fryer and the prime site of the importation of Western scientific and industrial technology into China in the late nineteenth century. A mammoth military enterprise that dated from the days of the Tongzhi restoration in the 1860s, the arsenal contained shipbuilding, weapons manufacturing, and various metallurgical facilities at its site south of the old city of Shanghai, as well as a technical translation bureau. Many Cantonese worked in the administration of the arsenal, which may have had something to do with Wu's finding a job there, beginning as a copyist and ending up working as a draftsman. Little is known of Wu during the many years he worked at the arsenal, but it is said that in 1888 he built by himself a scale-model steamboat that could and did sail on the Huangpu River—an event that was eventually the basis for an episode in his epic 108-chapter novel, *Ershi nian mudu zhi guai xianzhuang* (Strange events eyewitnessed in the past twenty years).[3] He made a journey to Beijing in 1891 to attend to the remains of his recently deceased uncle and brought his two young orphaned cousins back to Shanghai, events that also appear in thinly fictionalized form in the novel. He visited Tianjin on the way. In 1896 he went to Yichang to attend to the funeral of his remaining uncle, an event also fictionalized in *Strange Events*.

In 1897 Wu appears to have left his job at the arsenal. If we are to take the several comments on the arsenal and its products—particularly the scientific books translated by John Fryer—that are recorded in Wu's novels as representative of his own opinion, then his estimation of the operation overall was not high. In *Strange Events,* for instance, an arsenal employee, Fang Yilu, is introduced with little other apparent purpose than to express critical opinions of the arsenal and its management. After first harking back to how well the institution was run in its early days in the 1860s and 1870s, Fang proceeds to describe how badly it has declined.

The narrator then asks Fang if, at least, the translated books are not worth reading, and he receives the following response: "They are no use at all. I've read all the books he [i.e., Fryer] translated, and aside from those on astronomy, which I don't understand, all the books on acoustics, optics, electricity, and chemistry that I've read are incomplete. They go on and on, but they never illuminate the crucial points. They are fine if you only plan on using them as material to chat about, but if you want to use them to actually further your learning, forget it."[4] This is rather far from the general opinion of later scholars toward the arsenal and its works. As Mary Wright said of the enterprise: "The Kiangnan Arsenal represented a high degree of innovation in broad policy as well as in technology. The work of its translation bureau and language school is well known. In the opinion of a distinguished Chinese scientist of today [1941], the works translated there exceeded in quality those translated in all China during the subsequent half century."[5]

Upon his departure from his job at the arsenal, Wu reports that "in the Dingyou [1897] and Wuxu [1898] years, I closed myself up idly at home to nurse an illness." adding that "[f]or some time I had no desire to go out and socialize, spending my time only in reading newspapers, from which I learned much about current events."[6] Perhaps inspired by this close attention paid to newspapers, Wu soon thereafter went to work as a journalist himself and spent the next several years writing for and managing a succession of Shanghai newspapers, most of them small papers oriented toward the burgeoning entertainment industry in the growing city. Writing soon after he left the Shanghai newspaper arena in 1902, he noted: "[L]ooking back over the past five or six years, [I can see that] being in editorial charge of various small newspapers has been, in fact, a great impediment to my progress. I threw away five or six years of my time in this way."[7] Although Wu may have regretted the time spent as a journalist, it was probably indispensable to his development as a writer and participant in the Shanghai literary arena, if only for the vast number of stories he was in a position to hear and to use later in his novels. That other mainstay of late Qing fiction writing, Li Baojia (Boyuan, 1867–1906), had preceded Wu in journalism; in 1896 he had taken up the editorship of the *Youxi bao* (Recreation news), the most prominent and best-remembered of the entertainment papers. Among the papers that Wu managed or participated in were *Xiaoxian bao* (Leisure news), *Caifeng bao* (Folk song collector news), *Qixin bao* (Astounding news), and *Yuyan bao* (Fabulous news).

In the period shortly after departing from the arsenal, Wu busied himself for a time with a series of essays on current affairs, which, when collected together, he labeled *Jianyi waibian* (Jianren's somniloquy: The outer chapters), to which he added a preface in January 1902. When the collection was published in two small volumes in April of that year, the name was changed to *Zhengzhi weixin yaoyan* (Crucial words on political reform), a more precise—if less ironic—description of the contents. In the essays, he follows a political line fairly characteristic of the Shanghai scholars of the time: aware of the corruption and decline of the Chinese government and thus fully supportive of needed reforms, but also highly suspicious of Western motives and intensely mindful of the need to guard national sovereignty against the incursions of imperialist powers. He is at all times mindful of the need to steer a middle course between radical reform based exclusively on Western techniques and a stubborn adherence to indigenous ways and values.

In many ways, his collection is a characteristic product of the day, resembling, for instance, a compact version of Zheng Guanying's *Blunt Words in a Time of Prosperity*. He was, like Zheng, highly committed to the *ti/yong* prescription for Chinese reform and believed also that China possessed the *dao* while the West had the means of its implementation, or *qi*.[8] On the other hand, he was adamant about stressing that Western science and its Chinese translation at the time, *gezhi*, were both quite distinct from the term in *The Great Learning*, from which it was borrowed. Wu points out that the neo-Confucian classic was primarily concerned with personal cultivation, whereas science was considered strictly a matter of investigating external things and determining their natures, for which any number of potential translations would have served as well. Although Wu is unwilling to break completely with the notion of ultimate Chinese origins for the scientific method,[9] he does try to separate his sense of this from the cruder manifestations of the theory. Above all, Wu's work represents a commonsense evaluation of China's problems based on years of sharp-eyed observation from his privileged position at the primary point of the Chinese absorption of Western scientific and technical knowledge. Lacking any formal training in these fields, he nevertheless manifested the impressive degree to which an intelligent layman could appreciate the encroaching demands of modernity.

It is also important to point out just how closely Wu's broad and miscellaneous gathering of knowledge fits with Huang Ren's assessment of the nature of the writers and consumers of fiction: "those who write novels and those who read them know almost everything." In his final comments on the craft of fiction, written shortly before his death in 1910, Wu comes to an analogous conclusion. After noting his own lifelong habit of extensive reading, he observes that he could not seem to find a suitable form of expression until he settled upon writing essays that "rebuked the era and disdained common usage," a critical genre whose power impressed him. However, he continued: "Those who cared about me told me that it was a pity how scattered these shards of wisdom were, and that it was not easy [for readers] to bring the dispersed fragments together. A continuous piece of writing, on the other hand, would allow those who read to appreciate its value, not to mention being easy to collect; it might also be possible by this means to have [my message] prove somewhat more enduring. I thereupon endeavored to learn to write multichapter novels *(zhanghui xiaoshuo)*."[10] There was nevertheless to be an important difference between the two forms: Wu, in his admonitory essays, was able to fuse such things as essence *(ti)* and function *(yong)* seamlessly together, but when he entered the more demanding arena of narrative representation, he could not so easily dispose of the practical difficulties engendered by such fusions. If nothing else, the contrast between Wu's intentions and the work he actually produced provides a perfect example of the discrepancy between the theory and practice of fiction that was noted at the end of chapter 4.

It was also during this time that we find the first record of Wu's speaking at a public meeting. It dates from March 1901, when he participated in a demonstration at the Zhang Garden (Zhang yuan)—the preeminent public space in Shanghai at the time—against the liberal concessions China granted in signing its most recent treaty with Russia. In March 1902, Wu resigned as editor of the *Yuyan bao*, traveling to Hankou a month later to take up the editorship of the *Hankou ribao* (Hankou daily). This transition marks the end of his association with the Shanghai entertainment papers and the beginning of a brief sojourn into mainstream journalism. In July of the same year, he published in an entertainment monthly a short collection of fifty-seven satirical comments on Shanghai life, entitled *Wu Jianren ku* (Wu Jianren laments). Each entry contains an ironic observation of modern life in the big city, followed by the remark "Wu Jianren laments." The cynical tone of the collections is registered in the following entry: "I often thought to myself that the reason that China is not progressive and open and able to reform is its shortage of educated people. Suddenly, however, a different thought came to me: It is precisely because it contains too many educated people that China has been unable to be progressive and open and able to reform. Wu Jianren laments."[11] He does not hold himself exempt from censure and often turns a jaundiced eye upon his own shortcomings: "Wu Jianren of course has not made any progress, but I can clearly see that neither has anyone else. Wu Jianren laments."[12]

According to his 1910 preface, it was in 1903, during his sojourn in Hankou, that Wu took up the writing of fiction. He says that his motivation stemmed from a general discontent with the more orthodox forms of writing available to him, and from an inability to compose in the "imposing, masculine" style that could "shout up the winds, move mountains, seize the soul, and lament the spirits."[13] The results of his decision to turn to fiction were impressive, to say the least. By the time the eighth issue of *Xin xiaoshuo* was published on October 5, 1903, it contained initial chapters from three different novels that Wu was apparently working on at the same time: *Strange Events, Tongshi* (A painful history), and *Dianshu qitan* (The marvels of electricity). Each subsequent issue of this pioneering journal was to contain multiple chapters of these and other of Wu's novels, testifying both to his devotion to the form and to his extraordinary productivity.

It is perhaps from the amount of work he took on in this period that in the autumn of 1904 he was diagnosed with nervous exhaustion *(xuqie zheng);* he took a trip to Jinan in Shandong shortly thereafter. In March 1905 his only child, a daughter named Jingjing, was born, and at about that time he accepted the position of editor of the *Chubao*, the newly founded Chinese edition of the English language *Central China Post,* an American-owned newspaper also published in Hankou. Wu had not been on the job long when the question of the renewal of the discriminatory Chinese exclusion acts was due to come up in the U.S. Congress. In reaction to this, various Chinese patriotic organizations planned a boycott of American goods and interests in China as a way to pressure the U.S. government to revise the treaties.[14] Wu responded to this call in July by resigning his post at the American-owned newspaper and returning to Shanghai, a dramatic move widely reported upon in the Shanghai press at the time. Once back in that city, he was much in demand as a speaker at a number of the many patriotic rallies held throughout the summer of that year. In September he began the first serialization of one of his novels in a daily paper, the newly founded Shanghai newspaper, *Nanfang bao* (Southern news). The work was his new novel, *Xin shitou ji* (The new story of the Stone), which is the focus of chapter 6. Reflecting the exciting period in which it was being written, *The New Story of the Stone* stands out among Wu's novels as the work that most earnestly expresses Wu's intense concern with China's difficult situation in the world.

January 1906 witnessed the final issue of *Xin xiaoshuo*. Only the detective novel *Jiuming qiyuan* (Strange injustice to nine lives) ran in its entirety in the journal; the other works that had been appearing in serialization were eventually completed only in book form. In November of that year the first issue of *Yueyue xiaoshuo* appeared, with Wu and his good friend, the prominent translator Zhou Guisheng (1873–1936), listed as principal contributors. In his introductory words in that first issue, Wu mentioned that the purpose of the journal was to publish fiction that would provide moral uplift in trying times. Wu was primarily responsible for producing original fiction for the periodical, while Zhou was in charge of translating foreign work, then at the height of its popularity in China. Wu and Zhou produced only eight issues of this journal before it closed temporarily after the May 1907 issue was published. When the journal resumed in October, Wu and Zhou no longer had the primary responsibility for producing it, although they did continue to publish stories in it before it finally ceased publication in 1909. Most of the few commentaries that Wu wrote about the nature and goals of fiction were published on the pages of *Yueyue xiaoshuo,* where most of his short stories also appeared. In October of the same year, Wu published his most famous novelette, *Henhai* (Sea of regret), as a single volume through the Guangzhi Book Company in Shanghai. A tragic romance of only ten chapters, Wu wrote it all at once and later confided that it was his personal favorite among the fictions he had created.

For the remainder of his life, Wu continued not only to complete the novels he had begun but also to write new works of fiction at the same hectic pace he had pursued since 1903. There are few records of any further public activity in the years between 1907 and 1910. On October 21, 1910, he completed moving his small family to a new residence, and after celebrating the move with some friends, he went to bed and died from an asthmatic attack later that night. For all his frenetic writing, he is said to have had only forty cents to his name when he died, and funeral arrangements were left to his many friends. More of Wu's writings continued to be published posthumously for a considerable period after his death, providing yet more testimony to his extraordinary productivity and his great popularity in the *xiaoshuo* form he did so much to revivify.

The Late Qing Novel and Its Antecedents

Wu's best-known work of fiction continues to be not only by far his most extensive but also one of his first. *Strange Events* is not just Wu's longest and most famous work but is also considered to be one of the four landmark works of the late Qing novel.[15] It presents a thoroughly dismal picture of contemporary life among the upper classes, with a particular focus on the higher rungs of the nonmetropolitan bureaucracy. Many of the people and incidents depicted in the text are thinly disguised versions of actual people and the gossip about them, with a good number consisting of members of Wu's own family and his personal experiences. The twenty years mentioned in the title are the period beginning about 1884, the year of China's war with France and, not so incidentally, the time of Wu's arrival in Shanghai. These two decades also contain the crises of the war with Japan, the struggle on the part of the imperialist powers for expanded concessions in China in 1897–1898, the abortive "Hundred Days Reform" of 1898, and the Boxer Rebellion and the subsequent occupation of the capital by foreign troops in 1900.[16] From the perspective of the first few years of the twentieth century, then, the twenty years after 1884 could be seen from almost any perspective as uniquely disastrous for China.

The novel is also the earliest sustained first-person narrative in Chinese vernacular literature.[17] As such, it inevitably raises questions as to why this new mode of expression materialized on the scene when it did. Was it merely a response to the discovery that this type of narrative existed in the West, or did it fuse together portions of the Chinese literary tradition in an unprecedented way? Were there specific reasons that it spoke to new intellectual needs within the realm of Chinese letters? Although there seems to be no way to answer these questions definitively, *Strange Events* does fit at the end of a continuum of Qing-dynasty fiction that deals with the position of the writer himself, both in regard to the text he is creating and to the larger world. There certainly had been intimate accounts of personal life in Chinese narrative before the late Qing—*Fusheng liuji* (Six chapters of a floating life), by Shen Fu (1762–after 1809), comes immediately to mind—but such accounts were generally limited to detailed descriptions of household goings-on rather than to the sort of broad examination of public affairs we see in Wu's novel. In the end, however, the sudden implementation of an unprecedented narrative mode, however, calls attention to itself in such a way as to move to the foreground and address in a new way notions of the capacities and the range of writing that had been in play since as early as the 1750s—the middle years of the dynasty.

Overall, Wu's narrative in both form and content represents a rich and uneasy meeting of Western discourses on reform, collisions between new and old ways of thinking, and new modes of narrative representation. These are represented through, among other things, the first-person narration, a narrative trajectory close to that of the contemporary European bildungsroman,[18] the centering of the text in the liminal city of Shanghai, spatial manifestations of the hybrid cultural formations created in that city, as well as a strong focus on the means of travel between Shanghai and other parts of China. The result is a narrative in flux, both formally and in its representations, and the generally unhappy results of the juxtapositions among cultural elements show the underlying tensions and anxieties that inhere in the unprecedented social order that Wu represents.

The first-person narration serves in large part as the device whereby Wu can introduce autobiographical information and make it immediate and relevant, but the form itself cannot be sustained, as events continuously overwhelm it. The novel thus represents an attempt to come to grips with the new situation—via a developmental narrative of the times—that can never be successful. At the beginning the narrator plainly does not understand his circumstances, nor can he find a basis for gaining understanding, for the place that long-standing Chinese practice stipulates one is supposed to start, the family, is conspicuously unable to provide a base for him to work from—first because of the death of his father and afterward because of the perfidy of his uncle. He searches for other means of control and finds a number of them, which eventually enable him to gain some leverage on understanding and being able to act upon his surroundings. In the end, however, all these means prove illusory, as events continue to overwhelm him—resoundingly so by the end of the story.

Central to this new dynamic was an atmosphere at once of crisis and of utopian hope created by the radical disruption of the intellectual world as it had subsisted prior to 1895.[19] From this perspective, the novel appears to be torn between contemplating the problematics of individual perspective on the one hand and disclosing the more lurid forms of social behavior on the other, behavior now seen as threatening the very existence of the Chinese polity itself. Within this renewal project embodied by the introduction of a new type of narrative voice, however, lies an effort to gain leverage on the social process by building a platform for speaking that lies outside the perceived cultural norms of the time. In hindsight, these expectations were unrealistic to be sure, but they were built into the hopes embodied in the concept of the "revolution in the realm of fiction" itself. The key to gaining this leverage over a vast set of dismal social facts is the specter of the newly arrived foreign ideas, institutions, and material realities, like steamships and the telegraph. These foreign facts represented within the texts combine with formal devices (first-person narration, bildungsroman) of Western provenance to create a narrative trajectory in *Strange Events* that uncannily resembles Yan Fu's intellectual journey—a hopeful turn to Western methods (narrative and material) at the outset, only to be followed by profound doubts as the whether they can actually live up to the promise they seemed to hold out when first entertained.

The revolution in the possibilities for writing that the late Qing New Novel represents did not take place in a vacuum. Much has been said in twentieth-century China about the subordination of textual production to the concerns of a narrow political and intellectual orthodoxy under the Manchu Empire.[20] At least from the mid-Qing on, however, there had been considerable discussion of the act of composition itself and its relationship to officially sanctioned Confucianism.[21] Within the realm of narrative fiction prior to 1895, there seems to have been considerable space within which to discuss the problematic relationship between the act of writing and the normative discourses that had surrounded and situated writing since the institution of *Daoxue* orthodoxy in the Yuan dynasty. Although these texts were clearly critical in their perspectives on social practice and its distance from what moral norms demanded, they did not manifest the same desire to build a speaking position outside contemporary society that is so conspicuous in some of Wu Jianren's work.

The extent of the space available for the interrogation of norms can be understood from the presentation of the figure of the Stone in Cao Xueqin's mid-eighteenth-century novel, *Story of the Stone*. On perceiving itself to have had no place to fit during the construction of the sky, the Stone considers itself alienated from the cosmic process. This alienation in turn affords it the opportunity for—or, rather, forces it toward—an aesthetic contemplation of virtually all the attributes of its links to the world. The resulting comprehensiveness of the Stone's theorization of its relationship to its own act of writing is extraordinary: it is at once author of the text, the text itself, the subject of the story the text is telling, and the guardian of the ways in which it should be read. The world of the Stone, then, is a thoroughly textual one in which no aspect of the production of writing is left unproblematized.[22] It is also true, however, that the very complexity of the structure of the discussion indicates how delicate this subject was to broach and how difficult it was to find a position within the discursive norms of the time from which to mount an effective critique of cultural practices, or at least those that impinged upon the writing subject personally.

The novel *Rulin waishi* (The scholars), written slightly before *The Story of the Stone*, also has much to say about the act of writing, but it tends to break down the possibilities in a more schematic way. Less intent upon gauging the potential of a particular voice, it maps out instead the constitutive features of the possibility of writing from a variety of social positions. One of the interests the author, Wu Jingzi (1701–1754), shared with Cao Xueqin is measuring the possibility of writing that distances itself from what both authors see as a corrupt and corrupting state discourse. We thus meet in *The Scholars* a number of people who seek to keep their distance from the dominant ideology. One of the most vividly depicted is Qu Shenfu, referred to throughout as Young Master Qu (Qu *gongsun*), a youthful poetaster from a family distinguished for both scholarship and ethical behavior. The introduction of the Qu family immediately after the depiction of a series of mean men devoted to self-advancement through the examination system makes it seem all the more praiseworthy when we first encounter it. In chapters 10 and 11 of *The Scholars*, Qu *gongsun* is married to a certain Miss Lu, an attractive young woman who on first glance seems to stand as the perfect *jiaren* (beauty) to Qu's *caizi* (talent). At this point, however, the irony begins. Qu, as the reader has known from the point of the young man's entry into the story, is, not unlike Jia Baoyu, the protagonist in *Stone*, an adept at poetry who considers anything to do with the examination system unbearably vulgar. Miss Lu, on the other hand, lacking brothers, has been rigorously trained in *bagu*, the "eight-legged essay"—the complicated rhetorical form required for the imperial civil service examinations—and considers any form of writing not associated with the examination path to be contemptibly frivolous.

Like most of the book, this episode is satirical, but it is a satire so evenhanded that it seems impossible to assign a partisan role to the writing voice. Although this evenhandedness is a crucial feature of the novel as a whole—I shall return to it below—for the purposes at hand what is striking about the episode is the way in which it sets forth two characteristic and complementary discursive positions open to writers in the post-Song empire. Miss Lu is a caricature, and a vivid one, of the most enduring of models open to writers after the set of writing practices enabled by Zhou Dunyi's phrase *wen yi zai dao* (writing should convey the way) came to dominate Chinese letters in the Daoxue era—in other words, virtually the whole of the Ming and Qing dynasties. For his part, Master Qu is her polar opposite—a man who tries mightily to define himself as being other than an adherent of the state orthodoxy. His position can be said to be based on the notion, presented by Su Shi (1037–1101), of a *wenxue* meant to be dominant in letters but particularly open-ended in its function.[23]

It seems evident that Wu Jingzi's evenhandedness in presenting this binary encapsulates a feeling that both positions were unsatisfactory, but that they also represented an inescapable problematic. From the modern perspective, the critique of Miss Lu's position is the most readily apprehensible. Twentieth-century intellectuals have been so firm in their condemnation of *bagu* as an instrument of intellectual suffocation that it is nearly impossible for the modern reader to see it as anything other than the vulgar business that Master Qu holds it to be. But neither does the novel's account of Master Qu leave out the considerable economic and psychic costs to those who turned their backs on this most official of genres. What strikes one as most significant about the episode, however, is the extent to which it invests itself in the critique of the *wenren*, the man dedicated to the aesthetic writing alternative to official prose. This may be due to the simple fact that further satire of *bagu* would have been too cheap and thus unworthy of Wu Jingzi's supple talent, since criticism of the eight-legged essay had been a staple of literati complaints since at least the early Qing.[24] Nevertheless, the greater amount of detail devoted to lampooning Master Qu and his relatives the Lou brothers imparts a particularly ludicrous cast to the field of nonofficial writing they represent. On first consideration, this denigration of the *wenren* alternative seems surprising. Why should an author so obviously writing from outside the realm of official sanction not create for himself a refuge by privileging the tradition that seems to most closely parallel his own dispositions?[25] A closer look at Master Qu's attributes, however, begins to clarify the matter. After we hear about his family's probity, one of the first and most important things we are told about him is that his climb to eminence resulted from passing off as his own editorial work a treatise on poetics by the Ming poet Gao Qi (1336–1374) that had come into his hands in a shady fashion.²⁶

This would seem a broad hint that the writing voice considers members of the *wenren* or *mingshi* (scholar of note) traditions not to be what they present themselves as. This episode taints them with the suspicion that their cherished relationships with refined texts is based more on plagiarism than the elegant *(ya)* empathy they consider to be their defining characteristic. It even suggests that the air of refinement so carefully cultivated by these men is little more than a cover for this unsavory fact. Perhaps even more to the point, however, is the way in which Qu and his friends define taste and creativity as being functions of perpetual marginalization from serious concerns, or even straightforward superficiality. In other words, from the perspective of the fine minds of these conscientious objectors to government-sanctioned prose, to aspire to anything distinguishable as an idea is already to be thoroughly penetrated by vulgarity.

Given this analysis of the choices available to the educated, it becomes easier to understand why Wu Jingzi would want to avoid either condition. But the question raised by the text—only to be continually deferred by it—is whether it is possible to avoid falling into one pattern or the other in pursuit of some more intellectually satisfactory path. On the one hand, that Wu chose to depict Miss Lu and Master Qu as joined in a marriage frustrating to both suggests that the two options are meant to embody the sort of claustrophobic binary opposition so thoroughly analyzed in Western critical theory over the last two decades. On the other hand, Wu's very act of recognizing the ineluctability of the relationship between the two modes of writing—that there really were no other choices available—represents (minimal though it might be) a space for critical reflection in what seems at first glance to be a field barren of possibility.²⁷ In short, I would argue that the self-consciousness expressed by Wu in his description of the impasse that writers faced in itself embodies a crucial critical space. It is by its very nature aporetic, for he portrayed a literary arena that had no place for the position from which he was writing. Wu creates the space strictly by virtue of his subtle capacity to write it into existence, and he makes it clear even as he is creating it that writer and reader alike must battle formidable obstacles to keep it open. For all the iconoclasm inhering in his stance, however, Wu is writing from a position within the norms of his times; his work is an inside job, the guarantee of the novel's extraordinary finesse.

Strange Events

If Wu Jingzi portrays a world rotting from the head via the temptations of seeking office, Wu Jianren's *Strange Events* portrays a world gripped by a nearly universal corruption, in which everything turns up for sale sooner or later.²⁸ Behind this corruption lies a terrible breakdown of Confucian values, particularly those having to do with the family. The moral squalor of this period is represented through a large number of episodes; the more elaborate ones are personally witnessed by the narrator, and the many shorter stories are recounted to the narrator by people he meets in the course of his travels through a China shrunk by the new network of steamships and telegraph lines—from the perspective of this text, the most important material legacy of the coming of the West. Most of the stories are quite self-consciously lurid, reflecting the narrator's view that the human world he has encountered contains only "pests, beasts, and demons."²⁹ Within the rather gothic tone the narrative assumes, however, it portrays events with a great deal of power. There is a mixture of narrative timbre, from near burlesque to pure horror, carefully worked-out thriller, and heartfelt sympathy. There is even, from time to time, the presentation of exemplary characters. The meticulously observed psychological insights and fastidious attention to anecdotal detail characterizing the stories combine with this adroit manipulation of tone to make for what is on the whole a most compelling work.

There has, however, been a persistent unease in the critical evaluation of this text within China. For instance, the contrast between my own assessment of *Strange Events* and that of Lu Xun, written sometime between 1920 and 1923, could hardly be more extreme. Lu Xun's judgment of this novel is of a piece with his critique of the late Qing novel as a whole: "Although they were intent upon reforming the age and thus seem to be in the same category as novels of satire [such as *The Scholars*], their expression is superficial and their biting style is without any subtlety. More than that, however, they are full of exaggeration in order to accord with the predilections of the time. There is, then, a marked poverty to their skill and to their degree of tolerance. I have, therefore, put them in a special category I call 'novels of censure' *(qianze xiaoshuo).*"³⁰ His judgment of *Strange Events* itself is, if anything, even harsher. After initially praising the wide range of characters Wu Jianren included in his work and the author's unbending disposition toward a critical perspective, Lu Xun renders the following appraisal: "Unfortunately, his descriptions are too hurried, and he sometimes errs by overstating the evils he is depicting. His words disregard reality, and their power to affect people is thereby diminished. The result is merely a compendium of gossip, good only for providing those at loose ends with material for idle chatter."³¹

Writing in the years immediately after 1920, it was easy for Lu Xun to regard the late Qing novel as already part of the old order he was so determined to denounce. On one level, then, his disdain demonstrates the extent to which his thoughts on the novel partook of the same disposition as Liang Qichao and his epigones in regarding all extant Chinese fiction as unworthy of emulation. Lu Xun did, after all, participate in the commentary on fiction of that earlier time, however much he retrospectively thought himself apart from it.[32] But why did he single these texts out for condemnation as the concluding section of a larger project whose goal was to recuperate the tradition of Chinese fictional narrative? At this point, it would be premature to assay an answer to this question; it must await the discussion of *Strange Events* itself. Whatever the reason for Lu Xun's harsh words, however, they have stood as canonical ever since he uttered them, and critics feel compelled to cite this statement approvingly even if they are in effect engaged in a project to reverse his verdicts.[33] In other words, later critical evaluation of the late Qing novel in China rarely—until the last few years, at least—moved very far beyond the condemnation of the Chinese novel as a whole as voiced by Liang Qichao in 1898 and affirmed even more conclusively in 1915.

The strange—or perhaps more accurately, horrible—events that transpire in the novel are presented to the reader from the perspective of a young man, Jiusi yisheng—literally, "Nine deaths, one life," or more loosely, "Still alive despite multiple perils." Jiusi began keeping a diary from the age of fifteen, the year his father died. He does not present the diary directly to the reader, however. That act is performed by one Sili taosheng, or "Escapee from the jaws of death." He had procured the diary from a man on the street in Shanghai who was touting the work as being more instructive than a *shanshu,* or book of morality. Accounting for the source of Wu's use of the motif of stumbling across a valuable manuscript is difficult. As mentioned in chapter 4, the explosion of the late Qing novel included at least as many novels in translation as it did novels originally written in Chinese. In fact, Zhou Guisheng, one of Wu's closest friends and collaborators, announced in an essay published at the beginning of 1904—just at the time, in other words, when *Strange Events* was beginning to appear in print—that he had read several hundred foreign novels written in either English or French, the only two foreign languages he professed to know.[34]

Given this relatively easy access to translated European novels, it becomes difficult to establish the origins of all the motifs Wu deploys in his own narratives. It could be, for instance, that the idea for "discovering" a diary is either a borrowing from one of the translated Western novels circulating in Shanghai or, equally plausibly, a kind of secularization of the mystical process of discovering the narrative-covered Stone at the beginning of *The Story of the Stone,* or even some combination of the two. Considering the concatenation of narrative devices in Wu's work that were then prevalent in the Western novel, however, it would be impossible to deny that these Western motifs played at least a key catalytic role in Wu's creative process in composing *Strange Events*. Whatever its specific provenance, however, the stance the author employs to cast the novel as a diary found by obscure means serves a fairly conventional purpose in boosting the work's claim to greater actuality. The diary form also serves to place within the novel an observer who is self-consciously outside the events he is recording. The composer of the diary thereby serves as the emblem of an alienated, external point of view on domestic events, something that had lain behind the perception by Liang Qichao and his followers of the singular power of the novel in the West.

When we first encounter the author of the diary, we are almost immediately given signals of his immaturity and general incapacity to make the correct decision when confronted with a set of plausible alternatives. His inexperience, his newness to the scene, is thus set up as the novel's first theme. This unfortunate circumstance is conveyed in the text at the beginning of Jiusi's self-presentation, when the young man arrives in Hangzhou only to find that his father has died before the son was able to see him one final time. The death of the father immediately presents the problem of the disposition of his assets, and Jiusi must choose among three adult men who present themselves as credible candidates to assist in this task. To complicate the choice, each is quite frank in explaining to the boy why the others cannot be trusted. Jiusi ends up choosing precisely the two who are unreliable. One of them is his uncle, whom Jiusi's father's trusted shop assistant had warned him about. Jiusi, however, decides to honor Confucian principle in making his choice on the basis of the familial connection.

The journey to see the dying father, the father's death, and the distribution of the money take place in the second chapter, which is the first chapter of Jiusi's diary proper. The men to whom Jiusi entrusts his estate are both presented with substantial sums of money, and within a few pages the young man and the reader alike learn that the money has, at least for the time being, disappeared. Although this fact provides the reader with sufficient reason to begin to doubt the trustworthiness of the uncle, Jiusi himself admits to no inkling of a problem. Moreover, at the end of the same chapter, Jiusi refuses to believe that a man dressed as an official he encountered during a short sea voyage is in fact a thief—he must be shown the evidence for this in considerable detail before he will credit the accusation. The focus of all the significant events of this chapter[35] on the narrator's inability to adequately judge his own perceptions establishes a pattern that persists for the first segment of the book, which runs through chapter 18. Once the pattern is established, Jiusi continues to see events as happening in a world that he can make no sense of. He fails to reach appropriate conclusions about what he sees, and a more experienced person must tell him the meaning of anything that happens. Sometimes, as with his failure to understand his uncle's actions correctly, he almost seems to actively resist seeing, even when the evidence for making a judgment is presented in so many iterations that no one inside or outside the text other than Jiusi fails to perceive the actual intent of the uncle's actions.

Gradually, however, through a slow process of finding and learning from competent authority, Jiusi becomes able at least to make observations that help him deal with situations in a more efficacious manner. The key authority figure and mentor here is one Wu Jingzeng, known by his cognomen of Jizhi and introduced in chapter 3. Jiusi encounters Jizhi by chance in Nanjing, when they recognize one another as having been students at the same school. Jizhi, ten years Jiusi's senior, has gone on to win his *jinshi* degree and now has an official post in Nanjing. The older man first invites Jiusi to move into his household and by chapter 4 has offered him a position in his private secretariat *(mufu)*. Both these offers come in the nick of time, Jiusi having squandered what resources he had left in a fruitless attempt to gain audience with his uncle in order to inquire what has become of the substantial capital that Jiusi entrusted to him.

An emblematic episode, which not only shows Jiusi's ignorance and Jizhi's role in educating him but also introduces another important figure in the novel, begins at the end of chapter 4. On one of the first days Jiusi is on his way to work as Jizhi's office, he happens to walk by the Nanjing establishment of Gou Cai, a Manchu of high rank (and whose name is an obvious pun on a phrase meaning "dog talent"). Jiusi is extremely impressed by the marks of status and wealth on display, the elegant clothes, and the many attendants. Upon arrival at Jizhi's office, Jiusi remarks on what he has just seen, but Jizhi dismisses him with a contemptuous "You're always so easily impressed!"[36] and turns the conversation to other matters in a deliberate attempt to avoid talking about Gou Cai. It is only later, when Jiusi and Jizhi are alone, that Jizhi tells him about Gou Cai's actual circumstances, something he had been unwilling to do with other people present. Jizhi informs Jiusi that Gou Cai, though once a high official, had alienated his superiors and is now mired in poverty, something Jiusi finds impossible to believe:

> I said, "You must have spoken in error. When I saw him this morning escorting his guest to the gate, not only was everyone in brand-new clothes, but he had four or five men in attendance. How could he be in poverty?"
>
> Jizhi said with a smile, "You haven't been around very long, so how can you know what you're talking about? Manchus are masters of putting up a false front; no matter how poor they are, they'll still put up a front.... So when you consider that he was once a circuit intendant

(daotai), how could he not come up with new clothes and attendants? As for the clothes, he clearly went to some trouble to conjure them up, but do you know about his 'servants'? When guests come they are servants, but when there are no guests around they eat at the table with the family."

I asked, "Why is that?"

Jizhi said, "The reason is that they are all his nephews and cousins and that sort of person, who flocked to him when they heard that he had become an official. None of them expected him to get poor, and that they would be obliged to act as his servants in order to keep up appearances."[37]

For all the delicacy of the "Manchu question" during the years this novel was written, it is clear that this presentation places more emphasis on the absurdity of Gou Cai (and of Manchus in general) than on the urgent depiction of the national question as such.[38]

A turning point in the novel, however, occurs in chapters 18–20, when Jiusi returns from Nanjing to his home in the south in response to an urgent family telegram reporting that his mother is seriously ill. Upon arriving, he finds not only that his mother knows nothing of the telegram but also that she has not been sick at all. She does, however, hint darkly at family plots designed to swindle their branch of the family out of its remaining property. This, combined with Jiusi's own observations about the sinister environment at home, causes him to decide to dispose of the family property and to take his mother and the proceeds from the sale back to Nanjing with him. He accomplishes this successfully in spite of the machinations of various conniving family members and acquaintances, including one of the men who had earlier embezzled money from him at Hangzhou soon after his father's death.[39]

For all the good judgment Jiusi demonstrates in this episode, however, he still must rely on other people for information and advice. In this case, a relative of his Nanjing patron, Jizhi, provides him with the information on land prices that he needs to resist his family's absurdly low offer, and then the relative proceeds to buy Jiusi's land himself. So although Jiusi does not fail to figure out the correct course of action, he still would not have been able to act without crucial support from the Wu family. It is not until chapters 32–35 that Jiusi encounters a problem and actually works out the solution completely on his own.[40] The long episode takes place in Shanghai and begins with Jiusi's encountering Li Jingyi, a former clerk in Jiusi's father's store. Before he describes Li Jingyi in detail, Jiusi first notes that he had learned that Li was guilty of a series of horrible acts, thereby signaling the reader that Jiusi is not under any illusions about what he is dealing with this time. We soon learn that Li was complicit in the forced suicide of his own brother and that he subsequently sold his newly widowed sister-in-law into prostitution. The narrative that follows recounts Jiusi's successful efforts to find the young woman, Qiuju; reunite her with her "step" *(gan)* parents; and oblige Li to surrender his financial claims on her. As part of this process, Jiusi meets her "stepfather," Cai Lüsheng, and discovers him to be an upright scholar who has been unable to prosper in the cutthroat world of private secretaries in Shanghai.⁴¹ After solving Cai's problems, Jiusi in effect becomes his patron and finds him a job within Jizhi's establishment.

With this ultimate indication of Jiusi's learning and maturation, the diary would seem to fit the pattern of the standard account of a young man's education and intellectual growth, a form familiar in the West as the bildungsroman. The text to this point can be interpreted as being consonant with this genre. Although the narration of Jiusi's personal and family life had been somewhat sketchy before this episode, we do see him pursuing his uncle and talking at length to his mother and cousin about matters of real consequence, conspicuously including questions of how Confucianism was to be applied in these parlous times. And the text does, of course, constantly place in the foreground questions dealing with the broader issue of how Jiusi personally will cope with the difficult task of gauging events. At this point in the novel, however, Jiusi takes on a significant new role. Almost simultaneous with his rescue of Cai Lüsheng, Jizhi decides to set himself up as a merchant, with a chain of shops in Yangzi River ports. Jizhi is serving as an official, so it is illegal for him to engage in trade, and he asks Jiusi to manage the enterprise in his stead (chapter 40).⁴² Because the job entails extensive travel, it serves as the device by which Jiusi gains the opportunity to visit other parts of China and, most important, to collect more stories.

Having by this time achieved what might be called epistemological maturity, Jiusi is now in a position to evaluate the significance of each new story. The emblem of his ability to collect, to move between, and to follow up on stories is the modern steamship and telegraphy systems brought to China by the imperial powers. Jiusi moves about by steamship and communicates by telegram, very conspicuously tools brought from the West and presented as crucial means by which to understand this new and otherwise opaque age. These modern tools, knitting together a far-ranging narrative, figure so prominently in so many episodes that the reader is obliged to assume that the author is consciously investing them with positive thematic significance.⁴³

Once Jiusi takes this job and begins his travels, however, the narrative of his personal life diminishes significantly. When he achieves a certain level of knowledge, in other words, the details and concerns of his own life are allowed to recede to the margins. A position of wisdom in this novel thus seems to allow the narrator to effectively judge the events he encounters by their external face alone, and from this perspective introspection appears to be a manifestation of cognitive weakness. To a certain extent this loss of focus on his personal life might be explained by his travels, which inevitably separate him from friends and family. But this explanation comes up wanting in chapter 65, in which Jiusi returns to his old home with his mother and cousin for the purpose of his marriage. Whereas in the earlier chapters of the book we had extensive glimpses of the inner quarters of Jiusi and Jizhi's households, including long episodes in which Jizhi's wife appears, Jiusi's own marriage is dealt with tersely. We are told that he will marry, that he is teased a bit by his female relatives, and that he spends three years at home after the marriage, not one day of which is narrated. At the end of this time, he leaves home at Jizhi's call and does not return for the remainder of the novel. About his wife, or any detail of the three years spent with her, nothing is written.[44]

Jiusi's personal abstraction from the events he relates in the second half of the novel is indicated in a striking disclosure in chapter 60. Jiusi returns from a trip to Canton and gives his diary to his friends to read. They read about events the reader has just witnesses in chapters 57 and 59, but one of the friends notices that a tagline in the text apparently refers to an episode not recorded in the diary. Jiusi confesses that this is indeed the case and that he had written down the tag in haste so as to remind himself to write up the whole episode when he had more time.[45] What is significant about this event is the confession to us readers that when we thought we were reading about Jiusi's "real" journey to the south, and everything of significance about it, we were in fact reading only what had been set down in the diary. Calling attention to the tagline reminds us that we are reading only what has been chosen for us (for whatever reason) by a particular process of text production that must be kept analytically distinct from the actual events that make up Jiusi's travels. This episode indicates that the author of the diary is ultimately shown to have almost complete freedom to build the text from memories of his own choosing. There could be no firmer sign of Jiusi's self-chosen exteriority from the events that he chooses to narrate.

What Jiusi's Bildung has gained for him, in other words, is access to more stories, and his function in the text after he gains perceptual maturity is reduced in effect to collector of and witness to tales. To be sure, embedded within these narratives is a vast array of detail about life and habits, the practical ideology of the governing classes, and how that ideology relates to daily life, and each episode remains loyal to the theme announced by Sili taosheng in the very first chapter: "I had known that Shanghai was no good, but according to [this] book, although the world is wide, there seems to be no place anywhere that a human being can actually receive proper treatment."[46] The dramatic quality of the episodes does seem to become more powerful in the later chapters, as the level of behavioral depravity represented increases markedly. But the trajectory of the narrative provided by the focus on Jiusi's education in the early chapters seems to disappear, and his new intellectual control proves in the end to be, ironically, inadequate to the task of providing a new sense of order to the myriad events that he observes. In fact, his later position is actually inferior to his earlier one: at the beginning he was aware of his own limitations, and the resulting lack of control made sense. He also gradually gained consciousness of his own capacity to augment his knowledge and his own capacity to judge. Toward the novel's end, however, he knows much more, and his inability to make that knowledge work renders his situation all the more poignant.

There are two characters whose reappearance at various points in the novel serves as a moral gauge on events. These are Jiusi's reprobate uncle and the Manchu official Gou Cai.[47] The growing outrageousness of their behavior as well as that of the characters surrounding them signals the precipitous descent into moral chaos that increasingly marks the second half of the book. The reader and even Jiusi have by the later chapters long recognized the uncle's character flaws, but in chapter 82 Jiusi ferrets out the information that his uncle had taken his own wife's niece as a mistress, an action revealing a whole new level of depravity to the character. Although the uncle's perfidy had served from early on in the text as the very sign of the decay of Confucian family values, this transgression involves an even greater violation of these norms than anything that had happened previously. It is thus an important part of the demonstration in the final half of *Strange Events* that Confucian values have been eroded to their core.

The decline of the moral order is even more powerfully represented in the later depiction of Gou Cai. As described above, when Jiusi first encountered him in the early chapters, Gou served both as a prime emblem of Jiusi's inability to discern the difference between appearance and the true order of things and as a ready object of ridicule. He is still primarily an object of ridicule in his next significant appearance, in chapter 44, where he is invited to a party given by Jizhi. Gou Cai brings his concubine instead of his wife, an act almost unworthy of comment in those years, but he does allow her to dress as if she were his formal wife. When his wife hears of this, she crashes the party to visit physical mayhem upon both Gou Cai and the concubine, an event portrayed even more broadly than are the early episodes involving the Manchu.[48] Although the emphasis in this scene is on Gou Cai's absurdity, his act of moral transgression in jumbling family rules is an event that hints at more ominous consequences than had been his earlier show of simply putting on airs. Family values throughout the novel are depicted as being in decline, but their decline also serves as part of a Confucian moral economy in which the family is an index of the moral decline of society in general.

Gou Cai and his circle's level of transgression increases as the novel continues. Gou Cai next enters the narrative at the end of chapter 86, where his story becomes the principal focus of the novel for eight of the next ten chapters.[49] The core story in this sequence centers around the gift of the daughter-in-law of Gou Cai and his wife (the young widow of their recently deceased son) to a viceroy, one of whose concubines has just died. They do this in order to get back into official favor after Gou Cai's dismissal from office in a scandal involving a whole range of corrupt officials. In carrying out this outrageous act against both their own family honor and all the rules of Confucian rectitude, Gou Cai and his wife transcend simple buffoonery. The two of them are still the same absurd people, but their urgent persuasion of their daughter-in-law to accede to their wishes puts them at the wrong end of an important moral register, in which the stakes have suddenly become quite serious. At this point the tone of the text takes on a new gravity, as we see characters who had always seemed to be mere clowns suddenly put into the soberest sort of situation, a new juxtaposition that is extremely effective in conveying the queasy feeling of an encroaching moral chaos. As with the episode in which we learn that Jiusi's uncle had compromised the honor of a young female member of his own family, Gou Cai's actions here contribute to the complication of tone that the novel as a whole is undergoing.

Although Gou Cai's act gains him a temporary official reprieve, eventually a new viceroy takes office, and he is horrified at Gou Cai's violations of norms, dismissing Gou Cai from his official position yet again. Gou Cai later schemes to get rich by building and operating a mint, and when the governor of Anhui agrees to sponsor the project, Gou Cai's plan is put into operation. Although he eventually loses this job too, Gou Cai has in the intervening two years of managing the mint made so much money that he has been able to take "five or six concubines"—in this book a sure indication of sudden wealth. After a few more years on the official circuit, Gou Cai decides to retire to Shanghai with his loot. He has acquired a minor heart condition along with his money, and one of his motives for moving to Shanghai is to seek expert medical opinion. Upon arriving in the city, he visits Jizhi to get a referral to a capable physician. The physician whom Jizhi recommends, Wang Duanfu, diagnoses Gou Cai's illness as minor but is also puzzled that Gou continues to manifest symptoms. Wang concludes that someone in Gou Cai's household is trying to do Gou harm, motivating the physician to abandon the case lest he eventually be blamed for what he can already see will be Gou's untimely demise.

Although both Jizhi and Jiusi recognize Gou Cai as a person who is thoroughly compromised morally, they agree that only a family member greedy for Gou's money would try to poison him. Jizhi visits the Gou household and sets a trap, telling Gou Cai's only surviving son, Gou Longguang, that abalone is the one thing that will do great damage to his father's health. A week later Jizhi and Jiusi invite Gou Cai to dinner, along with Wang Duanfu. When abalone is served and Gou refuses it because he says that he has been having it served to him every day at home, Jizhi and Jiusi realize that they are witnessing an ongoing patricide. Jizhi tries indirectly to warn Gou Cai to leave home or to send his son away, but Gou does not catch the hints. After Gou departs, Jizhi informs Wang Duanfu of the trap and what he had learned from it, and the doctor, who had just delivered himself of a long after-dinner speech on the wisdom of separating parents from children, especially only sons, responds:

> "What did I tell you? So I wasn't doing anybody an injustice when I said what I did. But if you already had such firm evidence, why didn't you tell him directly just now, instead of beating around the bush as you did? To look at Gou Cai in action, you'd think he knew what he was doing, but in fact he's pretty ordinary in his understanding of things. There really isn't any reason to assume he'd get what you were hinting at."
>
> Jizhi said: "But if I had told him directly, it would have done damage to the relationship between father and son."
>
> Duanfu was furious and said: "Enough of that! Don't you think the 'relationship between father and son' will be even more damaged if you don't tell him directly?"
>
> Jizhi suddenly saw the truth to this and said: "You're right. I'll go see him tomorrow and tell him plainly."[50]

Perhaps the most striking thing about the encounter between Wang Duanfu and Jizhi is the contrast revealed between Jizhi's ordinary Confucian tact concerning family propriety and its inability to encompass the outrage that is being committed. The ineffectiveness of morality in the face of this greatest of all outrages against Chinese values is extraordinary, a crime explicitly linked in Chinese thought with utter decadence in political and social morality.[51] The offense is so great, in fact, that even the wretched Gou Cai wins our sympathy,[52] and Wang Duanfu's speech on the positive value of breaking up families, which seemed so scandalous as he was delivering it, now passes by unnoticed as being, at least in this case, a transparent statement of a situational truth. For all the horror of these final episodes, however, Jiusi maintains a relative distance from the events themselves—he continues only to observe and to report (note also that it is Jizhi who makes the effort to intervene on Gou Cai's behalf). This distance also keeps events at one remove from readers, if only because we are constantly being reminded that what is being recounted is only a set of stories.

The Gou Cai episode continues to become even more ominous. When Jizhi visits Gou Cai the next day to tell the wretched man of the plot against him, Jizhi is abruptly sent away after being told that Gou Cai is now too sick to receive visitors. The next day, he returns to the Gou residence, only to be told the same thing, and his many subsequent efforts to gain audience with Gou Cai are similarly unavailing. A few months later, he not unexpectedly receives word of the Manchu's death. Jizhi eventually learns the full details of the plot, which he duly communicates to Jiusi. It turns out that Gou Cai's son had not been able to make a satisfactory marriage for himself because of his family's tarnished image, and Longguang did not like the wife he was eventually obliged to settle for — although he got on very well with her brother. When Gou Cai rejected his request to take a concubine, Longguang and his brother-in-law took up with two of the senior Gou's consorts, thus giving the younger men ample reason to plot against Gou upon the older man's eventual return to Shanghai. By promising a share of the spoils once the older man died, Longguang and his brother-in-law enlisted the assistance of a shady doctor in their scheme, although when Gou Cai eventually died, they managed to swindle the doctor out of his share. Although Gou Cai's sorry fate represents a working out of the karmic consequences of his treatment of his daughter-in-law, the actual results are so dreadful as to constitute the moral nadir of the whole work.

On the other hand, Gou Cai's recurrence throughout the book does, as I discussed above, make his story more consequential than most of the other tales presented. In fact, Gou Cai's trajectory as a character turns out to be ominous for Jiusi as well, as the final two chapters, which follow hard upon Gou's tale and almost equal it in finality, make clear. These chapters contain an extremely decisive conclusion, a closure that is as sudden and powerful as it is unexpected. In chapter 107, Jiusi receives a letter from one of Jizhi's other employees telling him that his client Cai Lüsheng is now serving as a county magistrate in Shandong; at the same time, in the next county, we are told, the sudden death of an uncle and aunt of Jiusi's has orphaned their two sons. After notifying his embezzler-uncle of the situation, who characteristically advises him not to get involved, Jiusi sets off to rescue his two young cousins and then goes on to pay a visit to his old friend Cai.

Jiusi arrives in Shandong to bring the two boys back but in the process is robbed of the considerable sum of money he had been carrying. While all this is going on, he receives word that Jizhi's mother has died. When he arrives in the county under Cai's administration, he finds that Cai has been unjustly relieved of his magistracy, not to mention having been fined by the central government because he had distributed famine relief to the people of his *xian* (country) against the wishes of his fellow officials in the region. It is surely significant that these events, which unravel Jiusi and his social network, take place while he is traveling about inland Shandong, which lacks entirely his standard means of modern locomotion and communication. The sluggishness of travel by horse-drawn cart and his isolation from sources of news in this remote and, perhaps more to the point, completely traditional place are set in the foreground in this episode, ushering in a new mood in which Jiusi no longer has any control over the narrative whatsoever. Without access to modern transportation and the telegraph, Jiusi's ability to gather stories that reach beyond his own small circle suddenly grinds to a halt.[53] It is worth noting the contrast between the omnipresence of these new Western applied technologies in Wu Jianren's novels and the complete absence of them within the narrative of the nearly contemporaneous *Lao Can youji*. In spite of the early reference to the compass and its implicit Western origins—at least in its modern form—in Liu E's novel (not to mention Liu's historical role in espousing the importation of Western technology), the eponymous protagonist in that work travels about Shandong for a considerable period of time with no reference at all to any of these new, Western implements of communication and transportation.

After this decisive interlude in the interior, Jiusi returns to Shanghai to try to raise money for Cai, only to be told that Jizhi's commercial empire has suddenly and utterly crumbled. This collapse leaves Jiusi liable, for he had accepted responsibility for the firm when Jizhi was serving as an official (and was thus barred from commercial enterprise). The story ends with Jiusi's journeying upriver—incognito to avoid his creditors—in order to settle the affairs of the embezzler-uncle, who has also suddenly died. Upon returning to Shanghai, Jiusi goes to the house of Wen Shunong, Jizhi's trusted employee and the bearer of many of these bad tidings, and finds that the house has burned to the ground. Finally, Jiusi flees to his ancestral home in the south, but first he turns his diary over to Shunong, who is only at this point revealed to be the man from whom the wandering Sili taosheng had received the text in chapter 1.[54]

Aside from ending the novel on as sensational a note as possible, with death, lamentation, and corrosive pettiness on all sides of Jiusi, these final two chapters also abruptly restore his personal narrative to prominence. This sudden reappearance of Jiusi's story destabilizes the comfortable pattern that the novel had fallen into and renders it again as uncertain as it had been in the early chapters. If the attenuation of his personal narrative had coincided with a new sense of cognitive control on his part, how does the sudden return of his personal story to the foreground affect the overall shape of the narrative? It has seemed as if the text after chapter 40 was basing its determined collection and representation of tales on Jiusi's capacity to understand and organize them. In the final two chapters, however, Jiusi's own story sneaks up on him, as it were, in such a furious way as to cast doubt upon the idea that he ever had achieved the sort of capacity for practical understanding that he had seemed to manifest earlier. Furthermore, the overpowering force that marks the return of his narrative after its long abeyance suggests that some mechanism has been repressing it, which would help account for the nightmarish quality of its return. In short, the promise of the novel to both represent and bring about understanding of the world is substantially undermined by these concluding chapters.

This change of narrative pattern implies that the cognitive equilibrium that marked the novel during most of its latter part is more unstable than the narrative voice itself could ever be aware of. If the record of events themselves is throughout pessimistic, Jiusi's crisp way of thinking and writing about it had animated the grim account. In the final chapters, however, all the elements that had made up the new and enabled Jiusi to move about and to contemplate his own (and China's) situation—steamships, telegraphs, Western examples, new ideas about the role of women in Confucianism, the reformed novel, and, above all, his superior position outside events—collapse.[55] Even if the observed events never turned out well, the representation of a consciousness that could conceive of viable alternatives seemed to hold out a genuine prospect of improvement. This final collapse of perspective, however, provides a most graphic image of how even this promise has evaporated.[56]

The slow accretion of Jiusi's practical capacity for understanding achieved textual figuration in the first-person voice, the maturation of which represented the hopes for cognitive development. With the final collapse of this speaking position in the almost gratuitously brutal cutting down of Jiusi's status in the world, a sense of the instability of events and the corruption surrounding them fills the resulting vacuum. The final chapters demonstrate retrospectively, and with maximum force, the actual incapacity of Jiusi to manipulate or understand, even symbolically, the events that he witnessed over the years.[57] The leverage that an external position seemed to promise turns out to be nugatory. If the new nation demanded "national subjects" as a stable and active body of citizens, the very fragility of the former demonstrated how problematic would be this category of new citizen capable of bringing the nation into being. If, in other words, the new nation required national subjects in order to come into being, and national subjects required a nation in order to be able to create themselves, where was one to begin?

In being for most of its course in sympathy with Jiusi's critique of what he finds and with his desire to achieve practical understanding, the rhetorical posture of the text as a whole clashes with its own dire conclusion. On the one hand, then, the impasse of Wu Jianren's writing represents a particularly powerful instance of a resistance or even inability to produce the sort of comprehensive guide to the world that the contemporary critical discourse on the novel persisted in demanding of the form. On the other hand, the brutality of the ending signals the urgent desire in the writing voice for just such a transcendent position, even as it discloses its failure to locate one. The text comes to the conclusion that it cannot fulfill the demands of contemporary critics, even as it seems at some level to accept those demands. What the novel does not settle for, however, is the aesthetic mood of resignation characteristic of *The Scholars*, a book that remains content with creating a purely intellectual space somewhere between protest and disinterested contemplation of the folly of the human condition. *Strange Events* embodies, in other words, an outlook on the world frustrated by its own inability to create a representation that has any hope of affecting the world.

Perhaps it was this tacit admission that there was no real alternative to surrendering to the power of things as they were that so aroused the later ire of Lu Xun. Even if one were to grant him the truth of his highly problematic remarks about the lack of forbearance in the late Qing novel, his condemnation of this intolerance seems more than a little ironic if one seriously considers some of his own narrative work. It is difficult, for instance, to think of *The True Story of Ah Q* as exhibiting some vast reservoir of generosity toward its objects of scrutiny that is completely foreign to late Qing fiction. It is fairly evident from his remarks on *Strange Events* quoted above that Lu Xun's rejection of the work is based on what he perceives as its failure to present a sustained and comprehensive critique, its failure to gain, in short, a useful purchase on the unfolding of events. In a real sense, Lu Xun's frustration with the text is of a piece with the novel's evident frustration with its own inability to attain control over the events of its own representational universe. If, however, one understands Lu Xun's critique of the novel as based predominantly on aesthetic concerns (as most subsequent understandings of Lu Xun's remarks assume), it would be easy to lose sight of the ideological nature of his paradoxical argument with Wu Jianren. In other words, even the "hard-boned" Lu Xun (as Mao Zedong called him)[58] was unwilling to accept the foreclosure of the possibility of a hopeful future represented by the collapse of the external perspective in Wu's text.

The tendency to ascribe the novel's difficulties to simple aesthetic failure contributed to the notion that behind this failure lay a potential narrative fully capable of controlling a sufficient representation of events. Critics who took this line, such as Liang Qichao, seemed to be motivated by a Western-inspired vision that there existed somewhere a spectral text undergirded by a firm historical telos that would lift China out of the abyss. As we shall see, Lu Xun was clearly not the sort of person who indulged in such teleological fantasies, but even he seems not to have been able to make his peace with the radical epistemological uncertainty that marks the end of Wu Jianren's novel, however much Lu Xun's own fictional work was to echo it. Wu at least presented forthrightly the perplexity endemic to the bewildering period in which he lived. Most later efforts to build narratives of modern China would, in fact, foreclose on this fearful asymmetry by imposing a linear and external trajectory on the events they chose to depict. However, the need to find a way toward a new kind of control over a desperately amorphous situation—to "social-engineer"—was to grow on its own failure, in social practice as in literature, for utopian thinking seemed to feed on the progressive collapse of ordinary civic activity as the twentieth century drew on. Mirages from the West and succeeding reappraisals were invariably central to this process.

CHAPTER 6

Melding East and West

Wu Jianren's *New Story of the Stone*

"Those Chinamen knew what they were about," somebody added, "when they refused to let in our western civilization. They knew what it would lead to better than we did. They saw it as nothing but dynamite in disguise."
   Edward Bellamy, *Looking Backward*

The foreign settlements at Shanghai may have been grafted on China, but they have grown into the commercial, financial, and industrial organism of that country, and to remove them entirely would be like cutting a pound of flesh from a man's body.
   Thomas F. Millard, *China: Where It Is Today and Why*

*I*f the world encompassed by *Strange Events* had ultimately proved itself too big and complicated to comprehend, Wu tried again to come to grips with a global understanding of China, its situation in the world, and its multiplicity of internal problems in a different sort of novel begun about two years later, in 1905. In his *Xin shitou ji* (The new story of the Stone), Wu created a fictional realm less tied to his own experiences, where solutions could thereby, presumably, be more readily—or at least more dispassionately—imagined. This tractability of intention is enhanced by the fact that half the novel is set in a science fictional realm almost certainly inspired by Edward Bellamy's 1888 American novel of a socialist utopia. In both texts, fantasies are effortlessly realized, at least for much of the time. In borrowing two of the major characters (and one minor one) from China's most famous novel—the eighteenth-century *Story of the Stone*, by Cao Xueqin—Wu is also, somewhat paradoxically, able to bring a genuinely external perspective to bear on the issues of his time. Jia Baoyu, the protagonist of both Cao's original and Wu's version, represented an outsider's point of view in the original text, as a conscientious dropout from the orthodox, examination-based path to social success that had long been the norm for educated elites in imperial China. In this sense, Baoyu gains a double objectivity in being suddenly transported to the Shanghai of 1900.

In Wu's novel Baoyu proves early on to be a vastly quicker and more adept study than the Jiusi of *Strange Events,* capable of learning largely on his own and having only to see or hear things once to gain full comprehension. Baoyu, in contrast to the various scoundrels and frauds he encounters on his travels, also rapidly establishes himself in the reader's eye as a reliable practical and moral guide to the complicated turn-of-the-century scene. The source of Baoyu's intellectual authority poses an interesting question. Whereas Wu had relied on access to modern means of communication to enable Jiusi's Bildung in *Strange Events,* Baoyu is, by comparison, a figure profoundly imbricated in the culture of tradition, who even, for instance, has to puzzle out what it is he is reading the first time he comes across a modern newspaper. Is it, then, Baoyu's deep traditional learning that makes him so much more perceptive than the less-educated Jiusi? As we observed in the last chapter, in *Strange Events* the women of Jiusi's household had often been the repository of a clear moral sense thoroughly based in Confucian learning, but their inability to function fully in society, precisely because of gender restrictions, had rendered that moral capacity merely theoretical. Baoyu, on the other hand, is very much out and about and trying his best, moreover, to intervene for the good where he is able.

As we shall see, however, Baoyu's world collapses in the end just as surely as did Jiusi's, although for quite different reasons. *New Stone* goes so far as to create a utopian realm in a science fiction mode, where all China's problems look to be solved. This utopian scheme suddenly collapses of its own weight. Events at the end are just as overwhelming as in *Strange Events,* all the more so because of the suddenness of the revelation of failure. This brings up, in turn, another interesting question. All the novels we examine closely in this book are records of failures to construct a narrative world their characters can comfortably inhabit, and, in fact, all the work of the late Qing that has received critical approbation appears to belong in this category. As Denise Gimpel has shown, however, a wide variety of fiction was published in the late Qing that was situated in a significantly more benign social context.[1] It would seem, therefore, that situating narratives in as crisis-saturated a context as leading intellectuals perceived China to be facing at the time has been the sine qua non of canonization for late Qing novels and stories, however misprized that canon has been in the post–May Fourth critical environment.

Jia Baoyu in Shanghai: From *Wenren* to *Wenhua ren*

Whereas *Strange Events* had been set almost entirely in the 1880s and 1890s, *New Stone* bravely moves up to 1900, the momentous year of the Boxer Rebellion. *New Stone* also spends much of its time in Shanghai, taking questions posed by that city as one of the text's major thematic concerns. In the great port city, the years after 1895 witnessed not only an increase in civic consciousness but also vastly increased economic growth, particularly in the new industrial sector, secured by new treaties allowing foreign investment in industrial enterprises.[2] The resulting rapid expansion of a white-collar readership—consisting of the men staffing the new professions created by this economic expansion[3]—was accompanied by a burgeoning publishing industry. In the period immediately following Liang Qichao's 1902 call for the creation of a new fiction, much of the attention of this industry turned to the production of hundreds of new novels, both indigenous and translated from foreign languages. Whereas the foreign novels were devoted to a wide variety of subject matters, many of the homegrown texts, and particularly those that achieved both critical and popular esteem, were acutely concerned with the cultural and economic conditions that had been the occasion for their appearance.[4] A significant number of these latter novels also took the city of Shanghai itself—the zone of contact within which both the new readership and the new economic activity were concentrated—as the ideal thematic focus through which at once to observe and to comment critically upon the rapidly changing circumstances of the time, as well as the multiple contradictions the city had come to embody.[5]

Shanghai had also been one of the thematic foci of *Strange Events*, to which I shall regress briefly to show how that burgeoning city figures there. At the beginning of the introductory chapter, or "wedge" *(xiezi)*, of the novel, Wu Jianren had voiced a sense of how the new urban space of Shanghai had come to represent the modern transformations that were taking place rapidly in China by the late Qing. More than that, the city also served as the locus for the many anxieties engendered by reflection upon those changes:

> Shanghai is the gathering place of merchants and traders, a place where foreigners and Chinese mix and where human habitation is thick; ships come and go and the goods of the world are transported there. Add to this the very flower of Suzhou and Yangzhou [i.e., the prostitutes], who

have also migrated with their sights set on this large gathering of rich merchants and prosperous traders. They sail in and gather in the vicinity of Fourth Avenue, bedecked in a riot of color, contending with one another to be as extraordinary as possible. Those of the first rank are of course inquired after by noble young gentlemen, while even the lowly do have those who pursue them, greedy for a taste. So, what was sixty years ago a chunk of reed bank has been transformed into the most lively place in China.

. . . But these are small things: beyond this, there are frauds and swindles and gambling. In fact, there are all sorts of strange and rare things—things that one cannot even dream of—that all take place in Shanghai. So, what was sixty years ago a place of simple custom has become a refuge both for the frivolous and for the crafty.[6]

Wu's narrator duly notes the miraculous transformation that has taken place, as well as the powerful commercial engine that has driven it. Above all, however, he seems determined to demonstrate both the novelty and the singularity of Shanghai and, in particular, to persuade us that it has suddenly grown up out of nothing—an idea that much contemporary scholarship has been at pains to correct.[7] He also links in the same breath the extraordinary commercial growth and a seemingly inseparable observation of the dissolution of appropriate values in a miasma of shady dealings. Prostitution—in effect the commercialization of a realm of human activity that had been extensively regulated within the traditional value system—serves here as the figure of displacement that more than anything else ties together the new economy and the decline in social values. It is the most conspicuous marker of the ultimate power of money to shape society and the people in it. The opening page of *Strange Events* confines itself to describing "merchants and traders" and the prostitutes they support. As was illustrated in the chapter 5, however, the narrative goes on to provide numerous examples of official malfeasance and the generally sordid parallel lives of those with considerable education who are the hangers-on of those with government positions. If such men are conventionally regarded as leaders and social models, the extremely low behavior that Wu attributes to them is an ominous sign of the moral chaos lying just ahead.

Although most of *Strange Events* is given to intricate description of abuses in the official realm *(guanchang)*, there are a number of memorable passages of vicious satire directed against the self-consciously literary men, *mingshi* (or *wenren*),[8] who along with the merchants and traders patronize the houses of prostitution on Shanghai's infamous Fourth Avenue *(si malu)*, the universal Chinese sobriquet for what the foreign authorities had labeled "Foochow Road." In one of the most cutting portraits of these men, Jiusi, the novel's narrator, joins a group of poetasters and responds with utter amazement to the fatuously egotistical literary names they have adopted for themselves. He remarks:

> These [style-names that I have just listed] were only the strangest among them, and after hearing them once, I will never forget them for the remainder of my life. As for all the rest, they were named after poets and lyricists and Buddhist adepts in such profusion that I cannot possibly recall them all. They asked me my style-name *(biehao),* and I replied that I did not have one. The one named Mei said to me:
> "How can a poet not have a style-name? If one doesn't fashion a literary name for oneself, one's name will sink into obscurity. That was the reason ancient poets did this, which is why Li Bai [701–762] called himself the 'Green lotus hermit' *(qinglian jushi)* and Du Fu [712–770] styled himself Yuxi sheng [actually the style-name of Li Shangyin (813?–858), a poet who lived some hundred years after Du Fu]."
> I could not help exploding into laughter, and I suddenly heard someone say in a loud voice: "If you can't remember clearly, don't say just anything that comes to mind, or people will laugh at you." I all at once remembered that it is not a good thing to laugh at people to their face, so I rapidly resumed a serious demeanor. But I also heard the second person say: "Yuxi sheng is the style-name of Du Mu [803–852]; you misremembered because both of them are named Du." The one named Mei asked: "Then what is Du Fu's style-name?" The other one replied: "Isn't he the 'Hermit of Fan River' *(fanchuan jushi)* [actually, minus the "hermit" suffix, Du Mu's style-name]?"[9]

After beginning by correctly identifying Li Bai's literary name, the quality of the commentary supplied by these latter-day literati goes rapidly downhill, with the would-be *wenren* preposterously failing to recognize the actual referents of the names they had so enthusiastically adopted for themselves. Although the satire in this passage is a good deal cruder than that contained in most of the rest of the novel, its point could not be clearer: Wu Jianren is intent upon indicating that these paragons of letters, as they would like to think of themselves, know virtually nothing of the men and work they fancy themselves to be emulating.

The Qing-dynasty fictional discourse on the relative validity of the man of letters has a long history,[10] but in the earlier period, the issue had not focused on the question of the literacy of the *wenren*. Rather, the issue had been more about the role of these men of taste in society at large. For instance, in chapter 7 of *The Scholars,* the elegant and witty *mingshi* Qu Jingyu is introduced into the text when he tells a joke on a contemporary examination official in Sichuan (an episode set in the first decade of the

1500s). He reports that the official had been drinking with He Jingming (1483–1521, an archaist poet and member of the "Former Seven Masters" *[qian qizi]* of Ming literature), when He suddenly blurted out that "[the examinees] in Sichuan are like Su Shi's essays: they should all be graded as sixth-rate." To which the examiner responded: "I have been in Sichuan for three years and have been all around the province carefully testing candidates. I don't remember any Su Shi coming to take the exam."[11] In *The Scholars,* then, those scholars who devoted all their energies to passing the official exams are the ones marked as culturally illiterate; however unsuccessful Qu and those more or less like him turn out to be at ordering the world, there is no question about their knowledge of literary lore. The contrast with Wu Jianren's *wenren* from the passage quoted above could not be more stark. The frivolous men from Wu's novel are no longer even capable of performing their self-appointed task of maintaining the literary heritage, much less contributing anything to the maintenance of the governmental and social realm. If nothing else, Wu's caricatures demonstrate the extent to which the category of *wenren* had become devalued by the late Qing.

In *The New Story of the Stone,* which began newspaper serialization in Shanghai in late September 1905, Wu makes use of an extraordinarily familiar text to convey his rendition of the experience of the transformation China was undergoing in the period around 1900.[12] Because Wu always had so many different works in serial publication at the same time, the actual time of writing and precise circumstances of composition are almost impossible to pin down. In 1905, for instance, in addition to editing the newspaper in Hankou for the first half of the year and participating actively in the protest movement against the American Chinese exclusion acts over the summer, he had throughout the year chapters from four different novels being simultaneously published in Liang Qichao's *Xin xiaoshuo* and another one in *Xiuxiang xiaoshuo* (Embroidered fiction).[13] As I discuss below, however, 1905 was a particularly crucial year both in the history of Shanghai and in the course of Wu's own busy career, and it is thus likely that the patriotic political climate of the months preceding the publication of the first installments of the novel had a significant effect on its composition.

Given this context, Wu's choice to write yet another sequel to Cao Xueqin's enormously popular eighteenth-century novel is not easy to understand. Wu himself opens his text in a defensive mode, noting the many sequels to famous novels and voicing the fear that his effort will be another case of "adding feet to [the portrait] of a snake."[14] He nonetheless concludes his introduction by claiming that a writer must please himself and not care overmuch about the response of his readers: "If the readers say it is good, that is fine; if they think it is clownish *(chou),* that is fine too.

I won't be able to hear [the comments] in any case" (p. 2). I should note parenthetically the evident courage of such a stance in someone who was dependent upon the market for his work to make a living.[15] Moreover, given the negative attitude toward *The Story of the Stone* manifested in Wu's next novel, *Sea of Regret,* it is curious that he chose to emulate Cao's text at all. In chapter 8 of *Sea,* for instance, the moral paragon Chen Zhongai is taken by colleagues to the pleasure quarters but refuses to indulge in the proffered courtesans. When mocked by his friends for what they take to be his overdeveloped sense of propriety, Zhongai accuses them all of having been taken in by *Stone,* concluding, "People of later generations have more often than not taken *Stone* to task as a book that incites lust, but the sins of the work cannot be limited to the word 'lust' alone."[16] That the author inserts three marginal comments into Zhongai's discourse, applauding him (and himself) on the perspicuity of his comments, is convincing evidence that Zhongai's negative remarks reflect Wu's own opinion of the damage done by too much favorable attention paid over the years to Cao's novel.

For all his fears that *New Stone* will be merely another low-quality imitation of a superior original, Wu's work in many ways represents a daring innovation in the sequel genre. It is certainly true that, by writing still one more version of this beloved novel, Wu participates in an extremely familiar—and from the perspective of true connoisseurs of the novel, rather tiresome—Qing-dynasty practice. Most of the earlier sequels, however, had centered themselves on retelling Cao's love story by carefully maintaining the original setting and characters, merely trying to ingratiate themselves to the audience by making the ending happier.[17] Wu's departure from the ordinary sequel format may well be a reflection of his censorious attitude toward the original. In *Sea of Regret,* for instance, the first chapter is devoted to making a careful distinction between works that advertise themselves as novels of *qing,* "(appropriate) sentiment or feeling," and novels characterized by *mo,* "lechery," the latter of which he regards as being considerably more common. In making this discrimination, Wu adds a marginal note accusing *The Story of the Stone* of being a classic case in point.[18] His *New Stone,* in other words, may be at least in part a sincere attempt on his part to recast Cao's eighteenth-century epic in a more congenial moral register.

Whatever his motives, Wu's rendition makes a daring move in resuscitating only three of the male characters from the original and completely omitting the females who had been the great focus of Cao's text. And by making the three men—Jia Baoyu; his page, Beiming; and his ne'er-do-well brother-in-law, Xue Pan—serve as indicators of the vast changes between the eighteenth-century setting of the original and the contemporary period, he creates something quite original. The novel is constructed of two roughly equal but antithetical parts. The first twenty-one chapters bring the familiar characters to a transformed Shanghai and Beijing and other points in China that Wu knew firsthand. In these chapters, Baoyu repeatedly bears witness to the chaos of the modern and of the varieties of foolishness that have prevented the implementation of sound policy. The second half of the work—originally published only in the late 1908 book version of the text, more than a year after the serialization of the first half was completed—presents a completely contrasting ideal realm where this chaos has been resolved into order by resort to the creation of an overtly science fictional realm.

By bringing both Jia Baoyu and Xue Pan to contemporary Shanghai after a hibernation of some 150 years, the real shock of the transformations that Shanghai embodied can be distinctly registered by representing the responses of these two men to what they encounter there. Jia Baoyu, who in his earlier incarnation had been a young man dead set against joining the government or even entering into the discourse that would lead to officialdom, is suddenly transformed into someone with a burning devotion not just to understanding political economy but also to publicizing what he has learned. He is particularly intent upon figuring out why Chinese seemed to have been relegated to an inferior position in their own country. Xue Pan, for his part, adapts smoothly to the changed circumstances, registering no real sign of any surprise at them. He has made a good deal of money in trade since he has come to Shanghai, and he spends it liberally in instinctive pursuit of the same sort of mindlessly dissolute life he had led in the earlier novel. The Shanghai in which every human relationship appears to have become commodified turns out to be entirely suitable for Xue the consumer and his licentious style of life.

Xue Pan either genuinely does not sense, or chooses not to express, any amazement at conditions in Shanghai. Baoyu, on the other hand, is obsessed by the strangeness of what he observes and can hardly think about anything else. One of the things that strikes Baoyu immediately and continues to bother him greatly is the omnipresence of foreign goods for sale on the streets of Shanghai. In relaying his concern to Xue Pan, the latter expresses surprise that Baoyu is engaging himself with matters of commerce, to which the younger man responds: "This didn't come to me all of a sudden, but I have been thinking that if foreigners do nothing but sell things to Chinese, won't all of China's money eventually flow out to foreign countries?"[19] It is, in other words, the very novelty of the situation he encounters in Shanghai that forces him to consider things that had never occurred to him before. That these new things include much that has to do with commerce and trade demonstrates a new intellectual adaptability on Baoyu's part, as well as Shanghai's centrality to the emerging society and economy of modern China.

If Xue Pan proves himself to be quite recognizable even as he is perfectly adaptable to becoming a "merchant or trader" and a patron of the demimonde, the new Baoyu is harder to classify. In Cao Xueqin's novel, Baoyu had provided a virtual model of the *wenren,* or literatus: holding his nose at the official bureaucratic uses of the world, he had cultivated a private sensibility that even his father, strict and orthodox official that he was, had at times to admit—if only to himself—was elegantly representative of the type.[20] Baoyu's new interest in political economy thus hardly conforms to expectation, as even the oafish Xue Pan cannot help noticing and pointing out a number of times.[21] This abrupt transformation of Baoyu's character must be seen in the context of Wu's previous bitter depiction of the life of the would-be *mingshi* in Shanghai. If, in Wu's judgment, the aesthetic disposition of the *wenren/mingshi* has become devalued, and if Baoyu is to be a character with whom the reader can continue to sympathize, then the young man apparently must turn away from his old habits and points of view. Furthermore, the conversion of Baoyu probably suggests that for Wu Jianren at least, given the new situation facing China at the end of the nineteenth century, there seems to be no appropriate place for the old category of *wenren* in the urban culture emerging in Shanghai in those years. Whatever role that *wenren* had played in previous centuries, their attempt to reconstitute themselves in modern Shanghai can only be ludicrous, as Wu takes pains to demonstrate.

It is also of considerable interest that *New Stone* appeared in 1905, a year declared to have been a "memorable" one by F. L. Hawks Pott, an Episcopalian missionary and longtime head of Shanghai's St. John's University, in the title of chapter 18 of his 1928 *Short History of Shanghai.* This was the year both of the defeat a European power by an Asian one in the Russo-Japanese War and of the powerful boycott of American trade in protest of the Chinese exclusion laws put into effect in the United States.[22] The boycott was most effective in cities like Canton and Shanghai. As Hawks Pott sums up the result: "The year 1905 is a memorable one in the annals of Shanghai, as at that time a change in the attitude of the educated Chinese became evident, indicating that they were no longer willing to submit passively to what they regarded as an infringement of their rights."[23]

As will be remembered, Wu Jianren played an active part in the dramatic events of that year, resigning as editor at the American-owned *Chubao* in Hankou in protest against U.S. policy. Upon his return to Shanghai in early July 1905, he attended as featured speaker and even chaired numerous public rallies, speaking and writing in support of the boycott throughout the rest of the summer. Given that the first installment of *New Stone* was published in the Shanghai *Nanfang bao* on September 19,[24] the context renders Wu's decision to transform Baoyu into an urgent nationalist understandable. That the vicious satires of Shanghai *wenren* found in chapters 33, 35, and 38 of *Strange Events* were also first published in the October and November 1905 issues of *Xin xiaoshuo* lends further substance to taking 1905 as a formative period in Wu's view of appropriate social behavior for educated Chinese gentlemen facing new social and political circumstances.[25] There is an interesting irony involved in Wu's negative representations of Shanghai society, for 1905 was also the year in which active Chinese civic organizations were set up in both the Foreign Settlement and the Chinese city.[26] Perhaps—as we shall see in chapter 9—Chinese observers were generally skeptical about the motivations behind the creation of such bodies.

As Wu sets about representing the new era, however, the character of Xue Pan remains the same gross figure, fully recognizable as the same man who appeared in Cao's novel despite (or, perhaps, because of) his unwittingly becoming the perfect stereotype of the comprador.[27] It may be that the unreflective adaptability of Xue Pan's character signals the indispensability of a new sort of figure in the transformed order, one we might call (somewhat anachronistically) the *wenhua ren* (lit., "cultural person"), or critical intellectual.[28] Shanghai culture, for all its fearsome novelty, seems paradoxically to offer any number of easy new subject positions to those like Xue Pan who happily and uncritically accept whatever comfortable social role is offered to them. It is thus all the more important for those who are intellectually capable of seriously evaluating their own circumstances to develop their abilities for judging the changed surroundings in as critical a fashion as possible. Jia Baoyu, the perpetual outsider never content with the social role for which he was trained in his earlier incarnation, is thus perhaps ideally cast for a new role as critical intellectual.

For all Wu's contempt for the Shanghai-style *wenren*, however, there remains the difficult (if unasked) question as to what sort of education this new critical intellectual should be provided.[29] Could one not make the case that the earlier Baoyu's determination to experience a wide variety of texts, and not just utilitarian publications concerned with assisting young men to pass the examinations, provided crucial preparation for the role of independent evaluator he eventually plays after coming to Shanghai? The significance of Baoyu's ability to discriminate is underlined by its contrast with Xue Pan's enthusiastic conversion to the Boxer cause when he visits North China in early 1900.[30] Earlier, and almost as soon as he had settled into Shanghai, Baoyu had become acutely critical of Xue Pan's thoughtless and obsessive purchases of foreign-made "toys," such as watches and a phonograph. When they meet later in Beijing, however, and Baoyu scolds Xue Pan for the latter's foolish adhesion to the Boxer cause, Xue Pan becomes confused by what he regards as Baoyu's inconsistent response:

[Xue Pan said:] "I really don't understand your attitude. When we were in Shanghai, whenever you talked of foreign goods you became angry; but now that we have declared our opposition to the "Hairies" [foreigners] you disapprove. But if we succeed in wiping the Hairies out, then there will be no more foreign goods, and won't this be just what you wanted?"

Baoyu said: "How can you be so confused? My anger at foreign imports was simply anger at trading our useful money for their useless goods! I was also angry at us Chinese for not putting our minds to the task of learning how to manufacture these things ourselves. As for the foreigners, why should I hate them? As far as I can see, those folks [who joined the Boxers] all had their motives [for doing so], but what possessed you to join them?"[31]

For all his enthusiasm for the fruits of foreign technology and for the good life in Shanghai, in other words, Xue Pan has remained oblivious to any larger issue involved. And for all his evident disgust at the excesses evident along the Yangjingbang (the creek dividing the International Settlement from the French Concession that had by then become synonymous with the city's excessive aping of foreign ways), Baoyu has apparently absorbed a crucial message from his attention to the variety of new sources of information that now surround him: familiarity with the foreigners and their ways, learned in Shanghai, has enabled him to discriminate between mindless prejudice and a sensitive appreciation of the intricate demands of the new era. For all his stubborn refusal to succumb to the temptations offered up by Shanghai, Baoyu understands what he observes there much better than those like Xue Pan who go along with the creature comforts so easily available in the new metropolis. Baoyu's sedulity in familiarizing himself with writings about his new surroundings has paid off in allowing him to realize the ultimate futility of the Boxer movement and thereby keep an appropriate distance from it. Xue Pan, however, can do nothing more than simply respond to the immediate sensory stimuli of the madding crowd and plunge in headfirst, again amazed at Baoyu's response.

The new information available to Baoyu upon his return, as well as his attention to the nuances of his new situation, enables him to have an appropriate vantage point on the various (and contradictory) aspects of the presence of the foreign. For instance, even before he arrives in Shanghai, he discovers some books lying on a table in a room in which he is staying. He pays little attention to the books—a mixture of novels and writings on the classics—and instead devotes himself to the paper they are wrapped in, which turns out to be a recent edition of the Shanghai newspaper *Xinwen bao*. He picks it up, first just trying to figure out what it is: "Baoyu picked up the paper and stared at it, thinking to himself, 'Exactly how long has it been since I left home? Looking at this paper, it seems clearly to be something like the *Capital Gazette (Jingbao)*, except it not only carries official documents but also contains news from the outside. It seems to be issued daily.'"[32] The newspaper as an organ containing information that had been unavailable in earlier times has long been noted as an important feature in the development of modern Shanghai.[33] Baoyu discovers the press soon after his return and relies on it extensively to orient himself in the new and more complicated world he discovers himself to be a part of. In fact, upon returning from his adventures in Beijing, he remarks to his confidant in Shanghai, Wu Bohui, "I've been away from Shanghai for some time. Living in Beijing, because of the chaos and the lack of newspapers, I feel as if I've gone deaf."[34] One of the complications to which the newspaper introduces him is the presence of two calendars, with the Western year printed alongside the Guangxu-reign year at the top of each page. In Shanghai, it would appear, even the manner of keeping track of time has been transformed into something requiring careful consideration.

The unprecedented nature of the position of the West vis-à-vis China, in other words, demands an unprecedented sort of critical reflection, a dialectal attitude that can facilitate the difficult feat of simultaneously holding in mind a sense of the threat of the West and the capacity to appropriate things from it that can be of use to China. In a sense, this intellectual position is embodied in late Qing China only by the complicated diversity of the city of Shanghai itself; the place represents a new sort of society, which demands a new type of critical mentality to be able to make sense of what it means. For instance, the new concept of national identity is brought to Baoyu's consciousness only by the awareness of national differences forced upon him by seeing the array of people and jurisdictions in Shanghai. For all the seeming remoteness of the new concept of the nation, however, for Baoyu the awareness of it is never strictly an abstraction but is inextricably entwined with his immediate perceptions. One of the key factors contributing to Baoyu's newfound seriousness is, in fact, his having to come to grips with the differences he cannot fail to perceive between China and the foreign, as well as the omnipresent sense of Chinese inability to measure up, something he endeavors almost obsessively to get to the root of.

In an illuminating episode in chapter 7, Baoyu is invited out by friends of Xue Pan's to a restaurant liberally staffed with courtesans. Baoyu insists upon trying to get an answer to why Yangzi River steamers belonging to the Chinese-owned China Merchants' Steam Navigation Company employ only foreign captains. After trying to explain the intricacies of insurance underwriting, the host, Bai Yaolian (a clear pun on *"buyao lian,"* or "shameless"), interjects a comment that leads to the following exchange:

> "Not only is [the only Chinese insurance company at the time] unable to underwrite a whole cargo [and apparently no foreign company would have underwritten a cargo with a Chinese captain in charge], but no Chinese undertakings [of any kind] can be depended upon."
> Baoyu said: "What do you mean that no Chinese undertakings can be depended upon?"
> Yaolian said: "Well, to begin with, there is not a single Chinese person who can be depended upon."
> Without waiting for him to finish speaking, Baoyu interrupted coldly: "Everyone at this table today is Chinese, so we are doubtless all undependable. It is one thing to say that I am unreliable, but are you including yourself among those you are taking to task?"
> Yaolian said: "Although I am Chinese, I have a little bit of the temperament of a foreigner."
> Baoyu responded furiously: "Foreign piss is also pretty tasty, but since I've never been a foreign dog, I've never actually had the good fortune to taste it."[35]

Although Baoyu's response may seem at first to be merely his instinctive retort to what is, in the end, merely a personal insult, he soon reveals a more fundamental notion underlying his reaction:

> "Fortunately, according to him, all Chinese are unreliable. Otherwise, if they were able somehow to become dependable, wouldn't that just turn China into a foreign country? To sum up, then, since he understands the foreigners' language and their system of writing, anything that is foreign becomes better, and evidently he would like nothing better than to have foreigners for parents. But last night I sat up reading the whole night through and learned that what foreigners value most is patriotism. So I'm afraid that patriotic foreigners would have no use for this unfilial offspring [of China]."[36]

In other words, in the course of the intense reading Baoyu undertook in his effort to figure out Shanghai and his own position there, he has discovered the Western discourse on nationalism, a complex of ideas that confounds any simple intention to adopt foreign ways in a wholesale fashion. A clear paradox is outlined here concerning possible responses to the West: if one expresses too much enthusiasm for it and its ideas, one thereby violates one of the central tenets of Western strength that one is seeking to emulate, the power gained from the notion of community solidarity within the nation-state and of ultimate loyalty to it. Show too little interest, however, and the great tasks of reform will rest undone.

If, for someone as concerned with his nation as Baoyu, the problem that nationalism poses is easy enough to perceive, his response to Bai shows how the advent of European power brings up yet another set of issues. As Partha Chatterjee sets out this problem: "[W]hy is that non-European colonial countries have no historical alternative but to try to approximate the given attributes of modernity when that very process of approximation means their continued subjection under a world order which only sets their tasks for them and over which they have no control?"[37] Given the overwhelming dominance of the West at the beginning of the last century, Chatterjee's question would seem to be just as applicable to semicolonial China as to colonial India, and this is particularly true for Shanghai, where the presence of the foreign was that much more evident. Given that the idea that foreign technology ultimately sprang from Chinese sources had become generally discredited after about 1900, the source of the general popularity of science fiction in late Qing China[38] and the relevance of the science fiction episodes of *New Stone* become clear if one thinks of that genre as one of the few modes of writing available for thinking beyond the problem so eloquently posed by Chatterjee. It is perhaps only by inventing a utopian realm that knotty issues of domination and unilateral influence can be finessed, even if only momentarily and only in the imagination.

Intertwined with his contemplation of high national policy, Baoyu at all times exhibits an awareness of the implications of how social change impinges upon his personal life. For instance, early on in the section of the book devoted to Shanghai, Baoyu hears that one of the four famous prostitutes of Shanghai *(si da jin'gang)* is named Lin Daiyu,[39] Baoyu's soul mate in the earlier novel. He is stunned to learn this and becomes preoccupied about it to such an extent that his interlocutor cannot help noticing and stops the conversation. Baoyu can't figure out how this could have happened, and his reaction eventually leads to a frustrated state of suspense ("He thought about it first this way and then that, and his mind could not help becoming vexed"). This suspension is finally resolved three chapters later, when Xue Pan tells him that the *"daguanyuan"* (Grandview Garden) names (i.e., names of the women who lived in a garden compound of that name in Cao Xueqin's text) have been promiscuously adopted by all the courtesans in Shanghai, and that he should not worry about the "real" Lin Daiyu, who is safely dead.[40] Ironies abound in this resolution to Baoyu's anxiety, beginning with Xue Pan's easy assumption that Daiyu is better off dead than having returned as a prostitute. More profoundly ironic, however, is Xue Pan's revelation of the ubiquity of the Grandview Garden names on and around Fourth Avenue in Shanghai. If the "real" Lin Daiyu of Cao's novel has escaped the "fiery pit" of prostitution, the widespread commodification of her name does send a more general signal of the extent to which human relationships in general have been put at the mercy of mass commerce in a way unthinkable in the original *Story of the Stone*.[41]

The eerie resemblance between this episode and the brutal final scene of *Sea of Regret* only amplifies this message. In this scene, Zhongai discovers that his once-cloistered fiancée Wang Juanjuan has become a courtesan as a result of the chaos attending upon the Boxer Rebellion.[42] Particularly jarring is Juanjuan's sudden departure from the party room they are both in when she realizes that Chen has recognized her. Rather than showing any regret at her new identity and how she has disappointed her fiancé—or in other words, rather than recognize the vicissitudes that have driven her into her present circumstance—she chooses to deny her origins. Baoyu and Chen share a shocked sense that firm ground is being pulled out from under their feet. It is the sudden awareness of the contingency of what they had assumed to be firm identity in the face of the enormous changes taking places in China that gives each episode its particular force. Of special interest, however, is that both identity crises take place against the context of the inexplicable fall of a well-educated young woman into prostitution. Most disorienting of all, perhaps, the values surrounding the most urgent questions of personal integrity are shown to be acutely vulnerable to ready commodification. In both cases, also, the commercial capital of Shanghai serves as the most typical, if not the only, possible site of these deeply unsettling transformations of identity.

For all Baoyu's unease with the disposition of power and with various popular attitudes that he finds in Shanghai, the city proves to be the one place he visits in China where he can ponder and discuss the issues facing the country without the threat that discussion of the questions themselves will prove dangerous to those who engage them. For instance, the page Beiming is captured by the Boxers when he and Baoyu visit Beijing and is about to be executed on the suspicion that he is a Christian convert (*er maozi,* "subaltern hairy").[43] Even worse, when Baoyu visits Hankou in chapters 18–20 and makes some critical remarks about the educational philosophy of the local examination official that are overheard and reported, he is arrested and nearly executed (by informal murder in his prison cell at the behest of the evil official concerned).[44] The critical facility that he had developed with so much enthusiasm during his days in Shanghai—the location of the paradoxes and stimuli that engendered this faculty, in other words—proves to be not easily transported to the rest of the country. This was also, as we saw, very much the case in the concluding chapters of *Strange Events,* but it is something of which the characters themselves never seem to become fully conscious.[45] The hybrid environment of Shanghai seems to demonstrate itself indispensable in allowing for clear thinking about China's predicament in a new age.

The Civilized Realm

In suddenly finding his way in chapter 22 to what is portentously called *wenming jingjie,* or "the civilized realm" (apparently hidden off in a corner of Shandong Province), Baoyu enters a world in which the seemingly insoluble anxieties and difficulties of the first half of the book become suddenly and painlessly resolved. In constructing a utopia on Chinese soil, Wu more than anything else finds a way of coping with the challenge presented by the West: not only has China caught up with the West in technology and social organization in this zone of the ideal, but this technological development has also allowed the ultimate superiority of traditional Chinese values, which had seemed so threatened in the first half of this novel and throughout *Strange Events,* to reveal itself in full glory. In chapter 25, for instance, when Baoyu first sees the elegant flying machines that provide public transportation in the new realm, he comments on how their invention seems to have borne out the imagination of such things that he had read about in Chinese novels. His guide responds:

> "Actually, the creation of these machines was enabled in the first place because the ancients had the idea, which allowed us to think up the experimental method [to bring the idea to fruition]. The ridiculous Europeans and Americans, on the other hand, invented the [hot-air] balloon, which is both cumbersome and dangerous, but they persist in endlessly bragging about it. Do you see any way [these balloons] could even approach our [flying machines] in stability and general satisfaction?"[46]

In chapter 28, Baoyu moves on to inquire as to the intellectual and cultural underpinnings of this ideal order. His curiosity piqued by learning that the region completely lacks temples or churches, he asks:

> "But if there are no temples *(miaoyu)* or churches, are there any Confucian temples *(wenmiao)?*
> Lao Shaonian responded: "There is a portrait of Confucius in every school, but no Confucian temples."
> Baoyu said: "If there are no Confucian temples, then what religion do you follow in your realm? Are there any countries in the world *(tianxia)* that do not have a religion?"
> Lao Shaonian laughed and said: "You should add one word to what you just said, 'Are there any barbaric *(yeman)* countries in the world that do not have a religion?' To which I would respond, 'Are there any civilized countries in the world that do have a religion?' You should know that this thing called religion *(jiao)* is simply used to indoctrinate *(jiao)*

ignorant people. If the people all understand the cardinal principles of what is right *(dayi)*, on the other hand, what need is there for religion? But if you insist upon asking what religion we follow here, then we can only respond that we follow Confucianism. In our realm, however, we have home education from the time children are very small, and their mothers instruct them in practical ethics. Once they go to school, the first lesson is on self-cultivation *(xiushen)*. So no matter whether people are young or old, noble or humble, there is no one who does not follow principle *(xunli)*. The [cardinal virtues] of filiality *(xiao)*, brotherly duty *(ti)*, loyalty *(zhong)*, trust *(xin)*, ritual *(li)*, righteousness *(yi)*, modesty *(lian)*, and shame *(chi)* are all infused in the people's hearts. And this is why we adopted the word 'civilized' to be the name of our realm. . . . As for those on the outside who use the term 'civilized,' they are the exact opposite of what the term means. They insist on bragging to one another about how they are 'civilized countries'; they think they are fooling the world, but they don't know that we just laugh at them."[47]

With this discourse, Wu not only finds a way to posit a technical parity with the "civilized" countries of the West but affirms at the same time the moral superiority of the Confucian teaching in particular and of Chinese culture in general. Interestingly enough, this moral superiority is guaranteed by a set of local and informal practices thoroughly rooted in Chinese society, rather than any institutionalized religion of the sort that had been called for by a significant number of late Qing reformers.[48] All in all, these episodes in the civilized realm represent the ultimate wish fulfillment of *"Zhongxue wei ti, xixue wei yong"* (Chinese learning as the essence, Western learning as the application), that slogan so thoroughly imbricated in late Qing intellectual life and discussed in chapter 2.[49] By placing so much emphasis on the word "civilized" *(wenming)*, as well as by constant reference to the falsity of Western claims to this status, Wu clearly announces his ideal of recuperating the fallen position of China in the world: in appropriating the particular term *"wenming"*—extremely common in contemporary China, Japan, and Korea—and almost invariably used to signify Western origin, Wu declares his radical intention not just to abolish the invidious distinction between a progressive West and a backward China but also to reestablish the superiority of Chinese culture, however complicated the new context.

In presenting the spectacle of a technologically advanced civilized realm, Wu does not fail to give an account, cursory though it may be, of how these inventions were made possible. While discussing the reasons for the perfection of the Chinese flying machines, Baoyu suddenly inquires of his host:

"I have heard people say that without factions *(dangpai)* there is no competition, and without competition there can be no progress. In your realm everyone is of one mind, however, so of course there are no factions. How, then, did you manage to progress so quickly?"

Dongfang Fa said: "That is unsympathetic talk from those who know nothing about us. They want to have people in competition with them at every point, and only then are they willing to get down to work. If they have nobody to compete with, they just won't work, so they advance a theory of progress requiring competition. What they don't realize is that even without competition, as long as you can manage at all times not to be complacent with yourself *(buzizu de xin)*, there will be no lack of progress. Moreover, we do have factions, except that our factions are not among ourselves."

Baoyu responded in surprise: "If the factions are not among yourselves, then where are they?"

Dongfang Fa said: "Everyone in our own country composes one faction, while the other faction is, of course, made up of foreigners. If one is looking for competition, there is competition with foreigners; how can anyone say we have no competition?"[50]

The official history of progress in the civilized realm turns out to be an eclectic mix of elements of Confucian theories of communal unity combined with an idiosyncratic borrowing from social Darwinism: there is the obligatory competition and natural selection, but the competition is only with those from outside the national body. Wu can thus have his social Darwinist cake and eat it too: the painful demand for internal "survival of the fittest" can be displaced onto competition between China and the West, which, conveniently, China has already won by the time Baoyu has reached the civilized realm. In setting up his utopian China, in other words, Wu incorporates the key points of a corporatist nationalism that had first dawned on Baoyu when initially confronted with the new society and economy of Shanghai. Wu also reveals the inextricable bonds between nationalism and culturalism in China.

In spite of (or, perhaps, because of) the importance of the lessons to be learned from the new realm, for the most part the realistic account of contemporary China and the fantastical journey to the *wenming jingjie* are kept rigorously distinct from one another. Once Baoyu reaches the other realm, there is no commerce back and forth. Only in the book's final chapter does Baoyu return from the "civilized realm" to Shanghai and Beijing, although the episode is set off by conventional phrases clearly marking it as a dream ("Just as he was about to fall asleep, he saw . . .").[51] For those readers who might have missed the invocation of the dream convention, events become more fantastical as the dream draws to a close, as is the conventional practice with this motif.[52] In this case, the fantasy builds toward a vision of a prosperous and industrially developed modern China, with the lower Yangzi River now built up to resemble a vastly expanded Shanghai bund—ironically resembling many parts of that stretch of river today:

> In the time it took [Baoyu] to look up, he suddenly sensed himself to be aboard a steamer, one that was proceeding forward at great speed. Looking at both banks, he saw them covered with tall buildings, and the smokestacks arose like the trees in a vast forest. Unconsciously he said to himself, "Where is this? I've never been here before." Suddenly, he heard Bohui's voice coming from behind: "This is the Yangzi River!" Baoyu turned his head and asked: "Where on the Yangzi are there as many buildings as this?" Bohui said: "You don't know? Nowadays there are Chinese-owned factories covering both banks of the river all the way from Wusong to Hankou."[53]

At this point, in good dreamlike fashion, Baoyu suddenly finds himself aboard a fast train, which passes through vast expanses of well-kept agricultural lands. After reaching the capital of China (quite pointedly not identified by name here), he finds himself in the midst of an international peace conference being held there, a clear echo of the first chapter of Liang Qichao's famously incomplete and unsuccessful 1903 attempt at a political novel, *Xin Zhongguo weilai ji* (Record of the future of the new China).[54] At the conference, it is announced that the emperor of China will say a few words, and when the emperor ascends the dais, Baoyu is amazed to see that he is none other than Dongfang Qiang ("oriental strength," also known as Dongfang Wenming, "oriental civilization"), the rather mysterious figure who had served as Baoyu's guide to the civilized realm from the point of his first arrival there and in whose guest room Baoyu had just fallen asleep. The dream ends abruptly as Baoyu applauds and stamps his feet in appreciation of Dongfang's enthusiastic words announcing the coming era of world peace. In stamping his feet, Baoyu breaks through the floor and finds himself falling into an abyss, and the terror he experiences wakes him up. When he awakens, Baoyu finds himself still in the civilized realm, but the substantive contact between that realm and actual places in China that he had just visited turns out to have been only such stuff as dreams are made on.

In evaluating the frenzied conclusion to Baoyu's dream, it is important to note that this chapter represents the only actual meeting between the "real" China of the late Qing and the fantastic civilized realm; it also provides the only structural link between the first half of the book and the second. And at least with regard to the imagination of future urbanization—of all the things that Baoyu observes in his dream, by the way, this seems to impress him the most—we see an apparent projection of contemporary Shanghai, in which that modern city has, in effect, reached out to colonize the rest of China, albeit under Chinese ownership. But just at this point where we see the projected urban China of the future, the dream begins to expose itself most transparently as being only a dream, through a montage of random jumps wherein Baoyu suddenly finds himself first aboard a steamer, then aboard a train, then in the capital. Perhaps the best indicator of the instability of the union between the "real" China and the fantastical realm is the collapse of the illusion of communication between the two as soon as Baoyu begins to participate in it, even if only through the passive activity of applauding the emperor's idealistic speech. As David Wang has suggested, to a large extent this sequence of events serves to remind us painfully of the remoteness and inaccessibility of the utopian vision of the perfect Chinese order that Wu had so lovingly set out in the second half of the novel.[55]

Perhaps of even greater interest is that in Baoyu's final dream Dongfang Qiang (Wenming) turns out to be the emperor of China, for he had been the man in charge of the "civilized realm." Moreover, immediately after waking, Baoyu learns that Dongfang is none other than Zhen Baoyu, that spectral mirror image of Jia Baoyu in Cao Xueqin's original who had always been more committed to the norms of the Confucian ruling class and from whom the latter had done his best to keep his distance (it is also significant that the more earnest Zhen had haunted Jia Baoyu's conscience throughout the original novel). That Dongfang Qiang is identified as the enlightened and idealized ruler of the civilized realm, as the emperor of a new China, and as Jia Baoyu's alter ego is emblematic of a stunning collapse of narrative perspective into the single focalizing standpoint of Jia Baoyu himself. At some level, then, the whole utopian vision presented in the civilized realm is revealed to be nothing other than self-obsession and personal fantasy, with a single consciousness acting both as reflector of events and as only real agent upon them. The result is, in short, a situation very much like that depicted in Cao Xueqin's *Story of the Stone*, except that Wu Jianren has added a powerful dimension of an impinging statecraft to the sequel.

Moreover, as David Wang notes, since Zhen Baoyu has already overseen the successful reform of China and its subsequent progress, Baoyu "can only be a late spectator to what 'will already have' happened while he sojourned somewhere outside history."[56] The narratorial sleight of hand that allows Baoyu to witness both China's early twentieth-century backwardness as well as its presumptive transcendence of this state also renders Baoyu the embodiment of "belated modernity,"[57] where someone else has already done the work and he can only witness or copy what has been accomplished. To have the actual process by which the "civilized realm" achieved its utopian status disappear into a time warp that is never accounted for in any serious sense simply shows the imponderability of the process itself and casts doubt upon the possibility that it can ever be made to happen.

We can conclude that in Wu's *New Stone* the resurrected Jia Baoyu's perspective on the new order of things facing Chinese thinkers has been decisively shaped by his experience of Shanghai. He develops a powerful critical outlook, but it is perhaps the enormity of the new data that this critical mentality has enabled him to gather that overloads the transmission line between self-cultivation and ordering the world that was central to the neo-Confucian worldview.[58] The overload collapses the link between self and world in on itself, with all the points along the line of separation becoming blurred upon one another. In more mundane terms, this final admission that all the projections of future improvement in China's situation are based on the inventions of a single imagination hints at the unraveling of the social consensus that had, for better or for worse, been the basis for political order in late imperial China. If Baoyu's sojourn in Shanghai had alerted him to the existence of a stark new world that, for all the problems it presented, was still alive with possibilities, it also alienated him from the society he had come from in the first place. The disconnection represented in the novel between individual perception and the actual ways of the world might also serve as a forecast of the dangers inhering in investing too much reliance on the brave new world of "interiority" (or heightened subjectivity) that was beginning to come into vogue in the late Qing. As foretold by the impact of Lu Xun's madman *(kuangren)*, it was just this idea of the alienated perceiving mind that would sweep the whole of the literary stage by the early 1920s, partly out of emulation of Western forms of writing.[59] If interiority did in fact open new avenues of insight, the final failure of the actual and the ideal to be able to find any common ground in *New Stone* illustrates the dangers of solipsism and of an ultimate narrowing of perspective to an exclusive concern with the position of the cognizant subject.

In his two remarkable novels, then, Wu Jianren makes a complete circuit of the intellectual possibilities of his era. *Strange Events* focuses almost exclusively on behavioral defects, heavily relying upon the infrastructure supplied by the modern West to achieve its understanding. The novel grinds to a halt when it travels to a completely traditional realm without modern communications. *New Stone* attempts to be more upbeat, consciously contriving to achieve an understanding, even a union, between the realms of the wished-for modern and the desuetude of the present. The sudden collapse of this effort in the final pages of the text is all the more bleak for its abrupt admission of the impossibility of a successful fusion. If Yan Fu had found himself whipsawed between what seemed an airtight case for rejecting China's past and equally urgent ideological and moral needs to build upon it, Wu found himself in much the same situation, which is all the more poignant for building its case through its vivid representations of the exigencies of everyday life.

CHAPTER 7

Impossible Representations
Visions of China and the West in
Flower in a Sea of Retribution

Works of art . . . indifferent to their mode of presentation would negate their own concept.
    Theodor Adorno, "Extorted Reconciliation: On Georg Lukács' *Realism in Our Time*"

At the heart of the search for Chinese modernity in Chinese thinking and in some of China's most important intellectuals stands a huge paradox.
    Wang Hui, "Contemporary Chinese Thought and the Question of Modernity"

*I*n the autumn of 1895, after China's catastrophic defeat by Japan, the Zongli yamen (Office of Foreign Affairs) responded by instituting special classes within the ministry to teach foreign languages.[1] Zeng Pu, a well-connected young *juren* degree holder, went north from his home in Jiangsu to attend these classes. Zeng was one of the few who enrolled in the French section, a choice that was to have a significant impact on the rest of his life. For all the good intentions evident in instituting the new course of instruction, the classes quickly failed: the teachers, apparently officials returned from overseas duty, had no interest or skill in instructing, and the students felt they had better things to do than attend class.[2] Among the students, it seems, only Zeng Pu took the course seriously and devoted himself sedulously to learning French, sensing that knowledge of Western culture would be indispensable to successful reform within China. Even after the dissolution of the formal course, Zeng continued to study French on his own, embarking upon a course of self-study of works of literature and history written in that language.

After a short period in which he tried to educate himself in French literature, Zeng eventually encountered Chen Jitong (1851–1907), a graduate of the Fuzhou Shipyard School of Navigation who had studied in the French-language track there.[3] Chen provided Zeng the bibliographic guidance he had theretofore lacked, and from that point on, the younger man procured books in French. As he put it, "[I] developed a literary mania *(wenxue kuang)*, sleeping neither night nor day, until I contracted a serious illness. Once I became sick, I stayed sick for five years."[4] As is clear from the examples provided by Liang Qichao and Zhang Taiyan that were discussed in chapter 3, this almost religious sense of dedication to newly discovered Western cultural work is by no means uncommon in retrospective accounts by Chinese intellectuals of their activities in the 1890s, especially for the period after 1895, when defeat by Japan brought the realization that a more active engagement with Western political ideas and technological organization would be indispensable to national survival. Meanwhile, probably in early 1903, Jin Songcen had begun work on a political novel intended to track China's relations with Russia through a depiction of the Chinese envoy to that country, Hong Jun, including as a secondary character the concubine who accompanied him on his foreign travels, the famous courtesan Sai Jinhua (1874–1936). The first two chapters were published at the end of 1903.[5] In 1904, after having completed six chapters, Jin recognized his lack of sympathy with the novel form and turned the work over to Zeng Pu, then still recovering from his illness. Zeng had also become one of the founders of the Xiaoshuo lin she, a publishing house that was primarily devoted to translating Western fiction and in 1907–1908 published the fiction journal *Xiaoshuo lin*.[6] The two men agreed upon the general subject matter to be covered in the book's sixty projected chapters.[7]

Building upon Song's draft of the first six chapters, Zeng soon completed twenty chapters of the novel entitled *Niehai hua* (Flower in a sea of retribution). These chapters were published together in book form in 1905, and the work was immediately hugely popular with the urban reading audience. According to Zeng's own and thus perhaps overoptimistic estimate, the book went through as many as fifteen printings in the years following its first publication and sold close to fifty thousand copies, a vast number for the new publishing market that had arisen in Shanghai at the end of the Qing.[8] It was virtually unique for its time in not having been first serialized in a magazine, and the relatively sympathetic portrait it presents of Russian anarchists also sets it apart from the rather more conservative novels by writers like Wu Jianren, Li Baojia, and Liu E. As Zeng noted in his 1928 remarks on the text, "[T]he core meaning of this book consists of my view of how during the thirty years [covered in the text, 1868–1898], our China went through a huge transformation from new to old, consisting of one part cultural development *(tuiyi)* and one part political change. Phenomena both alarming and pleasing occurred in this period one upon the other."[9]

One of the most striking things about the novel is the prominence given to representations of the foreign, in both the unfolding of the plot and the development of the principal characters.[10] This figuration of a world that is at once beyond China but has also become, by the time the novel was written, profoundly imbricated with Chinese society is highly complicated. Part of this complexity arises out of a sharp awareness that indigenous knowledge would be lamentably insufficient in the new international age. As was the case with the novels of Wu Jianren discussed in chapters 5 and 6, there seems to be in *Flower in a Sea* a profound ambivalence about what the coming of the West means for China. Within the discourse of the novel, Western ideas, no matter how noble and practical they have proved to be in their native terrain, never seem to work once they are imported into China and grafted on to preexisting Chinese ways. When these Western practices come to China, for all the inevitability of their presence, they somehow come to embody a crudity and an amorality that cast doubt on the desirability and even the stability of Chinese participation in the Western-dominated new world order that was emerging in the late nineteenth century. In other words, something about the Chinese narrative context renders the universality of Western ideas problematic.

On the surface this anxiety about the positioning of Western ideas presents a paradox. For all the pressures that the Western powers exerted on the Qing at the turn of the century, China remained in control of its own organs of government and education. That so many powerful nations had interests in China made it exceedingly difficult for them ever to agree on any method of subjecting the huge country to colonial division. Moreover, in the radically transformed post-1895 political situation, what had been the minority position of the Yangwu movement could now easily envision itself as the new and suddenly influential majority in government. And it would be in charge of a bureaucracy that, while admittedly a shadow of its former self, was still staffed by more competent men than most governments the world had ever known.[11] The uphill struggle to appropriate Western technology and administration piecemeal that had been going since the 1860s could now metamorphose into policies of sweeping institutional change, something that not even the setback of the failed Hundred Days Reform of 1898 or the Boxer Rebellion of 1900 could really upset. Yet, for all the clear sense of utopian possibility that arose after 1895,[12] there remained an undercurrent profoundly pessimistic about the chances for successful adoption of the new, even among those who professed the most devotion to the need for change. In fact, the characteristic rhetoric of the later writings of Yan Fu, who had set in motion the road map for radical reform in 1895, seems to sound notes of pessimism alien to the discourse on the possibilities of adapting to the new as it had been conducted during the preceding thirty years.[13] Why was this?

In the recent large and influential corpus of writings on the impact of European colonialism both on the metropole and on the rest of the world, China in particular and East Asia in general have seldom been discussed.[14] The obvious reason for China's absence in this discourse is that China was never colonized; that is, foreign state powers never gained more than a token foothold within China's borders. The theories of subalternity and of the "colonial subject" that were developed primarily to describe characteristics of British India thus never seem to quite fit China: at the very least, outside of portions of a number of important cities, Chinese people were never subject to the rule of European colonizers. Neither the legal nor the educational structure ever had foreigners in ultimate command, and Chinese always remained the dominant language, both officially and unofficially. Those who were in a position to take upon command of the modernization of China were, therefore, Chinese, rather than colonial administrators. In principle, then, the resentments and resistances we can easily find in scenarios of colonial modernity should be absent, or at least greatly attenuated, in China. Yet this dark cloud remains. Perhaps the best approach to the question is to look at the agenda of modernization rather than at either the personnel in charge or any particular structure of power. In reviewing the demands of the agenda, the differences between the overt colony and China diminish sharply: an educational curriculum built around extended literacy and technical training, industrial structure, and rationalized administration are alike demanded, whether the agent of the demands is the colonial overseer or the national elite desperately trying to develop sufficient national strength to keep colonial power safely at bay.

In fact, one might even argue that holding on to indigenous agency actually made the problem of accommodation more acute. In a place like India, for instance, where the material demands imposed by external force for modernity were so evident and so equally unlikely to flag, it was always possible to hold on to a notion of national essence beyond the realm of practical statecraft and thus equally beyond the reach of the British Raj.[15] In China, on the other hand, the need for the agency of modernization to emerge exclusively from domestic institutions and people rendered issues of autonomy and their relationship to social function much more problematic. Perhaps an anecdote recounted by Yan Fu can help illustrate the problem. Writing in 1895 about how the Chinese military had tried to implement a policy of adopting Western techniques, he reports that the effort has been in vain and provides a specific example:

Some time ago, during the war with the French [in 1884], the Beiyang army contracted with several dozen German officers. By the time the agreement was settled, there was no further use for them [because the war had ended], so they were sent as training officers to various units. They saw the incompetence of our troops and sought to effect some reforms. Each unit commander where they were stationed, however, regarded them as inimical to his own interests and thereupon raised such a clamor as to have the advisers removed.[16]

In India, by contrast, the Indian army was accepted on all counts as a British organization, and its being run in British fashion generally ceased to be an issue (at least after 1857). Nationalists could, of course, conscientiously object to the institution as a whole, but that the army itself was run on British military lines was beyond contest. The choice, then, was between a thoroughly British establishment or some indigenous alternative completely uninflected by foreign ways. In other words, the question became whether one approved or disapproved of a modern army, not on the extent of the role assigned to foreign advisers. And given British domination of government and the economy, it was easy for Indian nationalists like Gandhi to posit a radical heterogeneity between the modern, British-organized segments of society and the traditional, indigenous sector. Once this distinction was accepted, a notion of building upon an Indian essence provided a clear (if institutionally fuzzy) path for nationalism to establish itself. In China, however, the situation could never be this clear-cut: the battle lines were drawn precisely on issues of political and economic sovereignty within the indigenous structure of the government, and it was never even theoretically possible to distinguish neatly between advisers who were counseling efforts toward a universal modernity and foreign agents intent upon stripping Chinese organizations of their closely guarded autonomy.

Given this built-in inclination, or even nationalist imperative, to resist reorganization on Western lines, reformers like Yan Fu came increasingly to take intransigent stands of their own, if only to resist the assertions eventually arising from the conservatives that to institute reform was tantamount to selling the nation off bit by bit. The various schemes of compromise that suggested a binary division between Chinese spirit and Western force—from *"Zhongxue wei ti, xixue wei yong"* (Chinese learning as the essence, Western learning as the application), discussed in chapter 2; to *"guocui"* (national essence) in the early years of this century;[17] and on to Liang Qichao's post–World War I attempt to valorize Chinese spirituality over Western materiality and Rabindranath Tagore's similar efforts during his early 1920s visit to China[18]—were all impatiently hooted down by reformers who had come to believe that change required the extra leverage of a radical rejection of any handhold the past had on the present. If, as Partha Chatterjee suggests, ". . . it is not just military might or industrial strength, but thought itself, which can dominate and subjugate,"[19] the amount at stake alone seemed to guarantee that the struggle over the redefinition of a newly destabilized self and its attendant social responsibilities would be far more fraught with trauma than a struggle in which both goal and agent could be located, if never comfortably so, at least definitely outside. It was precisely in regard to ambiguous circumstances like these that the Chinese Left came up with the formulation of "semicolonial" to refer to a situation in which nominal self-rule masked an underlying imperative to model oneself on the very imperialist regimes that one needed to resist in the first place.

The sharp ambivalence that *Flower in a Sea* manifests toward the representation of the foreign reflects the contradictory attitudes of late Qing thinkers toward the dramatically transformed circumstances that emerged in China after 1895. These divergent perspectives on the foreign are distinctly encapsulated in the paradox that Western language and learning presented to Chinese thinkers trying to work out the means of accommodation between China and the West in these years. Writers of the period seem to have been constantly struck by contrast between the apparent ease of becoming literate in the alphabetical languages of the West and the equally apparent difficulty for Chinese to master the intricacies of a body of knowledge that was so widely disseminated at all levels of society in the West. This contrast in turn refracts back on the internal structure of Chinese society and its relationship to epistemology: if the linguistic medium of Western learning is so simple, will more people in Chinese society be capable of mastering it? But if, from the contrary perspective, the essence of Western learning is so difficult to comprehend, who exactly will be able to gain intellectual control over this vital new body of knowledge? This problem in turn raises new questions. If there is to be a new regime of learning in China, who is going to be in charge of it? Will it be the old intellectual elite or some new group? Or—and I think this is the most worrisome question we see posed as a continuing subtext in *Flower in a Sea*—could it be possible that no one is qualified to do the job adequately? The need to master Western learning will not recede, but the possibility of actually doing so retreats to the utopian realm in the strictest sense of the word.

Nowhere is this contradiction more sharply rendered than in the depiction of the relationship between Fu Caiyun (the courtesan-turned-ambassador's-wife so transparently modeled on the famous Sai Jinhua) and Jin Wenqing (the fictional counterpart of Hong Wenqing, the Chinese ambassador to several countries in northern Europe), whom she accompanies to northern Europe in 1887. Caiyun is portrayed as someone who, although illiterate in Chinese, quickly masters foreign languages (in both spoken and written forms)[20] and is possessed of sufficient meretricious craftiness to deal with all the odd situations she and her husband, Wenqing, encounter in their travels outside China. For his part, Jin proves utterly incompetent to comprehend the new people and ideas he meets. For all his command of Chinese learning—he was, after all, *optimus (zhuangyuan)* in the Palace Examination of 1868—he is easily taken advantage of and often ends up a helpless fool once he leaves his homeland. Ironically, the person who most often takes that advantage is his young wife, Caiyun, who uses her easily gained knowledge of Western languages and customs to further her own interests, which are represented more often than not as being in opposition to those of her new husband. The couple thus represents in microcosm the paradox that scholars had been writing about for years before the novel was even begun. Caiyun, with no cultivation in domestic arts and letters, proves extraordinarily adept at mastering the external features of the West, while Jin, for all his learning and evident intellectual ability in the traditional sense, proves incapable of understanding even the most superficial aspects of Western knowledge, much less the fundamental ideas that would allow a deeper understanding of the mysteries of Western success in the world.

The vision of the West and its learning presented in the novel is thus a disheartening one for its early twentieth-century audience: only superficial tricks, which do nothing more (and nothing less) than empower the self-interested, can be mastered. The noble tradition of Chinese learning, on the other hand, not only seems to make it impossible to insinuate oneself into this new and more ignoble world but also offers no clues whatsoever as to how the deeper knowledge of Western technology and statecraft might be acquired. The body of knowledge now classified as indigenous is represented as being practically obsolete. The only replacement on the horizon, however, is a set of serviceable tools for getting on in the world that are as morally questionable as they are easy to acquire for those who are willing to forget their scruples or, more germane to this text, who never attained the level of personal cultivation that would have engendered scruples to begin with. Neither Caiyun nor Wenqing proves up to the task of striking a happy medium that would accommodate the full spectrum of Western learning on the one hand and the adaptation of Chinese ideas to the new era on the other. The true key to the West's knowledge—and, beyond that, to its power—is marked as lying outside both cognitive ranges. It thus stands as a frustrating reminder of Chinese inadequacy in the face of unprecedented challenge.

That the demarcations of the different types of learning and moral capacity are made strictly along gender lines faithfully reflects the usages of the times. For one thing, it was Western missionaries who initiated large-scale education for women, even though there was always the suspicion that it was of inferior quality to that provided for men.[21] Thus, since female education in the traditional Chinese curriculum, however extensive it may have been, achieved virtually no recognition in that discourse, the relative prominence of women who were educated in the missionary-sponsored foreign learning would stand out all that much more.[22] For another, to the extent that female education figured in educational discourse at all, it tended to be represented at the simple end of the continuum. For instance, the late Qing concern to extend the cultural franchise put great stress on the role of fiction in this process, basing itself on the old cliché that *xiaoshuo* was the province of the semiliterate—that is, women and children, categories that often were fused together by their constant simultaneous evocation. Finally, even if we read no further than the Pan Jinlian–Wu Song episode of *Shuihu zhuan* (the pivotal story around which the representations of depravity contained in the late Ming novel *Jin Ping Mei* are built), it is clear that on occasion women served the figural purpose in Chinese fiction of representing the antithesis to the normative order of the world of males.[23]

These three factors combine to create a sense that representing Caiyun as a readable totality is impossible, that there can be no resolution of her character any clearer than an intensely strange otherness. At first, in her customary environment, she is treated matter-of-factly, with all the disdain her low status implied. Once freed from that context, however, she adapts to the transformed situation like a genie out of the bottle: she can cope with new situations so well that she becomes a person of unpredictable consequence, such that the petty injuries meted out to her as a matter of routine in the past come back to fatally haunt Jin Wenqing.

Late Qing reformers often noted the substantial difference between Chinese and Western scripts that was one part of the paradox presented by Western learning. Writing sometime before 1894, for instance, Zheng Guanying sums up what he takes to be the important differences in relative difficulty:

> Chinese writing and speech are completely different from one another, but the shallowest of Western writing is simply speech. For this reason, not only can Western children read easy books after a few years of study, but they can compose letters, essays, and the like. In China, if a child is not of prodigious intelligence, I have never heard of anyone [any child] being able to write letters and essays after only a few years of study. We can thus know that the difference between Chinese and Westerners is not one between intelligence and stupidity but in reality is a matter of the difference in the difficulty of their written languages.[24]

For all the apparent ease of reading Western languages, however, translating them adequately into Chinese is quite another matter:

> For those with the ambition for Western learning, they can buy the translations produced [by the Tongwen guan and the Shanghai Translation Bureau (Shanghai fanyi guan)] and read them. They can thus follow their methods, experiment with them, and investigate them; it seems as if there is no difference from reading the actual Western books. There is, in fact, a serious discrepancy. Translating Western books into Chinese is something for which there is no alternative, but is just somewhat better than having no access to these texts at all. But the translations are far from perfect, for they give but a fragmentary picture. Moreover, the names and things in Western books invariably are things that China does not have, and the diction and tone of these works are completely different from Chinese forms of writing. For these reasons, there is always the concern that translation will result in words that fail to convey the meaning *(ci bu da yi)* or become a plausible corruption of a text. Beyond that, the number of Western books that detail each realm of knowledge is beyond count, and translations available now are but a tiny fraction of the whole. So how can we possibly grasp the essentials [through translations]?[25]

In spite of the ease of the Western languages in themselves, Zheng perceives a larger cultural gap. He blames much of it on a failure of educated Chinese to devote themselves to Western learning with the perseverance that is required, despite all their desire to know more about the West:

> Those with an ambition for Western learning are either content with a mere smattering of knowledge *(qian chang zhe zhi)*, or float over it hastily without specializing, or only grasp the superficialities to no substantial advantage. The upshot is that no one has mastered any technique that allows us to soar *(xiehang)* with the Westerners. Why is this? Because our languages differ. So although their language is easy and obvious in the extreme, not to mention highly detailed, we are still at a loss: we feel in the end that there are obstacles that prevent us from communicating, an awkwardness of accommodation that prevents us from gaining the essentials.[26]

Zheng Guanying expresses his feeling that, even if the Western languages themselves are simple, some essence in them lies just beyond translatability, without which the accumulation of discrete elements of knowledge is ultimately fruitless. It is hard not to see at work here the sort of totalistic thinking pointed out by such scholars as Lin Yu-sheng and Wang Hui and described in chapter 2.[27] For all the accessibility with which the West seems to present itself, Zheng and others writing at the same time persist in feeling that something persistently blocks Chinese understanding of new ideas. Based on the belief that Western languages are fundamentally simple, however, they also hold out the hope that a key exists that will provide total and unmediated access to the secrets of Western wealth and power if only the right sort of effort is put forth. The problem is that no one can seem to find the key to the sort of effort that is required.

For Yan Fu, this key seems to be science *(kexue)*. As he wrote in 1902:

> The reason Chinese politics becomes daily more deficient and shows itself as being incapable of surviving is that it does not base itself on science and thus diverges from universal principles and accepted practices. If one thus takes science as being identical with technology *(yi)*, then Western technology is in fact the root of Western politics. And even if one says that technology is not [in itself] science, then both politics and technology are derived from science, and they are like right and left hands.[28]

For Yan, then, science is the quintessence of the Western learning that must be adopted by China. In his assessment of how its transmission to China can be effected, Yan has much in common with Zheng. As the essay quoted above develops, Yan ends up putting even more stress on the general failure of piecemeal efforts to acquire Western knowledge. And despite his own significant efforts at translation, in this essay he stresses the need for people to master the original Western languages. Particularly germane to the purposes at hand, however, is the class inflection he puts on the ability to master his beloved science and the foreign languages and foreign ideas that underlie it:

> There are those who wish to use Chinese to teach Western learning, with the idea that, even though the knowledge comes from the West, if we use our language to teach it, it will become our knowledge. This sounds excellent, but I am afraid that in light of present circumstances it is premature. In the trading cities on the coast, where missionary instruction has taken place, one meets constantly with those who can speak and write Western languages.[29] But finding any capable of serving as science teachers is all but impossible—there are almost none. Those who wish to devote themselves to this learning *(zhi qi ye)* cannot translate without prior training, and even if they get hold of the books, those who would teach them cannot do so without first having a thorough understanding *(xin tong)*.[30]

Without disputing Yan's assertion of the shortage of qualified science teachers in China circa 1900, of interest here is his apparent dismissal of what was by then a reasonably extensive system of missionary-sponsored education, which had long been devoting considerable effort to secular topics, particularly mathematics.[31] Nor does he mention the extensive mathematics-based discourse on technological modernization that emanated from the Jiangnan Arsenal in the years after its founding in the 1860s.[32] One gets the impression, if merely from the pedagogical lexicon he employs, that the only training in Western studies that Yan Fu would regard as really to the point would be that based on the sort of intense education/cultivation long associated with mastering the Confucian classics. Any more pragmatic, or experiential, absorption of Western language and culture would be disqualified from the lofty and absolutely essential task of penetrating to the definitive essence of Western learning, defined by him here as an all-embracing science.

One way to explain Yan's distinction between varieties of knowledge of the foreign would be simply to regard it as an attempt to preserve the monopoly on knowledge so long claimed by those with traditional educations. There can be no denying that this is at least partly true, but I think that more is at work here. By implicitly dividing up capacity in foreign language into two types—one a profound understanding conferred by first grasping the essence of Western learning, and the other a far more casual bricolage[33] that lacks systematic application—Yan, like Zheng before him, creates under the rubric of science a special zone of rarefied knowledge of the foreign that will stand as a perpetual goad to the ordinary student who approaches the task of mastering foreign learning merely deductively. As part of the constant fear both men voice that too vulgar an approach will pollute any attempts to really master a highly arcane and all but unknowable West, the practical ability to naturalize Western knowledge regresses continually toward the horizon in formulations like these.

An episode that begins at the end of chapter 12 of *Flower in a Sea* captures with particular clarity some of the differences by which contrary modes of learning are articulated. As the new ambassador to Russia—among other titles in his portfolio—Jin Wenqing naturally is greatly concerned about working out long-standing problems between Russia and China. The definition of the Sino-Russian border had been a prime object of contention between the two countries for some time, but the issue had became particularly acute in the nineteenth century. Jin thus takes exact delimitation of the border as a special concern. When the mysterious "M. Pierre"—who figured prominently in the novel in an earlier episode involving a swindle of Jin's money that I will discuss presently—shows up at the embassy in St. Petersburg with a decrepit map purporting to be a draft of the secret official version held in Russian government archives, Jin is anxious to acquire it. The price is one thousand gold pounds, but to Jin that exorbitant fee is simply an index to the map's true value. As Jin is in the process of asking for a reduction in price, Caiyun suddenly enters and says to herself: "Fine, he ["Pierre"] has been hiding this from me, and here he comes again to try to get hold of the old man's money! I won't let this one pass!"³⁴ She inquires as to what is happening, and when Jin tells her what the maps are, she blurts out at him: "Right you are! I was just about to ask you how much gold these old pieces of rotten paper are selling for. The drawing on them is fuzzy and not much to look at, so don't get taken."³⁵

At this point, Wenqing explains his motives in some detail, situating himself firmly in the Chinese academic context as he does so:

> "Caiyun, smart as you are, this is something you do not understand. It was with great difficulty that I entreated this gentleman to secure this Sino-Russian map. In the first place, I acquired this map to straighten out our country's borders such that foreigners will not be able to occupy so much as one inch of our territory, and also so as not to betray the trust the emperor placed in me when he sent me abroad. In the second place, it will provide reliable material for my *Empirical Supplement to the Yuan History (Yuan shi buzheng)* that I have poured ten years of my life into and still not published after all these years. So now when I return to Beijing, even the famous geographer of the northwest, Li Shinong,³⁶ will have to admire my efforts. . . ."³⁷

Jin here announces himself to be the perfect scholar-official, for not only does he pursue the book in the national interest but he also has a profound academic agenda as well, and the book thus represents to him important cultural capital in the erudite world of metropolitan scholarship. He also announces himself to be completely within the ambit of traditional scholarly practice: everything about the method of learning he espouses here would have been recognized as valid throughout the entire late imperial period.

As her husband said, Caiyun does not understand any of this and proceeds to provide a sharply ironic commentary on Jin's sententious and self-regarding remarks:

> "Don't be so proud of yourself. All day you carry around a couple of tattered old books, going around muttering to yourself, talking some kind of incomprehensible language: all this 'double-sound words, triple-sound words, quadruple-sound words.' It's enough to fog up the mind and give me a headache. The one thing it does do is cause you to abandon your real work for three or four days at a time. All your talk about 'not so much as an inch of our territory!' If you ask me, even if somebody came and carried your own body away, you wouldn't pay any attention. I don't understand how, even if you get all the Yuan-dynasty names straight, you will assist the Qing in opening up the border and extending our land."³⁸

In this, Caiyun proves to be prophetic, for the maps turn out to be forgeries that considerably understate China's actual historical landholdings in the border region (a scandal recounted later in the book, beginning in chapter 20). All Jin's years of study of Chinese geographical books are unable, in other words, to see through a foreign forgery that even the uneducated Caiyun instinctively suspected. What's more, Caiyun's pessimism extends to the notions of textuality that were so key to Chinese learning's vision of itself. Not only does she assume that the carefully prepared maps are so much wastepaper, but she also impugns the significance of Wenqing's years of attempting to wring meaning from old books, in effect anticipating some of the more radical pronouncements of the early May Fourth movement by some fifteen years. After all, there are not very many steps between Caiyun's cynical dismissal of Wenqing's belief that all solutions can be found in old texts and the radical iconoclasm of Lu Xun's "Madman's Diary" ("Kuangren riji"), in which yet another look at the classics reveals the shockingly negative reading embedded there: namely, that the key to Chinese culture is a positive injunction to engage in cannibalism. For all the horror of the madman's discovery, however, his insight is still based on a notion of textual authority that Caiyun almost completely discounts, revealing her, perhaps, as the more radical iconoclast of the two; there is no question whatsoever that she is the more vulgar and poorly educated.

The attention this exchange between Wenqing and Caiyun draws to the difference in their linguistic registers should also be noted. Whereas Wenqing throughout the novel speaks in a plain colloquial for ordinary conversational exchanges, Caiyun's utterances here are laced with a particular coarseness. A good example is the sequence that begins with "Don't be so proud of yourself. All day long you carry around a couple of tattered old books, going around muttering to yourself, talking some kind of incomprehensible language." The original Chinese is even clearer: *"Laoye bie chuipang, ni yitian dao wan, baole jiben po shu, zuili jiligulu, shuoxie buzhong buwai de buzhi shemma hua . . . ."* The words she uses to express her distance from the elaborate classical idiom of which Wenqing is master mark her as a thoroughly vernacular person and as being homologous to the linguistic simplicity that contemporary scholars regarded as the hallmark of the Western languages, at least as spoken in the treaty ports, and of the uneducated urban folk who were able to master them.

If Caiyun demonstrates a superiority in practical intelligence, however, the more we learn about her, the more her practical abilities become linked to a questionable moral status. As the episode continues after several narrative digressions back to China, we see Wenqing thinking that his acquisition of Pierre's map will ensure his mark as a great ambassador. His exclusive attention on his book soon is revealed as costing him more than simply attention to his ambassadorial duties. As the novel narrates the events of a typical day at the embassy, we suddenly learn how Caiyun spends the time when her husband is at work on his book: "Every day after Caiyun had completed her toilette, it was almost invariably just about time for lunch. She then went into the dining room and ate breakfast with Wenqing. When Wenqing went downstairs to his study to work on his *Empirical Supplement to the Yuan History,* he left Caiyun upstairs to exert herself strenuously at amorous pursuits, which he neither saw nor heard about."[39] Although a prior chapter strongly hinted that Caiyun and Ah Fu, the youthful manservant assigned by Wenqing to attend upon her, have been engaging in illicit behavior,[40] this is the first time it is made so explicit. And though Ah Fu may have been her first dalliance, he is by no means her last. What is of particular interest here, however, is the structural dichotomy between Wenqing's traditional scholarship and Caiyun's infidelity. To the extent that Wenqing devotes himself to his scholarship, Caiyun, in almost direct proportion, takes advantage of his inattention to her to carry on with other men. That his scholarship no longer has any practical application has already been alluded to and becomes even more evident as the novel draws on. But this portion of the episode also demonstrates that such scholarship no longer has any effective moral or personal function either. In fact, instead of illuminating the world, Wenqing's scholarly activity blinds him to its actual nature, thereby providing the most ironic commentary possible on traditional scholarship's diminished status in the new realm of things.

Caiyun's introduction to foreign languages had come earlier, on the boat taking her and Wenqing to Europe. The sum of the episodes on the boat introduced the notions so pointedly depicted in chapter 13 that traditional Chinese education was of less than no utility outside China, and it strongly hinted that the foreign brought along with it a loss of moral bearings. Before going into this, however, it would be worthwhile to sketch in the background to how a courtesan became an ambassador's wife in the first place. Wenqing had met the girl at an excursion of his friends on a pleasure boat where each of them was accompanied by a courtesan. Wenqing had been shown Caiyun and told that she was the *"zhuangyuan" (optima)* of courtesans; she was thus the perfect match for him. The two of them were smitten with one another immediately and shared a sense that they had somehow known one another in the past.[41] Wenqing quickly took her as a concubine, even though he was still in mourning over the death of his mother. When he received his assignment to go to Europe, his principal wife, hearing that women in Europe were obliged to engage in numerous public functions, declined to go and suggested that Caiyun go in her stead, according her the privilege of wearing clothes appropriate only to the principal wife.

Caiyun thus from the very beginning of her life with Wenqing transgresses the role that traditional practice would have assigned her, something quite serious in China. There sumptuary laws and other badges and insignia of rank fulfilled a crucial function of social differentiation in a country so large and diverse that more subtle signs of hierarchical status, such as accent or fashionable clothes, could not be counted upon to serve that function. As will be recalled from chapter 5, a similar transgression of dress code occurs in Wu Jianren's *Strange Events,* in which Gou Cai's concubine's usurpation of the clothes proper only for the principal wife marks the first signal of the disorder in the clownish Manchu's household. The only thing that renders Caiyun's transgression palatable is the demands of Western usage, in this case diplomatic etiquette. The transgression is perhaps best emblematized by the contrast between the significance accorded their respective titles of *"zhuangyuan."* The initial pairing of Wenqing and Caiyun had been based on their mutual "primacy" in their respective social realms: Wenqing in the world of indigenous scholarship, and Caiyun in the demimonde of prostitution. Given the social hierarchy out of which both designations arose, Caiyun's status as *"optima"* would originally have been an ironic back-formation on the dominant male pecking order. It is a sign of the disruption brought about by the coming of the West that Caiyun's ability to negotiate the new order grows exponentially as soon as the couple reach Europe. As her capacities develop, Caiyun's primacy loses its original ironic framing, with Wenqing and his formal title of *"zhuangyuan"* now becoming positioned as merely the residual ornaments of a passing regime. In the transit to the West, the irony attached to her title has gradually become transposed to his.

The switching places of the two characters is not immediately evident. During the first stages of the sea voyage to Europe aboard the German ship *Saxon,* Wenqing seems to be still in his element, enjoying himself aboard the ship and paying visits to locally eminent Chinese whenever they reach a new port. Caiyun, for her part, is seasick at first, although she recovers enough while in port to go ashore and enjoy seeing new things. Toward the end of the voyage, Wenqing encounters the Chinese-speaking "Pierre" ("Biyeshike"), described as a "famous Russian Ph.D.," in the act of hypnotizing three Chinese men. Wenqing is curious about the technique and asks Pierre to have one of the men reveal something about himself that he would not otherwise tell. Pierre objects to the impropriety involved in this but proceeds to ask the man anyway, and the latter promptly reveals sexual improprieties between himself and his employer's second wife that prove embarrassing to hear for all present, not to mention prophetic of Wenqing's cuckolding at the hands of Ah Fu, who coincidentally disappears while the story is being told. As all this is going on, however, Wenqing remains firmly in control and oblivious to any implications the story might have for his own future. Instead, he banters with a colleague about the significance of hypnotism. At this point, Wenqing suddenly sees a beautiful young foreign woman emerging from a passageway. Wenqing is fascinated by her and thinks it would be extremely interesting were she hypnotized. He does not dare ask Pierre directly to do this but devises a ruse to have him do it. Wenqing says that he thinks Pierre's hypnotizing of the first three men was prearranged, and to prove the true efficacy of hypnotism, Pierre would have to demonstrate his craft on someone at random, suggesting the young woman who has just come out on deck.

Pierre, having his veracity challenged in this way, agrees to hypnotize the woman before he even has a chance to get a good look at her. He duly puts her under his control and enjoins her to bring over a tray and set it on a small table in front of Wenqing, which she does in a manner that captivates the ambassador designate. Once Pierre sees who his subject actually is, however, he becomes extremely distraught and urges all the witnesses not to tell the young woman what has happened when she comes out of her trance. After she leaves, Wenqing asks Pierre the reason for his agitation and is told that the woman he had just put under is a famous Russian personage, known for her learning, capable of a large number of languages, and generally not someone to trifle with. Upon being told that her name is Sarah (Xiayali)[42] and that her Chinese is excellent, Wenqing asks if Pierre might intercede by asking if Sarah would teach Caiyun a foreign language, something Pierre agrees to do after some persuasion. Wenqing learns the next morning that Sarah has, somewhat reluctantly, agreed to teach German to Caiyun, partly because they are all going to be in Germany for some time, so the lessons can continue. Sarah sets a wage of eighty marks a month. Caiyun is most enthusiastic and proceeds immediately to her first lesson. The text records Caiyun and Sarah as getting along very well and further remarks that "Caiyun was intelligent by nature, and within ten days could already communicate in the [new] language," an extraordinary feat by anyone's standard.[43]

The voyage and the events that take place on it mark the high point of Wenqing's powers of agency after leaving China. He seems at this point in the novel to be in control of the situations he encounters, and Caiyun plays only a small and rather passive role. The people who are later to cause him grief, notably the two women Caiyun and Sarah, are not threatening to him during all but the final stages of the journey. Neither is Ah Fu, who remains definitely in a subsidiary position. The reader who has read the book more than once, however, can share the dramatic irony of the old man's confessions under hypnosis about his dalliance with his master's concubine that no one in the text (or no first reader) can know. The storm clouds are building around Wenqing, but there is no way for him to know what they ultimately portend, much as China's leaders in the nineteenth century could not apprehend what their ignorance of foreign codes of knowledge would augur for them and their country in the long run. Moreover, as it was for the more competent of late Qing officials, it is difficult to nominate any particular shortcoming or even series of misjudgments on Wenqing's part that can be seen as definitive signs of a change in his fortunes. He simply acts in ways that seem at the time to be essentially unexceptional and that only retrospectively turn out to be recognizable as errors. Even his subterfuge in persuading Pierre to hypnotize Sarah, although it arises out of improper, voyeuristic impulse, brings about consequences out of all proportion to the magnitude of the act itself.[44] Significantly, the event that signals the end of Wenqing's fool's paradise comes just as the ship heaves in sight of Europe, in this case represented by the volcanoes of southern Italy.

What happens then is a shocking perturbation in the texture of the story as it has proceeded up to that point. In good storyteller style, at the end of chapter 9, just as Wenqing and Caiyun are getting out of their berths one morning, someone enters their cabin and demands in a cold voice that they answer a few questions, on pain of being shot. In turning the page to the next chapter, the reader discovers that the hand with the gun belongs to none other than Sarah, who has finally learned that she was hypnotized by Pierre and has now come to exact revenge on the ultimate agent of her humiliation. Speaking flawless Beijing Chinese, she generally insults the Chinese mandarinate ("Who would have thought that the more important a Chinese official was, the more inhuman he would be?")[45] and compares her own strength and determination invidiously with what she calls the "good-for-nothing *(worang)* ways of your Chinese women." Even as she utters this, however, the actions of Wenqing and Caiyun contrast with one another in such a way as to render ironic at least her remarks about Chinese women, if not about the officials: "Hard-pressed by [Sarah's] icy stare, Wenqing took several steps back and could say nothing at all. It was Caiyun who turned out to be the seasoned one; when she saw that things were not going well, she quickly stepped forward and grabbed Sarah by the shoulder."[46] Then Caiyun tries to explain that the hypnosis had only been a random act, something that only Wenqing and the reader know is not quite the truth.

Just as Sarah is about to reply, the ship's German captain, Zhike, enters the cabin, and the contrast between Wenqing's and Caiyun's responses impresses itself upon the reader yet again: "As Sarah was about to open her mouth, the door of the cabin squeaked open and a short and powerful foreigner pushed his way in. Wenqing was again startled and thought to himself: 'It's all over. We can't even take care of one person and here comes another!' Caiyun took in everything in a moment and had instantly recognized the ship's captain, Zhike. She shouted out as quickly as she could: 'Mister Zhike, come in here and mediate for us!'"[47] Whereas Caiyun can instantly size up the situation as it develops and recognize which roles everyone should play, Wenqing is seized with panic and cannot even identify who the relevant players are. Zhike duly intercedes with Sarah, carrying on a long conversation with her in German and requesting that she not create an international incident by offending the Chinese ambassador to both of their countries, Germany and Russia. She relents but demands that there be some compensation for the insult. The captain had seen the badge of her political party, the name and nature of which are not revealed to the readers or to Wenqing and Caiyun. Captain Zhike suggests that she seek from the ambassador financial compensation for her suffering that she can turn over to the empty coffers of her party. Because the conversation is in German, Wenqing of course cannot understand a word of it, but Caiyun follows it completely, as her rapid mastering of German now begins to pay off for her.

Realizing the Wenqing will most likely accept any course of action that the captain suggests, Caiyun alertly takes advantage of her new bilingual status. When Sarah suggests, in German, that the "contribution" of Wenqing amount to ten thousand marks, Caiyun tells Wenqing the actual request was for fifteen thousand, thereby ensuring herself a sizable profit from her brief intercession in the affair. As the discussion in German takes place, Wenqing is again described as being completely at a loss: "For his part, Wenqing had long since collapsed in alarm, and he sat trembling on a couch. Since he did not understand German, when he saw them depart, he was both afraid for himself and dreading the outcome." When Caiyun imparts to him the amount of his "contribution," he is horrified by the size of the amount and asks Caiyun if she might go to the captain and ask him to lower the sum. Her reply is blunt and decisive:

> "As for what just happened, if it had not been for me, you wouldn't even be alive by now. And now that you still have your life, you suddenly can't bear to part with your money! I advise you to save your energy. When somebody goes out on assignment, almost anybody can make eighty or a hundred thousand, so why are you getting so itchy about this little bit of money spent to save your life?"
>
> Wenqing had nothing to say.[48]

There has been an almost complete displacement here, with the initiative passing from Wenqing to Caiyun just as Europe comes within view. Caiyun's new capabilities would not be possible without her newly acquired German, but they certainly transcend the purely linguistic—she has been revealed as someone of great flexibility and intuition, who can adapt to new situations with ease. Her adaptability, in fact, seems to be in complementary distribution to Wenqing's helplessness in the face of the new and foreign. It is particularly noteworthy that although Caiyun's first instinct is to come to the defense of her new husband when he is placed in difficulty, she almost immediately figures out a way to turn her privileged situation to her own financial advantage, and at Wenqing's expense. Her almost instinctive selfishness cannot help but recall Yan Fu's and Liang Qichao's denunciations of the lack of a public spirit as a besetting flaw of the Chinese "national character." In other words, for all Caiyun's superficial ease at dealing with the foreign, Zeng Pu carefully represents her character in terms that progressive thinkers of the time were depicting as the fatal pollution resulting from unquestioned adherence to traditional behavior and its unexamined social debilities.[49]

The arrival at Europe also signals a transition in the narrative mode of the novel. Prior to chapter 10, although it was clear that Jin Wenqing was the narrative focalizer, the text was made up primarily of a diversity of stories and anecdotes about recognizable late Qing personalities. In this respect, it followed the form marked out by Wu Jingzi's classic eighteenth-century novel, *Rulin waishi* (The scholars), a form adhered to in broad outline by other late Qing works like Li Baojia's *Wenming xiaoshi* (Short history of civilization) and Wu Jianren's *Strange Events*. The emphasis in these early chapters of *Flower in a Sea* is on what we would now regard as gossip about famous people, particularly high officials, and it gives us penetrating sketches of the quirks of their personalities. Upon reaching Europe, however, even though the novel continues to provide interspersed anecdotes of goings-on in China, the story as a whole shifts to a concentrated focus upon Wenqing, Caiyun, and Sarah, with the plotlines concerning each of them carefully interwoven with one another. One is tempted to conclude here that even as the story resituates itself in Europe, the narrative mode effects the same type of transition as the story itself: it moves from the episodic linking together of anecdotes characteristic of the late Qing *Rulin waishi* tradition to the unity plot of high nineteenth-century European fictional realism. This conclusion only gains credence from Zeng Pu's responses to criticism of the novel, in which he invokes his dedication to narrative craft.[50]

The revelation of Caiyun's shabby moral position emerges virtually simultaneously with her capacity to maneuver in the world, and the two aspects to her character are thereafter impossible to distinguish analytically. For a summary of Caiyun's character as she begins to perform as an independent agent, with a change of gender and substitution of "courtesan" for "merchant," her disposition as recounted in the novel accords remarkably well with Yen-p'ing Hao's description of the image of the nineteenth-century comprador, quoted in the notes to chapter 6: "Like any marginal man, he had his limitations. He was shrewd and talented but not always honest. Not an independent merchant per se from the beginning, he hung his hopes for success too closely on his connections with foreigners and thus on China's unstable foreign relations. He was still generally associated with the 'parasitic' merchant and was criticized for deviating from social norms."[51] From this perspective Caiyun is just as far from escaping what the late Qing reformers perceived to be the flaws of traditional Chinese ways as is Jin Wenqing. Moreover, the utter incapacity for introspection or concern for values vouchsafed to her by her lack of Chinese education renders her particularly unlikely ever to move beyond her condition of moral depravity so as to achieve any sort of satisfactory intellectual synthesis.

For his part, Wenqing has the intricacies of Sarah's political persuasion explained to him directly after the incident is over. In demonstrating complete incomprehension of the Saint-Simonian socialist anarchism that she espouses, he reveals himself to be not just practically incompetent but also beyond the intellectual range of successful adaptation. In response to Wenqing's question as to what organization Sarah belongs, Pierre gives a detailed account in a utopian mode, including such visionary rhetoric as the following: "His [i.e., Saint-Simon's] point in establishing this organization was to transform false equality into real equality—with no nationalist thought, no racialist thought, no familialism, and no religion. [He intended] to abolish money, to prohibit inheritance, to burst open all sorts of barriers, and to break out of all fetters. The emperor is the enemy, and the government is a bandit. If the country has important matters it must cope with, everyone in the country should discuss them and find ways to manage them."[52] Wenqing's response and Pierre's reply to it throw further light on Wenqing's disposition and on the general situation in China:

> When Wenqing heard this, he was so shocked that he blanched as he said: "If [what they believe] is as you say, then it is flat-out rebellion and sedition *(da ni budao)* and they are an unlicensed party of insurrection. If these people lived in my country, they would long since have been subject to clear penalties. We simply would not have allowed them to pursue so boldly their damaging course of action!"
>
> Pierre smiled as he said: "There is a principle at work here. Its not that I wish to insult your country, but in fact your people, when compared with other individuals, seem to be younger and more immature. Just at the time when they are groping their way along, they know only that they should be ruled by the emperor. Have they even heard of natural rights and the universal principle of equal rights? So it's easy to use force to coerce them. If you compare them with [the people of] my country [i.e.,

Russia], although the political systems are very similar, the people there have been enlightened, and they are not so easily fooled."[53]

Because the time represented here is given as January 1888, much of the dramatic irony embedded in this exchange results from the narrative's having been produced some fifteen years later, when the views that Pierre describes and that Wenqing finds so horrifying had become commonplace among radical intellectuals.[54] As early as 1895 even the by-then relatively cautious Yan Fu—cautious, at least, when compared with post-1898 radicals like Zhang Binglin and Liu Shipei—hinted at views consonant with the Saint-Simonian anarchism to which Pierre gives voice.[55] The clearly implicit social Darwinism with which Pierre compares the Chinese and Russian peoples is even more in accord with post-1895 intellectual fashion. Wenqing's shock at the novelty of these views, though certainly appropriate to an educated person in 1888 (particularly a high government official), thus seems naive and behind the times when gauged by the standards of readers in 1904 and after. The real point here, then, is again to show how ill-equipped those with a traditional education and the strict moral teaching imbricated within it are to deal with new ideas: just as he is unable to foresee what is in store for him as the *Saxon* approaches Europe, Wenqing seems unable even to begin to comprehend the broad range of Western learning, much less to recognize the extent of its implications for the new world that was just then coming into being within China.

Much of the commentary in English on *Flower in a Sea* focuses on how Caiyun's gender conditions how she treats others and how others treat her. Hu Ying, in particular, has dealt with the figuration of women, as emblems of the new and the uncertain.[56] It must be stressed here, however, that the figuration of women in the novel, while dealing with the same issues, does not have a transparent relationship with whatever real struggles were going on at the time in China for female emancipation. As Partha Chatterjee says of this literary figuration: "The figure of woman often acts as a sign in discursive formations, standing for concepts or entities that have little to do with women in actuality."[57] The women in *Flower in a Sea,* and Caiyun more than any other, are deployed to represent certain choices available along the late Qing political spectrum. It would seem that the author manipulates female figures in this schematic way precisely because he regards them as eminently mutable and ultimately as lacking stable social natures. They thus constitute the emblem of difference for him and, as such, become the ideal vehicles for representing new and even dangerous versions of subjectivity. We might even see in Caiyun a replica of the figuration of the dangerous female whom Chatterjee describes in Ramakr̥iṣṇa's *Kathāmr̥ta:*

But in the particular context of the *Kathāmṛta* in relation to middle-class culture, the figure of woman-and-gold could acquire the status of much more specific sign: the sign of the economic and political subordination of the respectable male householder in colonial Calcutta. It connoted humiliation and fear, the constant troubles and anxieties of maintaining a life of respectability and dignity, the sense of intellectual confusion and spiritual crisis in which neither the traditional prescriptions of ritual practice nor the unconcretized principles of enlightened rationality could provide adequate guidance in regulating one's daily life in a situation that, after all, was unprecedented in "tradition." The sign, therefore, was loaded with negative meanings: greed, venality, deception, immorality, aggression, violence—the qualifications of success in the worlds both of commerce and of statecraft.[58]

In keeping with this schematic view of the female, Wenqing's hopeless conservatism is represented by a basic incapacity to comprehend any of this female mutability, best embodied in the his final statement to Pierre, just before they part ways in a cloud of mutual suspicion: "Well, its one thing if men act this way, but how can women violate female propriety *(bu jinshou guimen)* by coming out and behaving in this reckless manner?"[59] Wenqing's notion of woman as someone who stays inside is thus tied to his inability to read the changes that are coming in China's direction. It is also a key indicator that the image of a new mobility for women has become a figure for the transformation of Chinese society itself. There is, however, a transparent irony here: Caiyun's act of assuming the clothes of the principal wife and appearing in public in Europe, depicted as one of the triumphs of Chinese diplomacy because of the enthusiastic reception accorded Caiyun, would have to be precisely the sort of "violation of female propriety" that Wenqing is addressing here. And even as he is about to fall victim to the very circumstances he protests here, he seems unable to link his instinctive response to Sarah's behavior to that of his own concubine. As I have tried to show, the rhetoric of the novel is notably ambiguous about Caiyun's transgressions of the traditional female role; they are at once seen as inevitable in her new circumstances and the cause of much anxiety. Jin's response thus falls at one end of this continuum of response to the new but is also portrayed as particularly blind to its own context. In other words, the discourse of modernity as it develops in this novel is distinctly ambivalent: the coming of the modern is seen as inescapable, but it brings with it a terrible amorality that gives no indication of any ready capacity for either rectification or rationalization.

In the scenes leading up to Jin Wenqing's horrible death, he both realizes the full extent of Caiyun's infidelity and attempts to pressure her into making some sort of declaration of regret for her disloyalty to him.

Their failure to reach any sort of understanding in these final scenes is emblematic of a negative evaluation of the larger issue being figured throughout the novel: is there any way that the two kinds of knowledge represented by Wenqing and Caiyun can be brought onto the same horizon of understanding? Wenqing's full realization of Caiyun's perfidy is rendered all the more devastating by the public revelation of his error in accepting the validity of the erroneous maps he had sent back from St. Petersburg. When this comes to light, he is suddenly in deep trouble professionally, and when he learns the full extent of the trouble, he tries to take a brief rest, by himself and away from all the annoyances that surround him. While napping, he gets up in response to what he thinks is the noise of a mouse squeaking loudly, and when he goes out to chase it away, he suddenly faints and falls down. Caiyun is closest by and duly goes to attend him, only to be greeted by a cold, angry stare from a mute Wenqing when he reattains consciousness. When she reaches her hand into his bed to comfort him, he pushes it away angrily and blurts out: "Save your effort; now I recognize you for what you are!" And when she attempts to hand him a cup of tea, he slaps it away and spills it all over the bed. At this, she becomes angry in turn and throws the cup on the table with an angry snort.

This action angers Wenqing further, and he says to Caiyun: "How strange. You still have the nerve to sulk. All your defects are clear to me now, so just what kind of justification do you think you could possibly have?"[60] Caiyun responds coolly, described by the narrator with cruel precision: "Who would have thought that Caiyun would show no fear but would merely concentrate on picking her teeth and looking straight up into the air? She smiled slightly as she said: 'I don't disagree; my flaws are all out in the open and there is nothing I can say about them. But I want to ask you one thing: Am I your proper wife or am I a concubine?'" This distinction is crucial for Caiyun. She says that if she were his proper wife, she would be loyal to the death and would deserve the worst sort of punishment for any transgression. Because she is only a concubine, however, she feels very different. She tells Wenqing:

> You look at concubines simply as playthings. When we're getting along, you hug us and bounce us on your knee and call us all sorts of sweet names. But when things go bad, you chase us out or marry us off or even just give us to a friend. You might do anything. As for me, I have to say you've treated me pretty well, but you should have understood my basic nature, and you also should have understood where I came from. When you took me in, you never gave me any formal instruction in the moral regulations [proper to women] *(san cong si de qi zhen jiu lie),*[61] and so when I did a few things you didn't like, it shouldn't have come as such a sur-

prise.... And now you want me to give up my immoral ways and go straight *(gaixie guizheng)*. Ai ya! You can alter the course of rivers and move mountains, but it's hard to change someone's nature. I'm afraid you just don't have what it takes to make me serve you faithfully with everything I've got.62

This long expostulation transmits a shock of recognition to Wenqing: "each phrase was a knife, and each word drew blood." Caiyun's evocation of the class division between them strikes Wenqing particularly hard, evidently because he had given so little thought to it. Caiyun seems obsessed with it, however, at least insofar as it gives her license to behave in any way she pleases. A key part of her perception of this class difference is the lack of formal moral instruction given to someone of her station. She claims implicitly that these sorts of principles are only for those higher on the social scale than she. Later, after Wenqing has died and Caiyun has scandalized the Jin family with her failure to fulfill the proper role of widow by continuing to go out on the town, she begs to be released from her position in the household, explaining her own character in terms of extraordinary candor that are remarkably similar to, if less impassioned than, those she used to address Wenqing in the passage quoted above:

The master [i.e., Wenqing] always treated me with kindness. Since I am a person, how could I not be aware of this? So when he died and abandoned me midway through life, how could I not be sad when I thought of the feelings we had from almost a decade spent together? When the mistress [i.e., Wenqing's principal wife] said that I grieved properly during the mourning period [of forty-nine days] and intended to observe [the proprieties of widowhood], it's true, and it also expressed my true feelings. At the time, I wanted to strive to do something for him and to win him a good name. But I was given this evil temperament that needed to be busy all the time and craved pleasure, and when opportunities offer themselves, I just can't control myself. If you insist on keeping me here at home, I can't guarantee that some sort of ugliness won't happen, and once it reaches that point, it will be even worse for the master's memory. What's more, I spend freely, and because I never learned any of the principles of how to be frugal and because of my basic nature, once I arrived here, I got used to spending money lavishly.63

Caiyun's self-analysis, when contrasted with the well-bred environment in which she had been placed, raises a complex of issues. The first centers on the educability of that indeterminately large group of people below the Confucian-educated elite, which was, as we saw in chapter 4, cited as the one of the justifications for the attention to the novel in the late Qing intellectual world. As was clear from the moment Caiyun and Wenqing came within sight of Europe, to the extent that Caiyun represents this less educated group, that group was perceived within the rhetorical position of the novel to be much better able to handle the purely technical demands of the new world than the Confucian elite. The quintessential moral standing that had always been the central tenet of the Confucian teaching, however, is painfully absent in Caiyun's character once she is exposed to different opportunities. That Caiyun has lived in a proper household for such a long time and still seems not to have absorbed any of the deep moral tradition that such families took so much pride in sounds a profoundly pessimistic note as to the possibility for this morality to be inculcated in society as a whole.[64] The gap between *dao* and *qi* (implementation) that Chen Chi and many others had been so concerned with in the years before 1900, which was discussed in chapter 1, seems to have grown even more since the imperfectly or inadequately educated population has become involved.

It is important to note, however, that class difference is not the only thing invoked here, for early in the novel a concubine is introduced who is the model of widowly propriety. In chapter 3, as part of Jin Wenqing's triumphant homecoming after winning his degree, he and his friends visit the home of Chu Ailin, a courtesan and former mistress of the late Gong Xiaoqi, a character modeled after Gong Cheng (b. 1817), son of the famous iconoclastic scholar Gong Zizhen (1792–1841). When his friend Lu Renxiang (Bengru), also a *zhuangyuan* (based on the historical figure Lu Runxiang [1841–1915], *optimus* of 1874), first informs him that their group of friends is going to visit a courtesan, Jin is surprised, thinking that they should be above such vulgar pursuits. Another of the men in the circle explains: "I used to think this way myself, but later I learned that this Chu Ailin is not just a common whore who can be called out by anybody. Not only can she sing song sets *(daqu)* and short lyrics *(xiaoling)*, but she is also mentioned in the *Banqiao zaji*.[65] Moreover, her residence is filled with antiques, old paintings, and heirloom inkstones. She is a veritable female connoisseur!"[66] The contrast between Chu Ailin and Fu Caiyun could not be clearer here: whereas Chu is steeped in the cultural trappings of the Chinese tradition, there is almost no mention of such attainments in connection with Caiyun. In fact, the one place in the novel where Caiyun does demonstrate that she can sing is on the terrace of the Chinese embassy at St. Petersburg, accompanied by Ah Fu on the organ,[67] creating a spectacle portrayed as being as gross and déclassé as the character of Chu Ailin is refined.

These differences in cultural attainment between the two women serve as indices of more profound contrasts below the surface. Whereas Caiyun never fails to place her own interests ahead of everyone else's, most notably those of Jin Wenqing and his family, Chu Ailin goes to great lengths to defend the memory of her late consort. When Wenqing and Ailin meet, she realizes that she has met him before and asks him about a prior concubine he had had in Yantai before he passed the metropolitan examinations. Because Jin had callously discarded her, he does not wish to be reminded of the connection. He becomes irked and proceeds to ask Ailin a series of hostile questions. Instead of unmasking any hidden flaws, however, her coolness in response to Wenqing's truculence only demonstrates the true dignity of her character. He first asks her if she has not simply run out on Gong Xiaoqi, taking with her all the cultural artifacts that now surround her in her lodgings. She replies that he had sent her away to make her own living, because through his spendthrift ways he had been reduced to desperate poverty and could no longer support her. He gave her all the valuable things she has as souvenirs of his enduring affection. Wenqing goes on to press her on Xiaoqi's perfidy in accompanying the British to the Summer Palace in 1860 and advocating that the British burn it down. Wenqing assumes that Xiaoqi turned traitor strictly as a way of getting his hands on more money, a conclusion that Ailin immediately takes pains to dispel. She tells a long and lurid story of how Xiaoqi's father (clearly Gong Zizhen, although never explicitly named) had been seduced by a princess of a Mongolian Banner and had been poisoned for revenge by her family once they found out about it. Xiaoqi's actions in participating in the burning of the Summer Palace were thus to avenge the death of his father, even though father and son never got along very well. Chu Ailin thus seeks to promote Xiaoqi's legacy as a man of surpassing filiality, the cardinal Confucian virtue.

In Chu Ailin and Fu Caiyun we thus see two very different women, whose figuration runs in diametrically opposed directions. The novel seems to indicate that Ailin's moral strengths are as homologous with her cultural attributes as Caiyun's amorality is with her lack of refinement. Furthermore, the intense "Chinese-ness" of Ailin's public personality—notably her profound cultural attainment—is as marked as Caiyun's ease of connecting with, and ability to manipulate, the foreign. In analyzing the novel as a whole, then, this is yet another demonstration that the figuration of the female in late Qing fiction is never simple. As in Wu Jianren's *Strange Events,* the traditional female in *Flower in a Sea* embodies the best of the traditional virtues, more so than the men surrounding her, who are portrayed as distinctly problematic—Xiaoqi is a spendthrift who sold out his country for the sake of filial obligation and Wenqing is a faithless lover. Once the female is separated from familiar cultural practices, however, she suddenly becomes dangerous. Without the paraphernalia of traditional ways to hem her in, Caiyun becomes promiscuous both culturally and sexually. While she seems to represent the coming of the new order, her peculiar coldness to customary notions of reciprocity renders her a highly ominous model for the new, foreign-oriented age to come.

It is equally important to note that Caiyun does not simply represent the foreign per se. The Russian revolutionary Sarah, another woman who figures prominently in the text, stands in as someone who seems in most ways to be the emblem of the modern Western woman. As we saw when she threatened Wenqing and Caiyun over the hypnosis incident, she is portrayed as someone with a strong sense of herself and perhaps even a salutary model for Caiyun, who spends considerable time with her studying German as the *Saxon* approaches Europe. It is, for instance, noteworthy that Sarah tells Caiyun during the course of her dispute with Wenqing that she will continue to give German classes as before—the Russian woman is steadfast in holding that her dispute with Wenqing has nothing to do with the relationship between the two women.[68] Sarah, however, also figures as a person willing to subordinate any personal loyalties to the political program of the anarchist party, demonstrating the most steadfast loyalty to its goals, even to the point of attempting to assassinate the czar.

Sarah would thus seem to represent one end of the continuum of possible human conduct, in this case the commitment to the commonweal that Yan Fu and Liang Qichao had established as such a defining characteristic of Western social and political behavior. In analyzing Sarah, however, one must keep in mind Pierre's remarks to Jin Wenqing about the relationship between China and Russia. In saying that their political systems resemble one another, but that the Russian people had already "been enlightened" and "are not so easily fooled,"[69] Pierre is, in effect, putting China and Russia on an evolutionary continuum. If Germany and England are envisioned as being part of an incomparably different and more advanced world, then Russia is halfway between, with a political system similar to that of China but with a people that has already begun to wake up. Sarah can thus serve as a model of personal progress, and her ability to converse readily in both Chinese and European languages demonstrates her to be in many ways the mirror image of the flexible Caiyun. The clear difference in fundamental character between them, however, points to the vast differences in political awareness between the peoples of the two countries.[70]

As it is retrospectively introduced to the reader, Sarah's political behavior does have problematic implications for the more personal side of her life. Only after the events leading to her arrest does the narrator recount her personal history, in an extended sequence more characteristic of an adventure novel than of the rest of *Flower in a Sea*. To render a long and complicated story briefly and simply, Sarah, after initially being portrayed as a heartless opportunist, turns out to be both politically brave and personally loyal, demonstrating her profound affection for her lover before she is executed for her attempt on the czar's life. To make the contrast between Sarah and Caiyun as acute as possible, as soon as this long sequence relating Sarah's heroism is wrapped up, the narration switches back to an account of another of Caiyun's illicit affairs, this time with a dashing young German officer, Count Waldersee. The juxtaposition of episodes here only emphasizes the contrast between Sarah's selflessness and Caiyun's self-indulgent hedonism. The much-remarked-upon fact that Zeng Pu did not extend his narrative to the aftermath of the Boxer Rebellion in Beijing—where Sai Jinhua, the model of Caiyun, was rumored to have performed notable acts of public service—stands as another example of the author's determination to portray Caiyun in as selfish a light as possible.[71]

When juxtaposed with one another, the different developmental trajectories among these three female characters suggest three possibilities for behavior in the environment China found itself in at the end of the nineteenth century. Together they represent the polysemy of the figuration of the female: there exists a large range of possibilities, both good and bad. Chu Ailin represents a highly traditional image of the Chinese woman: she dedicates herself to personal loyalty, thereby exhibiting the best side of the private virtues set out by contemporary thinkers as emblematic of the Chinese character. Sarah, for all that she is obliged to betray her personal loyalty to her lover Kelansi, turns out to have done it all for a noble cause, for which she most admirably martyrs herself. In the end, her selfless dedication to the cause justifies any of the apparent harshness of her personal behavior. At any rate, the scene where Kelansi observes her crying over his photograph demonstrates that personal loyalty had always been a core element of her character. Caiyun, however, in her relentless pursuit of personal advantage, combines the worst of both the other worlds: she manifests a profound instinct for her individual interest, but without any of the personal loyalties that would give it the sort of social meaning that Chu Ailin so richly embodies. And in contrast to the imposing Sarah, the only principle Caiyun seems to stand for is advantage to her own self. For all the technical education (i.e., the instruction in German) she receives from Sarah, Caiyun in the end is as completely impervious to the grander, selfless side of Sarah's Westernized character as she was to the moral influences of the Jin household and its strict notions of Confucian propriety. Above all, Caiyun seems to figure the impossibility of the realization of the utopian potentials represented in the other two women. She is thus very much the embodiment of a characteristic late Qing frustration: a most vivid representation of the inability to bring about any local application of the virtues that have been discovered in a newly widened world.

PART III

The New Republic

CHAPTER 8

The Contest over Universal Values

> We see most past work through our own experience, without even making the effort to see it in something like its original terms. What analysis can do is not so much to reverse this, returning a work to its period, as to make the interpretation conscious, by showing historical alternatives.
> Raymond Williams, *The Long Revolution*

> For enlightenment is as totalitarian as any system.
> Max Horkheimer and Theodor Adorno, *Dialectic of Enlightenment*

The texts and subtexts of the major thinkers and the major novels in the last decade of the Qing may have disclosed a great deal of uncertainty about the changes unfolding in China, but there was still real enthusiasm abroad among Chinese elites that the various openings toward the "new" would effect substantive change for the better in their beleaguered country. As was pointed out in the introduction to this book, even foreign observers who were longtime residents in China shed their usual pessimism regarding developments in China to share in this general enthusiasm. Among the many reforms of the period, the numerous initiatives toward parliamentary government and local rule seemed to embody these hopes. A large mix of people participated in these efforts, including merchants, journalists, those who held high degrees in the examination system that had finally been abolished in 1905, and, perhaps most revolutionary, those who had received a modern education either at home or in Japan. As Min Tu-ki has observed in summing up his detailed study of the formation of late Qing provincial assemblies, "Although one may not agree that this was a 'bloodless revolution,' the traditional gentry did take over new functions, and new leadership within the gentry class shifted from the conservative gentry with high degrees and high rank to the enlightened intellectuals. Clearly, a new era had arrived."[1]

When the revolution that overthrew the dynasty eventually came in October 1911, it was natural that the "enlightened" sector of Chinese public opinion was virtually unanimous in its enthusiasm for future prospects. For one thing, as this chapter will make clear, there had come onto the cultural stage a whole new group of intellectuals with an impressive command of both Chinese and Western intellectual traditions. The pessimism about the acquisition of Western knowledge expressed by Yan Fu in the years around 1900, mentioned in the last chapter, seemed no longer to be operative. This new optimism is clearly expressed by Ye Shaojun (1894–1988) in his 1929 novel, *Ni Huanzhi*, when he described the reaction in the cities as the news of the revolt became known: "Hidden beneath the surface were countless hearts which had been aroused by these events and were now uneasy, apprehensive, hopeful, elated, yet unanimous in the belief that a great upheaval was fast approaching."[2] For all the hopes with which the revolution was greeted, it soon became apparent that it added up to little more than a coup,[3] and the rapid consolidation of the social status quo ante almost instantly deflated the hopes that serious change was in the offing.[4] In addition, the resultant political confusion brought about a number of serious losses of sovereignty to the foreigners,[5] something diametrically opposed to the hopes for increased Chinese sovereignty implicit in all post-1895 thinking, whether revolutionary or not. As Ernest Young has summed up the post-1911 situation: "A year after the revolution, a sense of failure was already infecting the country. The removal of the Manchus had not been the regenerating act that many had hoped it would be. The republic had not brought greater foreign respect for Chinese sovereignty. Reforms, though energetically pursued, had with few exceptions stalled."[6]

A striking, if only momentary, lull in the fervent cultural activity of the previous fifteen years attended upon this political disappointment. With the deaths of Li Boyuan, Liu E, and Wu Jianren and the failure of Zeng Pu to follow up on the success of *Niehai hua,* the activist trend represented by the advocates of the New Novel seemed exhausted. Thereafter, fiction took a lower profile, one that would have been regarded as retrograde by the earlier advocates of a fiction of social consequence. While patriotic themes continued to be popular, novels about romance (often with patriotic subtexts) came to dominate the literary arena, and many of these were written in the classical rather than the vernacular language. For instance, the success of *Yuli hun* (Jade pear spirit), by Xu Zhenya (1889–1937)—first when serialized in the Shanghai newspaper *Minquan bao* in 1912–1913, and when it was published as a single volume the next year—marked the advent of parallel prose to the *xiaoshuo* form. This almost certainly represented the spread to the novel of the parallel prose promoted by the Wenxuan school, discussed in chapter 3. It was, however, also something the advocates of the New Fiction from the decade before would have found antipathetic to the popularization raison d'être for the movement. In these years the Nanshe (Southern Society)—a literary group that had been founded in 1909 by men who identified themselves with the Tongmeng hui but that became active in Shanghai by 1911—is another indicator of the changed cultural environment. Although it burgeoned just as the revolution was in the offing, it neither specialized in fiction nor had as prominent a political profile as the nature of its membership would suggest.[7]

The rapid consolidation of power by military dictator Yuan Shikai (1859–1916) almost immediately followed the founding of the republic on January 1, 1912, resulting in a confused and profoundly depressing political scene that did nothing to clarify the cultural situation. The high hopes that had accompanied the overthrow of the Manchus had been dashed. Disappointment was particularly strong among the politically active class that had come to dominate cultural production after 1895, a class that included the writers and readers described in the previous chapters of this book. Even the characters in the novels discussed in chapters 5 through 7 display the characteristics of this group. The "second revolution," an effort that began in the spring of 1913 and was led by southerners representing (among others) the forces of reform against Yuan, was effectively crushed in less than six months, adding to the gloom.[8] Yan Fu and Liang Qichao, the twin beacons of reformist thought in the period after 1895, had, as shown in chapter 2, long since begun to have reservations about some of their initial extreme views. Even had they strictly adhered to the positions they had pioneered in the late 1890s, however, new voices gathering around the revolutionary party of Sun Yat-sen would have made them appear quite restrained in comparison.

Yan and Liang had become conspicuously more moderate in their political views in the intervening years,[9] even as the fire-breathing anarchist Liu Shipei had thrown his lot in with the Manchus in 1908. Yan and Liang thus had few new ideas to offer in these depressing times. In addition, because they had become voluntarily ensnared in what later commentators would unanimously regard as futile, even quixotic political activity, it was even less clear which voices of wisdom could be depended upon to offer guidelines to the troubling new situation. To make matters worse, as Yuan Shikai grasped for power in these years, he launched an active governmental effort to suppress the journalistic expression of opinion, an avenue of communication that had expanded greatly after the 1911 revolution. His efforts at limiting the circulation of public opinion achieved conspicuous and indeed unprecedented success, even in the semiprotected zone of the Shanghai Foreign Settlement.[10]

By 1915, however, intellectual life began to heat up again—whether because of or in spite of Yuan's continuing oppressive policies is difficult to say. At the heart of this renewed activity was, once again, a sense of cultural crisis, centering around the question of China's disadvantageous position in the world. As we have seen, this question had been on the intellectual agenda from at least the early 1860s, but it had now become even more urgent with the realization that the post-Qing Chinese state was weaker than ever. One of the most important debates that developed concerned the nature of the differences between China and the West, a question that had bedeviled both the Yangwu thinkers and Yan Fu alike. In the postrevolutionary period, however, a new constellation of intellectual opinion sprang up, with positions polarizing toward two distinct trends.

One side was generally the more moderate, basing itself on the notion that China's problems were only slightly different species of a genus of general questions affecting humanity at large and the modern world in particular. Solutions to these common issues could thus be found by looking at a broad spectrum of ideas from both China and the West, resulting in the gradual development of a hybrid culture. The more radical position held that China's problems were the result of a uniquely disadvantageous set of historical circumstances, which pushed in the direction of what Lin Yu-sheng has labeled "totalistic iconoclasm,"[11] or the substitution of a wholly new set of ideals and values for the old. Practically speaking, this meant that the iconoclasts came to embrace wholeheartedly the ideas that had animated the recent history and success of the progressive West. Given the severity of the political crisis, which extended to the fundamental nature and even the existence of a central state, these two options represented the polar ends of a spectrum that was all but unavoidable in any profound reexamination of the political options available to the new Republic of China.

It should also be noted that the inevitable instrumentality of the choice here could not help but shape the way in which contemporary thinkers perceived the differences between China and the West upon which they based their analyses. In other words, the disposition of each thinker toward the nature of and the possibility for change colored his views of where these changes were to come from and how they were to be effected. The question around which the cultural crisis had long revolved—namely, whether ideas were universal property or were products unique to a particular culture—thus dramatically came to the surface again. This time around it was to prove even more vexing and immediate than it had to all prior would-be reformers, from the Yangwu theorists after the 1860s to Yan Fu and Liang Qichao after 1895. The ensuing dispute came increasingly to dominate the sphere of public discussion that revolved initially around the Shanghai publishing industry and included Beijing after the reorganization of Beijing University in 1916. By 1920 this dispute would transform the public arena in ways that would have been unimaginable just a few years earlier and would, in fact, usher in a whole new intellectual regime in the period that followed.

As the debate over the proper mix between China and the West waxed in the years after 1915, there was a widespread feeling among all the contending parties that the stakes were now much higher than ever before. The continuing decline of the political situation even after the departure of the Manchus disabused anyone that any easy solutions were to be had. Beyond that, radical resolve was hardened by the unedifying spectacle of many of the former leaders of the anti-Qing revolution now having become part of the problem by virtue of their involvement with Yuan Shikai, and the sense that perhaps only by including new groups in the political process could there be any progress. At the same time, the beginning of the catastrophic European war in 1914, the rapid economic growth in urban China resulting from the need to produce the goods that Europe was no longer able to provide, and the accompanying expansion of a cosmopolitan elite with a vastly more sophisticated knowledge of the West and its ideas were giving rise to a new body of opinion makers. This group of men felt that it could much more confidently deal equally with Chinese and Western issues on the same intellectual horizon than had any prior generation of thinkers.

After 1915 this group split into two, which, although emerging from the same pre-1915 intellectual matrix, were each marked by very different modes of discourse. The eventual victory of the radical party that followed upon the events in Beijing on May 4, 1919, was to be decisive. For not only did it virtually eradicate the memory of the moderate position with which it had contended, but it also succeeded in powerfully insinuating the voice of radicalism firmly within the realm of literary criticism and practice. If the victory of the radical voice proved conclusive, in retrospect it hardly seemed inevitable in the years before 1919. At that time, the moderates seemed to have the more gifted writers, and their reasoning was almost invariably more carefully worked out. They also controlled the most prestigious and powerful organs of opinion. In the end, perhaps it was the characteristic signature of perilous times that the most extreme solutions proved to be, if not the most persuasive, then at least the most appealing to those stymied by China's myriad difficulties.[12]

It is not surprising that the first thinker to put the cross-cultural question back on the intellectual agenda was Chen Duxiu (1879–1942) in his radical new journal, *Qingnian zazhi* (Youth journal). The first issue appeared in Shanghai in September 1915, shortly after Yuan Shikai launched his bid to restore the monarchy.[13] It included an article by Wang Shuqian, entitled "The Question of the New and the Old" ("Xinjiu wenti"), in which Wang notes that the definitions of what is really new and what is really traditional have become hopelessly confused since the overt confrontation of reformist and traditionalist voices passed from the scene along with the former dynasty. Because everyone has now rallied to the cause of the "new," regardless of the actual content of its ideas, any clear political direction has become impossible to identify:

> Since the contention between New and Old arose in our country, no one has as yet been able to clearly define the two terms. During the former dynasty, China was clearly divided into reform *(weixin)* and conservative *(shoujiu)* factions that contended with one another and could never get along; it was an uproarious time for both concepts. Since the label of "conservative" disappeared along with the former Qing empire, people have come to regard the New as something almost sacred and inviolable and even those who actually advocate archaism *(fugu)* more often than not do so under the cover of "renewal," in order to secure respect *(yin yiwei zhong)*. When one examines the substance of their arguments, however, one finds that in all respects they are actually in conflict with the New. Because of this, all things seem to be both new and not new, old and not old, which is why we are in a period of confusion between New and Old. It therefore did not really matter if the arguments were right or wrong during the [former] period of contention between New and Old, since people could base themselves on their consciences in advocating their ideas. There was no dissembling, and the livelihood of the nation even depended upon this. Now that New and Old are muddled together, however, not only is the difference between right and wrong indistinct, but it is impossible even to distinguish the motives lying behind right and wrong. If things continue in this way, things will lead inevitably to a point where no one in our country will have a functioning consciousness *(jingshenshang zhi zuoyong)* any longer. I don't know how a country can stand under such circumstances.[14]

In other words, since the "new" had assumed an almost totemic power after the end of the Qing, it was difficult to mark out a distinct speaking position from which one could clearly distinguish new from old. The problem of how to break out of this rhetorical impasse, where all discourse tended toward a superficial consensus, occupies Wang's attention for most of the course of the article. How was a writer to gain the leverage to mark out distinct territory beyond this confusing middle ground? For Wang, this question is far from academic, because for him it constitutes the indispensable prerequisite to gaining intellectual leverage over China's creaking political situation in order to be able to implement any true social or political reforms.

Wang's solution to this problem is to declare the distinction to be spatial rather than temporal, something that had long been at least implicit in late Qing thought: "Let us now set up the boundary in this fashion: Let what is new be none other than the Western culture that has come from abroad; let what is old be none other than the indigenous culture of China."[15] At first, Wang seems to justify his taxonomy on procedural grounds only, arguing that it will not be possible to distinguish the true characteristics of either culture or, more importantly, to decide whether or not they can actually accommodate one another, unless they are kept analytically distinct and thereby understood on their own terms. Even as he establishes this argument, however, he immediately shifts its ground to the moral arena by setting out the valorized categories of human rights and equality as the essential and unvarying hallmarks of Western culture, at least since the French revolution of 1789: ". . . Once the view of human life changed, a substantial value was placed upon freedom, and human reason could be developed without restraint. Once the attitude toward the nation changed, despotism was abolished, and the spirit of constitutionalism achieved complete expression. This is what we are calling Western culture, and it is something that China never had before, so we are labeling it 'new.' That which is the opposite of this we are calling 'old.'"[16]

If Wang's distinctions still seem to have an ad hoc quality in this formulation, however, he concludes peremptorily that "the two [i.e., new and old] are completely at odds with one another, and there is no space between them for mediation *(tiaohe)* or compromise *(zhezhong)*."[17] China has no option, then, but to choose between one or the other of these two totalities. In his effort to find leverage for comprehensive reform, in other words, Wang makes the same absolute distinction between Western and Chinese cultural qualities that Yan Fu had made two decades earlier. Yan, as will be recalled, made this distinction a major vehicle in opening his comprehensive attack on late Qing intellectual and political life. Wang seems to echo that distinction here in his own attack on contemporary practices, even to the emphasis on freedom and equality as the essential qualities of the West.[18]

Chen Duxiu, in another article in the inaugural issue of his journal, makes precisely the same distinction as Wang does between the essential natures of the new and the old. The essay, entitled "The French and Modern Civilization" ("Falanxi ren yu jinshi wenming"), is shorter and considerably more melodramatic than Wang's, although much less rigorously argued, riddled as it is with factual errors and fanciful interpretations of European intellectual history.[19] In reasserting the uniquely Western nature of the new, Chen similarly attempts to follow Wang in moving the essential definitions of the terms of difference from new/old to Western/Chinese. He begins by flatly claiming that "that which can be labeled modern civilization *(jinshi wenming)* is the sole possession of the Europeans and is thus Western civilization, or it can also be called European civilization."[20] Chen isolates three entities as key to what he regards as an earth-shattering force—human rights, biological evolution, and socialism—and gives credit to the French for having given these ideas the force they possess in the modern world. If Chen's argument in the end turns out to be the same as Wang's, its failure to include any of the nuance that confers a good deal more depth on Wang's essay has perhaps given Chen's work more lasting force as a piece of propaganda. The very fuzziness of definition that Wang's argument attempts to address with some care seems to be answered by Chen with definitions as abrupt and dramatic as they are simplistic.[21]

Chen's decisive turn from heuristic distinctions for analytical purposes to essentializing cultural characteristics, a move that Wang in his essay is chary of indulging in, becomes a basic building block in Chen's cultural writings that follow. In his "Fundamental Difference in the Thought of Eastern and Western Nations" ("Dong-xi minzu genben sixiang zhi chayi"), published in December 1915 in the fourth issue of *Qingnian zazhi,* Chen elaborates on his basic decision to perceive fundamental differences between China and the West by bringing out in full the always-implicit invidious side of his arguments. For instance, when discussing the contrasts between the Eastern family-centered society and Western individualism, he almost casually makes such comments as "Loyalty and filiality represent the morality of a patriarchal *(zongfa)* society in the feudal period and comprise the persisting spirit of the *semicivilized (ban kaihua) Eastern peoples*" (emphasis added).[22]

For reasons that will be made clear below, it is quite likely that the bold cultural theorizing that characterized *Qingnian zazhi* may well have influenced *Dongfang zazhi* (The Eastern miscellany), which by then was quite established. The Commercial Press had begun publishing the latter authoritative journal in Shanghai in 1904, and by 1915 it had become the principal organ for educated public opinion in the country.[23] Given the later importance of Chen Duxiu's new journal, to say that it exerted an influence on other publications may seem a commonplace assertion, for later historians have retrospectively conferred upon *Xin qingnian* (New youth—the name of Chen Duxiu's journal after late 1916) a weight and power it almost certainly lacked in its early years.[24] In 1915–1916, however, *Dongfang* so far surpassed the new journal in influence and readership that one might well imagine the senior periodical simply ignoring the new upstart. But the fact remains that soon after *Qingnian zazhi* commenced publication, leading articles on the East-West cultural question suddenly start to appear in *Dongfang zazhi,* in its first issues of 1916. It is noteworthy that in the years and months immediately prior to late 1915, the main articles in *Dongfang zazhi* had been a mixture of policy discussion, general questions, and accounts of current events, but with few systematic comparisons between Chinese and Western culture and values. If anything, the theses and tone of these pre-1916 articles suggest that the pieces are based on a thoroughgoing assumption by their authors of the ultimate universality of ideas and values and the transparency of cultural communication, with China taken as just another player on the international stage.

The first articles directly engaging the difficult questions of cultural comparison between the West and China come almost exclusively from Huang Yuanyong (1885–1915), writing under the name "Yuansheng." Huang, who received the *jinshi* at the extraordinarily precocious age of nineteen, passed the last examination ever given for that degree, in 1904. He later became probably the leading journalist of the early republican period, serving as (among other positions) the Beijing correspondent of the Shanghai *Shen bao*.[25] Because of his skill and fame as a writer, Huang became implicated in Yuan Shikai's effort to declare himself emperor, and he departed Beijing for Shanghai when Yuan's attempts to enlist became too pressing. Huang soon thereafter felt he had to flee even Shanghai, and he was eventually assassinated in San Francisco on December 27, 1915. The Shanghai scholar Tang Zhenchang has recently offered persuasive evidence that Huang was killed by supporters of the republican cause; they objected to his earlier mockery of the revolutionary effort as much as to any endorsement he may have given Yuan Shikai in the early years of the latter's ascension to power.[26] In a set of posthumously published essays written after he had fled China in the fall of 1915, Huang focuses on China's dire straits in a way that sounds many of the same pessimistic notes expressed by Wang Shuqian and Chen Duxiu.[27] The key difference between them is that Huang's discussion is more carefully constructed upon a clear underlying theme of human similarity and a sense of the transparency of cultural communication. For all his stress on common humanity, however, Huang grants "thought," or ideology *(sixiang),* the vital role in ordering human activity and in creating cultural difference, ascertaining that the contrasts among cultures arose from different historical circumstances that in turn bring about distinct patterns of thought.

The most important of this set of articles is an elaborately embellished essay published in January 1916, entitled "Our General Malignancy" ("Guoren zhi gongdu"). Huang begins the piece with an intricate parallel construction that fully recognizes the extremity of China's current position: "Of all the people in our country, there is almost no one who does not think China is about to perish. But when they say 'is about to perish,' it is to avoid the taboo of saying that everyone believes China will indeed perish. But when they say 'will indeed perish,' they are also being polite; in fact, they believe that China has already perished."[28] Huang says he will set aside the question of whether these beliefs are true or not in favor of exploring the roots of the malady. In passing, he also mentions the uniqueness as well as the paradoxical implications of the discourse of autocritique in which he is even then participating himself: "Nowadays the politicians and scholars of other countries daily seek to extol the particular spirit of their nationals, while we [in China] consider it our most urgent task to research and seek out the particular malignancy that is universal among us *(wu guomin tebie zhi gongdu)*."

Huang develops his inquiry with logical precision and balance, carefully keeping in mind at all times the historical factors behind the malaise, as well as noting the universal factors underlying it. For instance, in setting the stage for his eventual diagnosis, he engages in a mock catechism on why Chinese society has come to be in its current sorry state:

> In China now there are many "doctors." The first of them said: "China's maladies result from a bad political situation." If one then asks why the political situation is bad, the response is "Because the authorities are bad." But one cannot say (at least in general) that a malevolent god has specially dispatched demons to torment China; these authorities of ours are simply other Chinese. So why are they as bad as this? To speak plainly, such moral lapses as self-indulgence, debauchery, peculation, and cruelty are but the common excesses of unlicensed human interests *(yisi);* all humans seek to further their own interests at the expense of others. Willfulness and self-indulgence that lead to malevolent behavior are thus simply human nature. Human nature is naturally predisposed toward wickedness and turns toward the benevolent only with difficulty.[29]

Although Huang is here engaged in the same project as the writers of *Qingnian zazhi*—that of trying to understand the roots of China's problems—he goes about it in a way that stresses a nature common to the whole human species. This clearly contrasts with the position of Chen Duxiu, who is engaged in a constant project of seeing China's difficulties as the result of some unique national perversity. Huang's discourse may also be indebted to the many discussions of Xunzi's philosophy that were popular at the time,[30] again a contrast with that of Chen Duxiu, who (at least consciously) is even at this early date attempting to establish the obsolescence of the Chinese intellectual tradition in its entirety. The root cause that Huang adduces as underlying all China's problems is "nothing other than vagueness in the realm of thought" *(sixiang jie zhi longtong eryi)*.[31] As for the nature of this vagueness, Huang admits, "I cannot really define it, but I can describe it well enough: it is everything without system, without substance, without character, and without distinctions. The phenomena it gives rise to are arbitrariness, despotism, stagnation, corruption, and following weakly along."[32] In a word, it is empty formalism.[33] In the latter half of the essay, in other words, Huang sounds themes that resonated long and loud in the New Culture movement that ensued shortly thereafter. What the radical voices of the movement omitted from their discourse, however, was the delicate nuance of Huang Yuanyong's careful presentation of the full richness of the context of a universal human history.

At the same time as Huang was engaging himself in a series of anatomies of China's particular problems, he also writes about the general malaise of the modern. In an essay entitled "Reflections" ("Xiangying lu"), published posthumously in *Dongfang zazhi*, he situates China's difficulties as part of a common modern problematic:

> Now the people of the civilized countries are also suffering from the vexations and disunity of [contemporary] intellectual life. Because of the omnipotence of science, religion and philosophy have become mere appendages to it, and so the [latter two] are not able to reach their fulfillment. As for the functions of science, it would seem to be more than sufficient for manufacturing *(zhiqi)*, but it is not up to promoting morality and nurturing one's character. It is just for these reasons that the more advanced that production becomes, and the greater the power of machines, the more difficult life becomes. The stimulation of the nervous system is even greater for them [i.e., those in the "civilized" countries] than it is for us. At this point, we have become neither new nor old, neither Chinese nor Western. Our old grain is exhausted and the new not yet ready for harvest, just as is the case with them. And what causes particular pain for us is the predicament of the nation, which is more extreme for us than it is for them. From the standpoint of a wise man, however, the sense of the experience of life and the anxieties produced are the same [for us as for them].[34]

Huang does not simplistically equate China and the West here, nor does he demarcate them as two completely different realms, the one of nature and spirit and the other of science, as Liang Qichao and Liang Shuming were to do with much fanfare a few years later. Instead, while not ignoring the clear differences, Huang subsumes the consequences of modernity under a sense of general human crisis, which he describes as achieving the same effect on the individual subject whether in China or in the West. Huang's use of the term "people of the civilized countries" *(wenming guo ren)* to refer to the West here seems simply to be following and thus naturalizing a convention that had been common since the late Qing. If any irony is implied, it is understated almost to the vanishing point. In this respect, his usage contrasts sharply with that of Wu Jianren a decade earlier in *The New Story of the Stone*. As outlined in chapter 6, Wu Jianren deployed the narrating voice in a manner that becomes extremely defensive about just which country should be accounted as truly "civilized," thereby registering his anxiety over the implications of the term itself. What allows Huang his uninflected use of the phrase is the underlying assumption in his discourse that the hurly-burly of modernity has rendered the "civilized" nations no better (or no worse) off than poor China, at least in respect of the affective life of their citizens.

Huang's most profound inquiry into the problems of China, and into the nature of its contrasts with the West, is contained in a long essay published as the lead article in the *Dongfang zazhi* issue of February 1916. In this piece, entitled "The Clash between New and Old Thought" ("Xinjiu sixiang zhi chongtu"), Huang begins by arguing a point precisely the opposite of what Wang Shuqian had dismissed as axiomatic in his contribution to the first issue of *Qingnian zazhi* in September of the year before: "Since the time that the importation of Western culture began, the clash between New and Old has never been as severe as it is today."[35] Huang notes that, after the 1898 effort at reform and the trauma of the Boxer Rebellion in 1900, almost everyone had assented to a reform program based to a large extent on the emulation of Western political ideas, and that "there was no one so devoted to the old ways as to raise the banner of restoring tradition *(fugu)*, as there is today." But, Huang says, this new group of traditionalists is equally steadfastly opposed by believers in evolution, and each side is of equal strength. According to Huang, what accounts for this new standoff is the shift of the locus of the reform effort from institutional matters like armaments and political systems to the realm of thought, which he defines as "the source from which every aspect [of society] emanates."[36]

Even as he establishes thought as a fundamental marker of difference, however, Huang is careful to add a long section on how all such differences are relative rather than absolute. He concludes this demonstration with a long citation from *Zhuangzi*'s "Qiwu lun" (The sorting that evens things out) as his source of authority: "Humans eat the flesh of hay-fed and grain-fed beasts, deer eat the grass, centipedes relish snakes, owls and crows crave mice; which [of the four] has a proper sense of taste?"[37] Huang comments, "One cannot know which has the proper sense of taste. The point is that if habits differ, then what each eats will differ. This serves to explain why, if thought differs, then behavior will differ as well." In other words, even while preparing himself to make his strongest statement on the historical roots of difference between China and the West, he prefaces the discourse with a strong assertion of ultimate cultural relativism. He thus makes clear that although Western thought may have a clear claim to instrumental superiority in dealing with the complexities of the modern age, this does not allow one to affirm its ontological supremacy. This distinction is easy enough to make, perhaps, but it is one that the radical reformers of the years to follow always strenuously denied.

As part of an evident delight in the rhetorical possibilities of his language,[38] Huang was never one to introduce his principal thesis without a long prologue that set out a complicated context for what was to come. In "The Clash between New and Old Thought," after establishing the importance of thought in culture and then expatiating at some length upon the relativity of cultural difference, he finally gets down to the business of defining Western thought and its fundamental differences with that of China. He first establishes the Renaissance and Christianity as the most important variables in the Western tradition and goes on to posit three stages of human thought: the unconscious period, the period of critical thought, and the period of theoretical synthesis *(xueshuo goucheng)*. At this point he once again sounds a note a similarity with the nascent radical reformers in declaring that "China at present is just moving from the period of unconsciousness into the period of critical [thought]." He attributes Europe's ability to fuse the drastically opposing strands of Christian intuitional piety and Greek skeptical empiricism to a tradition that has been the upshot of a long period of interaction among different civilizations. Interestingly enough, Huang grants substantial credit for this multiculturalism to the colonial policies of both the ancient Greeks and the modern Europeans, which resulted in increased contact with the ideas of other peoples and a disposition not to take the inherited ideas of one's own culture as absolute truth.[39]

Following upon this detailed historical evaluation, Huang concludes with a long list of the different qualities of the "new" and the "old," sorted into four general groupings. The third grouping is the most definitive:

> Number Three: The new is that which affirms this human freedom [to study and critique traditional morality]. Therefore, it fosters individual self-consciousness and individual liberation. The new thus affirms that the human race has its own human character *(renge)*. This human character consists of self-knowledge and holds that humanity has an absolute value and an independent purpose. It is not like an implement to be used by others, nor like a slave in service to others. If this [human character can be said to] have no value or purpose in itself, then the old [thinkers] can regard the human race as being made up of so many machines, good only for its instrumental use, and see each individual person as subject to the

service of others. Therefore, [under such a system] slavery is inevitable, and should a country [organized under these principles] perish, there is no reason to mourn it.[40]

Huang is careful here to phrase in strictly universal terms his argument on the inadmissibility of allowing humans to be regarded as vulnerable to subjugation to a larger principle outside of themselves. While the differences between new and old are easily seen as represented in the modern West and a depressingly hidebound China, respectively, his discourse allows for considerable voluntarism. For instance, that China now has a variety of cultures on its doorstep (or, perhaps more accurately, the cultures have already intruded themselves well into the house) would seem implicitly to indicate that the conditions for cultural critique are now fully present at home. Huang concludes with a warning based on this tacit understanding, one of the few places in the essay where explicit comparison is drawn between the West and China: "Alas! If our country in the present day should prove still able to close its doors and be self-subsistent and to keep these strange Greek and Christian [systems of] thought forever at bay, with no exchange back and forth, then our people will simply remain content in our old ways and in their enjoyment of life."[41]

After Huang's untimely death, Du Yaquan (1873–1933), the editor of *Dongfang zazhi* between 1912 and 1920 (and, perhaps not so incidentally, a pioneer of scientific education both in Shanghai and in his native Shaoxing),[42] resumed the major burden of cultural theorizing for the journal.[43] In so doing, Du protested—with some justification—his inability to continue the high standards that Huang had brought to the work he had so brilliantly begun. In an article published in the April 1916 issue of *Dongfang zazhi,* Du makes clear his debt to Huang in the title he chooses for the piece: "More Remarks on the Clash between New and Old Thought" ("Zai lun xinjiu sixiang zhi chongtu"). Like Huang, Du is at pains to advance the notion that differences customarily assumed to exist between China and the West are only "questions of degree" *(chengdu wenti)*. The reasoning that Du advances for this position, however, seems to be rooted in a somewhat more reified sense of the particular natures of the two traditions than had been the case with Huang: "To say that the intellectual clashes among our people are the result of the [overarching] clash between Eastern and Western thought is simply erroneous. . . . How can what we refer to as the new thought in China ever depart from the legacy of traditional Eastern thought? And how can what we refer to as the old thought ever remain completely stuck in the patterns of traditional Eastern thought and completely reject that of the West?"[44]

While Du, like Huang, certainly assumes the inevitability of hybridity here, the core of his argument seems tilted a bit more than Huang's toward assumptions about the fixedness of particular human characteristics that have evolved through historical difference. Thus, although he finds the evils of selfish desire *(liyu)* and personal will *(yiqi)* to be universal causes of political disruption, he also finds these problems to have been uniquely deleterious to China:

> People of our country have never paid much attention to social intercourse, so their opportunities to learn from one another have been few. Since education and the establishment of schools have not been widespread, the level of [socialization] has also been rather juvenile. Educators have only paid lip service to the training of character and the molding of personal qualities, so the result has been far from [what they have advocated]. Therefore, there are very few of our citizens who combine general knowledge with satisfactory personal qualities.[45]

Du gives an extensive account of how such bad human habits develop in all populations, but his nomination of "human desire" as one of the besetting social sins overtly recalls the theories on human nature originally advanced by Song-dynasty Confucian thinkers, as well as the extensive debate about the depredations of *renyu* (human desire) that had been carried on throughout the Qing dynasty.[46] In this sense, his remarks earlier in the article about how all thinkers in modern China, reformist and conservative alike, were inevitably attached in important ways to traditional values ring true at least in his own essay. If one can tease out a slight emphasis on an essential nature of Chinese culture in Du's article of March 1916, when compared at least with Huang Yuanyong's work that had apparently inspired it, the overall positioning of both men's work is on the common quality of the human experience. That difference, in Du's own words, is "a question of degree" rather than of essential quality.

By October of the same year, however, Du published a landmark article in *Dongfang zazhi* that was a significant departure from what had come before in that journal. Entitled "The Quiet Civilization and the Active Civilization" ("Jingde wenming yu dongde wenming"), the essay declares a basic reversal for Du from his earlier position: in the first paragraph Du proclaims that "as far as my opinion concerning Western civilization and our traditional civilization is concerned, the difference is *a matter of quality (xingzhi) and not one of degree*" (emphasis added).[47] In setting out the reasons for this abrupt switch of opinion, Du announces a number of themes that were to resonate greatly in the years to come:

> In recent years, the emulation of Western civilization on the part of our people has known no limits. From the great questions of the military and the state to the minutiae of daily life, there has been no area in which we

do not imitate the West. And as for our own traditional civilization, we have paid no attention to it at all. Ever since the beginning of the European war, however, the efficient instruments that were invented because of Western science have been used by the assorted Western nations to slaughter their fellow beings. The dimensions of this tragedy are unprecedented not only in our own history but in world history in general. For my part, I thus cannot help but entertain doubts about the Western civilization that I had once held in such high regard. As for those in our country who imitate Western culture, I will no longer be able to credit their expressions of faith in [Western] morality and its other achievements (*gongye*).[48]

It is noteworthy that Du begins his essay by expressing his frustration with the automatic emulation of the West that had been the calling card of Chen Duxiu's new journal almost from its inception. If, however, Du has now come to believe in an essential difference between the West and China, he still has not given up the notion of communication between the two. In fact, he maintains that now, instead of China's learning from Western experience, "[o]ur traditional civilization is just what is needed to remedy the defects of Western civilization."

The discourse that follows this stunning opening is built on many of the same assumptions that Huang Yuanyong and Du had earlier called upon to show how China had been marked by deficiency vis-à-vis the West. For instance, where Huang had seen the Western multiculturalism that had grown out of the facility of cultural intercourse and colonialism as the West's great advantage in the modern world, Du now sees only how this easy contact has resulted merely in persistent conflict, "leading to the present, in which there are still nation-states in contention." The upshot is the present great war. According to Du, China, because it never developed such notions of national difference, has been spared such enduring strife.[49] What Huang had analyzed as a negative attribute of the Chinese situation is thus now countered by Du's precisely opposite representation of the attribute as positive. In a similar fashion, Du now radically reinterprets Huang's analysis of the need for the concept of *renge*, or human character. He sees the Western notion of humanity as linked indissolubly with the concept of nationality, and because China has had no notion of the nation-state, the country has not developed any notion of what would now be termed the "national subject":

> So, aside from the notion of the natural individual, we have no fixed notion of human character. Everything is predicated on the individual as center, and family, friends, locality, country, the human race, indeed all creation, are seen as proceeding from near to far, from close (*qin*) to

distant *(shu)*, all as matters of degree and thus without conflict [among them]. In Western society, on the other hand, there is individualism to be sure, but there is also nationalism, class solidarity, communalism *(minzu zhuyi)*, all of which result in discord. The two ideologies of individual-as-center and nationalism-as-center have come to the point of strong contention in the present era.⁵⁰

Much of the remainder of the essay is devoted to showing how the two qualities of quiescence and activity will balance each other out in the end, thus leaving open the possibility of eventual reconciliation between the two cultures. For all that, however, Du has taken a major step in the direction of re-creating the sort of polar opposition between China and the West that *Dongfang zazhi* had generally seemed steadfastly to avoid in the years after Du had become editor. If nothing else, the way in which Du suddenly reverses the verdicts on the meaning of Western history that he had earlier agreed upon with Huang Yuanyong should cause later readers to beware of any essentializing of cultural qualities, almost regardless of how much historical evidence is provided. The wide variety of opinion Huang and Du evince concerning even as basic an idea as individualism alone should cause anyone to think twice about the validity of such concepts, based as they are on such a wide range of social and historical factors.

The question remains, however, as to how to account for Du's abrupt about-face. We can without doubt take Du's word that the accumulating evidence of the horror of the war played a major part in his reconsideration. His reaction may even have resulted from an awareness of the singular horror of the slaughter brought by the various offensives on the western front in Europe in the summer of 1916, although there is no indication in any of the other extensive articles or comments—many of them also written by Du—in the *Dongfang zazhi* of this period that these catastrophic events were attracting particular attention in China.⁵¹ On the other hand, a further look at Chen Duxiu's writings from the same period suggests another possible reason for Du's change of heart. For instance, in an article portentously titled "1916" and published in the January 1916 issue of *Qingnian zazhi*, Chen draws an unmistakably invidious distinction between the West and China: "For our people, from the beginning of history up until 1915, in politics, in society, in morality, and in academics, the sins we have committed and the insults we have endured cannot be washed away even with all the rivers of China. At this moment of extirpating the old and broadcasting the new, by all rights we should thoroughly repent, mend our errors, and renew ourselves." Given this entirely negative view of Chinese history, Chen goes on to advocate a most thoroughly radical means of renewal:

Let us create the most substantial of boundaries between 1915 and 1916: We shall regard everything from the founding of our nation until 1915 as ancient history; let all things from the past perish as of 1916, and everything hereafter begin with 1916. We should first exert new energy *(xinxue)* in order to present a new character, a new country, a new society, a new family, and a new nation *(minzu)*. Once we have this new nation, then we will begin to live up to our vows as humans *(chang yuan)*, we will begin to have enough value to interact with the white race *(yu xizu zhouxuan zhi jiazhi)*, and we will begin to have the qualifications to inhabit this piece of land we live upon.[52]

Although there is no direct evidence to justify the assumption, the depth of Chen's iconoclasm, expressed in a new Shanghai journal of opinion, may have been enough to rally Du Yaquan to a more steadfast defense of Chinese culture than he had ever given previously. Chen's evident efforts to remove any qualification or possibility of mediation in his demarcation of a progressive West and a decadent China may have pushed people toward the polarized positioning he seems to be demanding. If Chen has affected Du's opinions, however, he has done so in a manner precisely the opposite of his own radical intentions, by bringing Du an increased appreciation of the value of his own tradition.

For his part, Du continued to contribute occasional writings on comparative culture to his journal. In an April 1917 essay entitled "The Postwar Reconciliation of Eastern and Western Cultures" ("Zhanhou dongxi wenming zhi tiaohe"), Du once again begins his discourse complaining about the tendency of Chinese intellectuals to idolize the West. He immediately proceeds, however, toward a more evenhanded evaluation: "In all fairness, modern life in both East and West cannot be said to be satisfactory; neither can the culture of either East or West be considered a model."[53] He sees the need for a process of self-conscious selection in which the features most appropriate to modern life can be determined. The essay goes on to break down the various features of human life into their most important categories—economics and morality. Du credits the West with vast economic power, so vast, in fact, that it has led to an extraordinary hunger for resources and markets that has been quite harmful to the world. Given that the goal of Chinese economic thought has been merely to provide equal sustenance to the population of the country, China has not harmed anyone else, but neither has it been able to provide enough even for its own people. Du concludes that "as far as the economic situation is concerned, Eastern societies suffer from systemic anemia, while Western societies suffer from an extraordinary surplus of blood."[54]

As for morality, Du gives the West full credit for its moral energy in creating institutions like charitable societies and cooperative agencies, but he breaks down Western morality into two main streams: Greek rationality, human centered and logical; and Jewish religious piety, divinely oriented and mystical. He observes that the Middle Ages were dominated by the spirit of the latter, whereas the Renaissance saw the former regain the preeminence it had once commanded in antiquity. Du sees an excess of science and rationality as the problem that created the disastrous situation that led to the war, and he predicts that, after the war, Western instrumental rationality will have to be leavened with Jewish religiosity:

> However, when human thought undergoes a change of this sort, it must also witness a renewal. And in this period of thriving science, how can the divine authority of the old religion forcibly hold things together? Moreover, the tendency of modern men of culture toward Greek thought is ever clearer, so its power must not be underestimated. So the new era of Hebrew thought must be reconciled with that of the Greeks and have modern qualities at the same time. To revere heaven and be in awe of fate, even as one seeks to probe to the root of things and fulfill one's nature *(qiongli jinxing)*; to make consistent the purposes of the divine and the human and to unify the spirit and the flesh—these are not impossible tasks. Although China's moral thinking is close to that of Greece, the basis of our rationality *(lixing)* derives from heaven, and its function devolves unto people: apprehending the intention of heaven and applying it to human affairs; dealing with human affairs such that they accord with the intention of heaven; a mind on guard and fearful, with the intention of cultivating the self and serving the divine. These notions [of ours] are thus in accord with Hebrew thought. Therefore, after Western moral thought has reconciled Greek and Hebrew ideas, it will look much like the moral thought of our Eastern societies; I await this outcome anxiously.[55]

If one adds to this Du's notions that Chinese economic thinking has always been predominantly socialistic and that socialism will be the necessary reform in the Western economic realm to remedy the excesses of instrumental reason, Du sees reconciliation between the social ideas of China and the West as inevitable on a number of levels. Moreover, his logic puts China in the uniquely favorable position of being able to mediate the crisis arising out of the West's inability to balance the demands of the material and the spiritual. Du's principal thesis is also virtually identical to the notion of Eastern spirituality/Western materialism discussed in chapter 7. Ironically, for all his conscious efforts to conserve the past, his ideas here are years ahead of their time, for they were taken up by Liang Qichao only in 1919 after his disillusioning sojourn in Europe and by Liang Shuming in the early 1920s.⁵⁶ That Du has never been given credit for this idea is yet another demonstration of the way in which moderate voices were drowned out by the cacophony unleashed by the New Culture movement.

If the utopian nature of Du's aspirations for the future renders his discourse somewhat strained, Qian Zhixiu, in an essay entitled "Utilitarianism and Scholarship" ("Gongli zhuyi yu xueshu"), published in June 1918, sets out the bleaker side of the interaction between China and the West. According to Mao Dun, Qian was of the three subeditors of *Dongfang zazhi* under Du Yaquan and was a regular writer for the journal. He also replaced Du as the major force in editing the magazine for a time after Du was relieved of his duties and *Dongfang* was reorganized in late 1919, with the changes taking effect for the first issue of 1920.⁵⁷ Qian explains in his essay his views on the modalities of the introduction of Western ideas into China at some length. He believes the Chinese adoption of these ideas to be tainted by a lack of real conviction that results in an inevitable and deleterious instrumentality in their application. Qian sums up this tendency as utilitarianism and describes it as the great flaw in the relationship of China to the West, seeing it as lying behind all the reform ideas that had swept China in the forty years prior to 1918:

> Forty years ago, the theory of "enriching the country and strengthening the military" *(fuguo qiangbing)* favored riches and strength on the basis of their being effective in resisting foreign insult, winning battles, and bringing about economic self-sufficiency. It was the most elemental form of utilitarianism. Thirty years ago, there was the theory of sound scholarship and science *(gezhi shixue)*, which were advocated because they would lead to better armaments, further technology, and bring about the satisfactions of material civilization. This also did not depart from the pattern of utilitarianism. Twenty years ago, the theories of human rights and liberalism were espoused, along with constitutionalism and republicanism.⁵⁸

Although Qian's argument may at first glance resemble the sort of wholesale condemnation of Western ideas that had been the staple of late Qing conservative thinkers, Qian is quick to add an important qualification concerning the merits of the ideas in their own right:

> When human rights and liberalism, constitutionalism, and republicanism were implemented by Europeans and Americans, they may have been used to break free of the old system of feudalism and divine authority or to bring into being the ideals of humane justice. These are not things that can be simply encompassed by the notion of utilitarianism. But with us

it is different: we adopt these things because the flourishing peoples of Europe and America have passed through this stage, and since we wish to be on the same level of strength and wealth, we feel we cannot but follow in their footsteps.⁵⁹

The problem, then, is not with the quality of the Western imports per se but with the strictly instrumental considerations that motivate the Chinese advocates of Western imports. In fact, Qian holds that any idea not strictly related to the maximization of utility, whether from traditional China or even from the West, gets discarded because of this orientation. Qian concludes his general remarks on the subject with the mordant observation that the blatant practicality of China's adoption of utilitarianism is probably something that even Jeremy Bentham or John Stuart Mill would not have been able to imagine when they originally advocated utilitarianism. When Qian eventually gets down to his discussion of the conflicts between utilitarianism and scholarship, he takes the frankly elitist position that scholarship will be irreparably harmed if it takes only utility as its goal and that true scholarship can thus never be anything other than a pursuit of a highly educated and disinterested minority. Perhaps most controversially, however, he takes what he regards as a corollary stand — by opposing the elimination of elite education, with its classical language, and the introduction of a debased popular education and its use of the vernacular language as its vehicle of instruction.

There may be no definitive proof that the "neoconservatism" of *Dongfang zazhi* after the middle of 1916 was at least in part a reaction to Chen Duxiu and his new journal. On the other hand, there is incontrovertible evidence that Chen was very much aware that the older journal had begun to run articles pointedly at odds with what he was advocating in *Xin qingnian*.⁶⁰ In September 1918 Chen published "Questions Addressed to the Correspondents of the *Eastern Miscellany*" ("Zhiwen *Dongfang zazhi* jizhe"), which was a direct refutation of a number of articles recently published in Du Yaquan's journal. Chen paid particular attention to Qian Zhixiu's essay attacking utilitarianism. Possibly because Chen so flatly disagreed with Qian's assumptions about the basic nature of utilitarianism and the damage it had brought about, his polemic spends more time on what can only be called facile debating tricks rather than directly addressing Qian's substantive points. For instance, in trying to undermine the basis of Qian's opposition to utilitarianism, Chen breaks the Chinese word *"gongli"* into its component parts and asks rhetorically if Qian favors their opposites: "The opposite of *'gong'* (gain) is *'zui'* (hardship), and the opposite of *'li'* (benefit) is *'hai'* (harm). May I ask, since the correspondent of the *Dongfang [zazhi]* is opposed to utilitarianism (i.e., *gong-li*-ism), does that mean he favors "harmism" (i.e., *zui-hai*-ism)?"⁶¹ In keeping with the overall tone of the attack, Chen closes his essay with a snide provocation: "I beg the correspondent of the *Eastern Miscellany* to respond clearly to each of the questions I raise above. Please favor me with comments that take some pains to avoid vague imprecision and illogic. Vague comments are, after all, just what the former correspondent for the *Eastern Miscellany*, Huang Yuanyong, so scathingly denounced."[62]

In the December issue of *Dongfang zazhi*, Du Yaquan responds to Chen's critique in a considerably more intellectually rigorous manner than Chen's original attack:

> [In Qian's original essay] he said something on the order of "The theories of human rights, liberalism, constitutionalism, and republicanism advanced in Europe and America cannot be encompassed by the notion of utilitarianism, but when we advocate these, it is out of utilitarian motives." The correspondent of *New Youth* asked in response whether our correspondent was "opposed to human rights and liberalism" and whether he was "opposed to constitutionalism and republicanism." But to criticize a [merely] utilitarian advocacy of human rights and liberalism is not to be opposed to human rights and liberalism in themselves. . . . This is rather like criticizing studying only for the sake of passing the exams in order to become an official, which is not the same as opposition to study in itself; or like criticizing elections based on bribery, which is not the same as opposition to elections in themselves. The correspondent of *New Youth* should also take care to logically examine these assumptions [of his].[63]

The more moderate tone of Du's response is clear enough. His moderation in itself betokens an intention to argue the issues, rather than simply an effort to shut down his opponents through rhetorical flourish.

Chen duly wrote a rejoinder to Du's response, which was published in the February 1919 issue of *New Youth*. In this piece, Chen seems to have been affected by the gravity of Du's effort, for he tones down his sarcasm considerably, addressing the issues with a good deal more specificity and seriousness. There is still, however, no meeting of the minds, and the continuing differences between the two on the matter of utilitarianism illustrate the larger gap between them. As Chen inquires: "Where is [Qian's] error? It is at the point where the *Eastern Miscellany* correspondent fails to understand the value of utilitarianism and its achievements in the history of European and American civilization. He mistakes it for coveting the illicit and an unprincipled adherence to power and influence *(gouqie shili)*."[64] As Wang Xiaoming has said of Chen and his journal:

> The most fundamental characteristic of *New Youth* is the effective dominance of utilitarianism. In the foreword to the first edition of the journal

(fakanci), "A Warning to Youth" ("Jinggao qingnian"), Chen Duxiu earnestly sets out six hopes that he has, the fifth of which is for "utility and not empty formalities." He even goes so far as to affirm that in every aspect of the social reforms in Europe since the eighteenth century, "there was nothing that was not hell-bent on contributing to the single path of practical enhancement of the popular livelihood *(housheng liyong zhi yitu)*." In the next issue [Oct. 15, 1915], in "The Guiding Principles of Education Today" ("Jinri zhi jiaoyu fangzhen"), he even more strongly advocates a notion of what he calls "Realism" *(xianshi zhuyi)*, and [he] says that "applied to ethics and morality, this is called utilitarianism *(leli zhuyi);* in politics it is called the greatest good for the greatest number; in philosophy, empiricism or materialism; in religion, atheism; in literature and the arts, realism or naturalism." One should not underestimate this short utterance, for it in fact draws a tight cordon around the content of *New Youth*. From volume 1 to volume 6 [i.e., from 1915 through 1918], there was not one important article of advocacy or discussion that was not in the service of this notion of "realism," from "On the Literary Revolution" [by Chen] to the critique of "spirituality" *(lingxue)*. This was even more the case in the extensive discussions of "Mr. Democracy" and "Mr. Science."[65]

In fact, as we have seen, Du had been arguing from quite another position. He had fully acknowledged the importance of the qualities of the greatest good for the greatest number that Chen sees as the essence of utilitarianism in Western history. Instead, Du had argued against utilitarianism largely on the basis of the Chinese context, in which it had figured for him as simply a symptom of the lack of any enduring principle, or what might more readily have been referred to as opportunism. In insisting upon using a strict textbook definition of utilitarianism, and one that contains no reference to historical practice or the different situations of China and the West, Chen almost willfully ignores the point that Du is attempting to make. In other words, it is not that one is wrong and the other is correct about the meaning of the term, but that the two have completely different understandings of the implications of the term and are thus talking past one another.

It is important to note that the two do have in common one unspoken point: both are implicitly skeptical of the capacity of China to deal with the new world that has come to its door. To Chen, China's deficiency in this regard is reason enough to jettison the whole of the past and everything related to it. His despair for the present is masked by his enthusiasm for a future inspired by new light coming from the West. For their part, Qian and Du recognize that the situation is much more complex and that any self-imposed limitation to newly imported ideologies will merely reinforce the problems that the imported ideas are ostensibly intended to solve.[66] If, for instance, China's polity had come to be marked by a series of struggles of one against all in the name of personal survival, then the doctrine of utilitarianism imposed on this basic pattern will in all likelihood simply give license to more of the same self-serving behavior. The question remains, however, why Qian can so readily conceive of the features of utilitarianism as serving a positive function in the West but cannot adduce a comparable set of ideas to serve China in its time of crisis.

In summing up the import of the long course of this debate, we can draw a few conclusions. First, before the radical denunciations of Chen Duxiu and his colleagues in their new journal, both Huang Yuanyong and Du Yaquan had made extremely trenchant critiques of their own on Chinese politics and society. (It must be said, by the way, that the quality both of Du's argumentation and of his writing is never able to match that of Huang's.) Each of them, however, was careful to position his critiques in a context in which Chinese flaws were measured in terms of universal patterns of behavior. In fact, the critiques were found to be meaningful precisely to the extent that they could be perceived as particular species of general deficiencies in human society. Whether Chen believed this or not—and it is impossible to tell from his writings of this period—his early polemical writings were overwhelmingly focused on Chinese deficiency, with the international context beyond China invariably depicted as having an altogether more wholesome set of characteristics. Second, we can probably safely assume that Du's change of orientation vis-à-vis the legacy of Chinese tradition is at least in part a defensive reaction to the spirit of iconoclasm being manifested in *New Youth*. If this is the case, then Chen's apparent effort to polarize the difference between China and the West to the fullest extent possible was remarkably successful. We can fairly conclude that Chen was able to exercise a good deal of agency in shaping the discourse into a pattern of his dictation very early in his career as a radical polemicist. It must also be noted, however, that his effect on thinkers like Du Yaquan and Qian Zhixiu seems to have been precisely the opposite of what he had intended.

On the other hand, the critical importance of Huang Yuanyong's invocation of the common alienation of the modern world should not be overlooked. Although Huang subsequently censured the particular failings of China, his capacity to tune into the spirit of a nascent Western modernism and to plausibly include China within its universal orbit represents a real departure from the reformist discourse up to that point. It is perhaps the first credible theoretical notion of cultural equivalence in the period after 1895, when the question presented itself for the first time with such ineluctable pertinence. For, however casually Huang adduces his argument—indeed, one could argue that its breezy informality is precisely what renders it so compelling—it contains the seeds of demystifying any theory of the cognitive superiority of the West. Thus, when Du Yaquan finally emerges with his defense of Chinese culture, it may well be that Huang's easy equation of the modern in China and the West gave Du the room to question at the least the invidiousness inhering in Chen Duxiu's reinvocation of an essential difference between China and the West. That Du at the same time more obviously is reacting to and thereby reinscribing Chen's rigid theory of difference does not rule out the presence of Huang's ideas as a vital catalyst in the transformation of Du's thought.

Ironically perhaps, it was the paradox apparent just behind the controversy over utilitarianism that led toward this polarization in the first place. If Qian is correct in his assessment of the utilitarian motives for the adoption of Western ideas, then the ultimate subservience of these imported ideas to a domestically generated political and social agenda is the only logical conclusion. Moreover, it is a point on which he and Chen implicitly agree, although Chen would never admit it. For the radical reformers, however, the political apparatus's capacity for endurance is what forces them toward extreme positions: the only conceivable way for politics and society to escape being recaptured by tradition is to insist on the need for an absolute departure from it in a drastic delimitation of boundaries (or *huaqing jiexian,* the revealing phrase that would be so popular in the Cultural Revolution, half a century later). Thus we encounter the almost chiliastic tone of Chen's enthusiastic "1916." The insistence upon the creation of a completely new literature, which was to be the hallmark of the New Culture movement, results directly from this iconoclasm: there could be no illicit importation of traditional imagery into it, nor could there be any recognition of the debts the new literature and its theories owed to the activity of the decades immediately preceding it.

More than anything else, though, it was perhaps the Ministry of Education decree of January 1920 that eventually succeeded in definitively banishing the past: "[F]rom this autumn onwards, all national schools are to use the national language as the language of writing in the first two grades, in order to achieve the uniformity of the spoken and written word."[67] If Wang Yuanhua's surmise is correct, and Du Yaquan's dismissal as editor at *Dongfang zazhi* was due to his resistance to the wholesale adoption of the vernacular and the management's fear of possible consequences for the textbook market, then the extent to which cultural practice was affected by a short and simply worded government edict is remarkable. Within its scope was encompassed more than two decades of reform thinking about writing and its social functions. The edict was both a portent of things to come and a poignant ending to a period of extraordinary openness of contention about China's cultural future. It should be kept in mind, however, that precisely because of this determination to sever itself from its past, the new literature that grew up after 1920 would never be at peace with itself. As the critical writings of Qu Qiubai in the early 1930s demonstrate, the price of a rigorous iconoclasm was an eternal vigilance engendered by the fear that old forms and genres would always find a way to sneak in through an unguarded back door.

CHAPTER 9

Swimming against the Tide
The Shanghai of Zhu Shouju

[The bourgeoisie] compels all nations, on pain of extinction, to adopt the bourgeois mode of production; it compels them to introduce what it calls civilization into their midst, i.e., to become bourgeois themselves. In one word, it creates the world after its own image.
  Karl Marx and Friedrich Engels,
  The Manifesto of the Communist Party

What a pity it is that the moment foreign things reach China they change their color as if they had fallen into a vat of black dye.
  Lu Xun, "Suigan lu sishisan"

Critics have agreed that a sea change came about in the realm of fiction when Li Boyuan, Liu E, Wu Jianren, and Zeng Pu—the four great novelists of the late Qing—passed from the scene. All but Zeng Pu were dead by the end of 1910, with Zeng writing little beyond adding chapters here and there to *Flower in a Sea*. The critical consensus among scholars in China ever since has seen in the post-1910 period a complete transformation in the sort of novel produced, from the high seriousness of the New Novel to the arch-melodrama of the "mandarin ducks and butterflies" fiction genre, which pandered to an urban audience. For these scholars, nothing symbolized this change more sharply than the founding of *Fiction Monthly (Xiaoshuo yuebao)* at the Commercial Press in 1910. Although a few scholars, following the lead set by the pioneering work of Perry Link,[1] have begun to question whether post-1910 fiction can so easily be taken as merely frivolous entertainment, a powerful consensus has long mitigated enthusiasm for serious study of the diverse variety of Chinese fiction between the last work of Wu Jianren's and the stories that Lu Xun had published in *New Youth* beginning in 1918.

It is beyond the scope of this book to undertake a thorough reconsideration of Chinese fiction in this tumultuous period. Nevertheless, one of the most famous of the works written in these years at the very least lends credence to the idea that an intensely serious narrative work was going on. Beginning serialization in 1916, Zhu Shouju's massive novel *Xiepu chao* (Tides of the Huangpu [river]; hereafter referred to as *The Shanghai Tide*) is not merely a serious work. It is serious in a way that carries forward the critical examination of the coming of the West, its ideas, and its institutions to China, a subject that is the focus of this book. Zhu, like Wu Jianren in *The New Story of the Stone,* examines the question of the new influences on China as it is embodied in the new metropolis of Shanghai, but he examines it in more painful, scandalous detail. The theme that announces itself again and again in Zhu's work is related to the notion of utilitarianism discussed in chapter 8. If Qian Zhixiu was leery of the advent of utilitarianism in China even as Chen Duxiu welcomed it with open arms, Zhu's novel announces broadly that the crassest sort of utility has become the hallmark of the new era and has become firmly entrenched in Shanghai, a place where everyone depicted in the text thinks of other people strictly as means to achieving his or her own ends.

The second decade of the twentieth century was paradoxical for China. As Marie-Claire Bergère has noted: "Between 1910 and 1920, Chinese capitalism expanded rapidly. This was the golden age . . . of the national industries, a spontaneous capitalism that had begun to prosper in the aftermath of the 1911 revolution. But far from promoting the accession of a bourgeois power capable of encouraging the development of productive forces, this revolution ushered in an era of profound decline for the State."[2] All in all, Chinese industry achieved an annual growth rate of 13.8 percent between 1912 and 1920, and because a vastly disproportionate amount of this industry, as well as the financial institutions behind it, was concentrated in Shanghai, that city's economic growth was particularly explosive.[3] As noted in chapter 8, this economic growth was accompanied by a vibrant print and intellectual culture, but the continuing decline of the prospects for a strong state and for the moral order it symbolized weighed heavily on this more powerful public opinion. The failure of political institutions to match the progress of the economy was particularly evident in Shanghai. As Mark Elvin has noted:

> In 1912 and 1913 the prospects of social progress in Shanghai gradually darkened. The increase in crime that followed the 1911 revolution, the rise to power of underworld leaders connected with that revolution, the

destruction of much of southern Shanghai in the fighting of 1913 with the consequent loss of about a third of the municipal revenue, the reign of terror and demoralization that followed the victory of [Yuan Shikai] and the influx of his agents into the city, the forcible disbanding of the Merchant Militia, and then [in 1914] of the [Shanghai City] Council [founded in 1905] itself, brought an end to eight and a half years' effort to realize what the Council's leaders had called "the way of humanitarianism."[4]

Zhu Shouju's epic novel is, among other things, an exhaustive chronicle of these years and the depressing events that marked them. It is also a powerful example of the case to be made for linking the modern—and the "Western" that stands behind it—inextricably with moral dissolution.

Zhu Shouju, who wrote under the pen name "Haishang shuomeng ren" (The Shanghai teller of dreams), is, to the extent to which he is remembered at all, known for having written *The Shanghai Tide*. As Fan Boqun notes in an article on Zhu, however, little else is known about him. He was by most accounts someone who spent most—if not all—of his life in Shanghai, and he wrote three other long novels that were published in the late 1910s and early 1920s.[5] He was also a pioneer of the Chinese cinema, having written, directed, and produced a number of the most prominent early Chinese silent films, as well as having been a managing partner in two of the early studios. Interestingly enough, he was associated with several of the early silent films starring the famous actress Ruan Lingyu (1910–1935) in 1928–1929, but his name vanished from the annals of the Chinese film industry after 1930. He is said to have moved on from film to working in the steel industry, but there seem to be no surviving accounts of his activities after 1930. Neither his date of birth nor his date of death is known, although a clear photograph of him as a rather scholarly-looking and fairly young man survives.[6]

Zhu begins his hundred-chapter epic with a conventional enough invocation of the moral perils of the time and place in which he will situate his text:

> It has been said that on the banks of the Shen River [i.e., in Shanghai] a new atmosphere has come into being since the time of the Xinhai restoration [i.e., 1912, the year of the republican revolution]. From the scholarly and official elites at the very top, however, on down to the smallest peddlers and errand boys, everyone has donned a mask of falsity, and hypocritical behavior grows apace. This is even truer of the wild girls, lascivious women, and young dandies who trade on the concepts of "freedom" and "civilization"[7] to further their sordid schemes. With them, all notions of shame and decency have sunk without trace.[8]

Although such castigatory words about the moral laxity of Shanghai were common enough in the New Novels of the late Qing dynasty,[9] Zhu sounds a more ominous note of warning. In setting out the idea that things have declined even further after the revolution that overthrew the empire and was meant to usher in an era of reform and good government, Zhu resonates with the most despairing voices of his time. Even the contemporary jeremiads by Chen Duxiu against the decadence of traditional Chinese culture in his new magazine, *Xin qingnian,* at least held out the hope for reform if the appropriate Western models could be emulated, a possibility that Zhu's narrative seems to reject out of hand. At its most basic level, the novel struggles to give an account of a society in which political organization is unraveling even as urban wealth is palpably on the increase.

Zhu's text began serialization in the Shanghai newspaper *Xin Shenbao* (New *Shen bao*) on November 23, 1916—a paper that had commenced publication only three days before—and continued well into 1921. *The Shanghai Tide* proved popular enough that its first thirty chapters were vetted by the leading popular novelist Wang Dungen (1888–1951?) and published in two volumes in 1917 or 1918.[10] The entire work was published in book form in ten volumes of ten chapters each in May 1921 by the New People's Library (Xinmin tushuguan). Wang's preface to this edition claims that publication was undertaken at the request of the novel's many enthusiastic readers.[11] This edition, which cost 4 Chinese dollars—a considerable sum at the time—and contained a photograph of the author as well as illustrations for each chapter, went through four printings between May 1921 and September 1922.[12] The World Book Company (Shijie shuju) issued a five-volume edition in January 1924; it was already in its third printing by April 1924, and a fourth printing followed in August 1928. Based on this quite reliable publication history, one source's claim that the book version sold "more than ten thousand copies" is highly credible, making it a best seller by the standards of pre-1949 Chinese publishing.[13] Four prefaces by prominent "butterfly" writers—including Zhou Shoujuan (1894–1968) and Wang Dungen—praised the work as having a unique combination of liveliness and detail. Based on this critical and popular success, Zhu was completing a ninety-chapter sequel even as the original work was being published in book form; in this sequel the individual chapters are only about half the length of those in the original.

The book seems to have fallen out of favor after the 1920s, probably one of the many victims of the May Fourth determination to extirpate from serious consideration all the literature from the 1910s and 1920s that did not conform to the dictates for high seriousness promulgated by the New Culture movement. Although the novel has been reprinted at least twice in the 1990s,[14] it has received little critical attention since the 1920s, because the negative attitude first voiced by May Fourth critics regarding fiction that revealed scandalous stories "behind the scenes" (*heimu;* literally, "black curtain") has persisted right down to the present day. For instance, the author of a recently published monograph on the little-studied literature of the 1910s can barely bring himself to comment on the novel at all and ends up doing so only by way of an oblique dismissal of the possibility that it might contain anything of value: "Hedonistic men of letters had no way to resuscitate the dissolute (*fengliu*) manners of the prior generation, so all they could do was represent the silly shamelessness of their own cynical attitudes toward life."[15] The contemporary Shanghai writer Wang Anyi, however, wrote a short appreciation of the novel in 1990 that tellingly captures the mood of urban ennui in the work.[16]

Alone among her contemporaries, Shanghai writer Eileen Chang (1920–1995) repeatedly referred to *The Shanghai Tide* as an influence on her own fiction and lamented the critical and popular neglect in later years of such a powerful work of satire of the urban scene.[17] It is, incidentally, not difficult to find any number of correspondences between several of the characters in *The Shanghai Tide* and many of the more minor figures that populate Chang's stories. One might even say that Chang used the urban atmospherics of the Zhu's novel as a kind of living backdrop against which she set her detailed explorations of complicated individual subjectivities. Zhu's novel contains a comprehensive catalogue of Shanghai life in the years immediately after 1912, all the way from the political activity among the self-constituted elites to lurid depictions of the complicated lives centered on the pleasure quarters. One of the most important concerns of the book is to demonstrate the extent to which these two spheres overlap and to which they are both marked—or, rather, afflicted—by common patterns of behavior. In fact, the new sphere of private association that is such a prominent feature of late Qing civic life—not to mention a focal point for contemporary scholarship—seems, from the point of view of Zhu's text at least, to be proving itself almost totally corrupt.[18]

The City and Its People

As Zhu proceeds to illustrate his critique of the modern city, he focuses on the relationships between his characters and the elements of urban life that attracted Chinese to the "model settlement"[19] in the first place: the open entertainments, the most recent types of residence that guaranteed a theretofore unattainable sense of privacy, the ease of transportation and communication, and the unmatched possibilities for voluntary organization. Similar to Wu Jianren's description of the city, the result is a profoundly disquieting portrait of an urban milieu in which openings to the new come to resemble mere license and in which transformed personal and spatial arrangements appear to take the ground out from under the feet of everyone in the city. The consequences of this new anonymity were apparent in every sort of new urban enterprise in Shanghai. As Roberta Wue has written of the society of artists in the late nineteenth century: "No longer able to rely on family and local connections in the establishment of their careers, artists were also dealing increasingly with an anonymous clientele, ranging from customers walking into a fan shop and buying a work from an artist they did not know, to the anonymous public that bought their works in the form of magazines and books. This new order necessitated a public image or reputation, and self-promotion became correspondingly important for the celebrity artist."[20]

Above all, the novel generates an intense paradox in which new possibilities for private behavior can play out only in an arena of unprecedented public scrutiny. Some of the more striking ways in which new spatial and personal relationships bring about uncertainty can be seen in the following passage, an account of a night at the opera in which the behavior of the audience is considerably more noteworthy than anything that could possibly transpire onstage:

> By this time, the people coming to see the play had become so numerous that all the reserved boxes had filled up. There remained only the box in front of the one belonging to Ms. Shao and her party, in which sat a single person dressed as a maid, with the other seats all empty. Each seat had a program lying on it, signifying that someone had come and gone, with a teapot in front that had been sitting there steeping for some time. Numerous people unable to find seats sought to crowd in, and the maid had been obliged to dispatch them one by one—it was clear that she had been forced to assert herself more than once. Ms. Shao thought to herself: Who is holding these seats? If they're serious about seeing the play, they should've come earlier. It's so strange that some people insist upon showing up only after nine, as if they'd lose face by arriving earlier. In fact, spending all that money and only coming for an act or two doesn't quite seem worthwhile.
>
> Just as she was thinking this, an exotic perfume suddenly struck her nostrils, and turning around, she saw a beautiful woman of about twenty. She was wearing a silver-red crepe jacket trimmed with inch-wide strips of black satin, beneath which was a Western-style long skirt that reached to the floor. She was probably wearing leather shoes, accounting for the clicking sound she made as she walked. Around her neck was a pearl necklace, on which each pearl was as big as a soybean. She walked along the aisle behind the usher with a broad smile on her face, and when the maid saw her, the former abruptly stood up and said "Second Mistress." The woman flashed her bright eyes at the seats around her, saw how many

people had come to watch, and uttered a 'tsk-tsk' as she lowered herself slowly into her seat. The maid promptly took a small Yixing-ware teapot out of her bag, along with two Japanese porcelain cups. She had the attendant remove the teapot that had been set there earlier and brewed a fresh batch in the Yixing-ware, filled up one of the cups, and handed it to the beautiful young woman. The latter took the cup and asked the maid: "Has he still not come?" The maid replied that he had not. The woman smiled as she took a sip of tea and then took out a small gold compact and looked at her visage in its mirror. She clasped a tissue and proceeded at some length to apply powder to her face.

 At this point, a handsome youth of no more than twenty swiftly emerged from the boxes on the far right, walked behind the lady's box, and coughed softly. He was wearing a silver-gray jacket of bright silk and a bluish-white satin vest inlaid with black satin embroidered buttons. He wore a small hat in the foreign style, and his face was as white as snow, as if powdered. When the beauty turned her head and saw him, she conferred a glowing smile upon him. The young man took this opportunity to slip into the box, and the two of them then sat shoulder to shoulder, whispering to one another. Ms. Shao had already pretty much figured out what they were up to, and she thought to herself—In Shanghai people don't even bother to try to hide this kind of thing from others, so no wonder the saying goes that once you have drunk the waters of the Huangpu River, you will end up permanently befuddled. She also saw that the maid, seeing what her mistress was doing, had an alarmed expression on her face, although she dared not say anything. The maid merely continued to look all around, as if afraid they would be observed. As it happened, after a short time an usher led in a fat man with a small moustache. Upon seeing him, the maid's face blanched in terror, and she said softly: "Your husband is here!"[21]

 The cold materiality of the representation here should immediately disabuse the reader of any notion that there might be a world of genuine romantic feeling underlying these dazzling surfaces and careful costumes. The intense theatricality of the audience's behavior on this night at the theater also strikes the reader immediately—and the self-promotion implicit in the flaunting of personal appearance and response to being observed is equally evident. Moreover, the drama embedded in the bold entrance of the beauty and the subsequent arrival of her young lover attracts the attention of the reader and the people sitting in the audience alike. The respectable Ms. Shao provides a focal point, registering her shocked reaction to the goings-on being performed before her. The theatricality of the scene is intensified not just by the behavior being displayed but also by the novelty of the venue in which it transpires. Ms. Shao, for instance, almost seems more scandalized by her observation that "in Shanghai people don't even bother to try to hide this kind of thing from others" than by the behavior itself.

This brings to the reader's attention that what Ms. Shao is witnessing represents an apparently unprecedented confusion between the realms of private and public behavior. Much of her surprise is a function of the new institutionalization of the theater in Shanghai, beginning in the second half of the nineteenth century, as the most important locus of a series of public spaces.[22] Although China certainly has a long tradition of theatrical performance, rarely had these performances been so generally open. The mixing of genders in theatrical audiences, in particular, had more often than not been the object of repeated efforts at restriction. In the words of Tao-ching Hsu, "Theatre has never been a congenial place [for] Chinese women, and ladies of perfect decorum never went to it until the recent emancipation [i.e., in the twentieth century]. Emperor Ch'ien-lung [r. 1736–1796] . . . once prohibited all women to visit theatres, but at other times those women who were not fastidious could and did go to them. They were, however, at first segregated from the men."[23]

The free and apparently random gender distribution of this Shanghai audience provides a sharp contrast to earlier attempts to enforce either female abstinence from attending theatrical performances or, failing that, strict segregation of females. Similarly, the status of the "beautiful woman" remains ambiguous. Aside from the maid's mode of address, which identifies the woman as someone's secondary wife, we are told nothing else about her background. While she is clearly someone of taste and wealth—as indicated by her clothing, her being attended by a maid, and her fastidiousness in regard to her tea—the most striking thing about her is that she retains her anonymity in both Ms. Shao's eyes and those of the readers. None of us is in a position to find out who she is, whom she knows, or how she fits into the extensive urban society that had developed by then in Shanghai. More importantly, once the brief scene is concluded, she and her gentleman-friends vanish from the action for several chapters. This contrasts sharply with traditional narrative technique in both fiction and drama, where someone introduced with such elaborate effect instantly becomes a key player in the story.[24] The contrast between the surface, observable features presented in such detail and the complete absence of any hints as to the nature of the woman's private life indicates the extent to which the action described, while intensely public, hides unknowable private implications. For all the intensity with which behavior is observed, it remains stubbornly opaque. This scene, in other words, hints at a new world of urban privacy amid Shanghai's ever growing throngs of people, but the privacy is all but canceled out by its having been made possible only by the intense public scrutiny that surrounds it.

The maid most sensitively reflects another side of this realm of the private. Although the elegant young woman herself betrays no anxiety about the delicacies of her situation, the maid, on the other hand, demonstrates an acute awareness of the uneasiness of the balance between public and private here. Even as she goes about ordinary household tasks like making tea and preparing things for her mistress, the maid never fails to register the fear of the public exposure that she seems to sense must eventually come. With the coming of the husband, her fears seem about to be realized. A quick-thinking usher, however, adroitly handles the situation by making it seem that the young man had sat next to the beauty only because of the general lack of seats. Part of the usher's impromptu excuse is to pin the blame on the maid—quite contrary to what actually happened—for having been inattentive to her duties and thus not keeping the young man out as she should have done. While the husband, Wei Wenjin, is briefly introduced as a wealthy candidate for officialdom from Hubei, both the beauty and what we can only assume to be her lover remain anonymous, underlining the highly fraught anonymity of this particular portion of the new public sphere.

We next see the beauty in chapter 8, where we are finally given a bit more information about her. After being told again of her charms and of her large social circle within the community of Shanghai concubines, the reader is presented with a brief personal history:

> Speaking of her basic character, when she was still back in Hubei, she was very well behaved *(guigui jujude)*, but, for some reason, on coming to Shanghai she had contracted the general malady of the concubines from great houses. She came to have a number of affairs, all unbeknownst to Wenjin. One evening when attending the opera at the Grand Theatre, he had come across his concubine sitting shoulder to shoulder with a young dandy in their box but had had his suspicions allayed by the actions of the usher. It was easy to see from this that Wenjin had complete trust in her. His young concubine, however, had more than just one lover, some of whom were men of little consequence and whom I thus cannot be bothered to talk about. I will restrict myself to describing one [of her lovers] by the name of Zhao, also a man of the official sphere, whose name and influence in town were quite equal to those of Wenjin but whose appearance was almost infinitely superior to that of her husband.[25]

After first reminding readers that they have encountered this character before, the text proceeds to narrate the young Mrs. Wei's affair with Zhao, which takes place in a love nest the latter keeps in town. At the conclusion of the chapter, the narrator ostentatiously reveals that Zhao is "none other than Zhao Boxuan, the good friend of Wei Wenjin and the official

Shanghai bank examiner."[26] The couple's rendezvous point turns out to be a *shikumen* townhouse. Lu Hanchao points out in his book on everyday life in old Shanghai that at the time Zhu was writing *The Shanghai Tide*, the *shikumen* was assuming its final form as a small unit just big enough to accommodate a nuclear family, in contrast to the nineteenth-century *shikumen* that had been built to house the larger group of people that typically constituted an extended family.[27]

As the book proceeds, the *shikumen* appears repeatedly as the place where wealthy men place their concubines, once again marking the novelty of social relations in Shanghai. The pattern in China had been for all the wives of prominent men to live in one large household, but in *The Shanghai Tide* at least, a trend toward monogamy in individual families is balanced by concubinage that is becoming more private and segmented, with the women consigned to their own small residences. The origins of the women themselves also bespeak a new set of domestic arrangements. Most of the concubines in the text were originally from the ranks of Shanghai's high-class courtesans, a group noted for its relatively high degree of social agency.[28] As Gail Hershatter makes clear, the book was being written at the time in which pressure to simplify the relationships between courtesans and their clients into a straightforward exchange of sex for money was exerting itself in the courtesan world. As a result, the higher strata of courtesans, with their greater degree of control over their relationships with men, were disappearing from the scene.[29] To put this in cruder (or more contemporary) terms, it could also be regarded as the period when the old class of high-status courtesans, the *shuyu* and the *changsan*, were losing their privileged position in the "market." To the extent that we can rely on the evidence provided by *The Shanghai Tide*, however, it might be possible to see the roots of this transformation in a kind of mass "privatization" of this group of women. They were, in other words, marrying themselves off to the burgeoning group of prosperous men who were even then coming to dominate the civic life of an increasingly wealthy Shanghai.

The implications in this change in the nature of relationships between men and women among the newly wealthy Shanghainese are various and complex. On the one hand, the new disposition of the concubine in her own residence suggests more privacy and intimacy, away from the prying eyes and endless gossip of the extended family. This in turn can be seen as either a burlesque of or a downright sinister foreshadowing of the emerging nuclear family in the city, or both. On the other hand, the new social organization of the city itself, with the intense theatricality of its public spaces, suggests a paradoxically public format for this recently achieved intimacy. As people circulate in the city, they experience a new exposure to the public eye, as is powerfully symbolized by the sharp gaze of the members of the theatrical audience on one another. The denouement of the illicit relationship between Wei Wenjin's concubine and Zhao Boxuan eventually unfolds in chapter 40, in an episode that provides this uneasy jumble of private and public with its most pointed representation.

In the intervening chapters, many of the men and their consorts have come to reside in a single *shikumen* compound. They include Zhao Boxuan and his new concubine, and Wei Wenjin and the beautiful concubine he had brought with him from Hubei. Zhao's concubine is well aware that her husband is still carrying on with Mrs. Wei, but she cannot think of a way to expose them convincingly. A third concubine, with a grudge against Mrs. Wei, thinks of a scheme that results in a mixed group of four men and four women observing Zhao and Mrs. Wei make love through an uncurtained window. This ultimate form of theater is made possible only by the architecture of the *shikumen* row house, in which one unit's "garret room" *(tingzi jian)*—often used as a spare room rented or sublet to outsiders and famously the lodging place of impoverished writers—looks directly out on the window of the adjacent unit's master bedroom. The pathetic Wei Wenjin, having been told that Zhao has hired an ordinary streetwalker *(yeji)* for his evening's amusement, enjoys the scene intensely during the short time when the faces of the lovers are obscured: "Wenjin did not yet know that the woman was none other than his concubine, and [he] looked upon the scene with great satisfaction, pushing at Yunsheng with one hand and pinching Zhuoqu with the other. 'This is great fun! Mei Yuege was right after all: that woman just has to be a streetwalker—no ordinary woman could ever behave so shamelessly,' he said with a laugh."[30]

In this extraordinary scene the most private of acts has suddenly been transformed into yet another theatrical performance, and as with other theatrical performances presented in the novel, even here the gaze is quickly turned back upon the presumptive observer. The irony of Wei Wenjin's enthusiastic voyeurism becomes acute when the attention is suddenly focused back on him. And the *shikumen,* even now celebrated as the location that both housed and in a sense enabled the Shanghai *xiao shimin,* or petty urbanite, instead appears as the place where moderately wealthy men housed their concubines and where all the confusing elements of private and public show themselves at their worst. The new spatial arrangements that characterize the city take on a sinister ambiguity in scenes like this, with moral implications that are only too obvious. We can, to be sure, take this as nothing more than the mark of a difficult transition, but it is hard to ignore the ominous overtones of a fatal moral flaw lying at the heart of the nascent bourgeois city.

As was outlined in some detail in chapter 2, anxiety over the cultural implications of highly overdetermined notions of public and private is a constant in Chinese intellectual discourse after 1895, following upon Yan Fu's declarations that China had nothing like the modern Western public sphere. With the amplification of this message provided by Liang Qichao in his influential essay of 1902, "Xin min shuo," it retained its power for a long period thereafter. Yan and Liang's efforts to promote a sense of *gong* (publicness) most assuredly did not aim to encompass anything like what transpires in this scandalous tableau, but perhaps the scene observed through the *shikumen* window offers the most ironic possible burlesque of the unanticipated complexities involved in the transformation between what Liang had labeled a morality based on "matters between one private person and another" into one based on "matters between one private person and the group." The very crassness involved in representing these actions as being related to exalted notions of public and private is yet another index of Zhu's low estimation of manners in the "model settlement."

While it had been the norm for Chinese novels prior to 1920 to contain a large number of characters, the late Qing novel, following the form of that great masterpiece of mid-Qing satire, *The Scholars,* tended to present the individual stories of these various characters in discrete episodes, set out in consecutive chapters. *Haishang hua liezhuan* (Singsong girls of Shanghai), by Han Bangqing (1856–1894) and published in 1894, was the first to break this pattern.[31] Arguably the first novel set in Shanghai to take urban life as its theme, it breaks its stories into smaller, discontinuous pieces that initially lack indication as to which character or group of characters is to be the focal point of each episode. The noncontiguous arrangement of the novel's various narratives points to an entirely new form of social organization even in the 1890s—the profusion of stories chopped into fine pieces and spread over longer expanses of text surely reflects the hurly-burly and anonymity of the new city. Most Chinese fiction of the late Qing, however, continues to use discrete episodes in its representation, but *The Shanghai Tide* conspicuously follows in the tracks of Han Bangqing's narrative innovations.[32]

It would be difficult to argue that *The Shanghai Tide* contains a broader range of characters than the "social novel" of comparable scope —developed during 1902–1910 and represented by Wu Jianren's *Strange Events* as its virtual prototype—from which it stemmed. The mode of presentation of the characters' stories in Zhu's novel, however, is completely different. Instead of each character being treated in a single episode, the author adopts Han's "hypotactic" narrative arrangement in which the stories of the individual characters are spread out over much longer stretches of the text. Moreover, the narrative trajectories of a number of characters are thoroughly intermixed as the novel progresses. This new disposition of plot elements would seem to reflect the unprecedented complication of human interaction that characterized the dense and interactive urban space of Shanghai. This intricate narrative hypotaxis represents, in other words, the passing of the possibility of segmenting off stories into discrete parts, as had generally been the case with the Chinese novel prior to this time. A bewildering new social reality had brought about an important transition in narrative convention.

Aside from presenting characters as part of a large crowd, the novel employs various other motifs to further its representation of the modern city. To begin with, the language Zhu uses is an unadorned vernacular marked by a crisp rhythm that combines considerable information and a vivid sense of action. To choose a random passage, in chapter 32, Rushi, the concubine of one Kang Erjin, has become depressed at her husband's disregard for her. Turning to religion, she takes to going up to the terrace of her *shikumen* every night to burn incense:

> The next day, in the still of night when everyone was quiet, she went again to the terrace to burn incense. She repeated this for several days running. She had no way of knowing that two brothers by the name of Zhou lived next door. The older brother had already married, but the younger had yet to take a bride. The latter, seeing his brother and sister-in-law's conjugal bliss, could not help feeling sorry for himself in being neglected. The window of his bedroom faced out onto the terrace. That night he had extinguished the lights to go to sleep, but by the middle of the night he was still tossing and turning, for some reason not able to sleep; finally he sat up, fumbled in the dark, and found the matches. Just as he was about to light the lamp, he saw a flash of light on the terrace opposite and was scared, thinking: is this not a thief? He thought to go wake his brother and sister-in-law so that they could all go catch the thief, but he was afraid that the thief would be scared off by the noise; but he also felt too timid to try to catch the thief by himself, so since the thief was in someone else's house and had nothing to do with him, he could look on calmly. He would wait for [the thief] to come over and then would plan accordingly. Finishing this thought, he walked over to the window in his bare feet, took a closer look, and almost broke out laughing: this was no thief he saw, but rather a beautiful woman, prostrate in worship and burning incense; he could see her particularly clearly in the moonlight, and he recognized her as the concubine of the Kang household, whom he had often seen coming and going in her rickshaw and had admired for a long time; because, however, he felt himself to be a lowly toad who could not aspire to attain such a beautiful swan, he had not dared to harbor any vain hopes—that she had come out on the terrace to burn incense right outside his window was something he never expected, so what harm was there in catching an eyeful and thereby feeding his fancy?[33]

Here the rapid pace of the exposition, in which the background information on the younger Zhou brother is supplied via what is, in effect, an interior monologue, contributes to the sense of the city as a locus of random encounters.[34] Each action has its own sentence, giving the first half of the passage, with its many different actions introducing a new set of characters, a choppy effect. When the narration recounts the thoughts going through the younger brother's head, however, the sentences expand to provide a sense of the virtual simultaneity of his mental processes. The passage is filled with linguistic clichés, like that of the toad not daring to eat the meat of the swan, but the clichés are piled on top of one another so that they end up seeming to be just common lexical items. The Zhous in the contiguous townhouse merely advance the story of Rushi's unhappy relationship with her husband, but the younger brother's actions and the motivations behind them are nonetheless explained in considerable mimetic detail.

The novel's language is also able to engender an unprecedented sense of the kinetic, a reflection of the new sense of continuous motion in the city.[35] There are endless descriptions of comings and goings by rickshaw—a new mode of conveyance imported from Japan and pioneered on Chinese soil in Shanghai—but characters also travel by motorcar, something also quite new at the time the novel was written and virtually exclusive to Shanghai in the years before 1920.[36] One episode in particular is emblematic of the novel's focus on motion. After the failure of the "second revolution" in 1913, a group of insurgents that have taken refuge in the Foreign Settlement decide one day to forestall their boredom by hiring a motorcar for a drive. Unbeknownst to them, the car's driver has been bribed by agents of Yuan Shikai to kidnap them into the Chinese part of the city, where they are to be arrested. As the driver turns toward the Chinese city, however, the passenger sitting in the front seat notices that something is amiss:

> At this point, [the driver] pointed the car south, but the six people sitting in the sedan were laughing and talking and failed to notice. [Tan] Guohun, however, sitting in front as he was, clearly saw what was going on and asked the driver where he was going. The driver made no reply and continued to drive toward the French Concession. Guohun was furious and ordered the driver to turn around. The driver, pretending not to hear, actually increased his speed and in a moment had already passed over the New Western Bridge [over the Yangjingbang and into the French Concession]. Guohun knew that a short distance away lay the Chinese city and was taken aback, thinking that the driver's actions were highly suspect: not wanting to be driven into the Chinese city and fall into someone's trap, he took no heed of the danger involved and reached out his

hand for the car's accelerator. The driver held on to it for dear life and would not loosen his grip. By this time the car had already reached the Rue du Consulat, where a westbound streetcar was just then approaching. The driver and Guohun were concerned only with struggling with one another, while the policeman at the crossing was too busy waving the traffic on to notice and allowed them to continue on, such that they ran right into the middle of the streetcar with a resounding crash that shattered the windows on the streetcar, crushed the hood of the car, and smashed the motor so that it ceased to run. The driver of the automobile was thrown out of the car, where he lay on the ground unable to get up, his head covered with blood; because his seat was somewhat lower than the driver's, Guohun was not thrown out, but his head had been struck in several places by the shards of glass, and blood covered his chest; the six people inside the sedan had been thrown into a heap by the force of the collision.[37]

The sense of motion out of control is enabled here by the breathless pace of the run-on sentences that constitute the narrative once the rented automobile nears its collision with the streetcar. Anyone familiar with Shanghai would have been able to identify precisely where the accident happened, and it is presented with a visual immediacy that may, in fact, have been influenced by the cinema, which had already become a fixture of the Shanghai scene in those years.

The rush of urban life reflected so vividly in the novel's language is also reflected in the nature of the relationships the men in the book have with one another. Contrary to what we might have expected based upon the meticulously researched conclusions of Bryna Goodman,[38] there is almost no identification of native-place ties among this new group of men who have become the movers and shakers of the Chinese establishment of the city. Neither are we told much about the origins of the characters populating the text, where they came from, or what their familial backgrounds are. They group together in voluntary organizations in Shanghai, ostensibly in pursuit of noble civic goals, but the groups almost invariably turn out to be fronts for the furtherance of the basest of private interests—in this way they are precise representations of the selfishness lamented by Yan Fu and Liang Qichao more than a decade earlier. It must also be noted that for all of Zhu's satire of social arrangements that appear to be specific products of the new urban order, he is equally sharp in his critique of new voluntary associations formed for conservative purposes. The "Society for the Preservation of the Old Learning," for instance, is a group made up "primarily of the local gentry." Zhu continues, "[T]he rest were either poets or composers of traditional lyrics *(cike)* [i.e., *wenren* in Wu Jianren's sense of the term] . . . , and there was not one of them who was not a student of the Sage [i.e., Confucius]."[39] Once this group convenes, however, its principal purpose immediately becomes clear: a devotion to gluttony in which each member struggles to get a greater share than the others. There could hardly be a sharper revelation of the bankruptcy of traditional values, at least in their contemporary urban incarnation.

This general satire notwithstanding, the author does seem to make a distinction for newcomers to Shanghai from the interior provinces of Hubei and Hunan. In addition to the rube Wei Wenjin, one Ni Bohe, visiting Shanghai from his home in Hunan, presents a view of Shanghai through the eyes of an uninitiated rustic. He nominally comes to the city to celebrate the birth of a son to his nephew Ni Junren, but Ni Bohe concedes even to himself that "the reason he made the long journey was not simply for the sake of the small matter of offering his congratulations but because he had heard that since the time of the Restoration [i.e., 1912], Shanghai had become even more prosperous and splendid than it had been in the past."[40] Once he arrives, however, nothing turns out to be what he expected, and his visit ends up becoming one long farce. He is, for instance, bitterly disappointed upon being taken to the Zhang Garden. Since he had heard so much about it, he expected it to be a larger and more elaborate expanse than anything he had ever seen, and he has to be told by his nephew that anything on that scale would have been ruled out by the high cost of land in Shanghai.[41] Ni's capacity to evaluate the human circumstances that he encounters is invariably off the mark, and he is taken advantage of every time he takes any initiative. This is particularly true in his efforts to gain female companionship, as he repeatedly acts out a caricature of the country bumpkin meeting up with city sharpers. In this context, he becomes another Granny Liu visiting the Grandview Garden, one of the most famous episodes from Cao Xueqin's *Story of the Stone*.[42]

If his ability to evaluate the urban scene is always off the mark, Ni does leave one particularly evocative judgment before he flees back to the interior with his tail between his legs. Upon being taken south out of the Foreign Settlement into the old Chinese city, his initial impression is highly unfavorable: "He walked into the old city and saw the narrow streets packed with visitors, with peddlers crowding either side, their little stands so crammed in that you were in danger of running into them if you weren't careful. This was as far from the Foreign Settlement as the heavens were from the deep blue sea." The impression Ni registers here was one that was widely shared in this period among Chinese observers—both Shanghai residents and visitors from the hinterland. For instance, a leading article in the *Shen bao* in 1883 makes a long series of comparisons between the two zones that pivots around an extremely positive assessment of the Foreign Settlement. It eventually comes to a conclusion that invokes precisely the same cliché that Ni used to frame his comments: "If

The Shanghai of Zhu Shouju   245

the Chinese area is compared to the settlement, the difference is no less than that between the sky above and the sea below."⁴³

On being taken to the Yuyuan Garden, however, Ni suddenly feels a comfort that had eluded him in the crowded confines of the rest of Shanghai, whether the old city or the Foreign Settlement. As he seats himself in the pavilion on the little artificial hill in the garden, he muses to his guide:

> I think that the strength of the Western strip *(yangchang)* lies in its splendid display *(fanhua)*, while the strength of the old city lies in its subtle elegance *(youya)*. In trying to compare the two, elegance is of course not as sensational as display, although display is but transient, while elegance endures. If you consider it from the long-term perspective, however, you will realize that the old city is something people can take pleasure in, but the Foreign Settlement will merely be a place where people of a later time come to ponder past glories.⁴⁴

Aside from its eerie prescience concerning the post-1992 "Old Shanghai" craze in that city, this passage is one of the few places in the novel where the implicit pastoral alternative to the urban hustle and bustle depicted in the text actually emerges. For all the plangency of the image Ni evokes here, however, the question must remain: in what possible world can this more emotionally enduring place exist in a time when the overwrought Shanghai has been so clearly marked as the place of the future?

The extent to which the instability and evanescence of Shanghai's public voluntarism were imbricated with the vanity of theatrical display manifests itself most poignantly in the chapters that describe the so-called second revolution *(di'erci geming)*, that futile attempt by southern, or Guomindang, military units to overthrow the Beijing government of Yuan Shikai in 1913. As Zhu sets the scene in chapter 44, he describes the Guomindang as "[being composed,] of course, of a good many who are moved by righteous indignation, but also containing not a few who merely blindly follow anyone intent on making trouble."⁴⁵ The narrator immediately adds that the characters he will be tracking through the battle will be of the latter type, and he proceeds to tell a disheartening tale of the pursuit of personal financial interest diligently masquerading as patriotic fervor.

As the battle is about to begin, the southern army, for all the corruption at its core, overwhelmingly outnumbers the northerners holed up in the Jiangnan Arsenal by some twenty thousand to five hundred, so there seems scant prospect of defeat for the southern forces. The southern leader Li Pingshu is in the process of negotiating a withdrawal of the northern battalion from its besieged position, when, "like an unexpected bolt from the blue, another unit marched up from Nanjing to join the southern forces." The story continues:

> Its leader was Commandant Liu, the famously brave general of the early Restoration days, and as soon as he arrived, he advocated the use of force. The commander in chief also mulled over the notion that, considering how many troops and capable officers he had at his command, what harm would there be in annihilating several hundred of these northern soldiers in a single stroke? So he disregarded the painstaking efforts at mediation by Li [Pingshu] and gave the order to mobilize.[46]

General Liu and his troop seem to be a conspicuous exception to the general moral squalor on exhibit during the formation of the southern armies. The sight of this well-ordered unit is an inspiration even for the cynical captain Song Shiren, who serves as narrative focalizer at this point in the tale. Song catches sight of Liu's forces just a few hours before the attack of the southern armies on the arsenal is about to begin, and he is suitably impressed:

> As [Song] passed through the West Gate, [he] saw a newly arrived unit of the Liu forces shouldering their rifles as they marched along the road. The unit extended back for several hundred meters, in neat gray uniforms and in good order, with brightly polished equipment. Commandant Liu was mounted on his horse and carrying his sword, as awe inspiring as the iron tower he seemed to be emulating. When Song Shiren saw that this was the type of unit backing them up, he immediately took heart, his courage increasing a hundred times . . . .[47]

As readers have reason to expect after so many previous accounts of plans gone awry, the first attack of the southern army on the arsenal is a dismal failure, although the physical damage to the attackers is remediable. Somewhat strangely, however, "the Liu force that had come as a backup and was grouped outside the West Gate, while still formidable in its array, had not dispatched a single soldier the whole time." An explanation is immediately provided: "When [the Liu forces] later received reports of the defeat of the southern armies, they became even more reluctant to enter the battlefield. They waited instead for the northern troops to attack the West Gate, at which point the Liu forces would engage them in a battle to the death."[48] Throughout the pages that describe the preparation of the demoralized southern forces for the second day of battle and their eventual defeat even after some early successes, readers are provided with periodic glimpses of the Liu forces, always well turned out, and always well out of the line of fire.

At the end of the day, however, the Liu forces are exposed:

> The popular force *(minjun)* had turned victory into defeat, and over half its troops were either casualties or had run off. The Liu forces, having

received news about the initial success of the popular forces, had struck camp and moved up, only to be broken up by a combination of the fleeing southern troops and the cannon fire of the northern garrison. The cannon fire hit them so hard that they were deserted by their courage, turned around, and fled for their lives. They ran all the way to the French Bund, where they were stopped only by the guards at the French Concession, at which point they took stock and realized the full extent of their losses. It was only then that people become aware that the Liu force was but a sorry facade.[49]

The spectral Liu force, hovering at the edges of the battlefield for so many hours and being perceived as nothing so much as the guardian angel of the southern army, is finally revealed as just another fraud, even if slightly more elaborate. It had proved spectacularly convincing in its brief moment of sparkling theatricality but ultimately showed itself to be as lacking in legitimate organizational capacity as any of the other voluntary associations depicted in the novel.

A Novel of Resistance?

In coming to grips with *The Shanghai Tide* as a whole, it is important to avoid reading the work as a simple representation of pure gloom. As Meng Yue has suggested in her pioneering work on late Qing and early Republican magazines, there is a deep playfulness at work in the Shanghai culture of this period, a playfulness that persists in mocking the constant sense of crisis that dogs modern China.[50] For all the dire words of instruction presented in the novel, the constant layering of ironies both high and low undermines the solemnity of tone. Like the transience of the "foreign" city at Shanghai witnessed by the character Ni Bohe, *The Shanghai Tide*'s bitter satire of the new urban lifestyle is leavened by a presentiment that what is being observed is ultimately evanescent. This sense of impermanence is augmented by the novel's abrupt finale, in which a tidal surge of the Huangpu River (i.e., the *"xiepu"* of the title) floods the city, sending the characters to their homes and "just happening" to provide for the author an occasion to "wash the filth off my pen and rinse out a mouthful of wrongdoing."[51]

In attempting to analyze the source of this bitter and subverting mockery, it is tempting to tease out a parallel with Homi Bhabha's notion of mimicry:

> [T]he discourse of mimicry is constructed around an *ambivalence;* in order to be effective, mimicry must continually produce its slippage, its excess, its difference. The authority of that mode of colonial discourse that I have called mimicry is therefore stricken by an indeterminacy: mimicry

emerges as the process of a difference that is itself a process of disavowal. Mimicry is, thus[,] the sign of a double articulation; a complex strategy of reform, regulation and discipline, which "appropriates" the Other as it visualizes power. Mimicry is also the sign of the inappropriate, however, a difference or recalcitrance which coheres the dominant strategic function of colonial power, intensifies surveillance, and poses as an immanent threat to both "normalized" knowledges and disciplinary powers.[52] (Emphasis in original)

We might see in *The Shanghai Tide,* in other words, a turning of the tables on the sober bourgeois morality that the Europeans would have as the necessary handmaiden of "modernization," as a later set of scholars would label it. But, as with many such acts of undermining, the play cannot help but be painful, reminding readers of the full extent of the predicament even as it mocks it. Perhaps the key variable here is the wild card represented by the term "colonialism," which, much as Bhabha tries to undermine it, in his formulation seems fixed as one term of the stable historical binary of "colonizer/colonized." As Michael Hardt and Antonio Negri write of Bhabha, "We should be careful to recognize the form of the dominating power that serves as the enemy (and really the negative foundation) in this postcolonialist framework. Power is assumed to operate exclusively through a dialectical and binary structure. The only form of domination Bhabha recognizes, in other words, is that of modern sovereignty."[53]

For all the foreign presence in Shanghai, however, the binary of colonization never quite applies there as Bhabha would have it: the colonizing other is always well offstage and presents its challenges indirectly, however insistent they may be in the long run. But the knowledge, the power, and the discipline remain, stubbornly, in indigenous hands, something that, ironically enough, merely intensifies the inherent instability of the mimicry of the offstage presence. Everyone feels the ineluctable compulsion to become the other, but, at the same time, that very obligation requires the construction of a rigid sense of self and other that must be thoroughly mocked to maintain even the hope of independent agency outside the paralyzing binary. And if this social and political mimicry does not deploy the full strength of its sardonic force even when it comes to represent events concerning desperately pursued core questions of the basic constitution of the nation-state, then the tantalizing sense of difference that enables even the notion of independent agency threatens to disappear for good. There is a cost here: Zhu's bitter mimicry renders any notion of agency problematic in the world of realpolitik, thereby threatening to make all action seem futile. In other words, the novel must continually undermine its own representation of the inevitability of unilateral progress in the Western mode as the only way to keep its options open, spectral and fleeting as those options must ever remain.

When analyzed from this perspective, the issue facing those who would try to understand the challenges of the early Republican period boils down to the conflict-ridden process of constituting the national subject. This, in turn, rests on the problem of how not only to create an understanding of the necessity of maintaining a sense of the indigenous even under terrible pressure to adapt to the ways of the other, but also to retain the capacity to imagine the possibility of autonomy in the first place. This agonizingly paradoxical responsibility perhaps lies just beneath the intense bleakness that surrounds virtually all of the book's satire. It probably also accounts for my being able to read only three chapters of *The Shanghai Tide* at a time without getting queasy and, more to the point, the positively visceral negative response the text has received from the post-1920 reform party and its many progeny. For if the immanent task facing any single person in those times of cultural crisis was to maintain the possibility of entertaining enormously challenging, complicated, and contradictory ideas, then refusing to take the ideas seriously may well be the most effective negation of an unbearable burden. On the other hand, the repeated scenes of personal dissipation that represent this refusal are, in the most profound sense, ultimately dispiriting. For those responsible for the future of Shanghai and, by synecdoche, that of the rest of China, to be able to deny the discipline of a new world order only by idling their days away in frivolous and self-destructive amusements is the single most damaging thing that they could do. That this damage is self-inflicted simply makes it all the more horrible to witness and harder to bear.

How, then, to take the measure of this massive and complicated novel? In its rich accounts of the varieties of human frailty it is, if nothing else, a riveting work, and one that offers all manner of insight and information about the Shanghai in that odd twilight period between 1912 and 1920, when the city grew ever fatter even as the national polity was so plainly dissolving. It is also an immense work of more than fifteen hundred closely packed pages, with any number of complicated characters and extraordinarily intricate narrative progressions; it will almost certainly never be translated out of Chinese or even read by many people who aren't either students of the period, the place, or both. And there are few enough of those, even in China.

One might begin by comparing this work with epics of the cruelty of New York society in approximately the same period such as *The House of Mirth* and *Sister Carrie*. It is, in fact, most interesting that there are no narratives of personal cruelty in *The Shanghai Tide* that come close to the crushing of the lovely Lily Bart or the incredible shrinking of the amiable George Hurstwood. Yet how is it that I can read the sadistic narratives in the two American novels, if not exactly cheerfully, at least without feeling the need to put them down in despair every forty pages? What is the source of the general unease Zhu's text has seemed so generally to inspire? Perhaps it is that few characters appear therein who are even remotely lovely or amiable. It seems that, whatever the power of the negations and critiques we can discern in Zhu's scheme, they require being represented through the gratuitous waste of human resources, people throwing themselves away just at the time when their interventions should matter most. These lives of dissipation—waking up only by late afternoon, hitting the opium pipe first thing, then calculating one's affairs and how one will get the better of those in one's social circle—betray the worst sort of denial of the potential of self-cultivation, even in the strongest Confucian sense of that term.

The Shanghai of *The Shanghai Tide* is contemporaneous with the great days of *Dongfang zazhi* under Du Yaquan's editorship. The rich variety of the pre-1916 magazine represents a buoyant optimism regarding the possibility of a relaxed hybrid of indigenous and foreign elements, at least in Shanghai. In the name of change, however, the New Culture group launched an ultimately successful challenge to this idea that ended up obliging Du Yaquan to move to a conservatism that he had never identified with before. In *The Shanghai Tide,* however, this process of adapting to the new and then denying the validity of the mix takes place not sequentially but in the same time and space, and perhaps that is the major reason for the novel's grimly claustrophobic atmosphere. As had been the case in the late Qing, when the novels that authors actually produced in response to calls to save the nation were invariably more problematic than the appeals that had brought the texts into existence, Zhu's epic mocks the urban milieu that enabled Commercial Press and its many magazines to flourish. It seems to take bitter pleasure in demonstrating that what Huang Yuanyong—to name but one example—might have celebrated as hybrid possibility was in reality bastard catastrophe.

In a sense, *The Shanghai Tide* can be regarded as embodying much of what Liang Qichao said about the novel in his bitter denunciation of it in 1915, the year before Zhu's work began its long serialization:

> Today the power of the novel has increased exponentially from what it was ten years ago, a fact that no one can dispute. It is equally clear that this fact leaves the greater part of society's lifeline in the hands of novelists. And what do we make of today's so-called novel literature? Alas, I can hardly bear to say it, hardly bear to say it! Nine out ten [novels] do nothing other than incite robbery and debauchery or indulge in frivolous writing that is at once scathing and inconsequential. . . . In the past ten years, the level of social customs has plummeted, and how can this not be

due to the instigation of the class of "new novelists"? If we continue to be inundated with these works, then in a few more years China will not be able to avoid sinking under their weight.[54]

This frenetic passage could almost have been written with *The Shanghai Tide* in mind, from the complaints about "scathing" writing to the ominous imagery of flooding. Of course, from our current perspective Liang is confusing cause and effect, as was his wont when discussing the role of the novel in society. But the larger question of the role of representing a polity in flux is not so easily dismissed. If the novel is the place where social undercurrents and desires are most tellingly revealed, then *The Shanghai Tide* forcefully shows the extent of social transformation in this period even as it expresses the anxiety that a monster has been created. Old and new end up simply discrediting one another on the pages of the novel, ironically—at least in light of all the later criticism of the text as being no more than a manifestation and reinscription of the worst features of the old order—pointing toward the critique by Chen Duxiu of the society in which he found himself subsisting.

CHAPTER 10

Lu Xun and the Crisis of Figuration

> "No fanciful sagas, now," they warned. "We're not here for a good time or to nurture new literary talent. Make up a story, and you'll wish you hadn't."
> Policemen to Fang Yan in Wang Shuo's *Playing for Thrills*

> One might say . . . that the practice of confession creates the metaphors of innerness that it claims to explore: without the requirement of confession—one might overstate the issue— there might be nothing inward to examine. In other words, the very notion of inwardness is consubstantial with the requirement to explore and examine it.
> Peter Brooks, *Troubling Confessions*

Lu Xun embodies many of the paradoxes of the past one hundred years of Chinese literature. Long accepted as the most important writer of the modern *(xiandai)* period following 1917, he was also extremely active in the cultural activities of the final decade of the Qing, which he spent mostly in Japan.[1] Being born in 1881 meant that his life straddled the great transformations that have been examined in the earlier chapters of this book. He was, however, born a good deal later than most of the figures analyzed in the earlier chapters of this book, and, as we saw in chapter 8, the pressures militating against maintaining an always fragile balance between ideas perceived as indigenous and those perceived as imported had grown stronger as he entered his career as a story writer. But the era of his birth also afforded him the distinct perspective of being remarkably conversant in both the Western and the Chinese intellectual traditions, in a way that even one so painstakingly self-educated as Yan Fu—a full generation older—could never approach. Lu's extraordinary learning and profundity of insight caused him to be regarded as a key member of the radical reformers gathered around *New Youth* almost from the moment he reluctantly enlisted in their ranks in 1918. He was, however, also virtually unique among the group of mostly younger radicals of that period in holding on to the "*jindai* ethos" and expressing significant misgivings about the nature and the process of reform from the very outset of his participation.

As his parable of China as an iron room from which there is no escape would indicate,[2] much of this reluctance to participate stemmed from his fear that any movement for comprehensive change was bound to fail in the end. Past commentators have, however, paid far too little attention to the possibility that a crucial part of his foot-dragging may have been rooted in a sense that, given the characteristic dispositions of both the reformers and their opponents, even if victory were to be achieved and change duly brought about, the victory would prove in the end to have been Pyrrhic and the change far from what was hoped for. Because Lu Xun was very familiar with writing from and about the West, his skepticism about the applicability of borrowed ideas to China is in its own way every bit as thoroughgoing as that of the late Qing novelists or even Zhu Shouju.

In a review of Lu Xun's first collection of stories published in October 1923, two months after the book appeared, the critic Shen Yanbing (Mao Dun) noted the exceptional variety of its contents: "In the Chinese literary arena, Lu Xun is often the vanguard in creating 'new forms'; of the dozen or more stories in *Nahan* (Call to arms), almost every one is written in a new form."[3] Given the sense of the crisis facing China that Lu Xun felt, his restless experimenting with the short story form should be seen as part of his effort to come to grips with a difficult situation rather than as an exercise in pure aesthetics. This is not at all to deny his commitment to his art, but rather to emphasize the complexities involved in his struggles to represent and thereby somehow bring to resolution the most vexing questions of his time. In fact, as his negative remarks on the late Qing novel in his history of Chinese fiction illustrate, he was mindful of what he regarded as the artistic failures of that set of narratives, and his relentless search for formal innovation may well have represented an anxious attempt to escape from those flaws as he set out to write stories of his own.

As had been the case with Yan Fu's realm of ideas and with Wu Jianren's narratives, among Lu Xun's stories and essays are many that work out numerous notions and modes of writing that have clear antecedents or, at least, counterparts in the West. In his struggle to shape these modes of figuration[4] to his own purposes, Lu Xun left innumerable traces that show how the linguistic and imaginative resources at hand, even at their best, could still not enable him to work out a vision of past, present, and future that was anything other than a source of ongoing torment. This is, again, not to gainsay Lu Xun's aesthetic achievement or the sophistication of his understanding of the materials he was working with, but ultimately merely to point out his inability to be satisfied with his own efforts—perhaps no writing of any sort could accomplish what he hoped to accomplish with it. This chapter will explore Lu Xun's deployment of some of his most significant literary figures and tropes and will attempt to show at least a portion of his intellectual struggle in trying to bring them to bear on a stubbornly resistant contemporary situation.

The Years in Japan

Lu Xun's remarkable series of four early essays, written toward the end of the period he spent studying in Japan, already gives voice to an exceedingly pessimistic mood. In his influential "On the Power of Mara Poetry" of 1908, he explains the heroic quality of the European poets of resistance he has labeled the "Mara School," a name taken from the Hindu goddess of destruction and indicating a kind of satanic power. Then he concludes:

> Now survey China: Where are the warriors of the spirit? Is there a genuine voice to lead us to goodness, beauty, and vigor? Is there a warm voice to deliver us from this barren winter? Barren homeland, without a Jeremiah to compose a final lamentation as a legacy to the world. Unborn perhaps, or murdered by the public, or both—thus China has become desolate. Only for the body have great pains been taken, while the mind faded into the barrens; the onslaught of the new overwhelmed it. "Reform," said the public, a voice that confessed its habitual wrongdoing, as if to say, "We repent." Along with reform came the birth of hope; as we expected, scholars introduced modern culture. But after a decade of incessant introduction, consider what they've been coming back with: nothing, aside from how to manufacture cake and guard prisons. In China, perennially desolate, a second call for reform is virtually certain yet to come, given past history.[5]

With this utterance, Lu Xun sounds a characteristic late Qing note[6] that can be traced back to Liang Qichao's first article advocating the utility of the novel, which was published in 1898 and is discussed in chapter 4. Although Lu Xun has announced the power of heroic literature over the course of his essay, he concludes by lamenting the virtual absence of such a literature from China (at least since the demise of Qu Yuan two thousand years before). The root cause of this absence seems to be a lack of strong, individual voices capable of delivering the sort of jeremiad that could overcome a profound inertia.

For all the pessimism that Lu Xun voices here, equally significant is his apparent confidence—based, no doubt, on his firm conviction of the ineluctability of social evolution—that "a second call for reform" is bound to come, sooner or later. Presumably this new call for renewal will be vitally dependent upon a literary activism set in motion by an awakened set of individual voices. Such activism is easy to assume, given his view that reforms restricted to the material realm—as embodied in his mordant summary of that realm as "manufacturing cake and guarding prisons"—could not lead to any substantial improvements. There is every reason to believe that Lu Xun during his time in Japan regarded literature as the basic vehicle for any such spiritual reform, even if we consider only the retrospective account of his activities and development there in his 1922 preface to *Call to Arms*: "[I]t doesn't really matter how many of [the people of a poor and backward country] die of illness. The most important thing for us is to change their spirit, and since the best thing to change the spirit was of course (or so I thought at the time) literature, I therefore thought to promote a literary movement."[7]

This sense of a need for a new departure is expressed even more clearly in "On Cultural Extremes" ("Wenhua pianzhi lun"), an essay published shortly before "Mara Poetry." In the former article, Lu Xun extensively and approvingly cites nineteenth-century European thinkers like Ibsen, Kierkegaard, Nietzsche, and Stirner in support of an activist spirituality. Lu Xun argues that late Qing China had been misled by the fallacious idea that fundamental reform could be brought about by attending only to the material and utilitarian externals of nineteenth-century European economic development. He couples this to what Lung-kee Sun has called a "proto-modernist" idea—that the true genius of modern Europe lies in notions of radical individualism advanced by the thinkers Lu Xun cites to counter the all-pervasive materialism brought about by economic growth.[8] A persistent denunciation of materialism and mass society in favor of a notion of the vital role of a transcendent individual subjectivity runs insistently through the whole text of "Cultural Extremes": "Only those who are resolute and steadfast, and who can remain unmoved even when they encounter external [obstacles] can provide anchors for society . . . [and the enervated masses] can look to [such] men of determined will to provide the core of leadership in the future."[9] This praise for the power of subjective judgment brings about a consequential contempt for the meager competence of the crowd. After citing the public condemnation of Brutus and Christ as examples, for instance, Lu Xun concludes, "Therefore, right and wrong cannot be adjudicated by the masses; any adjudication by the masses will bring about incorrect results. [Neither] can political affairs be adjudicated by the masses, for their standards are inequitable and will not lead to happy results."[10]

There can be little doubt that Wang Hui is correct about this essay when he writes, "Lu Xun takes the structure of subjectivity as the only basis for his historical critique of society; he thereby takes the individual subjective consciousness as the foundation for the blueprints of his plans for national and social liberation."[11] For all the rhetorical flourish that Lu Xun brings to bear in this essay, however, a number of obvious contradictions protrude from the deceptively smooth surface of the discourse. The most glaring reveals itself in his conclusion that, should the reformist attitudes he advocates be adopted in China, "the people of our nation will attain self-awareness, their individuality will flourish, and this country that is now a heap of loose sand will become a nation of true human beings."[12] What could have been the source of this sudden ability of the entire population to gain the sort of awareness that Lu Xun had previously viewed as the exclusive property of the discerning few? There seems to be here a slippage here between what Wang Hui has identified as two quite distinct strains of individualism: that which regards all individuals as equal and that which stresses the rights of particular persons.[13] At the end of his essay Lu Xun appears to conflate the two, evidently generalizing the Nietzschean notion of rights pertaining to the superior individual to the whole population of a reimagined China. In the final analysis, perhaps, Lu Xun seems unable to bring himself to limit possession of the liberated subjectivities he describes in such fine detail to a specific subset of Übermenschen.

Part of the contradiction between the divergent ideas of individuality here can probably be best explained by resort to the weak sense of the ontological position of the individual in the Chinese revolutionary discourse of the time. For instance, Zhang Binglin, Lu Xun's acknowledged teacher and probably the leading radical voice of the day, had in October 1907 published an article in *Minbao*, a Japan-published journal of the contemporary revolutionaries, that touched upon the question of the status of the individual. Although the main point of this influential essay was to deconstruct the intellectual authority of the notion of the state by questioning its existence as an substantial entity, Zhang moves on, almost as an afterthought, to an analysis of the position of the individual in a cosmology heavily indebted to Buddhist ideas:

> One might ask: Given this [i.e., that all things other than atoms are constructed of smaller elements], since humans are also constituted of a combination of cells, how can they be said to have their own essential natures *(zixing)*? In response, strictly speaking, humans must also be called only factitious entities *(weiwu)*. In discussing humans in relation to one another, however, then they are all in a position of provisionality *(jiayou)*, and one cannot dismiss one provisional entity from the standpoint of another. If, on the other hand, the cells of one's body were to brazenly insist that humans were provisional, then a human would not

be in a position to refute this thesis. But in dealing with the nation-state *(guojia)*, the entity *(ziti)* [dealing with it] is not another nation-state but is rather a human vis-à-vis a nation-state. And while humans are factitious entities, they are rather simple *(danchun)* ones. In comparison with composite groupings [like nation-states], then, [humans] approach the [status of] the genuine *(zhen)*.[14]

Lu Xun's conviction of the illegitimacy of mass groupings was most probably influenced by Zhang's insistence upon the nonorganic nature of large political bodies, and both of the writers insist upon the right of the individual agent to offer a critique. In so readily allowing that the individual ultimately has no substantial ontological status, however, Zhang necessarily undermines the speaking position he is ostensibly advocating. In other words, a strong sense of individual agency is validated only in contrast to larger, even falser agglomerations, like the state. Thus any attempt at creating a powerful notion of individual agency must eventually run up against Zhang's confession that the self is not a constant entity. While this may seem a relatively minor concession on Zhang's part as he proceeds to undermine the power of the nation, when Lu Xun finds himself needing to construct a powerful notion of individual agency, the contradictions cannot, perhaps, be so readily set aside. If nothing else, this helps explain Lu Xun's paradoxical reluctance to set himself up as an individual authority, a reluctance that can be discerned even in his writings produced during his years in Japan and even more strongly in the years that followed.

This temporizing with the authority of individual agency is apparent even in the basic compositional mode of "Cultural Extremes": throughout a long piece of writing in praise of the power of the individual, Lu Xun almost never phrases any of his advocacy in his own voice. In the course of the essay, whenever he explains the rise of the powerful individual in Europe, he invariably cites Ibsen, Nietzsche, Stirner, or some other European as the authority for the perception. For instance, the full context of the passage quoted above is as follows: "Therefore, right and wrong cannot be adjudicated by the masses; any adjudication by the masses will bring about incorrect results. [Neither] can political affairs be adjudicated by the masses, for their standards are inequitable and will not lead to happy results. *Only with the appearance of the Übermensch (chaoren) will the world achieve its greater order (taiping)*" (emphasis added).[15] This final invocation of the superman reminds the reader that Lu Xun has not been directly presenting his own opinion but rather has been developing an argument of Nietzsche's in the preceding page of extremely dense classical prose.

The constant resort to the voice of Western authority here lends a certain irony and distance to what otherwise seems intended as not just a powerful statement of opinion but as a call for resolute action as well. Is there not more than a little irony lodged in the fact that this series of affirmations of the power of the subjective voice is almost never presented as issuing from the consciousness of the writing subject himself? In other words, there is inscribed here more than a little of the reserve and doubts about expressing strong views that come to be such prominent features of a number of Xu Lun's writings from the May Fourth period. Perhaps we can also see here, represented as clearly as we are likely ever to find it, the imbedded anxiety about adopting the voices of another historical tradition as one's own.

The careful structure of quotation built up here and the underlying tentativeness of address serve as constant reminders of Lu Xun's awareness of the foreignness of his sources. He clearly believes these voices speak to what the times demand, but he also seems determined to keep them at some distance, for which there may be yet another reason. The sense that the late Qing advocates of material reform had become possessed and emboldened by the ideas they sought to emulate runs strongly throughout Lu Xun's essay. In thus keeping the European at arm's length, he is perhaps also on guard against the possibility of becoming locked up in a new totalism of subjectivity as potentially dangerous as the one he is speaking against. Naoki Sakai has summarized Takeuchi Yoshimi's fundamental realization about Lu Xun: "[R]esistance has to be likened to a negativity, as distinct from negation, which continues to disturb a putative stasis in which the subject is made to be adequate to himself."[16]

The New Era

The new call to cultural reform that Lu Xun had anticipated did eventually come, seven years later, with the Chen Duxiu's founding of *Qingnian zazhi*—a journal notable for its focus on the need for a new individual consciousness—in Shanghai in September 1915. The iconoclasm that followed, in its determination to completely reformulate the horizon of Chinese thought, proceeded rather rapidly to simply deny the legitimacy of anything from within the intellectual regimes of the past. The radical voices that came to dominate the new journal were intent not so much upon denouncing any particular thinker or pattern of thought as they were upon announcing the theoretical impossibility of finding any validity or nuance in anything that had come before. Thus the *Xin qingnian* writers would have had to regard the elaborate moral nuance and awareness of the intense difficulty of choices that permeate the writings of Yan Fu, Zhang Binglin, and the early Lu Xun, if anything, as symptoms of the dread inertia of the old ways rather than as signs of serious mental engagement. One example of Chen's impatience with any hesitation can be found in his in late 1915 contrast between the European determination to engage in struggle as opposed to China's peaceable nature. He notes the efforts of the small nations of Belgium and Serbia at the beginning of World War I to resist much larger opponents, adding: "Their strength of character in resisting difficulty may be looked upon as a descent into madness by East Asian peoples; but if we could imitate them in even in the tiniest way, would the inferior *(liedeng)*, peace-loving, serenity-promoting, harmonious, and elegant East Asian peoples have fallen into the conquered position they occupy today?"[17] The radical force of the polemic of iconoclasm in the magazine was set out in some detail in chapter 8 and needs no further discussion here.

By 1918 Lu Xun had begun to publish, in *Xin qingnian* itself, writing in response to this radical call of 1915. The thoroughgoing iconoclasm of Chen and even the rather more thoughtful appeals of Lu Xun in 1908 can be seen, however, to have become muted by an undefined anxiety. The resulting hesitation is rendered most explicitly toward the end of Lu Xun's late 1922 introduction to his first collection of stories:

> So I finally agreed to write something for [Qian Xuantong/Jin Xinyi], and the result was my first story, "Madman's Diary." From that time on, once started I could not stop writing, and I would compose a short story–like piece to dispose of the entreaties of my friends *(yi fuyan pengyou de zhutuo)* until after a time I had more than a dozen of them.
>
> For my part, I thought I had long ceased being the kind of person who feels any great urge to express himself.[18]

It seems evident here that Lu Xun's hesitation had by this time extended itself even to the matter of whether he should write or not. It is not hard to see this as the logical outcome of the paradoxical combination of a firm conviction about the power of literature and a weak sense of his own individual agency as revealed in his hesitancy in 1908. Nevertheless, this reluctance stands in such stark contrast to the deliberate stridency of his peers as to suggest that new factors were involved.

The question of what occasioned this new sense of vacillation about the act of writing has over the years given rise to a good deal of speculation in the scholarship on Lu Xun. Lin Yu-sheng, for instance, in *The Crisis of Chinese Consciousness* set out the idea of a barely suppressed reservoir of commitment to the old morality. This created "a sense of guilt arising from the tension between two incompatible intellectual and moral commitments."[19] Marston Anderson in *The Limits of Realism*, on the other hand, argues that the Chinese literary world of the May Fourth period had an extravagant expectation regarding the powers of the newly imported literary idea of realism. Whereas for most of the writers of the "New Literature" this merely reinforced a predisposition to suffuse their work with a sense of political mission, in Lu Xun it occasioned a fine moral hesitation concerning the extent to which a writer has the right to represent human suffering.[20] In other words, if realism has the power to, as it were, legislate a new order, how far may a writer go in replicating in his created world the cruelties arising from the vicious stratifications of the old order?

In China a crisis in values followed the great reorientation of intellectual horizons after 1895, including an increased attention to Buddhist ideas. Given the essential fragility of the notion of personal identity that resulted, it is probably not surprising that a Lu Xun who was at least a decade older than the vast majority of those who began writing fiction after 1917 would remain tentative in the presentation of his own voice. Moreover, the effusion of subjective excess that marked some of the first-person narratives in the upsurge in novel production after 1902—such as the 1906 *Qinhai shi* (Stones in the sea), by Fu Lin, and the 1913 *Huangjin sui* (The money demon), by Chen Diexian (1879–1940)[21]—would have made (and did make) any serious writer wary of the dangers of literary self-indulgence.

A full reckoning of the ways in which Lu Xun's uncertainty manifested itself in narrative practice, however, has yet to be made. It is one thing to rely on the voices of others in announcing a general worldview as Lu Xun did in 1908, but in confronting the need to construct an entirely new set of fictional worlds, it is not so easy to take refuge in the constructs of other writers. I would thus argue that at virtually every level of narrative figuration Lu Xun was confronted with—or, perhaps more accurately, confronted himself with—an acute crisis of legitimization. In short, the combination of a tentative sense of the range of the individual voice, combined with a new notion of the power of narrative representation, created for Lu Xun a particular sort of hesitation when it came to the construction of his short stories.

In brief, the specific figural crisis I am referring to here consists of a systemic instability of the relationship between the means of constructing a piece of narrative and its possible referents in the social life of the period. Given the dual pressures of the general sense of fiction's authority, which dates back to Liang Qichao's writings after the failure of the 1898 reforms, and the fact that writers were caught up in the very social uncertainty they were trying to remedy, certain questions inevitably came up: would, for instance, writing in a certain way about society and the people living their lives within it have a kind of legislative power to reify the conditions being written about? If so, even if the author intended a critique of those social conditions, what moral burden did he assume by writing them up in certain ways? If, however, one was to assume that the novel could bring about dramatic social change, one had also to allow the form a wide-ranging power to intervene in social life. And what were some of the deeper implications of this notion for Lu Xun and his narratives?

This general crisis of signification makes itself felt at any number of levels in Lu Xun's stories. There are several narrative elements where the resulting impasse becomes definitive in shaping the author's fictional oeuvre, and they serve to contrast some of Lu Xun's narrative modes with Western ideas concerning narrative. One of these alternative avenues can be traced by examining an idea Peter Brooks develops in his important narratological work, *Reading for the Plot*. At one point in that work, Brooks, following Walter Benjamin, notes that "the meaning of a life cannot be known until the moment of death: it is at death that a life first assumes transmissible form—becomes a completed and significant statement—so that it is death that provides the authority or 'sanction' of narrative."[22] It is not hard to see the application of this idea to numerous instances in the Western novel. In the particular discussion at hand, Brooks takes Conrad's *Heart of Darkness* as his primary example. In that work, the structural importance of Kurtz, his death, and his deathbed vision of the "Horror" is something everyone knows well. The unremarkable nature of the structural imperative contained in Kurtz's demise is reflected in the fact that even to suggest some complicity in it or a sense of bad faith by the narrator Marlow (or the implied author behind him) can, as far as I know, be found nowhere in the extensive critical canon devoted to Conrad's novel.

It is precisely on a point almost identical to this, however, that Lu Xun places the main focus of his moral inquiry in a number of his narratives, or at least those in *Panghuang* (Hesitation), his second collection of stories, published in 1926. As Anderson has noted, the most prominent stories in this gathering feature "ironical mediating narrators" who "allow Lu Xun to posit the opening of a full critical examination of the social order and to explore its consequences."[23] In those works built around the death of a key character—almost invariably someone who is victimized by the normal workings of a cruel society and is, more often than not, a woman, by the way—the moral gnashing of teeth surrounding that death, as Anderson has noted, is extraordinary. As the summary remarks of the narrator in "Zhufu" (The new year's sacrifice) would indicate, Lu Xun certainly takes these deaths as foundational elements in the stories in which they take place. For at the very moment in the story when the narrator satisfies himself that Xianglin Sao is, after all, better off dead, he says: "At this point, however, the fragments of her life that I had heard and seen before that linked themselves up into a whole piece."[24]

As is equally clear from the story, Lu Xun also seems to respond to the idea of death as a structural imperative of narrative with an unmistakable shock and horror. His personal disinclination to see people sacrificed is expressed eloquently in a letter he wrote in 1925 to Xu Guang-ping (1898–1968), Lu Xun's former student and eventual partner, when he cites one of the grounds he assumes disqualifies him for a role in political leadership as "I am most unwilling to allow others to be sacrificed."[25] His stories bother themselves to the point of obsession with the question of moral responsibility for these deaths. Again and again these texts raise the disturbing question of whether the narrator/author will have to bear responsibility for killing someone off in order to become able to narrate that person's life with real authority. A constellation of issues hovers around each narrated death: how can one even entertain the possibility of the need for these deaths? Why would one have to? And, at the core, what might be the reasons for this sense of presumptive guilt? If nothing else, these questions contrast sharply with the ones Brooks raises about *Heart of Darkness*, which are all concerned with mimetic fidelity, as for instance: "The [key] question may then be whether Marlow can tell the story 'right' the second time around: whether the story that needs telling can properly be told at all, since proper telling may imply a conventional semantics and syntax that are unfaithful to Marlow's experience of Kurtz's experience of the heart of darkness."[26]

Karl Kao has pointed out that the key to the differences between the sort of issue Brooks focuses on and the obsessions one can locate within Lu Xun's narratives might be found in different epistemologies underlying the European and Chinese linguistic and literary traditions:

> Within the Chinese framework, where language presents the person (vs. represents the world) and knowledge is intended for moral efficacy (vs. for the definition of truth), reflexive issues could hardly be expected to be riveted on the question of mediation or the "relationship of fictionality to reality." With respect to both the premises of the expressive (presentational) theory and the pragmatic orientation of epistemology, the problematic will more likely turn up in the area concerned with the relationship of word and deed, with the moral and ideological implications of the agency.[27]

In this light it is perhaps no surprise that in Lu Xun's stories the question of whether the story *can* be told (and told faithfully) recedes before the question of whether it *should* be told, given the cruelties it will be obliged to body forth. The moral center of each story involving a character's death seems inevitably to return the focus to the morality of the narrator himself and then to the implied author behind the narrator. In other words, how much blame must the implied author take upon himself for giving finality to a particular construction of worldly facts by stipulating them to be so in his narrative? With this in mind, the concluding lines in "Guxiang" (My old home)—lines that critics have almost universally taken as the very emblem of possibility—may thus have a more sinister implication: "[Hope] is just like roads across the earth. For actually the earth had no roads to begin with, but when many people pass one way, a road is made."[28] In a China in flux between new and old, creating images of possibility through narrating them into being seems to embody the risk of actually bringing any number of monstrous creatures of the imagination closer to actuality. In one of Lu Xun's last short stories, "Shangshi" (Regret for the past), Juansheng contemplates shucking himself of the "burden" imposed upon him by his relationship with Zijun, a relationship he had exerted every effort to bring into being in the first place. Juansheng's elaborate fantasies underline the unsettling possibilities inhering in the imagination:

> Icy needles pierced my soul, sentencing me to a persistent, numbing pain. Life still held out many roads to me *(shenghuo de lu hai henduo),* and it came to mind that I still had not forgotten how to move my wings—the thought of her death suddenly occurred to me, but I immediately reproached myself and repented.
>
> Sitting in the public library, I could often make out a ray of hope, as a new road for my life stretched out before me: she would bravely come to an awareness of the situation and resolutely depart this wintry home . . . .[29]

In this chilling passage, the fearful destruction implicit in bringing the new into existence is virtually explicit, and it is linked ineluctably with death.

Thus, the narrator in many of Lu Xun's more important stories presents himself with a terrible choice. He may either "kill off" the old—and, he cannot help perceive, the people who inhabit that realm—by writing it (and them) off as something that urgently needs to be superseded. Or he may give the old regime continued life and thereby risk perpetuating it and denying the "second call for reform" that Lu Xun had looked to with such certainty in 1908. As Tsi-an Hsia wrote in his profound study of Lu Xun's morbid attitudes, "In his public utterances and creative writings, Lu Hsün did not seem to be so much horrified by death itself as by death as the symbol of a bygone age."[30] I would suggest, however, that it is the combination of the awful moral responsibility of having to "perform" death in narrative and the sense of death as symbol of overturning the weight of the past that confers upon death the particular intensity it has in Lu Xun's stories. In light of this, the absence of the subjective voice in "Cultural Extremes" suddenly seems as though it was the only way a younger Lu Xun could express ideas so prospectively disturbing. In speaking through others, Lu Xun could put off, for a time at least, taking a highly discomfiting personal responsibility for ideas that were ultimately to yield such devastating social consequences. In creating narratives, however, this responsibility for creating an individual voice to express his opinions could no longer be deferred.

Lu Xun never directly represents either the conflicting perspectives behind this omnipresent guilt in his stories or the China/West split that is a key feature underlying it. There is throughout the corpus of these texts, however, an unmistakable and pervasive sense of disconnect between the modern authorial/narratorial consciousness and other mentalities, necessarily of an earlier time, with whom he comes into contact. And as was so clear in the sharp debates outlined in chapter 8, "modern" means "Western" here, which was also the way the radicals of the May Fourth era overwhelmingly continued to define it. The emblem of this disconnect is the native who returns after so long that he feels himself to have no home; an automatic distance is established between him and everyone he meets, who are so carefully marked as also being remembered from earlier times. The writing voice is driven at once to anatomize these others, so as to understand why they have not or cannot become like him, but he is simultaneously tortured by a guilt that his act of anatomizing is a kind of murder. But whence, one may ask, comes this personal sense of guilt? Is not the "murder" actually the work of the cruelties and inadequacies of the old society? While the politically minded critic or ordinary reader may be content with this answer, the author/narrator constantly bothers himself about the nature of his implication within the old dispensation. In other words, as separate as he feels himself to be from the past, is he not bound to it in ways he cannot even begin to understand? And, in sorting through Lu Xun's conflicts here, one cannot, as with Yan Fu before him, pass over the complex exigencies of seeking refuge from the uncertainties of modernity in some sort of nationalistic identity, even as the substance of that identity must largely be denied.

Before consigning the figure of death to simply being the specter of guilt, however, we must first deal with "Ah Q zhengzhuan" (The true story of Ah Q). In that longest of Lu Xun's stories, the miserable eponymous main character can achieve consciousness only at the moment of his own death—a clown unexpectedly given the chance to "peep over the edge" and perceive of meanings he had never so much as imagined before. Even as he is presented with this insight, however, he is given no chance to make use of or even fully to process mentally what he sees at that moment. This marks the terrible inscription of the necessity and pathos of the death of the old. It lies at the point of juxtaposition of the horror that Ah Q suddenly can see, his inability to make out anything from it, and the final narrated inconsequence of his existence. Can there be any redemption in this? If so, what might redemption mean, and could it ever be worth the price? In Lu Xun's 1926 account of how the story came to be written, he seems to express the contradictions embodied in the character in the way he remembers how he decided to finish him off. One moment he seems to take the whole matter quite casually: "After about two months' work on [the story], I really felt like ending it, but I really can't remember clearly . . . [how I ended as I did]." Soon thereafter, however, he hints at a darker purpose: "Actually, the 'grand reunion' was not conferred upon him so casually as all that."[31] In other words, death retains its sting even in a setting that Lu Xun seems to be doing his best to render farcical.

There are thus dilemmas inhering in any possible representation of attitudes toward the past, as well as in the impossibility of avoiding the creation of painful nodes of plot in writing fiction. Given such dilemmas, one might think that the best way out of it would be to fashion ambiguous situations or narrators who temporize by steadfastly putting off any decision at all and thereby allow for a dispassionate examination of all the possible alternatives. Indeed, as I suggest above, this can arguably be taken as Lu Xun's motive in hiding behind the words of others in "Cultural Extremes." In the narrative world of Lu Xun, however, the moral demands of narrative seem to oblige a more direct confrontation of all major issues that are broached. In two of his most important stories, "New Year's Sacrifice" and "Zai jiulou shang" (In the wineshop), for instance, the dramatized narrator in each text quite explicitly avoids commitment by refusing to choose between two highly fraught possibilities. Ironically, this failure to choose is presented to the reader as the most cowardly and wrong of what turns out to have been *three* choices all along. This weak third option, whose craven nature is revealed only at the end of each story, presents itself as being vastly the worst thing to do in any possible moral universe.

In "Wineshop," for instance, Lü Weifu, the self-pitying old friend of the unnamed principal narrator, turns out in the end to be in effect shoring up the old by teaching material that was central to the curriculum of traditional education. The reader eventually understands, however, that Lü's behavior is far superior to the opting out of any commitments at all on the part of the primary narrator, whose smirking sense of superiority to the earnest Lü casts him in the worst possible moral light. The similarly unnamed narrator in "New Year's Sacrifice," while on the surface apparently taking a role of little consequence in the demise of Xianglin Sao, nonetheless manages to convince the reader of his culpability. More than anything else, this effect results from the fervency with which he repeats his denials that the poor woman has any moral claim on him whatsoever. The ultimate transparency of the falsity of his denial is most clearly revealed in his final expression of the conviction that she is better off dead anyway: "[T]hose who enjoyed life must have wondered at her for wishing to live on; but now at last she had been swept away by death. Whether spirits existed or not I did not know; but in this world of ours the end of a futile existence, the removal of someone whom others are tired of seeing, was just as well for both them and for the individual concerned."[32]

The irony in this statement stands out brutally even in its subtlety. By voicing statements that seem virtually identical to the thoughts of the people in the text whom he had initially found morally horrifying, the narrator reveals himself to be trapped between the near ineluctability of drawing such conclusions and the full dread of actually having done so. A famous passage from *Heart of Darkness* invokes a similar sort of irony: "The conquest of the earth, which mostly means the taking it away from those who have a different complexion or slightly flatter noses than ourselves, is not a pretty thing when you look into it too much. What redeems it is the idea only. An idea at the back of it; not a sentimental pretence but an idea; and an unselfish belief in the idea—something you can set up, and bow down before, and offer a sacrifice to."[33] By invoking the theretofore unthinkable notion that the noble ideas undergirding the imperialist enterprise are as fetishistic as any of superstitions it was pleased to think of itself as eradicating, Marlow suddenly reveals the full horror of colonialism: its cruelty is exceeded only by its hypocrisy. Even as he comes to this realization, however, Marlow at no point in this disquisition hints at any complicity on his own part. He maintains an independent position as detached observer, a secure subjectivity able to keep its distance from the horrors he observes going on around him. In "New Year's Sacrifice," on the other hand, Lu Xun's narrator exposes his own conscience as being finally no less concerned with his personal psychic comfort than were the inhabitants of the village from whom he had sought to distinguish himself in all ways for most of the story. At no point does he give any indication that he realizes the implication of his remarks for the position of superiority vis-à-vis the town's inhabitants that was an article of faith for him at the beginning of the story. Marlow, in other words, stands outside events as he passes negative judgment, a position Lu Xun's narrator is never permitted to achieve.

Guilt about one's role in manipulating characters caught in unfortunate circumstances, so evident in the treatment of Xianglin Sao, is one thing, but a similar anxiety about the propriety of creating utopian visions in general seems less easy to understand. This is especially true when one considers that, while external factors govern the dystopian regime that occasions authorial resistance, the utopian vision that would lie opposite to it would be, by definition, something arising finally out of authorial interiority, a zone that in Western narrative writing has generally been represented as an area of considerable freedom. Lu Xun, however, appears to bring to this particular subjective function the same sense of caution that he brings to other manifestations of the individual voice. The extraordinary manipulation of the working of memory in "My Old Home" presents the clearest case of this. To begin with, the most striking thing about the utopian longing that suffuses this text is its composition in a mode one would not expect to find in a literature of iconoclasm: instead of voicing hope for the future, utopianism in this story is expressed as a longing for a vanished past, which invariably presents itself to the narrator as incomparably superior to the fallen present.

The distance between the two is, in fact, at first represented as an agonizing difficulty in recalling the exact nature of those prior days. As the narrator says to himself while drawing near his native place after an absence of twenty years: "The hometown I remember is not like this at all. My hometown was better by far. But if you ask me to recall its beauty or to speak of its good parts, I have neither any images nor any words to express them."[34] Eventually his mother's mention of Runtu, someone he recalled from childhood, brings the memories flooding back with vivid definition: "Right then, a marvelous picture suddenly flashed into my mind: a round, golden moon suspended in a deep blue sky and under it the sandy verge of the sea . . . ."[35] Upon having this recollection, he sums up his feelings: "Now that my mother mentioned his name, it suddenly rekindled all my memories in a single flash, and it seemed as if I were able to see my beautiful home."[36] Immediately thereafter, however, he encounters "Bean-curd Beauty," another person from his past, but in this case someone he had not remembered at all until she rudely reminded him of her existence. The narrator's lapse of memory brings about a distinctly unpleasant meeting, for she draws bitter attention to his failure, as well as to the sociological implications of one of his status ignoring someone of hers.

This momentary dose of reality fades away with the news that Runtu has arrived at the narrator's house. The narrator looks forward to this reunion with the greatest of anticipation, but when the two actually meet, they are both tongue-tied, at least until Runtu breaks the ice by recognizing the narrator as "Master" *(laoye)*. This decisive declaration of social difference sends a shiver through the narrator, closing off once again the possibility of recalling the beauty of his old home. At the end of the story, hope is rekindled for a third time in the narrator's mind, this time while he is on the boat heading back to the city. The comfort on this occasion comes to him through his consideration of the possibility that the next generation might not fall victim to the cruelties of life in the same way that he and Runtu had. Given the disappointment that each earlier access of hope had brought about, however, the narrator immediately recoils from the impulse, saying to himself, "When I thought of hope, I suddenly became afraid."[37] The disappointments that arise out of the collisions between his nascent optimism and the ways of the world eventually seem to oblige the narrator to regard hope as a reckless subjective indulgence.

In short, each utopian projection, however foreshortened, is immediately stymied by an abrupt encounter with a bitter reality that renders any prospect for the implementation of change exceedingly remote. The ways in which the historical Lu Xun shared these anxieties about utopian projections with the narrators in his stories hardly needs to be remarked upon.[38] The complex examination of the possibilities and pitfalls of memory in "My Old Home" can be taken as a transparent metaphor of the author's own process of representing his own subjectivity. The devastating disillusion that overcomes that story's narrator each time he allows positive memories full play in his mind surely provides a privileged insight into the nature of the reservations Lu Xun expressed about committing himself to the act of writing narratives based on attempts at individual confession.

Authorial awareness of the delusions inhering in confessional writing has often been noted by critics. For instance, as J. M. Coetzee has said of what he takes to be Dostoyevsky's views on this matter as expressed in *The Idiot*, "Because of the nature of consciousness . . . the self cannot tell the truth of itself to itself and come to rest without the possibility of self-deception."[39] As Peter Brooks has commented on this process, Dostoevsky himself envisioned but one way out of the impasse thus created: "faith and grace . . . , punishment, penance, and ultimately . . . redemption." Brooks goes on to ask: "But about a world, or a writer, for whom faith and grace are not viable concepts? Is the confessional discourse without faith and grace condemned to being nothing but the sterile, unending unmaskings of the underground 'paradoxicalist'?"[40] Whether Lu Xun was aware of the comforts of the notion of divine grace is impossible to say, but it is probably safe to assume that even had he learned of them, he would have regarded them as illusory at best.[41] The fearful possibility of a sterile and unending cycle of confession and introspection, on the other hand, seems to torment him at every step of the way in the creation of his first-person narratives.

In the most general sense, Lu Xun's bleak vision of social alienation may at first glance seem familiar enough to the modern audience. Georg Lukács, for instance, in his early *Theory of the Novel* proposes that the novel form itself uniquely embodies a sense of the dissolution of a prior social totality: "[I]n all other genres . . . affirmation of a dissonance precedes the act of form-giving, whereas in the novel it is the form itself."[42] One can readily see how such an analysis might seem tailor-made for a story, told from a modern perspective, of an inability to reconstruct a past that has receded hopelessly out of reach, like "My Old Home." As Paul de Man long ago pointed out, however, Lukács's vision of formal dissonance is ultimately redeemed by a sense of the power of time to embody the meaning that has been lost, something that seems to be explicitly ruled out in Lu Xun's writings:[43]

> This victory is rendered possible by time. The unrestricted, uninterrupted flow of time is the unifying principle of the homogeneity that rubs the sharp edges off each heterogeneous fragment and establishes a relationship—albeit an irrational and inexpressible one—between them. Time brings order into the chaos of men's lives and gives it the semblance of a spontaneously flowering, organic entity. . . . Beyond events, beyond psychology, time gives [the characters in novels] the essential quality of their existence . . . [and] cancels out the accidental nature of their experiences and the isolated nature of the events recounted.[44]

If I may sidestep for the moment the question of the general validity of Lukács's notion of the function of time in the novel, it does seem safe to say that it is precisely such moments of transcendental temporal fusion that Lu Xun cannot bring himself to embrace. To cite only the case of Ah Q's sorry demise and the infinitesimal moment of enlightenment that preceded it, here Lu Xun almost sadistically mocks the notion of any salvation offered by the expanse of time. If Lukács's assumption of the redemptive power of time depends upon a sense of its inexhaustible supply, the fearful brevity of Ah Q's moment of consciousness demonstrates just how little time Lu Xun felt he had to work with. It is as if he is squeezed between a stagnant China and a (Western) modernity advancing rapidly into the future, in which the rush of time, rather than offering ultimate redemption, is itself the major source of anxiety. If calling attention to this fact is painful for Lu Xun, he stills feels it imperative to create a sharp and unbridgeable temporal break between the present and the past so as to be able to represent China's predicament. In short, however much he might have wished to invest reminiscence with a wealth of feeling, Lu Xun's evident sense of that past's dysfunctionality caused him in his hard fictional world to suppress any romantic musings like those of Lukács on the healing powers of time.

Lu Xun's experience is perhaps shared by intellectuals caught up in the squeeze between their natural affections for their home cultures and the pressures to "modernize" exerted by the example (and/or coercion) of the West. It is striking, for instance, how closely the musings of Indar, the tormented Oxbridge-educated East African Indian of V. S. Naipaul's powerful novel of postcolonial dislocation, *A Bend in the River*, parallel those of the narrator of "My Old Home." Indar speaks to Salim, his much less-educated friend of youth, in regard to coping with one's feelings about the past: "'You [must eventually] stop grieving for the past. You see that the past is something in your mind alone, that it doesn't exist in real life. You trample on the past, you crush it. In the beginning it is like trampling on a garden. In the end you are just walking on ground. That is the way we have to learn to live now. The past is here.' He touched his heart. 'It isn't there.' And pointed at the dusty road."[45] Of particular interest here is the contrasting parallel with the image that concludes "My Old Home." Whereas the narrator of Lu Xun's story speaks wistfully of trampling out new paths upon the earth where nothing had existed before, Indar is more forthright in seeing through to the inevitable demolition of any and all historical memory that must inevitably be a part of this move. In other words, the very past that at so many junctures of the story holds out the only possible source of comfort for the narrator must be ruthlessly paved over, both from Indar's perspective and from that of "Brother Xun" himself.

But for all the clarity with which Indar realizes what he must do, through the course of the novel he, like Brother Xun, can never succeed in tying himself off from memories that continue to call to him of a "beautiful home." Salim's practical-minded fiancée, Kareisha, describes Indar's torment, in the final time that Indar's name is mentioned in the text:

> ". . . He [Indar] had got a simple idea. The idea was that it was time for him to go home, to get away.
>
> "And that's how it has been with him. From time to time that is all he knows, that it is time for him to go home. There is some dream village in his head. In between he does the lowest kind of job. He knows he is equipped for better things, but he doesn't want to do them. . . . He doesn't want to risk anything again. The idea of sacrifice is safer, and he likes the act."[46]

Aside from the uncanny resemblance of this description to the character of Lü Weifu in "In the Wineshop," the passage also discloses a curious contradiction, which is that, for all his fixation upon his "dream village," Indar is, by birth and upbringing, a third-generation resident of an East African city. He can thus have no concrete memory of any actual village in which he has ever resided. Kareisha actually seems unclear even as to which continent this village might be on: is it in the East African country that is his natal place or the India that is his ancestral homeland? Although Indar can talk more boldly of the need to trample on the past than Lu Xun's narrator, they are both obsessed by recurrent visions of a utopian space. In Indar's case, however, the torment is perhaps rendered the more acute by his utopia's being purely the product of his imagination. He is, on the other hand, never subject to the disenchantment of the actual that befalls the narrator in "My Old Home" upon his revisit to the actual place that had inspired his nostalgia.

The Madman and His Discontents

If traumatic encounters with the imperialistic West form the evident material ground of both *Heart of Darkness* and *A Bend in the River,* the actual presence of specific references to the West are scarce in Lu Xun's narrative work. As I have attempted to argue, however, the figural presence of the West and its new ideas spectrally hovers over the construction of each of Lu Xun's stories. Only in "Kuangren riji" (Madman's diary) — Lu Xun's first story published in *Xin qingnian* in 1918 and conventionally regarded as the first work of the New Literature of the modern era — does the image of the West become considerably more palpable, though in the end it remains only an abstraction. It is nonetheless an abstraction that carries an immense discursive weight, being all the heavier precisely because of the vagueness of the reference to it. The embedded nature of the "absent cause" of an anxiety occasioned by the coming of the West is even more striking when the basic material of the story is taken into account: it is, as J. D. Chinnery has observed, a narrative built on a careful awareness of the behavior of a clear schizophrenic, the sort of character who would not generally overlook any potential source of threats to his person.[47]

"Madman's Diary," told in diary form in thirteen mostly short segments following a brief introduction by a friend of the diary's writer, develops as an extended metaphor of the cruelty of traditional Chinese society. Taking as its central image the figure of cannibalism, the story clearly marks itself as a highly critical account of the Chinese past, but one formulated as being immanent within the tradition itself. All specific references in the text — from the mention of history books as being everywhere overwritten by "virtue and morality" *(renyi daode)* to the invocation of figures from Chinese history and the classics, like Yi Ya, a man of antiquity who purportedly cooked up his own son to indulge his lord's culinary curiosity, and the famous pharmacologist Li Shizhen (1518–1593) — are to indigenous events and persons. Even the references to Xu Xilin, a revolutionary anarchist executed in 1907, and to "four thousand years of history" serve to specify the story and to bring it down almost to the date of its composition.

The narrative's move into an evolutionary discourse in section 10, however, suddenly hints at a set of ideas beyond the ken of the local framework of the earlier sections. The narrator underscores this reference when he admonishes his older brother: "Brother, probably all barbaric peoples *(yemande ren)* ate some human flesh in the beginning. Later, because their ideas changed, some stopped eating human flesh and, being intent on improving themselves, changed into humans, real humans *(zhende ren)*."[48] The diary's writer then compares to beasts *(chongzi)* those who have "refused" to take this step, and thereby sharpens the contrast between the "real humans" and all others. The diarist goes on to draw his conclusion from an obvious social Darwinian point of view, including the following general appeal:

> "You can effect a change, a change issuing from sincerity. You must realize that in the future the world will have no place in it for those who eat human flesh.
> "If you don't change, then you will all devour one another. And if a number of you are still alive, you will be extinguished by the real humans, just as wolves have been exterminated by hunters, just as it was with beasts!"[49]

Much of the power of the allegory contained within this story, at least to begin with, stems from the generally unambiguous metaphorical referents set out as the story develops: Chinese history has over its great length disguised its predatory nature with false expressions of morality, and anyone—in this case, the "madman" himself—who has the temerity to point out the obvious will be threatened with the most extreme ostracism. Indeed, as Wang Xiaoming has noted, Lu Xun is generally inclined to be obvious about the meanings of the figures he employs:

> [The symbolic figures just enumerated] are clearly purposeful designs, each one as clear as can be and instantly recognizable for what they are meant to suggest. At times the author seems to be afraid his readers will not understand the point, so he intentionally emphasizes the symbolic meaning of such figures. For instance, at the beginning of "The Eternal Lamp," he uses such inflated language to introduce the various hermetic characters that it is clear that he is pointing out to you that they epitomize the morbidly flawed Chinese people. He even uses narratorial comments as footnotes, as at the end of "My Old Home," where he is at pains to disclose the motive behind Runtu's taking away of the incense burner. If we can say that, in general, novelistic symbols issue from a powerful lyrical impulse on the part of the author, the symbols issuing from Lu Xun's pen are just the opposite, demonstrating just how deeply rationality imposes itself upon his emotions.[50]

The invocation of the "real humans," however, complicates this scheme by abruptly revealing the debt the general allegory bears to these spectral beings: their entry on the scene retrospectively reveals that what seemed at the outset to be a critique on strictly indigenous terms had all along been sanctioned by an implicit contrast with these more highly evolved others. The question then arises as to who these beings represent: is the allegorical scheme one in which humans in general are being compared with some superior ideal? Or is the scheme one in which the historical Chinese are contrasted with an equally historical set of more highly evolved people, in this case inevitably the same Western people from whom emanated the theory of evolution that sets the tenor of these final segments of the story?

The specificity of the rest of the allegorical scheme would argue in favor of the latter interpretation over the former, which, however, does not end the questions posed by this enigmatic text. For instance, was, then, modern Chinese literature—and the variety of new styles and modes brought into being to convey it—set in motion by an act of the most devastating invidious comparison? And are the terms of this contrast so powerful as to necessitate that all subsequent writing fall within its shadow, as Frederic Jameson's much-maligned essay on the omnipresence of "national allegory" in Third World literature would suggest?[51] As fundamental as these questions are, the deliberate vagueness of the diarist at this juncture in his text combines with the surplus of narratorial anxiety engendered by the overwrought tone of the story to render these issues as continuing sources of worried inquiry rather than as moments leading toward closure.

The interiority opened to the reader through these diary entries, a form universally signifying introspection, is drawn back relentlessly to analysis of the social terms on which it is based. It is as if the author will not allow himself the indulgence of wallowing in bootless rounds of self-examination, afraid from the beginning that there might be nothing there to discover. This forestalled interiority can be fully appreciated only by comparing Lu Xun's segment with the concluding section of the tale of a Russian madman by Nikolai Gogol, the namesake of Lu Xun's story. In Gogol's concluding entry, the narrator has a fantasy of escaping from the earth and sees a montage of scenes as he departs. He finally focuses on a particular house and asks: "And isn't that my mother sitting by the window? Mother, save your wretched son! Let your tears fall upon his sick head! See how they torture him! Hold me, a poor waif, in your arms. There's no room for him in this world. They are chasing him. Mother, take pity on your sick child. . . ."[52] The reference to the scene of the pietà here could not be more obvious; the promise of redemption offered by the mother suggests the divine overtones of the image, the same divine grace, in other words, that Brooks sees Dostoevsky falling back upon to provide ultimate salvation for his tortured characters.

Images of extermination of those who can't or won't keep up with the "real humans" haunt the final segments of Lu Xun's story: the fear and shame of the implications of modernity manifest themselves all the more powerfully for their having been muffled in tentative forms of representation. Thus, at the beginning of his short career as an author of narrative fiction, Lu Xun constantly signifies the quandaries inhering in the form he has chosen: the foreign origin of the problematics he finds himself involved with is a primary source of tension, and that tension is amplified by the structural inability to tie these elements into a unity that can definitively shape the questions themselves, much less provide any definitive answers. While these difficulties function like grains of sand caught in an oyster and lead to spectacular narrative results, the results themselves are constructed so as to offer continual reminders that the process of literary creation set in motion by these irritations was enabled only by real pain.

Afterword

The preceding chapters have in common the attempt to work through a few of the components of what most scholars refer to as the coming of "modernity" to China. This general historical process has been the site of a vast amount of research over the past fifty years, both inside and outside of China, and if there has been any scholarly consensus at all, it is that the process was never easy, something with which my study is in full accord. Beyond this sense of the pain and suffering of the period, however, academic opinion varies. I have chosen to focus on a particular set among the discursive possibilities offered by the period between 1895 and 1919 and have found that each one I have examined (plus who knows how many more) has carried its own charge of anxiety and inconclusiveness. Moreover, most of the ideas and texts that I looked at had in common a pervasive sense that what thinkers took as the Western way had demonstrated its superiority and that China, therefore, necessarily took a subordinate position. But once this conclusion was reached came the concomitant and nagging demands as to how each idea could be accommodated with its Chinese counterpart in any prospective universal spectrum of concepts, a universality demanded as integral to the conceptual process that enabled the invidious comparisons in the first place. The painful difficulty of this accommodation is the story of this book. It is the story of a process of hybridization be sure, but a conflicted and unstable mix with no ready resolution at hand.

The whole process did start, in the wake of the shocking events of 1894–1895, with a burst of a sense of possibility enabled by the decisiveness of the defeat by Japan, and the resulting feeling that all openings needed to be explored. The impression of potential was in effect enabled by the multiplicity of options that appeared suddenly on the horizon to those who thought they now had for the first time license to entertain seriously a full range of ideas from the West. Following the initial—if inevitably—tortured conviction of new opportunity in the period immediately after 1895, however, the continuing political weakening in China led to a progressive and apparently paradoxical narrowing of the perception of possibility in the years that followed. Options were tried and invariably found wanting—the differences in wealth and power between China and the Western powers virtually guaranteed failure, at least in the new geopolitical context. But these successive failures made irresistible the pressure to scapegoat that which had already been tried, and because indigenous institutions and patterns of thinking were most evidently extant in China, they became the target of blame. Given the tremendous influence of nationalism, however, something of the past needed to be affirmed, even as concrete examples of preexisting practices and ideas were denounced as a drag on the necessary hope for change.

This gradual constriction of the range of hope can perhaps best be represented by a comparison between Yan Fu from the beginning of the period under discussion and Lu Xun, writing toward the end of it. Yan Fu, at the start of his career as polemicist after 1894, perceived new opportunity as a particularly open field—everything was possible if only new ideas received the proper response within China. This openness, however, was occasioned by a new awareness of a wide range of ideas he thought of as having an exclusively Western origin, such as the notion of freedom and a sense of public spirit *(gong)*. But much of what he was declaring to be absolutely new turned out upon second thought actually to be robustly present in Chinese historical practice—something particularly obvious in the case of *gong*. As his blindness to that fact receded, his sense of possibility could only narrow. This was true irrespective of whether he compromised his sense of novelty by accepting the Chinese precedents for his ideas or, conversely, merely ruled out anything from the reform agenda that could be traced back to native roots. In the end, Yan moved toward the former course, while the latter remained the rebellious province of each new generation of radicals.

For his part, Lu Xun as early as his 1907–1908 writings—barely a dozen years after Yan Fu's opening shots—gives evidence of what at first seems to be a mysterious vacillation but turns out, upon closer inspection, to be a strict self-limitation. This hesitation becomes even more marked in his post-1918 work. The stark choice of accepting either that it was unlikely for any reform idea not to have some indigenous trace attached to it or that all new ideas had to be vetted such that all elements of the old be purged—the formula that Yan Fu put on the table and that all those who followed had to make their peace with—eventually emerges as the source of Lu Xun's limitations on himself and his hesitancy to indulge in overt advocacy. His sense of disappointment, evident as it is, is muted by the enormity of the choice he faced, and the upshot was that he ruled out any too grandiose speculation about future prospects. So while the madman's plaintive cry of "you should change, change from the bottom of your hearts" essentially echoes the optimism of the early Yan Fu, the more constricted context that had been created by the ongoing failure of any reforms to take hold, and in which Lu Xun was stuck, led toward portending the impossibility of any such redemptive change of heart. And once this impasse is realized, then the narrator in "My Old Home" provides the perfect symbol of Lu Xun's own reticence—if the chance that hope will be thwarted is so great, one had best be wary of embracing it too ardently in the first place. The result is a series of painful silences and withdrawals lying just beneath the surface of his narratives. He is acutely aware of these silences and of their cost to hopeful aspiration, and he duly punishes himself for them. In the end, however, he cannot allow himself to be more positive.

In between these two majestic figures, most of the study is devoted to a few of the major narrative works produced in the interim. Narrative form was the place where this struggle over the nature and definition of the "new" left its most tangible legacy. It is a powerful symbol of the age, posited initially by Liang Qichao and soon thereafter by those who followed in his steps as something new, but malleable and familiar at the same time. It was thus, at least theoretically, the ideal site in which to invest hope—by representing the novelty of reform possibilities but also being something deeply rooted in the Chinese mentality. Liang's writings demonstrate the inherent contradiction in his advocacy, but the urgency of the situation confronting China prevents him from recognizing the paradoxes he constructs, much less suggesting any way to resolve them. In other words, the explosive plasticity of the form itself seemed to offer the chance to square the circle by representing both what was actually there and where the future was supposed to lead. That this was easier to set out theoretically than to portray in convincing narratives shows, again, the intractability of the problem.

Although even to mention what follows risks falling into the teleology I am so intent upon warning against, it would be foolish to deny the legacy of this period for later events in modern Chinese history. Is not the Cultural Revolution, for instance, in which neither foreign imports nor legacies of the Chinese past are admissible, in some way a logical extension of the intellectual impasse already on display as early as Yan Fu's writing from the late 1890s? Does not literature throughout the rest of the century continue to hold out for itself the hope that it can represent the unsatisfactory present and the glorious future at the same time? Examples could be multiplied, but the point is that although the period between 1895 and the late 1910s in many ways prefigures the future, it still has a unique character that calls for its own standard of evaluation.

Joseph Levenson long ago outlined the theoretical advantages Marxism brought as solution to the intractable dilemma posed by the need to import Western notions of the nation-state and all it entailed, and the opposing but equally pressing demand of the nationalist imperative for something Chinese. The power of Marxism in this respect lay in its capacity to trump these vexatious questions, all of which revolved around the irresolvable issue of ultimate origins of the concrete histories of discursive formations. But the solution, whereby Marxism could at once originate in and be critical of the West, was durable only to a point, and it was not long before characteristic seams began to show through the patchwork garment that was Chinese Marxism. In the Cultural Revolution these problems broke through, and the Marxist "solution" has not worked well ever since. It therefore comes as no surprise that a number of Chinese scholars have returned to the late Qing and early Republican (or *jindai*) period to explore the diversity of ideas to be found there.

It is thus not simply coincidence or fashion that the post-1989 period has seen a stunning outpouring of empirically rich and analytically sharp studies from China on this period and its intellectual manifestations. From one perspective, it is perhaps only the security provided by the now substantial distance from the "semicolonial" that has allowed scholars the freedom to trace out the problems involved in such a clear-eyed way. A deeper purpose, however, is also at work. With the *jindai* period as the last age before Western intellectual paradigms started to drive the world of Chinese thought, scholars now look there for substantial alternatives to the much-bruited-about "end of history." As embodied by the work of such talented thinkers as Wang Hui, who has just completed a major project that attempts to critically evaluate scholarly traditions from before the great watershed of the late 1910s, this research proceeds not by ignoring the West and its ideas but by exploring the genuine differences between them and the indigenous notions that still flourished in the late empire and early republic.

Notes

Unless otherwise stated, translations of quotations are mine.

Introduction

1. Wright, introduction to *China in Revolution*, pp. 1–3.
2. Martin, preface to *The Awakening of China*, vi.
3. For the most recent example, see Gimpel, *Lost Voices of Modernity*, pp. 27–29.
4. Liu's words seem an uncanny echo of Lord George Macartney's characterization of China in January 1794, toward the end of the latter's famous mission to China: "The Empire of China is an old, crazy, First rate man-of-war, which a fortunate succession of able and vigilant officers has contrived to keep afloat for these one hundred and fifty years past, and to overawe their neighbors merely by her bulk and appearance, but whenever an insufficient man happens to have command upon deck, adieu to the discipline and safety of the ship. She may perhaps not sink outright; she may drift some time as a wreck, and will then be dashed to pieces on the shore; but she can never be rebuilt on the old bottom" (*An Embassy to China*, pp. 212–213).
5. Liu E, *Lao Can youji*, pp. 1–2. Translation from Shadick, *The Travels of Lao Ts'an*, p. 2.
6. Mao's full phrase to characterize pre-1949 is "semifeudal, semicolonial." For a concise description, see Hershatter, *Dangerous Pleasures*, pp. 7–8.
7. The Ottoman Empire is, of course, another example of this process, although its historical links with the West were vastly more substantial than in the case of China and Japan.
8. Cohen, *History in Three Keys*, p. 212.
9. As part of his effort to define neocolonialism, Philip Altbach notes that is "more difficult to describe [than traditional colonialism]," but he goes on to say: "[I]t does not involve direct political control, leaving substantial leeway to

the developing country. It is similar, nevertheless, in that some aspects of domination by the advanced nation over the developing nation remain" ("Education and Neocolonialism," p. 452).

10. See, for example, Jonathan Spence's recent *Search for Modern China,* perhaps the most successful comprehensive history of post-1600 China ever published. The second section of the book, entitled "Fragmentation and Reform," duly begins with 1840 but concludes with the overthrow of the Qing in 1911–1912. Of course, Joseph R. Levenson, in his *Liang Ch'i-ch'ao and the Mind of Modern China,* alerted us to this great transformation almost fifty years ago, and Mary Wright followed up by initiating a series of highly detailed examinations, but later scholars have tended to stay at either end of the continuum or to look at events in this zone as representing either continuity with "tradition" or, more frequently, the advent of "modernity."

11. Sakai, "Modernity and Its Critique," p. 477.

12. In an article generally dismissive of post-1949 Chinese historiography, Albert Feuerwerker notes the difficulties implicit in basing the periodization of national history on an event sparked by foreign intervention. See Feuerwerker, "China's History in Marxian Dress," pp. 26–27, 31–34.

13. A conspicuous exception is Douglas R. Reynolds' *China, 1898–1912,* a heroic attempt to provide the final decade of the Qing with a unique identity of its own. Even Reynolds, however, does not include the period between 1912 and 1919.

14. I will take up the first of the *ti/yong* question in detail below. Levenson's focus on the late Qing can be gauged qualitatively by the fact that pp. 49–129 of a 163-page text of the first volume of his trilogy, *The Problem of Intellectual Continuity,* is set in the late Qing (Levenson, *Confucian China and Its Modern Fate*). For a summary of Chinese views of the period as failure, see Luke S. Kwong, *A Mosaic of the Hundred Days,* pp. 2–4.

15. While I agree with Wang's findings in this important study of a profusion of literary diversity in the late Qing, I can't help thinking that the term "modernities" prejudges the period as being a backward extension of the overt desires to catch up with the world developed by the "May Fourth generation."

16. Schwartz, "The Limits of 'Tradition versus Modernity,'" p. 46.

17. Reynolds, *China, 1898–1912,* p. 1.

18. Wright, introduction to *China in Revolution,* p. 63.

19. Schwartz, "The Limits of 'Tradition versus Modernity,'" p. 46.

20. For a perceptive critique of the intellectual damage caused by such binarisms, see Wang Hui, "Contemporary Chinese Thought," esp. p. 157.

21. There was, for instance, the *Zouxiang shijie congshu* (Collectanea on moving toward the world), a series dating from the early 1990s in which reprints of important writings of late nineteenth-century thinkers were published.

22. The pioneering work on this movement is Mary Wright's *Last Stand.*

23. Xie, "*Xing shi congshu zongshu*," p. 3.

24. Hu Shi's extraordinarily tendentious *Baihua wenxue shi* (History of vernacular literature), in which he attempted to show that all Chinese literature worthy of the name was written in the vernacular, is one of the most conspicuous examples of bending history to a presentist agenda. That he only wrote the first volume can perhaps be taken as evidence that he had a hard time convincing even himself of the validity of the enterprise.

25. Yang Nianqun, *Ruxue diyuhuade jindai xingtai*, p. 5.

26. Duara, *Rescuing History from the Nation*, pp. 66–67.

27. Levenson, *Confucian China and Its Modern Fate*, p. 108.

28. Berman, *All That Is Solid Melts into Air*, p. 35.

29. On this term, see Lydia Liu, *Translingual Practice*, p. xix.

30. Ibid., p. 39.

31. The idea that modern Chinese history can be most fruitfully explored in indigenous terms was given its most careful justification in Paul Cohen's *Discovering History in China*. A more recent explication of this idea in a reform thinker's terms can be found in Xiaobing Tang, "'Poetic Revolution,' Colonization, and Form at the Beginning of Modern Chinese Literature."

32. This thesis has been advanced by Chen Xiaomei in her book *Occidentalism*. Chen focuses, however, largely on the period after 1920, in which a new dynamic had come to operate.

33. This thesis was given its initial currency by Edward Said in *Orientalism* (1978) and has given rise to an entire rubric of critical studies since.

34. On journalism's view of itself as vital to the reform effort, see Judge, *Print and Politics*, p. 7.

35. One of the best accounts of the centrality of Hegelian thinking to Europe's sense of its historical mission can be found in Robert Young, *White Mythologies*, esp. pp. 1–20.

36. See Hegel, *Introduction to the Philosophy of History*, pp. 94–95.

37. Williams, *The Long Revolution*, esp. pp. 28–40.

38. Readings, *The University in Ruins*, p. 70.

39. Moretti, "Conjectures on World Literature," p. 58.

40. Luce Irigaray, "This Sex Which Is Not One," p. 100.

41. Ibid., p. 106.

42. Butler, *Gender Trouble*, pp. 31–32.

43. Bhabha, "Signs Taken for Wonders: Questions of Ambivalence and Authority under a Tree outside Delhi, May 1817," in *The Location of Culture*, p. 119.

44. Reischauer and Fairbank, *East Asia*, p. 293, quoted in Ernest Young, *The Presidency of Yuan Shih-k'ai*, p. 20. The classic definition of the dichotomy is to be found in Levenson, *Liang Ch'i-ch'ao*, pp. 109–122.

45. Reynolds, *China, 1898–1912*, p. 194.

46. For instance, in *The Presidency of Yuan Shih-k'ai*, Young notes: "Admissions

of borrowing from Japanese experiences were understandably rare in the wake of the [1915] Twenty-One Demands" (p. 305 n. 82).

47. Zhang Zhidong, *Quanxue pian (Waipian),* "Youxue, di'er" (Studying abroad, no. 2), p. 117.

48. See Ernest Young, *The Presidency of Yuan Shih-k'ai,* p. 202.

49. Dickinson, "An Essay on the Civilizations of India, China, and Japan," pp. 71–72. Dickinson's perspicuity as an observer of the Chinese scene can perhaps be ascertained from his comment made no later than November 1913, in distinct contrast to the contemporary observations of many of his fellow foreigners, that Yuan Shikai "will not appear to history to be more than an astute and tenacious opportunist" (p. 72). On the generally favorable views toward Yuan held by John Newell Jordan, His Britannic Majesty's minister to China at the time, see Ernest Young, *The Presidency of Yuan Shih-k'ai,* pp. 169–170.

50. On the celebration of May Fourth as a powerful movement toward enlightenment, see Schwarz, *The Chinese Enlightenment,* esp. pp. 1–11. For the self-imaging of the May Fourth intellectuals, see Wang Xiaoming, "Yifen zazhi."

51. McDougall, *Fictional Authors, Imaginary Audiences,* p. 36.

1. China as Origin

1. For a detailed analysis of the history of this discussion, see Quan, "Qing mo de 'xixue yuan chu Zhongguo shuo.'" There was considerable satire of these views in post–May Fourth literature. See, for example, Lu Xun, "Gushu yu baihua," 3.213. In reading in his father's sinological library in preparation for a speech on Sino-Western relations, Fang Hongjian, the protagonist of Qian Zhongshu's *Weicheng,* encounters numerous absurd assertions of Chinese epistemological preeminence; see pp. 33–35.

2. Paul Cohen, *Between Tradition and Modernity,* p. 180.

3. Traces of the idea did remain, however, for a number of years thereafter. As I will show in chapter 6, one of Wu Jianren's most important novels seems to build from this premise, and the prominent jurist Xu Qian (1871–1940) was arguing as late as 1911 for the Mencian origins of democratic thought, which were discovered by Western thinkers only much later. Xu does not, however, posit a causal connection between the Chinese discovery and later Western development of the idea. See Judge, *Print and Politics,* p. 62.

4. Zhang Zhidong, *Quanxue pian (Waipian),* "Huitong di shisan" (Intercommunication, no. 13), p. 160.

5. For a concise account of the Kangxi emperor's scientific career, see Kessler, *K'ang-hsi and the Consolidation of Ch'ing Rule,* pp. 146–154.

6. Literally, "heaven-origin unit." Joseph Needham refers to this as "the unity symbol (I [yi]) placed at the left-hand top corner of the counting board before the beginning of the most important parts of the operation of [indeterminate analysis]." It first appears in the calendrical calculations of Qin Jiushao in

his 1247 treatise, *Shu shu jiu zhang* (Mathematical treatise in nine sections). See Needham, *Science and Civilization in China*, vol. 3, pp. 40, 42.

7. From *Chi shui yi zhen* (Pearls lost in the Red Sea), quoted in Quan Hansheng, pp. 218–219.

8. From *Kangxi zhengyao* (Key policy documents of the Kangxi period), quoted in Quan Hansheng, "Qing mo," p. 219.

9. The best account of the school of evidentiary research is to be found in Elman, *From Philosophy to Philology*.

10. See, for instance, "Ziming zhong shuo" (On the alarm clock), in Ruan, *Yanjingshi ji*, pp. 700–701.

11. Joseph Needham's attitude toward claims of Chinese origins is a good indicator here. He is more than willing to entertain Chinese claims to independent development of algebra (although he remains considerably more skeptical about claims of Chinese influence on the West), but he is abruptly dismissive of most of the nineteenth-century claims. See Needham, *Science and Civilization in China*, vol. 1, p. 48.

12. On the Gujing jingshe, see Elman, *From Philosophy to Philology*, pp. 124–125.

13. On Fang Dongshu, see Huters, "From Writing to Literature," pp. 77–81.

14. Feng Guifen, "Zhi yangqi yi," in *Jiaobinlu kangyi*, p. 197. Much of the remainder of this essay is translated in Wright, *Last Stand*, p. 65. Wright cites the 1885 edition of Feng's work, to which I have not had access, but she incorrectly gives the title of the essay from which it was taken as "Cai xixue yi" (On adopting Western learning), the essay that actually precedes "Zhi yangqi yi" in the collection. It is worth noting that in this text Feng in many ways demonstrates himself to be ahead of his time. Although compiled by Feng in 1861, this collection of essays circulated for many years only as a manuscript passed among reform officials. First printed in its entirety in 1883, it achieved its greatest influence in the late 1890s, with the Guangxu emperor distributing one thousand copies to high officials as part of the reform effort of 1898. See Dai Yangben, "Feng Guifen yu *Jiaobin lu kangyi*," pp. 2–3.

15. Edkins, *China's Place in Philology*, pp. xix, 11.

16. De Lacouperie, *The Languages of China before the Chinese*, p. 3.

17. Wang Tao, "Yuan xue."

18. An extraordinary and remarkably balanced eyewitness account of these battles can be found in Martin, *A Cycle of Cathay*, pp. 143–201. John Newsinger has a fine revisionary analysis of this war in his "Elgin in China."

19. For an account of the key events of these years, see Wright, *Last Stand*, pp. 12–20.

20. *Chou ban yi wu shimo*, Tongzhi 46.45a (p. 4499). Reprinted in *Yangwu yundong*, 2.24.

21. *Yangwu yundong*, 2.24. The set of memorials covering the 1866–1867 debate over the Tongwen Guan's curriculum is one of the best-covered events in

the English-language historiography of nineteenth-century China. There is an excellent account in Wright, *Last Stand,* pp. 243-248. See also Kuo and Liu, "Self-strengthening," pp. 528-531.

22. *Yangwu yundong,* 2.25.

23. The documents advocating reform were translated and published in the Shanghai *Court and Consular Gazette* and immediately reprinted in the *North China Daily News (NCDN)* and the *North China Herald (NCH).* A translated version of the court document submitted on January 28, 1867, for instance, appeared almost in full in the *NCDN* issue of March 12 (p. 2687) and was reprinted in the *NCH* issue of March 16 (pp. 43-44). Some indication of their impact—at least on Western educators—can be gleaned from the fact that John Fryer clipped later articles on the subject published in the editions of May 1867 and January 16, 1868 (before he went to work as a scientific translator for the Chinese government in March 1868), and maintained them in his files. See Bennett, *John Fryer,* pp. 22-23.

24. For an excellent study on Woren, see Li Xizhu, *Wanqing baoshou sixiang.*

25. *Yangwu yundong,* 2.30. The translation is my own; other translations can be found in Jerome Ch'en, *China and the West,* p. 429, and in Teng and Fairbank, *China's Response to the West,* p. 76. The empress dowager Cixi also echoed these sentiments during an emergency audience held at court in June 1900 to discuss official policy toward the Boxer rebels. Interrupting a minister speaking against the Boxers, she countered: "Perhaps their magic is not to be relied upon; but can we not rely on the hearts and minds of the people? Today China is extremely weak. We have only the people's hearts and minds to depend upon. If we cast them aside and lose the people's hearts, what can we use to sustain the country?" Quoted in Esherick, *Origins of the Boxer Uprising,* p. 289.

26. *Shi run,* literally, "to fail to insert intercalary months within the lunar calendar at the appropriate times."

27. *Yangwu yundong,* 2.45.

28. From Liu's *Yingyao siji* (Private diary of the journey to England), quoted and translated in Hu Ying, *Tales of Translation,* p. 1. This sense of complete otherness manifested by Chinese observers of the West was matched by Western observers of China in the same period. As J. O. P. Bland recalled in 1912: "[I]n our earlier geographies and text-books, China figured generally as a sort of fantastic topsy-turvy land, a land of pagodas and pigtails and porcelain, where people ate birds' nests and chow dogs, where merchants and missionaries struggled eternally with elusive mandarins, against a background of willow-pattern serenity chequered by periodic cataclysms. The Chinaman, as an individual, was regarded as a bundle of hopeless contradictions . . ." (*Recent Events,* p. 4).

29. David Pong in his *Shen Pao-chen,* p. 333, estimates that those in favor of technologically based reform in that body were always a relatively small minority.

30. Min Tu-ki cites a letter of Li Hongzhang's in which the statesman discussed a petition he made to Yixin in 1874, pleading for the construction of railroads. Although Yixin agreed that such a plan would be a good idea, he was ada-

mant that "there would be no one [within officialdom] to implement it." Min, *National Polity and Local Power*, pp. 65–66.

31. For a detailed account of these events focusing on Woren's role, see Li Xizhu, *Wanqing baoshou sixiang*, pp. 159–186.

32. For the specifics of Woren's relationships with young scholars, see ibid., pp. 173–78.

33. For more detail on how the Zongli amen reform worked out, see Mary Wright's accounts; Kuo and Liu, "Self-strengthening"; and Kwang-Ching Liu, "Politics, Intellectual Outlook, and Reform."

34. Ding and Chen, *Zhongxi tiyong*, p. 140.

35. This line of argument also was prominent in the new Shanghai newspaper, *Shen bao*. For some examples, in this case tracing Western ideas about popular education back to the Chinese classics, see Mittler, *A Newspaper for China?* pp. 163–164.

36. See Liang, "Xixue shumubiao houxu," p. 740.

37. It is important to note that Wang Tao, one of the first Chinese to attain a high level of literacy in both Chinese and English, seemed to change his mind on this question. In his writings of the 1870s and 1880s he voiced the orthodox view about ultimate Chinese origins (see Ding and Chen, *Zhongxi tiyong*, p. 145). In a later text, however, Wang takes issue with the notion that algebra was imported into Europe from China. For a translation of Wang's statement on this matter, see Paul Cohen, *Between Tradition and Modernity*, pp. 177–180.

38. I follow here A. C. Graham's translation of the term; see Graham, *Disputers of the Tao*, pp. 41–45. The idea that a diaspora of Mozi's disciples and theories lies at the heart of Western ideas of science and religion is most fully developed in Huang Zunxian, *Ribenguo zhi*, "Xueshu zhi" (Treatise on learning), as quoted in Xiong Yuezhi, *Xixue dongjian*, p. 718.

39. For the consonance of these works with the categories used in science fiction, see Ming, *In Search of a Position*, chaps. 3–4.

40. Actually, Jesuit writings of the seventeenth century had already had recourse to the flames of Qin Shihuang to explain the disappearance of any number of religious and scientific phenomena. See Hart, "The Jesuits as Missionaries of Science," pp. 28–29; cf. the claims made by Xu Guangqi (1562–1633) for the loss of Euclidian thinking in the Qin holocaust: "Xu's assertion of the loss of mathematical treatises and the decline of Ming mathematics was not an evaluation of the development of Chinese mathematics of which he knew little, but part of a theory that asserted the original meaning of the classics—lost in the burning of the books in the Qin dynasty—had been recovered in Jesuit teachings" (Hart, p. 38). For the Jesuits' arguments on the religious doctrines lost, see Gernet, *China and the Christian Impact*, p. 28.

41. There is a textual variant here. The 1894 edition in 5 *juan* says *"tiandi"* (the earth), whereas the 1895 edition in 14 *juan* says *"tianxia,"* or "realm."

42. At first glance, the *dao/qi* distinction seems difficult to differentiate from

the *ti/yong* dichotomy. As Min Tu-ki explains, however, "... the *tao-ch'i [dao-qi]* idea stresses the universal *tao* (that is, no specifically Chinese *tao* is assumed), while the principle/utility [i.e., *ti-yong*] dichotomy emphasizes specific Chinese values *(chung [zhong])*. Since *tao-ch'i* tends to center on an argument for the unity of *tao* and *ch'i*, it was easy for its advocates to accept Western culture and institutions as *ch'i*, thanks to the universality of *tao* itself" (Min, *National Polity and Local Power*, p. 85).

43. *Runwei*, literally, "interregnum."

44. Chen Chi, "*Shengshi weiyan* xu," p. 304.

45. On Kang, see Hsiao, *A Modern China and a New World*, pp. 409–435.

46. Wang Zhichun, "Guang xuexiao," p. 829.

47. This theme was also set out as early as 1861 by Feng Guifen in his *Jiaobinlu kangyi*.

48. This a remark attributed to Confucius in the *Hanshu*, based on the notion of cultural dispersal of the fruits of a central civilization to the periphery and the need to recover them from there.

49. Chen Chi, "*Shengshi weiyan* xu," pp. 305–306; the term *"da yitong"* is a New Text expression signifying the unity of all peoples under a more active Confucianism. See Yang Zhijun, *Wuxu bianfa shi*, p. 40, and Elman, *Classicism, Politics, and Kingship*, passim.

50. Zheng Guanying, "*Shengshi weiyan* zixu," p. 51.

51. Quoted in Ye, "*Youxuan jinyu* ping," p. 86.

52. Tang Zhen, *Weiyan*, 1.8b.

53. An allusion to the *Guliang zhuan* (The Guliang commentary), in *Shisan jing zhusu* (2.2392a) 7.28, "Xi gong er nian." The story is also in *Han Feizi* "Shi guo" (The ten faults), in Han Fei, *Han Fei Tzu*, trans. Burton Watson, pp. 51–52.

54. Zheng Guanying, "Xixue" (Western learning), in *Shengshi weiyan*, pp. 75–76.

55. In the 1920s, for instance, the poet-scholar Guo Moruo (1892–1978) asserted similarities among ancient China, ancient Greece, and Germany but discarded any notion of influence. See Guo Moruo, "Lun Zhong-De wenhua shu."

56. Xiong Yuezhi in his comprehensive *Xixue dongjian*, p. 722, notes the paradox involved here.

57. Sakai, "Modernity and Its Critique," pp. 476–481.

58. Xiong, *Xixue dongjian*, p. 723.

59. For Zhang's explanation of his thesis, see the extensively annotated version of his 1904 essay that introduced his *Qiushu* (The book of compulsion): "Xu zhongxing" (The origin of names and races), in Zhang Binglin, *Zhang Taiyan xuanji*, pp. 194–263. On the source of these ideas having been through Japan, see Bernal, "Liu Shih-p'ei and National Essence."

2. Appropriations

1. Zeng Pu, *Niehai hua* (1990), p. 15.
2. The best account of Yan's life and of his translations of English works into Chinese is to be found in Schwartz, *In Search of Wealth and Power*.
3. Hao Chang goes so far as to label this a "crisis of orientational order." See Chang, *Chinese Intellectuals in Crisis*, p. 8.
4. "*Sui*" roughly means "years old plus one."
5. The letter itself bears no date. For the reasons behind assigning the 1902 date, see Yan Fu, *Yan Fu shi wen xuan*, p. 155 n. 1.
6. Yan's quotation here is from *Lunyu* 19.23, a text originally posing a metaphor for the difficulty of comprehending Confucius' learning, sequestered as it was behind extremely high walls. Yan takes some liberties with the original wording, thereby stressing the aptness of the analogy to one who has never had the chance for an official position. Translation based on Lao, *The Analects*, p. 156.
7. Yan Fu, "Yu Liang Rengong," *Yan Fu ji* 3.516.
8. "Yuan qiang" had been significantly amended by the time it was republished in 1901. See Niu and Sun, *Yan Fu yanjiu ziliao*, p. 472.
9. The actual wording is "toward the end of spring in *jiawu*" (*jiawu chunban*), which would more correctly refer to early 1894. It is seems likely from the context, however, that Yan is referring to events that transpired in the winter of 1894–1895.
10. Yan Fu, "Yu Liang Qichao shu," *Yan Fu ji* 3.514.
11. See Mittler, *A Newspaper for China?* p. 166, for some of the complications involved in breaking with the old notion of Chinese origins of important ideas. As Mittler finds in her reading of *Shen bao*, it seems to have become safe after 1895 simply to declare Western superiority, but some examples from 1882 and 1892 say the same thing, at least when talking of education. The idea of ultimate Chinese origins, however, continues to be featured in *Shen bao* articles, as Mittler shows on pp. 163–165.
12. *Yan Fu ji* 1.1.
13. Although the slogan *"Zhongxue wei ti, xixue wei yong"* (Chinese learning as the essence, Western learning as the application) has been almost universally attributed to Zhang, the closest he actually came to this in *Quanxue pian* was the following: "the old learning as the essence, the new learning as the application; neither can be emphasized at the expense of the other" (*jiuxue wei ti, xinxue wei yong, bushi pian fei*). Zhang Zhidong, *Quanxue pian (Waipian)*, "Shexue disan" (Village schools, third essay), p. 121.
14. Yan's attack comes in a 1902 letter to the editors of the periodical *Waijiao bao* (Foreign relations), in which he is extremely abrupt: "The differences between Chinese and Western learning are as clear as the difference in appearance between the races. We cannot force them to resemble one another. Therefore, Chinese learning has its own substance and function, as does Western learning. If they are kept separate, they will both subsist, but if they are combined, they will

both perish. Advocates who insist upon wishing to combine them such that they become one entity, with one substance and one function, are simply not making sense. How can one expect that just by saying such things they can thereby be implemented?" ("Yu *Waijiao bao*," *Yan Fu ji* 3.559). A number of important contemporary voices also saw problems in this formulation. Even the Yangwu theorist Zheng Guanying, for instance, in his preface to his *Shengshi weiyan* expresses similar sentiments:

> Excellent are the words of Zhang Jingda: "Although their rituals, music and cultivation are all inferior to China's, Westerners in establishing their countries all have essentials and nonessentials *(benmo)*, and in gradually attaining to wealth and power, they have their substance and function. Educating talent in schools, discussing policy in legislatures, the sovereign and people being united, high and low of one mind, devotion to matters of substance *(shi)* and abstention from the frivolous, once a plan is established to then make a move—these are all the essentials. Steamboats and firearms, guns and mines, railroads and electric wires—these are all the functions. Were China to abandon the essentials and pursue the functions, no matter how we hasten, we will still never catch up. Even if we succeed with ranks of iron ships and have railroads going in every direction, will these be enough to rely on?" This discussion truly hits the target. ("*Shengshi weiyan* zixu," p. 51)

As Min Tu-ki has noted, "Principle *[ti]*/utility *[yong]* as a formula for modernization has generally been denigrated in both the late Ch'ing and the Republican contexts" (Min, *National Polity and Local Power*, p. 55).

15. *Yan Fu ji* 1.2.

16. The passage is quoted in chapter 1 above. Chen Chi, "*Shengshi weiyan* Chen xu," p. 304.

17. In a letter he composed in 1891, Kang Youwei stated virtually the same sentiments. In Hsiao Kung-chuan's paraphrase: "In China the 'Three Bonds' became the ruling principle of social life; in the West equality became the cardinal principle" (*A Modern China and a New World*, p. 535 n. 50).

18. *Yan Fu ji* 1.3.

19. Judge, *Print and Politics*, p. 63.

20. Liu E, *Lao Can youji*, p. 83. Shadick, *The Travels of Lao Ts'an*, p. 98, translates "*gong*" as "disinterestedness." For textual information on the novel, see Wong, "Notes on the Textual History of *Lao Ts'an yu-chi*."

21. One can note an immediate explosion of this new discourse on the disposition of "*gong*" and "*si*." An article entitled "Gongli shuo" (On public profit) that was published in the Shanghai newspaper *Shen bao* on January 9, 1897, for instance, devotes itself to showing how the pursuit of profit in the West is in the public good, unlike in China, where profit is strictly a personal pursuit. See Mittler, *A Newspaper for China?* pp. 144–149.

22. That the characters of young women in Wu Jianren's *Ershi nian mudu zhi guai xianzhuang* become the spokespersons for a specifically Confucian reform is one early indicator of this gender marking of ideas. See, for example, chapter 21, where the protagonist's female cousin gives him instruction on how Confucian verities need to be reinterpreted in modern times (pp. 149–151). The key text in redefining certain traditional cultural values as female is Liang Qichao's "Lun nüxue" (On female education), part of his influential 1896–1897 essay "Bianfa tongyi" (Comprehensive discussion on reform). For an excellent analysis of the genderization process, with traditional China depicted as female, see Hu Ying's introduction to her *Tales of Translation*. Note also Chen Duxiu's categorization of gender in his essay "Yijiuyiliu" ("1916"): "For all of humanity, men are the conquerors and women the conquered; Caucasians are the conquerors and non-whites are the conquered; among Far Eastern peoples, the Mongols, Manchus, and Japanese are conquering peoples and the Han are the conquered people" (p. 172).

23. *Yan Fu ji* 1.31.

24. Liang, "Xin min shuo," p. 113.

25. It must be noted, however, that this formulation seems to represent a revision of Liang's idea from only a year or two earlier—in 1900—where Liang had noted the value assigned to *gong* in Chinese thought, and the corresponding condemnation of *si*, as well as the importance of *si*, or self-interest, in the development of Western democracy *(minquan)*. See his "Shizhong dexing."

26. *Yan Fu ji* 1.26.

27. *Yan Fu ji* 1.3, p. 5.

28. As Wang Hui says in a slightly different context: "The point from which Yan Fu's advocacy of 'Western studies and science *(gezhi)*' is the pursuit of wealth and power, so his understanding of science *(kexue)* has a distinct utilitarian coloration to it" ("'Sai xiansheng' zai Zhongguo de mingyun," p. 73). For an English translation of this article, see Choy, "The Fate of 'Mr. Science' in China"; the relevant passage is on p. 21.

29. Here Yan makes a number of references to the Dynastic Histories: (1) "By the seventy years [following] the beginning of [Han] Wudi's reign, the country had no problems, and when there were no floods or droughts, then there was self-sufficiency for every person and family" (*Han shu* 24a—Ban Gu, "Shi huo zhi" 4, 4.1135). (2) "Wang Mang submitted a memorial that said: 'In the era of the sages there were many worthies in the country, so in the time of Tang and Yu [i.e., Yao and Shun], every household could be enfeoffed'" (*Han shu* 99a—"Wang Mang zhuan" 69a, 12.4089). (3) "In the time of Kings Cheng and Kang [of the Zhou, 1115–1053 BCE], the realm was at peace, and punishments were not used for more than forty years" (Sima, *Shiji* 4—"Zhou benji," 4.42, p. 68b).

30. *Yan Fu ji* 1.24. The critique of the contemporary West implied here is spelled out more explicitly in chapter 10 of Zeng Pu's *Niehai hua*, where the Russian "Pierre" explains the viewpoint of the Russian anarchists, based on an in-

terpretation of Saint-Simon's egalitarianism: "Contemporary people talk extravagantly of equality, but it is only a facade. If one gets to the truth of the matter, the real power in the world is mostly in the hands of the rich, with very little for the poor. The capitalists loom large and the working people figure for very little. Where is the real equality here?" (1990, p. 90).

31. On this point, see Wang's essay "Yan Fu de sange shijie," pp. 34–35:

> When comparing China and the West by explaining the features of modern Western thought, "China" is a negative image and value. If, however, one pursues the investigation more deeply, I also think that these "negative" images and values have already penetrated [Yan Fu's] understanding of the "positive West." This leads me to believe that Yan Fu's revelation of the premises underlying European thought of which the European thinkers were themselves unaware, such as the notion of collective strength and nationalism, cannot in fact exhaust the limits of his own thought. In the worldview constructed by Yan Fu, *there exist a certain logic and a set of values that directly conflict with these premises.* (Emphasis added)

For the idea that Yan reveals aspects of Western ideas that their originators had not noticed, see Hartz, introduction to Schwartz, *In Search of Wealth and Power,* pp. vii–ix.

32. The former phrase dates to the early 1930s and is primarily associated with Hu Shi. See Chow, *The May Fourth Movement,* p. 332. The latter phrase was coined by Lin Yu-sheng in his *Crisis of Chinese Consciousness.*

33. *Yan Fu ji* 1.49.

34. "Pi Han," *Yan Fu ji* 1. 34. Note that here Yan shares his conviction of the evils of post-Qin China with Chen Chi and the Yangwu theorists. See chapter 1 above.

35. *Yan Fu ji* 1.52.

36. Yan Fu, "Yi *Tianyan lun* zixu," *Yan Fu ji* 5.1320.

37. Ibid.

38. Sima, "Sima Xiangru liezhuan," *Shiki kaichu* 117.104 (p. 1232d).

39. *Yan Fu ji* 5.1319–1320.

40. *Yan Fu ji* 5.1320. Writing a few years later, Liang Qichao is considerably more explicit about the problems involved in claiming Chinese origins: "I despise the shoddy scholars who toy with words and are ever anxious to engraft Western learning upon Chinese learning under the pretext of introducing new things but who, in fact, want to preserve [the old ones]. They nurture a slavish spirit in the intellectual world." Liang quotes himself in his *Intellectual Trends in the Ch'ing Period,* trans. Immanuel C. Y. Hsü, p. 104; original in *Qingdai xueshu gailun,* p. 89.

41. Levenson, *Confucian China and Its Modern Fate,* pp. 112–113.

42. *Yan Fu ji* 1.4.

43. Hegel, *Introduction to the Philosophy of History,* p. 91.

44. Marx, "The Future Results of British Rule in India," p. 659.
45. Dirks, *Castes of Mind,* pp. 52, 82.
46. Martin, *The Lore of Cathay,* p. 388.
47. Ibid., p. 395.
48. Ibid., p. 8.
49. Bland, *Recent Events,* p. 1. For a sympathetic assessment of Bland's character that stresses his understanding of the Chinese situation, see Trevor-Roper, *The Hermit of Peking,* pp. 30–33. For Liang Qichao's similar comments, see Xiaobing Tang, *Global Space,* p. 36.
50. Bland, *Recent Events,* p. 2.
51. Ibid., p. 13. For a contemporary version of what is essentially the same story, compare Paul Cohen's account: "If, from the fact that Japan defeated China in 1895 and went on to become a world power while China continued to flounder in weakness, we conclude that Japan's 'response to the west' was rapid and successful, China's, slow and unsuccessful, we ignore a fundamental fact about modern Japanese history, namely that Japanese modernization had begun long before the arrival of the Westerners" (*Between Tradition and Modernity,* pp. 148–149).
52. Quoted in Tanaka, *Japan's Orient,* p. 21.
53. Liang, "Xin min shuo," p. 106. Translation modified from de Bary, *Sources of the Chinese Tradition,* 2.94. See also Xiaobing Tang, *Global Space,* pp. 25–26.
54. Chatterjee, *The Nation and Its Fragments,* p. 76.
55. Wu Jianren, *Xin shitou ji,* p. 52.
56. *Yan Fu ji* 2.425–426.
57. Yan is probably referring here to the arrest and cashiering of Zhang Peilun (1848–1903), the son-in-law of Li Hongzhang (1823–1901), and Li's nephew for peculation in sending defective ammunition to the Chinese fleet in the summer of 1894, during the early stages of the war against Japan. See Morse, *International Relations of the Chinese Empire,* pp. 33–34.
58. *Yan Fu ji* 1.30.
59. While the editors of the *Yan Fu ji* point out that these translations came from foreign papers both in China and abroad, it should be noted that the Shanghai *North China Daily News* and the *North China Herald* (the weekly edition of the *NCDN*), by far the most important foreign newspapers in China at the time, also carried extensive reprints from the foreign press and that were always labeled as such. In other words, just because a translation in the *Guowen bao* was cited as coming from a newspaper in Europe or America did not rule out its having been obtained from the *North China Herald.*
60. Yan Fu, "You ru sanbao," *Yan Fu ji* 1.82.
61. On Michie, see Britton, *The Chinese Periodical Press,* pp. 77–78.
62. See Michie, *Missionaries in China.* One indication of the lack of interest in how Yan felt about contemporary Western opinion of China is that Schwartz makes only two brief mentions of Michie in his book on Yan Fu, *In Search of Wealth and Power.* The Chinese sources are silent on the matter, and the translation by

Yan seems never to have been reprinted in any of the retrospective editions of his work published in the decades after his death.

63. See Zhou Wu, *Zhang Yuanji*, p. 59.
64. Yan Fu, "*Zhina jiaoan lun* tiyao," *Yan fu ji* 1.55.
65. Schwartz, *In Search of Wealth and Power*, p. 50.
66. Ibid., p. 240.
67. Qian Zhixiu, "Gongli zhuyi yu xueshu," in Chen Song, ed., *Wusi qianhou*, p. 57.
68. Wang Hui, "Yan Fu de sange shijie," p. 33.
69. Wang Hui, "'Sai xiansheng' zai Zhongguo de mingyun," pp. 71–72. See also Choy, "The Fate of 'Mr. Science' in China," p. 20.
70. Liang, *Intellectual Trends*, p. 114 (*Qingdai xueshu gailun*, pp. 100–101).
71. For Lu Xun's praise of Yan Fu, see Lu's "Suigan lu ershiwu," 1.295.
72. Hu Shi, *Sishi zishu* (Autobiography at forty), quoted in Greider, *Hu Shih and the Chinese Renaissance*, p. 26.
73. Hu Shi, "Dao yan," 1.3–4. Earlier in his career Hu had taken a more benign attitude toward Yan's translations, as in his 1923 "Wushi nian lai," pp. 24–27.
74. Fu Sinian, "Yishu ganyan," p. 532. Fu's criticism of Yan bears a striking resemblance to Zeng Pu's critique of Lin Shu, the famous stylist who rendered foreign novels into classical prose, without knowing any foreign languages himself. In taking Lin to task for not being more selective, Zeng characterizes him thus: "If we could remove those works [he translated] that are without value, reduce his tendency to translate all the work of one author, and add the representative works of great authors, *even if his translations were too free and thereby approached infidelity*, his achievement would have been more satisfactory than it now is" (emphasis added). Zeng also says in regard to Lin's renderings: "[T]hey will have no great influence on the future of Chinese literature. The guiding principle in translating should be to extend our own literary territory, and not to show off our own stylistic skill" ("Zeng Mengpu xiansheng fu Hu Shizhi," pp. 418–419.
75. Quoted in He Lin, "Yan Fu di fanyi," p. 238. He Lin is here quoting Zhang from his article entitled "*Shen bao* guan 'zuijin zhi wushi nian'" ("The last fifty years" of *Shen bao*).
76. Zhou Zhenfu in Yan Fu, *Yan Fu shi wen xuan*, p. 99. Zhou's notes to this text, which runs barely more than two pages, contain at least seven explicit refutations of Yan's "forced interpretations" (pp. 97–98).
77. Pusey, *China and Charles Darwin*, p. 56.
78. *Yan Fu ji* 1.16.
79. Schwartz, *In Search of Wealth and Power*, p. 36.
80. See ibid., pp. 70–71, where Schwartz points out how Yan had realized "[t]he wonderful paradox of the West . . . [,] that self-interest and the interest of the social organism reinforce one another."
81. Levenson, general preface to *Confucian China and Its Modern Fate*, p. xv.

The marginalization that I am referring to, however, lies in the rejection of any claims to the universal in Yan by Chinese thinkers who came after him, not in any sense in Yan's part of his own inadequacy. As far as I can see, Yan never hints at any regrets that he lacks what we would now refer to as discursive authority to reach an audience outside of China, which Levenson seems to wish to claim for him. One could, perhaps, just as readily detect a bit of projection here on Levenson's part: why must one be condemned to be but a historian of China, rather than a universal theorist of the general historical process?

82. See, for instance, the entries in Niu and Sun, *Yan Fu yanjiu ziliao*. Of the two sections that each occupy about half the book, the first is entitled "Yan Fu's Life and Literary Activities" ("Yan Fu shengping ji wenxue huodong"), and the second, "Research Essays on Yan Fu's Translations" ("Yan Fu fanyi yanjiu wenzhang"). There is no section devoted to his "thought" or general intellectual activity.

83. See Qian Zhongshu, "Lin Shu de fanyi."

84. Zhou Zhenfu, *Yan Fu sixiang shuping*, pp. 211–212. Note that on p. 24 of the same work Zhou sketches out a periodization of Yan's intellectual life. He categorizes the period between 1895–1899 as that of "complete Westernization," but this seems less than a good fit with many of Yan's thoughts in his preface to his translation of *Evolution and Ethics*.

85. See the examples cited by Quan, "Qing mo," pp. 221, 223, 224. Ding and Chen note the underlying pattern of this argument: ". . . in following out the logic of 'Chinese origins for Western learning,' it becomes a theoretical rejection of 'China is not as good as the West,' as well as a theory of cultural archaism, in which 'the present is not as good as the past.'" (*Zhongxi tiyong*, p. 151).

86. The architecture of this argument even coincides with the essential position of Song neo-Confucianism, with its claim of an interrupted *daotong*, or line of transmission from the sages that only thinkers starting with Han Yu (768–824) had been able to resume after a long hiatus. See Birdwhistle, *Transition to Neo-Confucianism*, p. 40. Daniel Gardner suggests another point in common between Song and late Qing scholarly motivation, namely resistance to accepting ideas of foreign origin: "Thus, Confucians stressed some ideas found in Buddhist teachings, but at the same time they were eager to reject any suggestion, however slight, that they had been influenced by the foreign doctrine. Indeed, that eagerness to reject such suggestions suggests how threatening they were" (*Chu Hsi and the Ta-hsueh*, p. 14).

3. New Ways of Writing

1. For the details of the *Subao* case, see Rankin, *Early Chinese Revolutionaries*, pp. 88–95.

2. Jiang, one of the editors of the State Historiographer's Office, after 1765 compiled this book from original documentary evidence to which he had access.

It is thus considered an early and authoritative source for official actions during the Qianlong period.

3. Dai and Zeng were both executed by the Manchu government for sedition. Zha died in prison after being sentenced on the same charge, his body being desecrated after his death.

4. Wang Fuzhi was a patriotic scholar who never gave up his loyalty to the Ming state and, in his scholarship, expressed persistent opposition to non-Han rule of China.

5. Zhang Binglin, "Dongjing liuxuesheng huanying hui," 1.269. A translation is available in Shimada, *Pioneer of the Chinese Revolution,* pp. 28–43, but it contains a significant number of translation errors.

6. Bergère, "The Issue of Imperialism," p. 270. See also Bergère, *Sun Yat-sen,* p. 98.

7. For an extensive list of this lexicon and a critical discussion of it, see Lydia Liu, *Translingual Practice,* pp. 259–378.

8. *Yan Fu ji* 1.126. For an alternative translation, see Schwartz, *In Search of Wealth and Power,* p. 34.

9. The locus classicus is *Lunyu* (Analects) 11.2. The four categories *(sike)* are *dexing* (virtuous conduct), *yanyu* (speech), *zhengshi* (government), and *wenxue* (culture and learning).

10. On the *Wanguo gongbao* and the Guangxue hui, see Zhu Weizheng, *Qiusuo zhen wenming,* pp. 62–95. See also Britton, *Chinese Periodical Press,* pp. 53–55.

11. Allen and Ren, *Wenxue xingguo ce,* p. 5.

12. See Huters, "From Writing to Literature," pp. 89–96.

13. The literary scholar Huang Ren (1866–1913) was the first fully to explain the European origins of the term. See his "Zhongguo wenxue shi" (History of Chinese literature), in Tang Zhesheng and Tu, *Huang Ren,* p. 67.

14. The Tongcheng scholar Wu Rulun (1840–1903) used the term in its older, broader sense as late as 1898, but as we shall see below, many other writers adopted the new sense of the word soon after 1895. Raymond Williams in *Keywords* (pp. 150–154) has traced the evolution of the word "literature" in English and found a similar change of meaning, from "letters" in general to a more restricted use for "imaginative writing" or "creative writing," occurring under the auspices of Romanticism.

15. Hsiao, *A Modern China and a New World,* pp. 97–122.

16. Schneider, "National Essence."

17. On the political side to this movement, see Polachek, *The Inner Opium War.*

18. This phenomenon was pointed out by Qian Zhongshu (1910–1999) in his 1932 review of *Zhongguo xin wenxue de yuanliu,* by Zhou Zuoren (1886–1967), pp. 11–12, cited in Huters, *Qian Zhongshu,* pp. 15–16. Recently Stephen Owen has explored the modern consequences of this in "The End of the Past," pp. 171–173.

19. See Huters, "From Writing to Literature," pp. 83–89.

20. These two phrases are almost invariably trotted out in any defense of the need for embellished writing. The former can be found in *Lunyu* 15.41, and the latter in the *Zuo zhuan*, "Xianggong" (Duke Xiang) 25.

21. Yan Fu, "*Tianyan lun* yi liyan," *Yan Fu ji* 5.1321.

22. For a brief summary of the May Fourth critique, see Chow, *The May Fourth Movement*, pp. 276–277.

23. Wu Rulun, "*Tianyan lun* xu," 4.144–145.

24. Ibid., 4.145.

25. Wu Rulun, "Da Yan Jidao," 4.151.

26. Hua Hengfang, "Xue suan bitan" (Notes on learning mathematics), quoted in Wang Yangzong, *Fu Lanya*, p. 39. This passage has also been translated by Wang Yusheng and included in his essay "Hua Hengfang," p. 380.

27. An excellent discussion of Lin Shu and his translations is to be found in Hu Ying, *Tales of Translation*, pp. 67–103.

28. Zheng Zhenduo, "Lin Qinnan xiansheng."

29. Lin Shu, "*Sakexun jiehou yingxiong lue* xu," 4.162.

30. Lin Shu, "*Kuairou yusheng shu* xu," 4.165.

31. Lin Shu, "*Zeishi* xu," 4.166.

32. On the post-1901 changes in the examination system, see Ayers, *Chang Chih-tung*, pp. 211–216.

33. Li Xiang, "Lun Tongcheng pai," p. 3b.

34. An excellent introduction to the history of the parallel style can be found in Knechtges, introduction to Xiao Tong, *Wen xuan*.

35. Huters, "From Writing to Literature," pp. 85–86.

36. The following account of Liu Shipei's life is based largely on the detailed biography in Zarrow, *Anarchism and Chinese Political Culture*, esp. pp. 32–45.

37. Wu Fang, "Liu Shenshu xiansheng xiaozhuan."

38. For a detailed profile of the *Minbao* and its contents, see Zhao Jinyu, "Minbao." This article is marred by the author's apparent determination to pay as little attention to Liu Shipei as possible.

39. Zhao claims that each number went through four or five printings and sold as many as forty to fifty thousand copies. Ibid., pp. 504–505.

40. This breakup is surrounded by any number of lurid stories about its nature and causes. Wu Fang, for instance, claims that He Zhen and her "lover" Wang Gongquan (described as her nephew by Zarrow, *Anarchism and Chinese Political Culture*, p. 34) poisoned Zhang's tea. See Wu, "Liu Shenshu xiansheng xiaozhuan," p. 404.

41. Martin Bernal claims that Liu Shipei had already gone over to Duanfang before he ever arrived in Tokyo, and letters turned up in 1934 supposedly demonstrating that Liu joined forces with Duanfang during a trip to China in December 1907. I follow Zarrow in his skepticism. For the evidence, see Zarrow, *Anarchism and Chinese Political Culture*, p. 269 n. 10.

42. Bernal, "Liu Shih-p'ei and National Essence," p. 104.

43. Ibid., pp. 101–102.
44. Liu Shipei, *Lun wen zaji*, p. 118 (chap. 10). Translation also in Denton, *Modern Chinese Literary Thought*, pp. 88–89.
45. Williams, *Culture and Society*, pp. 30–43.
46. Tan, "Sanshi ziji," p. 204.
47. See, for instance, Doležolová-Velingerová, introduction to *The Chinese Novel*, p. 6. See also Li Ruiteng, *Wan Qing wenxue sixiang lun*, p. 84. Li does, however, note the contradictions in Liu's position.
48. Liu Shipei, *Lun wen zaji*, pp. 109–110 (chap. 2).
49. Ibid.
50. For similar sentiments in modern Britain, see Williams, *The Long Revolution*, pp. 156–172. As Williams notes, "the argument about [literary] quality and the argument about democracy are here so deeply intertwined as to appear inseparable" (p. 158).
51. Li Ruiteng, *Wan Qing wenxue sixiang lun*, p. 84.
52. Liang, *Intellectual Trends in the Ch'ing Period*, trans. Hsü, p. 102; original in *Qingdai xueshu gailun*, pp. 85–86. The translation here is based on Hsü's.
53. Hu Shi, "Wushi nian lai," p. 32.
54. Qian Jibo, *Xiandai Zhongguo wenxue shi*, p. 337.
55. For more on Yao Nai and the Tongcheng school, see Huters, "From Writing to Literature," pp. 70–83.
56. Liang, "Sanshi zishu," p. 280.
57. Ibid., p. 281.
58. Paul Cohen, "Christian Missions," pp. 587–588. Cohen provides no source for this remark.
59. Published in 1850, this book is one of the first texts on world geography produced in China. For information on Xu and his work, see Hummel, *Eminent Chinese*, pp. 309–310.
60. Liang, "Sanshi zishu," p. 280.
61. Hu Shi, "Wushi nian lai," p. 35. For a rare positive assessment of the "eight-legged essay," see Qian Zhongshu (Qian Jibo's son), *Tan yi lu*, pp. 32–33. Even Hu Shi is quite tolerant of the form in this section of his essay: "To say this genre [i.e., the 'new style'] is influenced by *bagu wen* is something that many people will not wish to hear. In fact, however, to say this is not to be completely pejorative."
62. Qian Jibo, *Xiandai Zhongguo wenxue shi*, p. 338.
63. Note Edward M. Gunn's reference to Hu Shi on this point, in *Rewriting Chinese*, p. 305 n. 21.
64. Liu Shipei, "Lun jinshi wenxue zhi bianqian," 4.427.
65. Furth, "The Sage as Rebel," pp. 125–128.
66. Li Ruiteng, *Wan Qing wenxue sixiang lun*, p. 85.
67. See Galik, "Studies in Modern Chinese Intellectual History." See also Bonner, *Wang Kuo-wei*, pp. 102–110.

68. Wang Guowei, "Wenxue xiaoyan," 4.3780.
69. Bonner, *Wang Kuo-wei*, p. 92.
70. Ibid., p. 103.

4. New Theories of the Novel

1. On this new urban culture, see Bergère, *The Golden Age*, pp. 37–60.
2. See Cai, "Wan Qing xiaoshuo lilun chulun."
3. Yuan, *Zhongguo wenxue guannian de jindai bianqe*, p. 183. On Liang's relationship with the *shijie geming*, see Tang Xiaobing, "'Poetic Revolution,' Colonization, and Form," esp. pp. 248–254.
4. Wu Wenqi, *Jin bai nian lai*, pp. 28–31. Qian Zhongshu's withering account of the vulgarity of the result is briefly outlined in *Tan yi lu*, p. 24. See also Kamachi, *Reform in China*, pp. 178–181. Schmidt, *Within the Human Realm*, pp. 47–77, contains the most detailed account in English.
5. Yuan Jin, *Zhongguo wenxue guannian de jindai bianqe*, p. 183.
6. The best account of the Chinese novel over the course of the nineteenth century can be found in David Wang, *Fin-de-siècle Splendor*.
7. For the highlights of this text, see Huang, "Ribenguo zhi," 4.117–118. In his later years, Huang expressed his enthusiasm for fiction to Liang Qichao, but this was after the New Fiction movement was well under way.
8. For Qiu's complete text, see Guo Shaoyu and Wang, *Zhongguo lidai wenlun xuan*, 4.168–172. For the date of composition, see Li Ruiteng, *Wan Qing wenxue sixiang lun*, pp. 183–184, 202.
9. See C. T. Hsia, "Yen Fu and Liang Ch'i-ch'ao," p. 232.
10. See, for instance, Zhou Zuoren's assessments in his 1918 "Ren de wenxue," 1.219–225; a translation by Ernst Wolff is available in Denton, *Modern Chinese Literary Thought*, pp. 151–161. Note that while Zhou's condemnations are against Chinese literature in general, his specific examples are all from the realm of *xiaoshuo*.
11. Yuan Jin, *Zhongguo wenxue guannian de jindai bianqe*, p. 191.
12. John Fryer to Henry Venn, letter of March 8, 1864, excerpted in Dagenais, *John Fryer's Calendar*, 1864, p. 3.
13. Dagenais labels the letter from which this quotation is taken as being from Bishop George Smith (the Anglican prelate at Hong Kong) to Henry Venn and dated September 28, 1863. I think this is mistaken, as the letter seems to have been written by Fryer himself, and the date is almost certainly 1865. Given that the letter contains a reference to waiting in Shanghai for "the river to be open" before being able to proceed to Beijing, it was probably written in January or February. In Dagenais, *John Fryer's Calendar*, 1863, p. 1.
14. Fryer to Venn, letter of July 4, 1865, in Dagenais, *John Fryer's Calendar*, 1865, p. 3.

15. Venn to Fryer, letter of February 27, 1865, in Dagenais, *John Fryer's Calendar,* 1865, p. 1.

16. Fryer to Venn, letter of July 4, 1865, p. 2.

17. The best account of this scandal—to which I am greatly indebted—can be found in Wang Yangzong, *Fu Lanya,* pp. 13–17.

18. Bennett, in his *John Fryer,* p. 15, incorrectly identifies the newspaper Fryer edited as the *Jiaohui xin bao* (Mission news); Jonathan Spence in *To Change China,* p. 145, follows Bennett.

19. Fryer to Smith, Elder & Co., letter of July 31, 1868, in Dagenais, *John Fryer's Calendar,* 1868, p. 7.

20. Fryer to brother George, letter of February 6, 1868, in Dagenais, *John Fryer's Calendar,* 1868, p. 1.

21. For a highly favorably assessment of this organization in the 1860s and early 1870s, see Wright, *Last Stand,* pp. 211–212.

22. For figures and a description of the way the translations were done, see Wang Yangzong, *Fu Lanya,* pp. 33–38.

23. A good account of the founding of these educational institutions can be found in Bennett, *John Fryer,* pp. 46–55.

24. See Fryer's long report in Dagenais, *John Fryer's Calendar,* 1887, pp. 5–7.

25. Quoted in Yuan, "Wenhua yu xinli de bianyi," p. 35. The complete text can be found in Wang Yangzong, *Fu Lanya,* pp. 116–117. An alternative translation is in Dagenais, *John Fryer's Calendar,* 1895, pp. 7–8.

26. Yuan, *Jindai wenxue de tuwei,* p. 173. For a detailed account of the background of and response to Fryer's call, see Patrick Hanan ["Anonymous"], "The New Novel before the New Novel."

27. Chang, *Liang Ch'i-ch'ao,* p. 71.

28. See Bennett, *John Fryer,* pp. 43–44.

29. *Chinese Recorder* 27 (March 1896), pp. 142–143; reprinted in Dagenais, *John Fryer's Calendar,* 1896, p. 4.

30. See, most conspicuously, *Chinese Characteristics,* by Arthur H. Smith, an American Presbyterian. This exhaustive catalog of Chinese character flaws was published first in Shanghai in 1890 and in the United States in 1894. For many years thereafter, it appeared on basic reading lists as an introduction to China for the casual reader.

31. For a summary of the publishing history and reception of Bellamy's novel, see Yuan Jin, in Chen and Yuan, eds., *Jin sibai nian Zhongguo wenxue sichao shi,* pp. 340–341. See also Hanan, "Missionary Novels," pp. 439–440.

32. Liang, "Lun youxue," 1.51.

33. Chang, *Liang Ch'i-ch'ao,* p. 118. The text Chang is discussing is "Xixue shumubiao houxu," 1.740, in which Liang says that "one should realize that the various schools of the Zhou and Qin dynasties had already discussed much of the Western learning of today."

34. *Yan Fu ji* 2.439–440.

35. Yan Fu and Xia, "Guowen baoguan," 4.205.
36. Ibid.
37. Kang, "*Riben shumu zhi* zhiyu," pp. 13–14.
38. The profound influence of this article was first affirmed by A Ying (Qian Xingcun) in his 1937 *Wan Qing xiaoshuo shi*, p. 2.
39. Liang's identification of the long-lost *Yu chu* as the originary text in the genre is presumably based on the *Han shu* commentary by Yan Shigu (581–645), which cites "Western Metropolises Rhapsody" *(Xijing fu)*, by Zhang Heng (78–139), to the effect that "the nine hundred *xiaoshuo* begin from *Yu chu.*" See *Han shu*, p. 1745. Zhang Heng's line can be found in "Xijing fu," in Xiao, *Zengbu liu chen zhu wenxuan*, 3.23b.
40. Liang, "Yi yin zhengzhi xiaoshu xu," 1.743.
41. See Hsia, "Yen Fu and Liang Ch'i-ch'ao," p. 232, for the translation and a discussion of the obvious exaggeration that marks Liang's analysis of the novel's power in the West.
42. On Qu Qiubai's determination to see nothing useful in the literary languages available to Chinese writers in his day and his utopian calls for completely new forms, see Huters, "The Difficult Guest," pp. 135–149.
43. Hsia, for instance, poses the question in "Yen Fu and Liang Ch'i-ch'ao," pp. 230–231.
44. The principal imitators include *Xiuxiang xiaoshuo* (Embroidered fiction, 1903–1906), *Yueyue xiaoshuo* (Monthly fiction, 1906–1909), and *Xiaoshuo lin* (Forest of fiction, 1907–1908).
45. Ouyang, *Wan Qing xiaoshuo shi*, pp. 2–4.
46. See Chen Pingyuan, *Ershi shiji Zhongguo xiaoshuo shi*, pp. 41–42.
47. Liang, "Lun xiaoshuo yu qunzhi," 1.382.
48. Ibid., 1.385.
49. Xia, *Wan Qing shehui yu wenhua*, pp. 71–72.
50. Chang, *Liang Ch'i-ch'ao*, p. 232.
51. For a succinct account of this revival, see Chang, *Chinese Intellectuals in Crisis*, pp. 12–15.
52. Chang, *Liang Ch'i-chao*, pp. 236–237.
53. Liang, "Xuyan" to *Xin Zhongguo weilai ji*, p. 2.
54. Liang, "Gao xiaoshuo jia," 4.218.
55. Wu Jianren, "*Yueyue xiaoshuo* xu." Zeng Pu, author of the novel *Niehai hua* (the subject of chapter 7), also credited the new popularity and respectability to Liang. See Zeng Pu, "Zeng Mengpu xiansheng fu Hu Shizhi," p. 417.
56. On Di's career as a journalist, see Judge, *Print and Politics*.
57. Di, "Lun wenxueshang," 4.237. Lu Xun, on the contrary, in his "Wenhua pian zhi lun," is intent upon drawing attention to the dangers of the utilitarianism he saw pervading Chinese intellectual life in the first decade of this century. It should be remembered that Lu Xun regarded himself as a profoundly isolated voice.

58. Cai, "Wan Qing xiaoshuo lilun chulun," p. 415. For a specific instance of this way of reading the traditional novel, see Wang Zhongqi, "Zhongguo lidai xiaoshuo shi lun," 4.259–260. For Xia Zengyou and "Yan Fu's" thesis on this point, see Hsia, "Yen Fu and Liang Ch'i-ch'ao," p. 230. The most famous example of such a reading of a Qing novel is, of course, Cai Yuanpei's *"suoyin"* (hidden meaning) school of *The Story of the Stone,* in which the family relationships depicted in the novel are taken as a network of political allegory. For a brief description of Cai's approach, see Rolston, *How to Read the Chinese Novel,* pp. 482–483.

59. Anon., "Lun xiaoshuo zhi jiaoyu," 1.187.

60. Hu Shi, "Wushi nian lai," p. 76.

61. Tao, "Zhongguo wenxue zhi gaiguan," p. 241.

62. Tao, "Lun xiaoshuo zhi shili jiqi yingxiang," p. 226.

63. For a useful summary of Huang's work in literary history, see Doleželová-Velingerová, "Literary Historiography," pp. 137–143.

64. Zheng Yimei, "Huang Moxi," p. 372.

65. Huang Ren, "Zhongguo wenxue shi," pp. 67–69.

66. Huang Ren, "Xiaoshuo xiao hua," p. 302.

67. In chapter 18 of Zeng Pu's *Niehai hua* (1990), p. 185, the character representing the linguist Ma Jianzhong (1844–1900, author of the grammar book *Ma shi wentong* [Ma's comprehensive treatise on letters]) is quoted in thinly fictionalized form about the importance of novels in the world and about China's inferiority in that category.

68. Lee and Nathan, "The Beginnings of Mass Culture," pp. 387–388.

5. Wu Jianren

1. Wu Jianren, *"Yueyue xiaoshuo* xu."
2. Wang Yiliang, "Qichi shenqu da zhangfu."
3. Wu Jianren, *Ershi nian,* pp. 219–224 (chap. 29). This edition, published in first-list simplified characters, is both well annotated and easily accessible. An abridged English translation of approximately one-third of the 108-chapter text, by Liu Shih Shun, is available as *Vignettes from the Late Ch'ing.* The translation focuses on the early chapters and omits most of the commentary by the characters on the import of the events they are witnessing. It also leaves out many of the personal episodes of the narrator and most of his evaluations.
4. Wu Jianren, *Ershi nian,* p. 228.
5. Wright, *Last Stand,* p. 212.
6. "*Jianyi waibian* xu," in *Wu Jianren quanji* 8.3.
7. *Wu Jianren ku* (1902), 8.231.
8. See, for example, *Jianyi waibian,* in *Wu Jianren quanji* 8.12–13. See also Zheng Guanying, "Zhongxi hebi pinpan."
9. See, for instance, *Jianyi waibian,* in *Wu Jianren quanji* 8.107.
10. "*Jin shinian zhi guai xianzhuang* zixu," 3.299.

11. *Wu Jianren ku,* 8.229.
12. Ibid.
13. *"Jin shinian zhi guai xianzhuang* zixu," 3.299.
14. A full account of this movement can be found in Guanhua Wang, *In Search of Justice.*
15. The others are Liu E's *Travels of Lao Can,* Li Baojia's *Guanchang xianxing ji* (Exposure of officialdom), and Zeng Pu's *Flower in a Sea of Retribution.*
16. In his study of *Strange Events,* Chen Xinghui calculates that, in fact, only fifteen years elapse during the course of the novel. But Chen also allows that Wu seems to have every intention of giving a comprehensive account of the twenty years in question. See Chen Xinghui, *"Ershi nian mudu zhi guai xianzhuang" yanjiu,* pp. 54–55.
17. Patrick Hanan makes a case for regarding Karl Gützlaff's *Huizui zhi dalue* (General treatise on repentance), published in the 1830s, as the first Chinese novel written in the first person. Although this may be technically true, the exotic authorship of the book, its rapid disappearance from the scene, the limitation of what little circulation it did enjoy to the periphery (both geographically and demographically), and its religious tract-like nature would argue that it be relegated to a different category from that of Wu's work. Hanan, "Missionary Novels," pp. 430–431.
18. The most provocative and informative study of this form is Moretti's *The Way of the World.*
19. For a philosophical perspective on the sense of utopianism that pervaded the late Qing, see Metzger, *Escape from Predicament,* esp. pp. 191–231.
20. These concerns have been most succinctly summarized in Zhou Zuoren's 1932 series of talks at Furen University in Beijing recorded by Deng Gongsan and published two years later as *Zhongguo xin wenxue de yuanliu.*
21. For one account of such discussions from the 1770s through the 1830s, see Huters, "From Writing to Literature."
22. Cao and Gao, *Hong lou meng,* 1.2–7. The English translation is that of David Hawkes; see Cao, *The Story of the Stone,* 1.47–51. Note that the text elides any account of the act of transcription itself.
23. For a description and analysis of the history of *wenxue* in the Northern Song dynasty (1126–1275), see Bol, *"This Culture of Ours,"* and Fuller, *The Road to Eastslope.*
24. For some examples, see Ropp, *Dissent in Early Modern China,* pp. 93–100, 114–116. For an account of Wu's own critique of the examination system, see pp. 101–113.
25. Among other targets in this section, Wu Jingzi sharply mocks the literati critique of the Yongle emperor of the Ming, a public focus of *shi* resentment from circa 1500 on. See Elman, "The Formation of 'Dao Learning,'" pp. 78–81. See also Wu Jingzi, *Rulin waishi,* pp. 87, 93; a translation can be found in Wu Jingzi, *The Scholars,* pp. 143, 147–148.

26. The manuscript was among the effects of Wang Hui, a treacherous and corrupt official who had succeeded Qu's grandfather in office some years before the transaction. Wang presented his few books to young Qu as he was fleeing from the authorities. See Wu Jingzi, *Rulin waishi,* p. 86; *The Scholars,* pp. 140–141.

27. Marston Anderson has written with great perception on the related topic of the difficulty the novel encounters in representing ritual *(li)* as a space uncontaminated by the great issues of the day; see "The Scorpion in the Scholar's Cap." Anderson built upon the earlier work of Shuen-fu Lin, "Ritual and Narrative Structure."

28. The first sixty-five chapters of *Strange Events* were first published in installments in *Xin xiaoshuo* between August 1903 and December 1905, after which they were published as a book in eight volumes by the Shanghai Guangzhi Book Company in December 1906. The remaining chapters were published in three volumes that appeared at different times in March 1909 and August and December 1910.

29. Wu Jianren, *Ershi nian,* p. 5.

30. Lu Xun, *Zhongguo xiaoshuo shilüe,* 9.282. A different translation can be found in Lu Hsun, *Brief History of Chinese Fiction,* p. 372. The translators render *"qianze xiaoshuo"* as "novels of exposure."

31. Lu Xun, *Zhongguo xiaoshuo shilüe,* p. 286; *Brief History,* p. 379.

32. Lu Xun had translated two of Jules Verne's novels in his early years in Japan and had written a critical preface. See Lee, *Voices from the Iron House,* pp. 12–13. In addition, the episode in "Ah Q zhengzhuan" (*Lu Xun quanji* 1.522; translation in *Lu Xun: Selected Works* 1.147–148) in which the unarmed eponymous protagonist is arrested by a huge number of troops and police officers very much resembles a similar episode in *Strange Events* (*Ershi nian,* pp. 486–490, chaps. 61–62). Because of Lu Xun's participation in late Qing intellectual life, it is difficult to understand the passage in *"Nahan* zixu" where Lu Xun claims that during his years in Tokyo he was the only Chinese of his generation to be interested in literature (*Lu Xun quanji* 1.417; *Selected Works* 1.35). Only if we read this comment within the context of his manifest discontent with the direction chosen by Chinese intellectuals in the period immediately following 1895 does this make sense. This feeling of alienation is most clearly expressed in his essays written in Japan in 1907–1908 such as "Wenhua pian zhi lun," which is discussed in chapter 10.

33. This can be seen most clearly in the 1937 *Wan Qing xiaoshuo shi,* by A Ying (Qian Xingcun), p. 16, in which the later critic's plain attempt to praise the novel cannot overcome Lu Xun's negative judgments, which are cited at the beginning of A Ying's own evaluation. It is worthy of note that when Hu Shi talks of traditional Chinese fiction in his article "Wenxue gailiang chuyi" of 1917 (i.e., written at least three years before Lu Xun's negative judgments), he includes Wu Jianren on a short list of three worthy writers—Wu, Shi Naian (reputed author of *Shuihu zhuan*), and Cao Xueqin. See Hu Shi, "Wenxue gailiang chuyi."

34. See Zhou's contribution to *Xiaoshuo conghua* (Collected words on the

novel), which Liang Qichao put together in 1903 and published in the first and second issues of *Xin xiaoshuo*. *Xiaoshuo conghua* can be found in A Ying, ed., *Wan Qing wenxue congchao: Xiaoshuo xiqu yanjiu juan* 1.347. Zhou wrote at the same time that he had read some three hundred Chinese novels, including a hundred of "recent composition and newly translated [from Western works]."

35. Liu Shih Sun summarizes these events on p. 1 of *Vignettes*.

36. Wu Jianren, *Ershi nian*, pp. 29–30.

37. Ibid., pp. 43, 47. An English version of this episode can be found in *Vignettes*, pp. 13–14, 23, 26. Note that here, as elsewhere, the revelations about Gou Cai are delayed by the admixture of other plot elements, perhaps a simulacrum of the long period required for Jiusi to learn the true face of things.

38. The relative mildness here toward the Manchus becomes especially clear if the treatment of Gou Cai is compared with the fulminations of the revolutionaries against Manchu rule that were published at virtually the same time as the novel. The racialist opinions of Zhang Binglin are a good example, for which see Rankin, *Early Chinese Revolutionaries*, pp. 54–56.

39. Liu Shih Shun, *Vignettes*, pp. 71–85.

40. Ibid., pp. 147–164.

41. This episode is relatively well represented in *Vignettes*, pp. 149–164. Characteristically, however, the personal information about Cai Lüsheng has been completely omitted.

42. Ibid., p. 179.

43. Some of the more conspicuous examples of the foregrounding of these modern means of communication in the text include the tale told in chapters 51–52 (*Vignettes*, pp. 223–135) of the director general *(duban)* of the steamship company (probably a thinly disguised Sheng Xuanhuai [1844–1916], the actual *duban* of the China Merchants Steam Navigation Company [Lunchuan zhaoshang ju] in those years). Another such example is the story of the intricate model steamship employed in chapters 29–30 (*Vignettes*, pp. 131–137) to point out the corruption in governmental manufacturing enterprises.

44. *Vignettes* sums all this up in a few paragraphs on pp. 286–287.

45. Wu Jianren, *Ershi nian*, p. 476.

46. Ibid., p. 3.

47. For a slightly different view of the function of these two characters in the text, see Doleželová-Velingerová, "Typology of Plot Structures," pp. 42–45.

48. Liu Shih Shun, *Vignettes*, pp. 191–195.

49. *Vignettes* (pp. 349–371, 379–392) contains a detailed account of these episodes.

50. Wu Jianren, *Ershi nian*, p. 833.

51. See, e.g., *Mencius* 3B.9: "When the world declined and the Way fell into obscurity, heresies and violence again arose. There were instances of regicides and parricides. Confucius was apprehensive and composed the *Spring and Autumn Annals*" (trans. Lau, p. 114).

52. For a different perspective on this episode that emphasizes the black comedy and "dark laughter" inhering in these events, see David Wang, *Fin-de-siècle Splendor*, pp. 216–218.

53. There is an interesting parallel with Wu's most famous short novel, *Hen hai* (The sea of regret), first published in 1906. The novella is the story of the disruption of the prospective marriages of two young couples by the Boxer Rebellion in 1900, but the proximate cause of the breakups is the sudden disappearance of modern means of communication, in this case the railroad between Beijing and Tianjin. One couple then must rely on carts and canal boats, with the result that they become hopelessly separated from one another.

The determination of the Boxers to rip up the railroads and tear down the telegraphs is a backhanded indicator of their importance. The wall-poster doggerel translated by Joseph W. Esherick in his *Origins of the Boxer Uprising*, p. 300, is eloquent on this point:

Rip up the railroad tracks
Pull down the telegraph lines!
Quickly! Hurry up! Smash them—
The boats and the steamship combines.

54. These events are summarized in Liu Shih Shun, *Vignettes*, pp. 405–408.

55. As Paul Cohen makes clear, these tools of communication were specifically marked for destruction by the Boxer rebels. See Cohen's *History in Three Keys*, pp. 47–48. The foreign presence in China was equally obsessed with maintaining modern means of communications. After the trauma of the Boxer Rebellion, the treaty powers insisted upon inserting elaborate provisions in the 1901 Boxer Protocol to protect the access of these means of communication by their legations in Beijing. See Millard, *China*, pp. 227–232.

56. Doleželová-Velingerová offers a different evaluation of the import of the novel as a whole: "The meditations offered in the non-action sequences suggest, however, some hope: the crisis of values is temporary. Chinese society requires a reexamination of its traditional values. Perhaps, when properly interpreted and adapted to the crisis of the times, these values, enriched by practical Western learning, could survive the crisis and provide a new ethical basis for China" ("Typology of Plot Structures," p. 49).

57. This pattern was to appear frequently in Chinese literature produced after May Fourth. Perhaps the most famous example is the main character in Qian Zhongshu's exceptional novel, *Weicheng* (Fortress besieged). For that character, Fang Hongjian, knowledge of his own situation always comes too late. See Huters, *Qian Zhongshu*, chap. 6.

58. Mao's actual words were as follows: "Lu Xun was the commanding general of the Chinese Cultural Revolution; he was not only a great writer but also a great thinker and great revolutionary. Lu Xun had the hardest bones, without the

least bit of servility or obsequiousness, the most valuable sort of temperament in a colonial or semicolonial people" (Mao Zedong, "Xin minzhu zhuyi lun" [On the new democracy], in Li Zongying and Zhang, *Liushi nian lai Lu Xun yanjiu* 1.282).

6. Melding East and West

1. See Gimpel, "Were They Really Reading Disraeli?"

2. For a succinct summary of these events, see Coble, *Shanghai Capitalists,* pp. 14–15.

3. On the growth of this class of readers, see Xiong, "Lue lun wanQing Shanghai."

4. The best general survey of this publishing activity is contained in Chen Pingyuan, *Ershi shiji Zhongguo xiaoshuo shi,* esp. pp. 65–94.

5. For instance, in a *Xinwen bao* editorial of August 1903, "On Shanghai Customs" ("Lun Shanghai fengsu"), the editors ask, "Is Shanghai a civilized place, or a foreignized place, or a model for China's interior, or a harmful trap?" Quoted in Mittler, *A Newspaper for China?* p. 338.

6. Wu Jianren, *Ershi nian,* p. 1.

7. Xiong Yuezhi in "Lishi shang de Shanghai" and Linda Johnson in *Shanghai: From Market Town to Treaty Port,* to name only two, have demonstrated the continuity of urban custom at Shanghai over the centuries.

8. The question as to whether these two words refer to the same group of men is interesting in itself, although far beyond the scope of the present chapter. I base my equation of them here on a line at the conclusion of chapter 12 in Wu Jingzi's *Rulin waishi* (The scholars): "Because of this event, there is something to be learned: Young gentlemen of leisure close their doors and fail to inquire after matters of the world; *mingshi/wenren* change pursuits and seek success in the examinations" (p. 130).

9. *Ershi nian,* pp. 266–267 (chap. 35). Similar satire of contemporary men of letters can be found in chaps. 9, 33, and 38.

10. See, for instance, Martin Huang, *Literati and Self-Re/Presentation,* esp. pp. 29–36.

11. Wu Jingzi, *Rulin waishi,* p. 70; *The Scholars,* p. 120.

12. The first nineteen-plus chapters of *Xin shitou ji* (the portion of the novel in which Jia Baoyu and company tour the "actual" China of 1900) were originally published at irregular intervals in *Xiaoshuo lan,* a literary supplement of the Shanghai newspaper *Nanfang bao* (*NFB;* Southern news), beginning on September 19, 1905. The serialization suddenly ceased with *NFB* issue 195 (March 12, 1906), which contained the initial installment of chapter 20. This final installment was succeeded by the notation "incomplete" *(weiwan),* which in earlier *NFB* issues had indicated the unfinished status of the particular chapter being carried that day. The *NFB* apparently published no more of *Xin shitou ji.* It ceased publishing any fiction at all, for that matter, until issue 344 (August 14, 1906) began the seri-

alization of a novel entitled *Fan zhentan* (The anti-detective). The *NFB* itself, after several indications of financial instability (e.g., see the editorial note in English on p. 4 of issue 345, August 15, 1906), eventually ceased publication after November 5, 1907, with 785. A virtually complete run of the newspaper is held in the Shanghai Library and is readily available on microfilm there. The complete text of *Xin shitou ji*, with illustrations for each chapter, was published in four *juan* by the Gailiang xiaoshuo she in November 1908, with the annotation *"shehui xiaoshuo"* (social novel) on the cover.

13. Wang Junian, "Wo Foshan ren nianpu," in Wu Jianren, *Wo Foshan ren wenji* 8.345–350.

14. Wu Jianren, *Xin shitou ji*, p. 1. Wu was certainly correct in anticipating negative critical comment on writing a sequel. See, for instance, A Ying's dismissive remarks in *Wan Qing xiaoshuo shi*, pp. 177–178.

15. For all his lack of ready money at the time of his death, Wu did make a good deal from fees for his many writings, something that seems to have been in precarious balance with his free-spending nature.

16. Wu Jianren, *Henhai*, 5.58. See also Hanan, *Sea of Regret*, p. 176.

17. See, for instance, Lu Xun, *Zhongguo xiaoshuo shilüe* 9.238. See also Lu Hsun, *A Brief History*, p. 315.

18. Wu Jianren, *Henhai*, 5.3.

19. Wu Jianren, *Xin shitou ji*, pp. 36–37.

20. See, for instance, Baoyu's first tour of the Grandview Garden *(daguanyuan)* in the company of his father in chapter 17. Although Jia Zheng repeatedly scolds the boy while demanding literary names from him, as they near the end of the tour, the elder Jia's literary followers "could see that he [i.e., Zheng] was not displeased" (Cao, *The Story of the Stone*, trans. Hawkes, 1.342).

21. See, for instance, *Xin shitou ji*, pp. 34, 40, 58–59, 63. This transformation of the characters from Cao Xueqin's novel into paragons of modern seriousness is not limited to Wu Jianren's sequel. The 1909 sequel by "Nanwu Yeman," also entitled *Xin shitou ji*, has Lin Daiyu becoming a professor in Japan, with Baoyu signed on as her enthusiastic student. For all the change in their characters, however, the relationship between them continues. See David Wang, *Fin-de-siècle Splendor*, p. 29.

22. For details on the boycott, see Guanhua Wang, *In Search of Justice*. On the general political significance of the boycott, see Bergère, *The Golden Age*, pp. 50–51. See also Goodman, *Native Place, City, and Nation*, pp. 183–195.

23. Pott, *A Short History of Shanghai*, p. 164.

24. Wang Junian, "Wo Foshan ren nianpu," in Wu Jianren, *Wo Foshan ren wenji* 8.343–344, 348.

25. Ibid., 8.349.

26. See Elvin, "The Administration of Shanghai," p. 245.

27. Cf. Yen-p'ing Hao's description of the nineteenth-century comprador (also quoted in the text of chapter 7): "Like any marginal man, he had his limitations. He was shrewd and talented but not always honest. Not an independent

merchant per se from the beginning, he hung his hopes for success too closely on his connections with foreigners and thus on China's unstable foreign relations. He was still generally associated with the 'parasitic' merchant and was criticized for deviating from social norms" (*The Comprador*, p. 11).

28. *"Wenhua ren"* is a term that has come into use only in the 1990s, presumably as an alternative to the label *"zhishi fenzi"* (intellectual), a term regarded as compromised by heavy use in state discourse and as an anachronism for the late Qing period. Among other reasons, I have decided to use *"wenhua ren"* in order to highlight the transformation of the meaning of *"wen"* in the late Qing. If the term was primarily associated with personal cultivation in the neo-Confucian period, the widespread use of neologisms originally used primarily in Meiji Japan, like *"wenhua"* and *"wenming,"* signifies the expansion of the connotations of *"wen"* into a wider and more public realm. For an example of a usage similar to mine, see Xiong, "Lue lun wanQing Shanghai."

29. On the general issue of the *wenren* in late Qing Shanghai, see Catherine Vance Yeh, "The Life-style of Four *Wenren*."

30. On p. 34 of *Xin shitou ji*, Wu makes a mistake in placing Baoyu in Shanghai in early 1901, instead of 1900 *(gengzi nian)*, the actual date of the Boxer Rebellion.

31. Wu Jianren, *Xin shitou ji*, p. 108. Xue Pan had earlier expressed a similar surprise at Baoyu's desire to study foreign books; see *Xin shitou ji*, p. 87.

32. Ibid., p. 9.

33. The earliest study of the press in Shanghai can be found in Britton, *Chinese Periodical Press*. See also the important study of *Shen bao* by Mittler, *A Newspaper for China?*

34. Wu Jianren, *Xin shitou ji*, p. 129.

35. Ibid., p. 48.

36. Ibid., p. 52.

37. Chatterjee, *Nationalist Thought*, p. 10.

38. See David Wang, *Fin-de-siècle Splendor*, pp. 252–258.

39. Wu Jianren, *Xin shitou ji*, p. 20.

40. Ibid., p. 40.

41. My thanks to Paola Zamperini of Amherst College for this important insight.

42. Wu Jianren, *Henhai*, 5.78; Hanan, *Sea of Regret*, p. 204.

43. Wu Jianren, *Xin shitou ji*, pp. 103–104.

44. After Baoyu talks back to an official, the official accuses him of being in league with the Boxers, a fairly common way in those days of exacting revenge against someone you didn't like. See Paul Cohen, *History in Three Keys*, p. 238 n. 65.

45. Although they take little note of the fact, the troubles that the principal characters of *Henhai* encounter on their flight from Beijing coincide with the destruction of the railroad to Tianjin and their consequent need to resort to older and more cumbersome means of transportation.

46. Wu Jianren, *Xin shitou ji*, p. 193.

47. Ibid., p. 220.

48. On Kang Youwei's attempts to establish Confucianism as a state religion, see Hsiao, *A Modern China and a New World*, pp. 105–122. For Zhang Binglin's arguments for installing Buddhism as the Chinese state religion, see his "Dongjing liuxuesheng huanying hui," pp. 269–280.

49. Lu Shudu discusses Wu's commitment to this idea in his preface to his collection of Wu's writings. See Wu Jianren, *Wo Foshan ren wenji* 1.20.

50. Wu Jianren, *Xin shitou ji*, pp. 274–275.

51. Ibid., p. 313.

52. Perhaps the most famous example of this motif is Lin Daiyu's dream in chapter 82 of *The Story of the Stone*, which ends just as Baoyu inserts his hand into his chest cavity, seeking in vain to locate his heart therein (4.62–65).

53. Wu Jianren, *Xin shitou ji*, p. 315.

54. Reprinted in A Ying, *Wan Qing wenxue congchao* 1.1, p. 3. This novel was inspired by Edward Bellamy's popular American novel of 1888, *Looking Backward*, which was translated and serialized in a Shanghai newspaper in 1891–1892. See David Wang, *Fin-de-siècle Splendor*, p. 254.

55. David Wang, *Fin-de-siècle Splendor*, p. 283.

56. Ibid., p. 282.

57. The term is that of Gregory Judanis in his *Belated Modernity and Aesthetic Culture*.

58. On the continued relevance of this theme in modern China, see Wang Hui, "Zhongguo jin-xiandai sixiangzhong."

59. Jaroslav Prusek's writings of the late 1950s and early 1960s are still valuable resources in setting out this trend toward more subjective writing. The most important of these are collected in Prusek, *The Lyrical and the Epic*.

7. Impossible Representations

1. There is some discrepancy between various accounts as to how these classes were constituted and who attended them. Zeng Pu's own retrospective account completed in 1928, "Zeng Mengpu xiansheng fu Hu Shizhi xiansheng de xin," is appended to *Niehai hua* (1990), pp. 414–415. The person responsible for setting the course in motion was Zhang Yinhuan (1837–1900), a powerful official in the ministry and a former ambassador to the United States.

2. This course of instruction was merely a continuation of the long history of reformers' attempts to induce talented students to study foreign subjects, beginning with the attempted reform of the Tongwen guan in the late 1860s, described in chapter 1. For W. A. P. Martin's disappointment at the number and caliber of students, see his *Cycle of Cathay*, pp. 297–299. See also his *Lore of Cathay*, p. 17: "[Wenxiang] induced the throne to open the doors of the College [i.e., the Tongwen guan] to Chinese who were high-class graduates in letters; but the haughty graduates declined to enter."

3. On Chen Jitong, see Catherine Vance Yeh, "The Life-style of Four *Wenren*," pp. 435–449.

4. "Zeng Mengpu xiansheng fu Hu Shizhi," p. 415. For a more detailed and rather less melodramatic account of Zeng's illness (in which the illness lasts only three years and has a recognizable etiology), see Zeng Xubai (Zeng's son) "Zeng Mengpu nianpu," pp. 165–166.

5. Jin was one of the founders of the journal *Jiangsu* in the spring of 1903, and he implies that he composed his novel for publication in it. See Han Liangsheng (Fan Yanqiao), "Jin Songcen tan *Niehai hua*," p. 147.

6. On the 1904 date, see Cui, "Dongya bingfu fangwen ji," p. 142. See also Zeng Xubai, "Zeng Mengpu nianpu," pp. 167–168, where the son claims that Zeng Pu's publishing house started the craze for translated fiction. Chen Pingyuan in his *Ershi shiji Zhongguo xiaoshuo shi*, pp. 28–32, convincingly demonstrates that translations of foreign novels far outnumbered original works in the late Qing. See also Zhang Bilai, "*Niehai hua* de sixiang he yishu."

7. For Jin's account of this process, see "Jin Songcen tan *Niehai hua*," p. 146.

8. For these statistics, see Zeng Pu, "Xiugai hou," p. 408. These figures are repeated by A Ying in his *Wan Qing xiaoshuo shi*, p. 22.

9. Zeng Pu, "Xiugai hou," pp. 409–410.

10. The textual history of the novel and its textual variants is highly complicated, but the questions at issue in this chapter are not affected by this history, so I will not go into it here. For the best summary of the textual history, see the "Tiyao" (Synopsis) contained in the *Wan Qing xiaoshuo daxi* edition of the novel, 1984), pp. 1–2 (separate pagination in this section), reprinted in the Wenhua (1990) edition, pp. 1–2 (also separate pagination). The Wenhua edition also contains considerable supplementary material that throws light on the history and reception of the work. For more detail on the textual history, see Catherine Vance Yeh's dissertation, "Zeng Pu's 'Niehai hua,'" pp. 1–41. See also the materials collected in Wei, *Niehai hua ziliao*. It is worth noting, however, that, as with the critical hostility to the final forty chapters of *Shitou ji*, there is a strong moral element in the condemnation of Zeng's later (1920s) revision of the text. See, for example, Wang Lixing, "Zeng Pu jiqi *Niehai hua*."

11. Interestingly enough, the fifty-nine-part television drama produced in China in 2003, *Zouxiang gonghe* (Toward a republic), recognizes this: the portraits of such high officials as Li Hongzhang, Sheng Xuanhuai, and Zhang Zhidong are all highly complimentary, leaving the impression of men of great talent struggling with an intractable situation.

12. Thomas Metzger in his *Escape from Predicament*, pp. 210–226, provides the definitive account of late Qing utopianism.

13. On the relative ease with which *gezhi* was discussed in the Jiangnan region prior to 1895, versus the sense of *xixue* as being an impenetrable realm of knowledge in the years after the war, see Meng, "The Invention of Shanghai," pp. 50–110.

14. Notable exceptions to the silence on the issue include two recent books:

Lydia Liu's *Translingual Practice* and Prasenjit Duara's *Rescuing History from the Nation*.

15. Partha Chatterjee has worked out a three-stage theory of the development of nationalism within colonial modernity. The first, which he calls the "moment of departure," depends on an "awareness—and acceptance—of an essential cultural difference between East and West." Chatterjee goes on to say, "Modern European culture, it is thought, possesses attributes that make the European culturally equipped for power and progress, while such attributes are lacking in the 'traditional' cultures of the East" (*Nationalist Thought*, p. 50). The exclusive binarism of this distinction would seem to be a product of overt colonial conquest. In China's case, where the anxiety was centered in the question of whether sufficient power could be maintained to avoid colonial conquest, allowing this sort of binary to govern the conception of the relationship would have been to give the game away. Brett de Bary has noted the difficulties that Japanese intellectuals have had in making practical distinctions between things Western and indigenous. As she says of those attempting to make a critique of Westernization in Japan, "distinguishing between foreign elements to be repudiated and the indigenous strata to which Japanese could 'return' (a distinction which, in any event, did not neatly conform to a 'material' vs. 'spiritual' dichotomy) proved to be no easy task" (introduction to *Origins of Modern Japanese Literature,* by Karatani Kojin, p. 2).

16. Yan Fu, "Jiuwang juelun," 1.48.

17. On "national essence" thinking, see Schneider, "National Essence."

18. On Liang's postwar efforts, see chapter 8 below; on the criticism of Tagore, see Stephan N. Hay, *Asian Ideas of East and West.*

19. Chatterjee, *Nationalist Thought,* p. 11.

20. On this point there is a clear divergence between the fictional Fu Caiyun and the historical Sai Jinhua. By her own admission, Sai Jinhua could never write any German. See Shang and Liu, "Sai Jinhua benshi," p. 523.

21. See, for instance, Paul Cohen, "Christian Missions," p. 583: "Although there were unquestionably great variations in the quality of the female education thus provided, it has been claimed that, as late as the eve of the 1911 revolution, Protestant institutions were still the only ones in China at which the educational opportunities for women were roughly comparable to those available to Chinese men."

22. For a sampling of some of the considerable evidence on the extent of female literacy in late imperial China, see the essays collected in Widmer and Chang, *Writing Women.*

23. Andrew Jones in his essay "The Violence of the Text," p. 580, sets out the moral economy of that novel: "If *yi* is the primal (and distinctly patriarchal) *totem* of the bandit community at Liangshan, sexuality is its attendant *taboo*. And to the extent that females embody the threat of sexuality, they become the agents of the corrosion of the cardinal virtue." See also Ahern, "The Power and Pollution."

24. Zheng Guanying, "Huaren yi tong xiwen shuo."

25. Ibid., p. 284. Wu Jianren in his *Ershi nian mudu zhi guai xianzhuang,* pp. 227–228, includes a devastating critique of both the methods and the results of the translation work done at the Jiangnan Arsenal. For his critique of the obsolescence of the arsenal's work, see his *Xin shitou ji,* p. 81 (chap. 11).

26. Zheng Guanying, "Huaren yi tong xiwen shuo."

27. Lin Yu-sheng, *The Crisis of Chinese Consciousness;* Wang Hui, "'Sai xiansheng' zai Zhongguo de mingyun."

28. Yan Fu, "Yu *Waijiao bao,*" 3.559.

29. For a fictional example of a comprador who is virtually illiterate in Chinese but is said to be proficient in "foreign languages" *(yanghua yangzi),* see the case of Bai Yaolian in Wu Jianren's *Xin shitou ji,* discussed in chapter 6.

30. Yan Fu, "Yu *Waijiao bao,*'" 3.561. Like many utterances from the late 1890s, this echoes a comment in Feng Guifen's *Jiaobinlu kangyi* made as part of his effort to institute rigorous training in foreign languages: "Nowadays those familiar with barbarian affairs are called 'linguists.' These men are generally frivolous rascals and loafers in the cities and are despised in their villages and communities. They serve as interpreters only because they have no other means of making a livelihood. Their nature is boorish, their knowledge shallow, and furthermore, their moral principles are mean" (excerpted in Teng and Fairbank, *China's Response to the West,* p. 51). For similar remarks by Liang Qichao, see his "Xixue shumubiao houxu," 1.738.

31. For the most complete account of missionary education, see Lutz, *China and the Christian Colleges,* esp. pp. 67–68.

32. On the development of this discourse, see Meng, "The Invention of Shanghai," pp. 75–88.

33. The term "bricolage" derives from an analysis set forth by Claude Lévi-Strauss to define a particular sort of orientation toward work: "The 'bricoleur' is adept as performing a large number of diverse tasks; but, unlike the engineer, he does not subordinate each of them to the availability of raw materials and tools conceived and procured for the purpose of the project. His universe of instruments is closed and the rules of his game are always to make do with 'whatever is at hand . . . .'" Also, "It might be said that the engineer questions the universe, while the 'bricoleur' addresses himself to a collection of oddments left over from other human endeavors . . . ." See Claude Lévi-Strauss, *The Savage Mind,* pp. 17, 19.

34. Zeng Pu, *Niehai hua* (1990), p. 115.

35. Ibid., p. 118.

36. Li Shinong is said to be based on the prominent and very conservative Cantonese official Li Wentian (1834–1895). See Hummel, *Eminent Chinese,* p. 494.

37. Zeng Pu, *Niehai hua* (1990), p. 118.

38. Ibid., p. 115.

39. Ibid., p. 138.

40. Ibid., pp. 106–108.

41. For a virtuoso tracing out of the intertextual relationship between the

depiction of this meeting in *Niehai hua* and the meeting between Jia Baoyu and Lin Daiyu in the eighteenth-century masterpiece *The Story of the Stone,* see Hu Ying, *Tales of Translation,* pp. 57–60.

42. I follow Hu Ying, *Tales of Translation,* in translating the character's Chinese name "Xiayali" as Sarah Aizenson, a fictional version of the actual Russian anarchist Sophia Perovskaya (1853–1881), whose story circulated widely in China in this period. (See, for instance, Lingnan yuyi nü shi's *Dongou nü haojie* [Female heroes of Eastern Europe], an incomplete novel first published in *Xin xiaoshuo* in 1902.) For more on Perovskaya's image in late Qing China, see David Wang, *Fin-de-siècle Splendor,* pp. 166–168.

43. Zeng Pu, *Niehai hua* (1990), p. 84.

44. This disproportion between action and result recalls the category of Ming short story that Patrick Hanan has labeled the "folly and consequences" story, of which the various tales subsumed under the general title of "Fifteen Strings of Cash" is probably the best known. For a catalog of these stories, see Hanan, *The Chinese Vernacular Story,* pp. 59–68.

45. Zeng Pu, *Niehai hua* (1990), p. 87.

46. Ibid.

47. Ibid., p. 88.

48. Ibid., p. 89.

49. On post-1898 critiques of the reactionary nature of women in Chinese society, see Judge, "Reforming the Feminine," pp. 160–170, and Hu Ying, "Naming the First 'New Woman,'" pp. 183–188.

50. Hu Shi's critique of *Niehai hua* as being merely an inferior imitation of the episodic form of *Rulin waishi* is most instructive here. Zeng, in his response, is at pains to remind his readers that he attempted something far more complex, at least in terms of plot structure. See Zeng's "Xiugai hou," pp. 408–409. Hu's attempt to limit Zeng's achievement simply to imitating the characteristically "traditional Chinese" structure of Wu Jingzi's classic recalls the May Fourth efforts to portray Yan Fu as the hopeless victim of traditional discourses, as was discussed in chapter 2.

51. Yen-p'ing Hao, *The Comprador,* p. 11.

52. Zeng Pu, *Niehai hua* (1990), p. 90.

53. Ibid.

54. For examples of revolutionary rhetoric after the turn of the century, see Rankin, *Early Chinese Revolutionaries,* esp. pp. 80–81. For a study of anarchism that encompasses a slightly later period, see Dirlik, *Anarchism in the Chinese Revolution.*

55. "If we wish to strengthen ourselves, then we must not allow ourselves to become captivated by books written by men of ancient times, and this principle applies even more strongly to the laws promulgated after the Qin dynasty.... Because rulers in post-Qin times are precisely what is being referred in the remarks [of Zhuang Zhou] about 'the greatest robber steals a nation [and becomes the

king]' [*Chuang tzu,* trans. Watson, p. 110] And from whom did they steal it? Why, from the people" (Yan Fu, "Pi Han," 1.35).

56. Hu Ying, *Tales of Translation.* See also Zamperini, "Fu Caiyun."

57. Chatterjee, *The Nation and Its Fragments,* p. 68.

58. Ibid., pp. 68–69.

59. Zeng Pu, *Niehai hua* (1990), p. 91.

60. Ibid., p. 212.

61. Literally, "three followings, four virtues, seven chastities, and nine sacrifices." The first two generally enjoin male precedence in the household, whereas the final pair stress the need to hold on to chastity and death before dishonor. For a discussion of the *san cong,* see Ko, *Teachers of the Inner Chambers,* pp. 6–7.

62. Zeng Pu, *Niehai hua* (1990), p. 213.

63. Ibid., p. 275.

64. The contrast between Caiyun and the character Xianglin Sao of Lu Xun's 1924 story "Zhufu" (The new year's sacrifice) could not be more profound: the peasant woman Xianglin Sao has absorbed all the Confucian precepts of proper female behavior so completely that even her fellow clan members are amazed.

65. This represents an inexplicable anachronism, for the *Banqiao zaji* (Miscellany of the plank bridge), by Yu Huai (1616–1696), is a late sixteenth-century account of the Nanjing pleasure quarters that is marked by a strong and sensual nostalgia. That its elegant tone was much imitated by early twentieth-century writers in romanticizing their visits to such quarters may account for this odd reference. For more information on Yu Huai and his book's influence, see Wai-yee Li, "The Late Ming Courtesans: Invention of a Cultural Ideal," in Widmer and Chang, *Writing Women,* pp. 46–49.

66. Zeng Pu, *Niehai hua* (1990), pp. 19–20.

67. Ibid., p. 139.

68. Ibid., p. 89.

69. Ibid., p. 90.

70. My thanks to Xiaobing Tang of the University of Chicago for drawing my attention to the problematic aspects of the representation of Russia in the novel.

71. See for instance, Wei, "Guanyu Sai-Wa." That Sai Jinhua is rumored to have interceded with Waldersee, the German commander of the Boxer Expeditionary Force, on behalf of the residents of Beijing would change the perspective on the story of her adultery with the German officer.

8. The Contest over Universal Values

1. Min, *National Polity and Local Power,* p. 171.

2. Yeh Sheng-tao, *Schoolmaster Ni Huan-chih,* p. 14. See also Mao, *Wo zouguo de daolu* 1.73–75.

3. On the generally nonradical nature of the republic revolution, see Ernest P. Young, *The Presidency of Yuan Shih-k'ai*, pp. 27–30.

4. Among the most precise and bitter satires of the rapid quenching of revolutionary fires is Lu Xun's "Ah Q zhengzhuan" (The true story of Ah Q), particularly chaps. 7–9, 1.135–154. See also Yeh Sheng-tao, *Schoolmaster Ni Huan-chih*, p. 18: "But disappointment followed at once. Yes, the town ran up the white flag and fell to the Revolution; [Ni's] pigtail was sheared off as the headmaster's had been: but that was all. Nothing else appeared to be changed." For a foreign sense of the disappointment over the results of the revolution, see Bland, *Recent Events*, pp. 50–108.

5. Ernest P. Young, *The Presidency of Yuan Shih-k'ai*, pp. 42–48.

6. Ibid., p. 105.

7. For an excellent summary of the research on the Southern Society, see Hockx, *Questions of Style*, pp. 35–46.

8. On the second revolution, see Ernest P. Young, *The Presidency of Yuan Shih-k'ai*, pp. 129–137.

9. For an evaluation of Yan Fu's political activities in these years, see Schwartz, *In Search of Wealth and Power*, pp. 215–215, 223–228. For a succinct summary of Liang Qichao's interactions with the Yuan Shikai government in the years after 1912, see Zhu Weizheng, "*Qingdai xueshu gailun* daodu," pp. 13–14.

10. For an account of Yuan's draconian press policies and their success in reducing the number of newspapers published in China from more than 500 to 130 (and in Shanghai from 15 to 5), see Ma, *Shanghai xinwen shi*, pp. 422–439.

11. Lin Yu-sheng, *The Crisis of Chinese Consciousness*.

12. Not for the first time do we see this result. For a summary of the radical real-life response to the debate in Liang Qichao's 1902 novel, *Zhongguo weilai ji*, on whether or not China needed a revolution, see Xiaobing Tang, *Global Space*, pp. 136–137.

13. The magazine was published under the name *Qingnian zazhi* between September 15, 1915, and February 1916 (*juan* 1.1–6). It was then suspended until November 1916, when Chen, now at Beijing University, resumed its publication as *Xin qingnian* with *juan* 2. See Chow, *The May Fourth Movement*, pp. 44–45. On the restoration of the monarchy, see Ernest P. Young, "The Hung-hsien [Hongxian] Emperor," pp. 179–180.

14. Wang Shuqian, "Xinjiu wenti," p. 8. I was unable to locate any further information about the identity of Wang Shuqian.

15. Ibid., p. 10.

16. Ibid.

17. Ibid.

18. This discourse should be taken into account in the theorizing about the change from "culturalism" to nationalism in modern China, a transition that is customarily regarded as taking place when China realized it was no longer *tianxia* ("all under heaven") but merely one nation among others. The first half of this for-

mulation is not problematic, but the obsessive classification of the world into East or West in the years represented in Wang's article casts real doubt that "among" is the proper preposition to describe the perception of China's new position in the world, which is taken almost invariably as one-half of a rigid China/West binary.

19. For instance, Chen's granting credit to France for giving life to all the key concepts of Western civilization would probably not be found credible by most historians (or, at least, most historians of Anglo-Saxon or Teutonic origin). A predilection for the instant transformation represented by the French Revolution rather than for the slow development of English constitutionalism is, however, characteristic of Chen's thinking after 1915.

20. Chen Duxiu, "Falanxi ren," p. 136.

21. It must be said that even on the pages of *Qingnian zazhi* and *Xin qingnian*, Chen shows himself capable of another, entirely more subtle type of argument. For an example, see Chen Duxiu, "Kongzi zhi dao."

22. Chen Duxiu, "Dong-xi minzu genben sixiang chayi," p. 167.

23. For a brief profile of *Dongfang zazhi* (and Shanghai periodical publishing in general) in these years, see Lee, *Shanghai Modern*, pp. 47–52.

24. The best indication *Xin qingnian*'s small influence in its early years is the famous case of one of the editorial group, Qian Xuantong (1887–1939), who tried to elicit controversy in March 1918 by writing, under the fictitious name "Wang Jingxuan," a letter attacking the journal and its editorial policies. See Chow, *The May Fourth Movement*, p. 66. It is also worth recalling Lu Xun's reminiscence of Qian's visit to Lu sometime in 1917, when Qian was attempting to get Lu to participate in the journal: "They were bringing out *New Youth*, but since there did not seem to have been any reaction, favorable or otherwise, no doubt they felt lonely" ("*Nahan* zixu" [Personal preface to *Call to Arms*], 1.419; translation from *Lu Xun: Selected Works* 1.37). For a general evaluation on *Xin qingnian*'s early years, see Wang Xiaoming's "Yifen zazhi" and its translation by Hockx and Huters, "A Journal and a 'Society.'"

25. One source even maintains that Huang's dispatches from Beijing to the Shanghai papers marked the beginning of the modern system of newspaper correspondents in China. See Zhong Birong, "Huang Yuanyong."

26. Tang Zhenchang, *Tang Zhenchang sanwen*, pp. 98–106.

27. Huang's writings were collected by his colleague and friend Lin Zhijun in 1919 and published in four *juan* as *Yuansheng yizhu* (Writings left by [Mr.] Yuansheng). The work has been republished a number of times, including in the *Minguo congshu* published in the 1980s by the Shanghai shuju. Lin's preface contains a good deal about Huang's life and ideas. For an evaluation of Huang's career and ideas, see Qian Jibo, *Xiandai Zhongguo wenxue shi*, pp. 422–424.

28. Huang Yuanyong, "Guoren zhi gongdu," p. 1. The idea of China's imminent demise had been abroad for some time. In a famous article published in July 1911 in the Hankou *Dajiang bao*, for instance, Huang Kan (1886–1935), a phi-

lologist and then revolutionary student of Zhang Binglin's, wrote: "In the current Chinese situation, everything seems dead, everywhere is a realm of death; the disease is beyond cure. But society high and low is in a daze, unaware of the approach of the time of death" ("Daluanzhe jiu Zhongguo zhi miao yao ye" [Chaos would be the best medicine for China], quoted in Fang Hanqi, *Zhongguo jindai baokan*, pp. 526–527).

29. Huang Yuanyong, "Guoren zhi gongdu," p. 3.

30. For instance, a "Letters" *(wenyuan)* section of *Dongfang zazhi* was begun in January 1916. In October of that year the magazine began a series of articles on the philosophers of antiquity, beginning with an essay entitled "Reading Xunzi" ("Du Xunzi"), by the prominent poet and critic Chen Sanli. See also Wu Yu, "Du Xunzi shu hou." Contemporary focus on Xunzi can be traced back to the influence of Zhang Binglin and to Yu Yue before him. Zhang had "praised [Xunzi] as the man who proposed basic ideals for the politics of his day." Even before 1900, Zhang wrote an essay entitled "Zun Xun" (Honor Xunzi), which was published in the original edition of *Qiushu* in 1900 or 1901. See Shimada, "Confucius in the Era of the 1911 Revolution," in his *Pioneer of the Chinese Revolution*, pp. 110–111. For a detailed account of intellectual attitudes toward Xunzi in the 1895–1900 period, see Zhu Weizheng, *Qiusuo zhen wenming*, pp. 333–350.

31. Huang Yuanyong, "Guoren zhi gongdu," p. 4.

32. Ibid., p. 5.

33. Ibid., p. 6.

34. Huang Yuanyong, "Xiangying lu," 3.1. Cf. Liang Qichao's comments written during his journey to Europe in 1919 and published as *Ouyou xinying lu* (Impressions of travel in Europe):

> As a result of the development of science, the organization of industrial production underwent fundamental innovation. Changes were carried out at such a fast speed, with such sudden force, and also on such a large scale, that people were always and everywhere at a loss when they tried to make their inner lives agree with their outer life. The most obvious example is the drastically opposing ways in which urban life in the present and village life from before are experienced. (Quoted in Xiaobing Tang, *Global Space*, p. 181)

35. Huang Yuanyong, "Xinjiu sixiang zhi chongtu," p. 1.

36. Ibid., p. 2.

37. Translation by A. C. Graham in Zhuang, *Chuang-tzu*, p. 58.

38. In his introduction to Huang's collected work, Lin Zhijun notes Huang's delight in and facility with the classical language, but he also mentions Huang's expressions of frustration with the available linguistic forms. See Lin Zhijun's preface in Huang Yuanyong, *Yuansheng yizhu*, pp. 9–10. In spite of what to this reader, at least, is a conspicuous success in composing a vivid and precise classical prose,

Huang himself wrote in "Xiangying lu," 3.1: "The dead language of the classics is insufficient to develop new ideas."

39. On this point, one can see a clear contrast between Huang's calmness when describing colonialism and Liang Qichao's voice in "New Historiography." See Xiaobing Tang, *Global Space*, pp. 77–78.

40. Huang Yuanyong, "Xinjiu sixiang zhi chongtu," p. 5.

41. Ibid.

42. According to Shen Yanbing (Mao Dun), when Shen joined the Commercial Press in 1916, *Dongfang zazhi* was lodged in the science bureau *(lihua bu)*, where Du Yaquan was chief editor. Mao, *Wo zouguo de daolu* 1.98.

43. After having virtually disappeared from view in the decades after 1920, Du has received renewed attention in recent years. See, for example, Xu and Tian, *Yixi ji*, and Gao Like, *Tiaoshi de zhihui*. In "Incomplete Modernity," Leo Lee also discusses Du at some length. Probably the most important piece of writing in reviving interest in Du is Wang Yuanhua's "Du Yaquan."

44. Cangfu (Du Yaquan), "Zai lun xinjiu sixiang zhi chongtu," p. 2.

45. Ibid., p. 5.

46. For a good summary of the status of *yu* (desire) in late imperial thought and literature, see Martin W. Huang, *Desire and Fictional Narrative*, pp. 23–35. The question of the position of human desire in the social order is a major theme present even in the late Qing novel *Lao Can youji*, begun in 1904 by Liu E (Tieyun); see the translation in Shadick, *The Travels of Lao Ts'an*, pp. 99–102.

47. Cangfu, "Jingde wenming yu dongde wenming," p. 1.

48. Ibid.

49. Ibid., p. 2.

50. Ibid., p. 3.

51. For instance, an article entitled "Da zhanzheng xuji shiyi," by "Gao Lao," which is more often than not another of Du's pseudonyms, contains no mention of any particular horrors in its account of the war for the first nine months of 1916.

52. Chen Duxiu, "Yijiuyiliu," p. 171. Although it is beyond the scope of this chapter to delve very far into the issue, the simplicity of the demotic classical Chinese in which Chen's essay is composed gives one pause as to the actual justification for the movement for vernacular literature that was to blossom in *Xin qingnian* in 1917. To the extent that the move to the vernacular was advocated as a move to simplicity, it is hard to imagine any prose more transparent than Chen deploys here. It is not difficult to share Edward Gunn's conclusion about the vernacular movement: "As discussed by its various proponents and practitioners, baihua writing was endowed with several, sometimes contradictory, principles and goals. Yet it is important to note that it was in its origins, and in a major portion of its appeal to intellectuals, a political act" (*Rewriting Chinese*, p. 38).

53. Cangfu, "Zhanhou dongxi wenming zhi tiaohe," p. 2.

54. Ibid., p. 3.

55. Ibid., p. 6.

56. For a concise summary of Liang Shuming's arguments on the difference between China and the West, see Alitto, *The Last Confucian*, esp. pp. 82–125. On the relationship between Liang Shuming and Liang Qichao, see Xiaobing Tang, *Global Space*, pp. 174–196.

57. Mao, *Wo zouguo de daolu* 1.109, 145. Wang Yuanhua speculates that Du was dismissed in 1920 because of his opposition to using the vernacular, something vital at Commercial Press because of the official mandate to use the vernacular in school textbooks, which had always been the main source of income for the press; see Wang, "Du Yaquan." The diary of Zhang Yuanji, the general manager of the Commercial Press at the time, contains a revealing entry for October 22, 1919, in which Zhang complains about Du's editorial policy, stating that he was, "in fact, too prejudiced in favor of the old ways" (*shi tai pian yu jiu*) (*Zhang Yuanji riji* 2.889). Mao Dun notes that the new nominal editor of *Dongfang zazhi* after its 1920 reorganization was Tao Xingcun, who had connections with Zhang Yuanji. Mao Dun maintains, however, that Qian was the person in substantial charge of the magazine (*Wo zouguo de daolu* 1.145).

58. Qian Zhixiu, "Gongli zhuyi yu xueshu," p. 1.

59. Ibid. Qian is by no means alone in expressing such sentiments. Lu Xun, in several of his "Random Thoughts" from 1919, expresses himself with extreme cynicism concerning the reception of Western ideas in China. For instance: "What a pity it is that the moment foreign things reach China they change their color as if they had fallen into a vat of black dye" ("Suigan lu sishisan," 1.330; translation from *Lu Xun: Selected Works* 2.39). Also, "Whatever foreign thought is like today, it at least smacks of liberty and equality, mutual aid and coexistence. There is therefore no place for them in an intellectual realm filled with self, with the wish to 'take over,' to monopolize everything, and to quaff all the wine in time and space" ("Suigan lu wushijiu," 1.356; translation based on *Lu Xun: Selected Works* 2.50). See also the discussion of Benjamin Schwartz' critique of Yan Fu's views on liberalism in chapter 2 above.

60. For a new journal to gain leverage by spending an inordinate amount of space attacking a more established one is not a new tactic in Chinese political journalism. For instance, the newer *Minbao* (People's journal), the official organ of the Tongmeng hui, devoted nearly forty articles between October 1905 and June 1908 to denouncing its archrival Liang Qichao. See Xiaobing Tang, *Global Space*, p. 146.

61. Chen Duxiu, "Zhiwen *Dongfang zazhi* jizhe," p. 402.

62. Ibid., p. 407.

63. Cangfu, "Da *Xin qingnian* zazhi jizhe."

64. Chen Duxiu, "Zai zhiwen *Dongfang zazhi* jizhe," p. 481.

65. Wang Xiaoming, "Yifen zazhi," p. 192; "A Journal and a 'Society,'" p. 9.

66. Huang Yuanyong makes an explicit comparison along these lines. Using the example of a person with blood poisoning, he says, "[First one] must provide a medicine to clean the blood, and only then can one begin to effect a cure. Otherwise, no matter how marvelous the drug one uses, it will only nourish the germs

and simply lead the patient to death that much sooner" ("Guoren zhi gongdu," p. 2).

67. Originally published in *Jiaoyu zazhi* 12.2 (1920), quoted in Chen Pingyuan, "Literature High and Low," pp. 130–131.

9. Swimming against the Tide

1. Link, *Mandarin Ducks and Butterflies*. The most important recent works include Denise Gimpel's *Lost Voices of Modernity* and Yuan Jin's *"Minquan su* yanjiu."

2. Bergère, *Golden Age*, p. 63.

3. For figures and examples, see ibid., pp. 70–83.

4. Elvin, "The Administration of Shanghai," p. 261.

5. Only one of these novels—*Cizhong renyu* (The talk of the town), written in two sections and first published in 1918—is available in the Shanghai Municipal Library.

6. See Fan, "Guanyu Haishang shuomeng ren." The illustration is the frontispiece of the edition of *Xiepu chao* held in the library of the Institute of Chinese Studies at the University of Heidelberg.

7. For a discussion on how the term *"wenming"* functioned as a marker of the foreign in all types of contemporary writing, see chapters 6 and 8.

8. Haishang shuomeng ren, *Xiepu chao*, p. 1.

9. See, for instance, Wu Jianren's famous opening passage to his epic novel *Strange Events* (translated in chapter 6) and Liu Shi'e's *Xin Shanghai* (New Shanghai) of 1909, to name only two among many.

10. This edition (in the Shanghai Municipal Library) contains no publishing information. However, its preface, by Zhuang Renqiu, is dated "the *dingsi* [year 1917]," and Wang Dungen mentions having read a story by "Haishang shuomeng ren" in *Libailiu* (Saturday) "the year before last." Since the first run of *Libailiu* was published between 1914 and 1916, Wang's remarks must have been made between 1916 and 1918.

11. See Wang Dungen's preface to *Xiepu chao*. In his introduction to the first installment of the newspaper serialization on November 23, 1916, Wang had also praised Zhu as being "good at writing novels [and] penetrating *(wosuobuzhi)* in his depiction of social phenomena."

12. The fourth printing of this edition, dated September 9, 1922, is available in the Shanghai Municipal Library but is missing the illustrations. The University of Heidelberg's Institute of Chinese Studies library has a copy of the same edition, and it contains all but four of the illustrations at the opening of each chapter, as well as the author's photo.

13. Yan Fusun, "Haishang shuomeng ren."

14. In addition to the two-volume Hunan wenyi chubanshe edition of 1998, Shanghai guji chubanshe published a three-volume edition in 1991. The former, however, lacks the original prefaces, which were included in the 1991 edition.

15. Liu Na, *Shanbian*, p. 169; for Liu's equally dismissive comments on "behind-the-scenes literature," see pp. 152–154. For a more positive appreciation of *Xiepu chao*, see des Forges' dissertation, "Manufacturing Shanghai."

16. Wang Anyi, "Shanghai de gushi."

17. See Yuan, *Yuanyang hudie pai*, pp. 127–128.

18. For an overview of voluntary associations in the late Qing, see Sang, *Qingmo xin zhishijie*, esp. pp. 288–299. The best account in English of this activity is Strand, *Rickshaw Beijing*.

19. Linda Johnson has determined that the Foreign Settlement had as early as the 1850s become "what the British liked to call the 'Model Settlement': a showcase for Western progress and technical innovation, with drains, gas lighting, public water closets, firmly surfaced roads, raised sidewalks for pedestrians, and even, finally a municipal water supply." She adds, "Its most enduring innovation, however, was the self-governing municipality, installed in 1854. It was, in many ways, more modern than most English towns at home" (*Shanghai*, p. 343).

20. Wue, "Making the Artist," pp. 9–10.

21. Haishang shuomeng ren, *Xiepu chao*, pp. 29–30.

22. See Meng, *The Invention of Shanghai*.

23. Hsu, *Chinese Conception of the Theatre*, p. 25.

24. Cao Xueqin's *Story of the Stone* provides a good example. For instance, when Baoyu is first introduced in the novel, the description of his appearance and garb takes up almost two pages of text (see 1.100–101). Eileen Chang also devotes a good deal of attention to the physical description of her major characters when they first appear in her stories.

25. Haishang shuomeng ren, *Xiepu chao*, p. 100.

26. Ibid., p. 103.

27. On the history of the *shikumen*, see Lu Hanchao, *Beyond the Neon Lights*, pp. 143–160.

28. See Hershatter, *Dangerous Pleasures*.

29. Ibid., pp. 42–43, 64–65.

30. Haishang shuomeng ren, *Xiepu chao*, p. 536.

31. For an account of the thematic concerns of this novel, see David Wang, *Fin-de-siècle Splendor*, pp. 89–100.

32. Another exception to the standard pattern is Zeng Pu's *Niehai hua*, which, as Zeng himself was at pains to point out, was consciously different in disbursing it characters throughout the text rather than concentrating their stories in a particular section—in Zeng's words, not "taking a single thread and stringing pearls on it one by one until the end until it becomes a necklace." See Zeng Pu's 1918 "Xiugai hou", pp. 408–409.

33. Haishang shuomeng ren, *Xiepu chao*, pp. 303–304.

34. The concept of interior monologue has been developed in English most extensively by Dorrit Cohen in her *Transparent Minds*. Given the lack of inflection for person in Chinese, the linguistic features characteristic of the form are quite

easy to produce in Chinese and can readily be found throughout late Qing and modern Chinese fiction.

35. In his research on late nineteenth-century Shanghai painting, Jonathan Hay has found an "up-to-date effect of dynamic immediacy" that might be likened to the sense of the kinetic in Zhu's novel. See Hay's "Painting and the Built Environment," p. 82.

36. According to Shanghai Tushuguan (*Lao Shanghai fengqing lu* 3.168), fourteen hundred automobiles were registered in Shanghai as early as 1912.

37. Haishang shuomeng ren, *Xiepu chao*, pp. 661–662.

38. Goodman, *Native Place*.

39. Haishang shuomeng ren, *Xiepu chao*, p. 41.

40. Ibid., p. 127.

41. On the Zhang garden and its historical context, see Meng, "Re-envisioning the Great Interior."

42. See chapter 6 in Cao, *The Story of the Stone*.

43. *Shen bao*, October 27, 1883, quoted in Elvin, "The Administration of Shanghai," p. 247.

44. Haishang shuomeng ren, *Xiepu chao*, p. 153.

45. Ibid., p. 589.

46. Ibid., p. 602.

47. Ibid., p. 603.

48. Ibid., p. 604.

49. Ibid., p. 610.

50. Meng, "A Playful Discourse."

51. Haishang shuomeng ren, *Xiepu chao*, p. 1396.

52. Bhabha, "Of Mimicry and Man: The Ambivalence of Colonial Discourse," in *The Location of Culture*, p. 86.

53. Hardt and Negri, *Empire*, p. 145.

54. Liang, "Gao xiaoshuo jia," 4.218.

10. Lu Xun and the Crisis of Figuration

1. The best overall account of Lu Xun's life can be found in Wang Xiaoming, *Wufa zhimian de rensheng*. The best account in English is in Lee, *Voices from the Iron House*.

2. See Lu Xun, "*Nahan* zixu," 1.419; translation in *Lu Xun: Selected Works* 1.37.

3. Mao, "Du *Nahan*," 18.398.

4. "Figuration" is used in Genette's general sense of a figure's being the "gap between sign and meaning." See Genette, *Figures of Literary Discourse*, p. ix.

5. Lu Xun, *Lu Xun quanji* 1.100; Denton, *Modern Chinese Literary Thought*, pp. 108–109.

6. The remarkable "Reform Edict" issued by the Qing imperial institution on January 29, 1901, for instance, expresses many of the same ideas: "Those who

have studied Western methods up to now have confined themselves to the spoken and written languages and to weapons and machinery. These are but surface elements of the West and have nothing to do with the essentials of Western learning. . . . If China disregards the essentials of Western learning and merely confines its studies to surface elements which themselves are not even mastered, how can it possibly achieve wealth and power?" (Reynolds, *China, 1898–1912*, p. 203).

7. Lu Xun, "*Nahan* zixu," 1.417; translation from *Selected Works* 1.3.

8. *Lu Xun quanji* 1.44–57. For Sun, see "Lu Xun: China's First Protomodernist."

9. *Lu Xun quanji* 1.55. The translation is my own but is based on that of Kowallis, "Concerning Imbalanced Cultural Development," p. 142.

10. *Lu Xun quanji* 1.52.

11. Wang Hui, "Lu Xun (shang)," 1.124.

12. *Lu Xun quanji* 1.56.

13. Wang Hui, "Lu Xun (shang)," 1.119.

14. Zhang Binglin (Taiyan), "Guojia lun," p. 362; originally published in *Minbao* 17 on October 15, 1907. For the best account of Zhang's thought in this crucial period, see Wang Hui, "Zhang Taiyan's Concept." My discussion here is based on Wang's.

15. *Lu Xun quanji* 1.52.

16. Sakai, "Modernity and Its Critique," p. 501.

17. Chen Duxiu, "Dong-xi minzu."

18. *Lu Xun quanji* 1.419. Cf. Lu Xun's remarks in his 1926 essay, "'Ah Q zhengzhuan' de chengyin," 3.377: "I was simply complying with the wishes of some friends: when they asked me to write, I wrote."

19. Lin Yu-sheng, *The Crisis of Chinese Consciousness*, p. 149.

20. Anderson, *The Limits of Realism*, pp. 80–92.

21. The person behind the pen name "Fu Lin" remains unknown, but the text is available in *Zhongguo jindai wenxue daxi (1840–1919)*; see Fu Lin, *Qinhai shi;* for an English translation, see Patrick Hanan, *The Sea of Regret*, pp. 21–100. Chen Diexian's novel has been reprinted in *Zhongguo jindai xiaoshuo shiliao huibian;* see Chen Diexian, *Huangjin sui;* Hanan's English translation, *The Money Demon*, was published 1999.

22. Brooks, *Reading for the Plot*, p. 246.

23. Anderson, *The Limits of Realism*, p. 88.

24. *Lu Xun quanji* 2.10.

25. Ibid., 11.32; the letter is dated March 31, 1925. I thank Eileen Cheng for bringing this letter to my attention.

26. Brooks, *Reading for the Plot*, pp. 255–256.

27. Kao, "Self-reflexivity," p. 66.

28. *Lu Xun quanji* 1.485.

29. Ibid., 2.124.

30. Tsi-an Hsia, "Aspects of the Power of Darkness," p. 153.

31. *Lu Xun quanji* 3.380.
32. Ibid., 2.10; translation from *Selected Works* 1.174.
33. Conrad, *Heart of Darkness*, p. 10.
34. *Lu Xun quanji* 1.476.
35. Ibid., 1.477.
36. Ibid., 1.479.
37. Ibid., 1.485.
38. Again, the best account of the relationship between Lu Xun's life and work can be found in Wang Xiaoming's *Wufa zhimian de rensheng* (The life that cannot be faced), the title of which alone speaks volumes.
39. Quoted in Brooks, *Troubling Confessions*, p. 48.
40. Brooks, *Troubling Confessions*, p. 49.
41. For a critical account of Lu Xun's relationship with missionary discourse, see Lydia Liu, *Translingual Practice*, pp. 45–76. For a critique of Liu's critique, see the review by Huters in the *Harvard Journal of Asian Studies*.
42. Lukács, *The Theory of the Novel*, p. 72.
43. De Man, "Georg Lukács's *Theory of the Novel*," pp. 51–59.
44. Lukács, *The Theory of the Novel*, p. 125.
45. Naipaul, *A Bend in the River*, pp. 112–113.
46. Ibid., p. 244.
47. Chinnery, "The Influence of Western Literature."
48. *Lu Xun quanji* 1.429. See *Selected Works* 1.48 for a slightly different translation.
49. *Lu Xun quanji* 1.430–431. See also *Selected Works* 1.50.
50. Wang Xiaoming, *Wufa zhimian de rensheng*, pp. 302–303.
51. Jameson, "Third-World Literature." The first of many critiques of Jameson can be found in Ahmad, "Jameson's Rhetoric of Otherness."
52. Gogol, "The Diary of a Madman," p. 28.

Glossary

a er re ba da 阿爾熱八達
Ah Fu 阿福
Aiguo nüxue 愛國女學
bagu wen 八股文
Bai Yaolian 柏耀廉
Bainian yijiao 百年一覺
baishi 稗史
Ban Gu 班固
ban kaihua 半開化
Banqiao zaji 板橋雜詁
Baozhen 吳寶震
Beiming 焙茗
benmo 本末
bi 筆
Bianfa tongyi 變法通議
biehao 別號
bu jinshou guimen 不謹守閨門
bujie 不解
Bungaku kōkoku saku 文學興國策
buru ren 不如人
buyao lian 不要臉
buzizu de xin 不自足的心
Cai Lüsheng 蔡侶笙
"Cai xixue yi" 采西學議
Cai Yuanpei 蔡元培 (1868–1940)
Caifeng bao 采風報
caizi jiaren 才子佳人
Cao Xueqin 曹雪芹 (1715–1763)
Chang, Eileen 張愛玲 (1920–1995)

chang yuan 償愿
changsan 長三
chaoren 超人
Chen Jitong 陳季同 (1851–1907)
Chen Li 陳澧 (1810–1882)
Chen Qianqiu 陳千秋
Chen Zhongai 陳仲藹
Cheng 成
chengdu wenti 程度問題
chi 恥
Chi shui yi zhen 赤水遺珍
chongzi 蟲子
chou 丑
Chu Ailin 褚愛林
Chubao 楚報
Chunqiu 春秋
ci bu da yi 辭不達意
Cian 慈安 (1837–1881)
cike 詞客
ciqi yuan bi 辭氣遠鄙
Cixi 慈禧 (1835–1908)
cizhang 詞章
da ni budao 大逆不道
Da xue 大學
da yitong 大一統
dagong 大公
daguanyuan 大觀園
Dai Mingshi 戴名世 (1653–1713)
Dajiang bao 大江報

"Daluanzhe jiu Zhongguo zhi miao yao ye" 大亂者救中國之妙藥也
danchun 單純
dangpai 黨派
dao 道
dao/qi 道/器
daotai 道台
daotong 道統
Daoxue 道學
daqu 大曲
dayi 大義
Deng Gongsan 鄧恭三
Deng Shi 鄧實
dexing 德行
Dianshu qitan 電術奇談
dianxue 電學
di'erci geming 第二此革命
dingsi 丁巳
Dongfang Fa 東方法
Dongfang Qiang 東方強
Dongfang Wenming 東方文明
Dongfang zazhi 東方雜誌
Donghua lu 東華錄
Dongou nü haojie 東歐女豪傑
Dongwu daxue 東吳大學
Du Fu 杜甫 (712–770)
Du Mu 杜牧 (803–852)
Duan Yucai 段玉裁 (1735–1815)
Duanfang 端方 (1861–1911)
duban 督辦
er maozi 二毛子
fakanci 發刊詞
Fan zhentan 反偵探
fanchuan jushi 樊川居士
Fang Dongshu 方東樹 (1772–1851)
Fang Hongjian 方鴻漸
Fang Yilu 方佚盧
fanhua 繁華
fei xiaoshuo ye 非小說也
fengliu 風流
Foshan shuyuan 佛山書院
Fu Caiyun 傅彩雲
Fu Lanya 傅蘭雅

Fu Lin 符霖
fugu 復古
fuguo qiangbing 富國強兵
Furen 輔仁
Fusheng liuji 浮生六記
Fuzhou mawei chuanchang chuanzheng xuetang 福州馬尾船廠政學堂
Gailiang xiaoshuo she 改良小說社
gaixie guizheng 改邪歸正
gan 乾
gang 綱
Gangjian yizhi lu 綱鑑易知錄
Gao Qi 高啓 (1336–1374)
gengzi nian 庚子
gezhi 格致
Gezhi huibian 格致滙編
gezhi shixue 格致實學
Gezhi shuyuan 格致書院
gong 公
gong 功
Gong, Prince (Gong qinwang) 恭親王 (Yixin 奕訢)
Gong Cheng 龔橙 (b. 1817)
gong de 公德
Gong Xiaoqi 龔孝琪
Gong Zizhen 龔自珍 (1792–1841)
gongdu 公牘
"Gongli shuo" 功利說
gongye 功業
Gou Cai 苟才
Gou Longguang 苟龍光
gouqie shili 苟且勢力
guanchang 官場
Guanchang xianxing ji 官場現形記
guangxue 光學
Guangxue hui 廣學會
Guangzhi 廣智
Guanzi 莞子
gudai 古代
guigui jujude 規規矩矩的
Gujing jingshe 古經精社
gulei 故壘

Guliang zhuan 穀梁傳
Guo Songtao 郭嵩燾 (1818–1891)
guocui 國粹
Guocui baocun hui 國粹保存會
guojia 國家
Guomindang 國民黨
Guowen bao 國聞報
guwen 古文
Guwenci leizuan 古文辭類纂
guya 古雅
hai 害
Haishang hua liezhuan 海上花列傳
Han Bangqing 韓邦慶 (1856–1894)
Han *jue* 漢爵
han wanniu chong wandong 汗萬牛充萬棟
Han Wudi 漢武帝
Han Yu 韓愈 (768–824)
Hankou ribao 漢口日報
Hanxue 漢學
He Ban 何班 (Zhen 震)
He Jingming 何景明 (1483–1521)
heimu 黑幕
Henhai 恨海
Hong 虹
Hong Jun 洪鈞 (1840–1893)
housheng liyong zhi yitu 厚生利用之一途
Hu bao 滬報
Hua Hengfang 華蘅芳 (1833–1902)
Huai Nanzi 淮南子
Huang Jie 黃節
Huang Kan 黃侃 (1886–1935)
Huang Ren 黃人 (Moxi 摩西, 1866–1913)
Huangjin sui 黃金祟
huaqing jiexian 劃清界限
huaxue 化學
hui yin hui dao 誨姪誨盜
"Huitong di shisan" 會通之十三
Huitou kan jilue 囘頭看紀略
Huizui zhi dalue 悔罪之大略
I *(yi)* 一

Jia Baoyu 價寶玉
jian'ai 兼愛
Jiang Biao 蔣標 (1860–1899)
Jiang Liangqi 蔣良騏 (1722–1789)
Jiangnan zhizaoju 江南製造局
Jianren 吳趼人
Jianyi waibian 趼廛外編
jiao 教
Jiaohui xin bao 教會新報
jiaoyu 教育
Jiaoyu zazhi 教育雜誌
jiawu chunban 甲午春半
jiayou 假有
Jin 晉
Jin Ping Mei 金瓶梅
Jin Songcen 金菘岑 (1873–1947)
Jin Wenqing 金雯青
jindai Zhongguo 近代中國
Jingbao 京報
"Jinggao qingnian" 警告青年
jingji 經濟
jingshenshang zhi zuoyong 精神上的作用
Jingzhong ribao 警鍾日報
"Jinri zhi jiaoyu fangzhen" 今日之教育方針
jinshi 進士
jinshi jia 金石家
Jiuli 九黎
Jiuming qiyuan 九命奇緣
Jiusi yishing 九死一生
jiuxue wei ti, xinxue wei yong, bushi pian fei 舊學為體, 新學為用, 不使偏廢
juan 卷
kaihua 開化
kaiming pai 開明派
Kang 康
Kang Erjin 康爾錦
Kangxi zhengyao 康熙政要
kaozheng 攷證
kexue 科學
kuangren 狂人
"Kuangren riji" 狂人日記
laoye 老爺

Laoye bie chuipang, ni yitian dao wan baole jiben po shu, zuili jiligulu, shuoxie buzhong buwai de buzhi shemma hua . . . 老爺別吹滂，你一天到晚抱了幾本破書，嘴裏唧唎咕嚕，說些不中不外的不知甚麼話 . . .
leli zhuyi 樂利主義
li 利
li 理
li 禮
Li Bai 李白 (701–762)
Li Baojia 李寶嘉 (Boyuan 伯元, 1867–1906)
Li Hongzhang 李鴻章 (1823–1901)
Li Jingyi 黎景翼
Li Pingshu 李平書
Li Shangyin 李商隱 (813?–858)
Li Shanlan 李善蘭 (1810–1882)
Li Shinong 黎石農
Li Shizhen 李時珍 (1518–1593)
Li Shuchang 黎庶昌 (1837–1897)
Li Timotai 李提摩太
Li Wentian 李文田 (1834–1895)
Li Xiang 李詳 (1858–1931)
lian 廉
"Liang Shanbo" 梁山泊
Liang Shuming 梁漱溟 (1893–1988)
Libailiu 禮拜六
lidao 理道
liedeng 劣等
Liezi 列子
Lihua bu 理化部
lilong 里弄
Lin Daiyu 林黛玉
Lin Lezhi 林樂知
lingxue 靈學
Liu, Commandant 劉司令
Liu Shi'e 劉士諤
Liu Xihong 劉錫鴻
liu yi 六藝
lixing 理性
liyu 俚語

liyu 利慾
Lou brothers 婁兩公子
Lu Jiuyuan 陸九淵 (1139–1193)
Lu Renxiang 陸仁祥 (Bengru 犇如)
Lu Runxiang 陸潤庠 (1841–1915)
Lun baihua wei weixin zhi ben 論白話為維新之本
Lun fojiao yu qunzhi zhi guanxi 論佛教與群治之關係
Lun nüxue 論女學
Lun Shanghai fengsu 論上海風俗
"*Lun wenxue zhi shili jiqi guanxi*" 論文學之勢力及其關係
"*Lun xiaoshuo zhi jiaoyu*" 論小說之教育
Lunchuan zhaoshang ju 輪船招商局
Lunyu 論語
lunzhu 論著
Ma Jianzhong 馬建忠 (1844–1900)
Ma shi wentong 馬氏文通
Mei 梅女士
Mei Gucheng 梅穀成 (1681–1763)
Mei Yuege 媚月閣
Mencius 孟子
miaoyu 廟宇
Minbao 民報
mingjiao zuiren 明教罪人
mingliu 名流
mingshi 名士
minjun 民軍
minquan 民權
Minquan bao 民權報
minzu 民族
minzu sixiang 民族思想
minzu zhuyi 民族主義
Miss Lu 魯小姐
mo 魔
mombu daijin 文部大人
Mori Arinori 森有禮 (1847–1889)
Mozi 墨子
mu hua 慕化
mufu 幕府
Nahan 吶喊

Nanfang bao 南方報
Nanhai 南海
Nanshe 南社
Nanwu Yeman 南武野蠻
Nanyang gongxue 南洋公學
Ni Bohe 倪伯和
Ni Huanzhi 倪煥之
Ni Junren 倪俊人
niewu 臬兀
Ouyou xinying lu 歐遊心影錄
Pan Jinlian 潘金蓮
panghuang 彷徨
pianti 駢體
qi 器
qian chang zhe zhi 淺嘗輒止
qian qizi 前七子
Qian Xuantong 錢玄同 (1887–1939)
qianze xiaoshuo 譴責小說
Qin 秦
qin 親
Qin Jiushao 秦九韶
qing 情
qinglian jushi 青蓮居士
Qingnian zazhi 青年雜誌
qiongli jinxing 窮理盡性
Qiu Tingliang 裘廷梁 (1857–1943)
Qiu Weixuan 邱煒萲
Qiuju 秋菊
Qiushu 訄書
qiuzhe shixin xiaoshuo qi 求著時新小說啓
"Qiwu lun" 齊物論
Qixin bao 奇新報
Qu *gongsun* 蘧公孫
Qu Jingyu 蘧景玉
Qu Qiubai 瞿秋白 (1899–1935)
Qu Shenfu 蘧駪夫
qun 群
Qunxue 群學
qunzu 群族
qusi 屈私
Ren Tingxu 任廷旭
renge 人格
renyi daode 仁義道德
Ruan Lingyu 阮玲玉 (1910–1935)
runwei 閏位
Rushi 如是
Sai Jinhua 賽金花 (1874–1936)
san cong si de qi zhen jiu lie 三從四德七貞九烈
san gang 三綱
Sanmiao 三苗
Shang 商
Shang *yi* 商彝
Shanghai xin bao 上海新報
"Shangshi" 傷逝
shanshu 善書
shehui xiaoshuo 社會小說
Shen Fu 沈復 (1762–after 1809)
Shen bao 申報
"*Shen bao* guan 'zuijin wushi nian'" 申報館最近五十年
Sheng Xuanhuai 盛宣懷 (1844–1916)
shenghuo de lu hai henduo 生活的路還很多
shengjing xianzhuan 聖經賢傳
"Shexue disan" 設學第三
shi 實
shi chuan 失傳
shi dafu 士大夫
"Shi huo zhi" 食貨志
shi li qiu ye 失禮求野
Shi Naian 施耐菴
Shi run 失閏
shi tai pian yu jiu 實太偏于舊
Shibao 時報
shijie geming 詩界革命
Shijie shuju 世界書局
shikumen 石窟門
Shitou ji 石頭記
shiwen 時文
shoujiu 守舊
shu 疏
Shu shu jiu zhang 數書九章
Shuihu zhuan 水滸傳
Shun 舜

shuobu 說部
shusu 菽粟
shuyu 書寓
si 私
si da jin'gang 四大金剛
si de 私德
si malu 四馬路
sike 四科
Siku quanshu zongmu tiyao 四庫全書總目提要
Sili taosheng 死裏逃生
Sishi zishu 四十自述
sixiang 思想
sixiang jie zhi longtong eryi 思想界之籠統而已
Song Shiren 宋使仁
Su Shi 蘇軾 (1037–1101)
Subao 蘇報
Suiren shi 燧人氏
suoyin 索隱
ta 他, 她
taiping 太平
taiping rizi 太平日子
Tan Guohun 譚國魂
Tang 唐
Tang Caichang 唐才常 (1867–1900)
Tao Xingcun 陶惺存
ti 悌
ti 體
tian yuan yi 天元一
tian, di, ren 天, 地, 人
tiandi 天地
tianxia 天下
Tianyi bao 天義報
tiaohe 調和
tiegua 帖括
tingzi jian 亭子間
"Tiyao" 提要
tong 通
tong ru 通儒
Tongcheng 桐城
Tongmeng hui 同盟會

Tongshi 痛史
Tongwen guan 同文館
tuiyi 推移
tuoqi 唾棄
Waijiao bao 外交報
Waipian 外篇
Wan Qing xiaoshuo daxi 晚清小說大系
wan Zhou zhuzi 晚周諸子
Wang Chuanshan 王船山 (Fuzhi 夫之, 1619–1692)
Wang Duanfu 王端夫
Wang Dungen 王鈍根 (1888–1951?)
Wang Gongquan 汪公權
Wang Guowei 王國維 (1877–1927)
Wang Jingxuan 王敬軒
Wang Juanjuan 王娟娟
Wang Kaiyun 王闓運 (1833–1916)
"Wang Mang zhuan" 王莽傳
Wang Niansun 王念孫 (1744–1832)
Wang Yangming 王陽明 (1472–1529)
Wanguo gongbao 萬國公報
Wei 魏
Wei Wenjin 魏文錦
weiwan 未完
weiwu 偽物
weixin 維新
wen 文
Wen Shunong 文述農
wen yi zai dao 文以載道
wenci 文辭
wenhua ren 文化人
wenli ziju 文理字句
wenmiao 文廟
wenming 文明
wenming guo ren 文明國人
wenming jingjie 文明境界
Wenming xiaoshi 文明小史
wenren 文人
wenwu 文物
Wenxuan 文選
wenxue 文學
wenxue kuang 文學狂

"Wenxue xiaoyan" 文學小言
wenxue zhi zui shangcheng 文學之最上乘
Wenyan 文言
wenyuan 文苑
wenzhang 文章
wenzi 文字
Wo foshan ren 我佛山人
worang 窩攮
Woren 倭仁 (1804–1871)
wosuobuzhi 無所不至
Woyao 吳沃堯
Wu Bohui 吳伯惠
wu guomin tebie zhi gongdu 吾國民特別之公毒
Wu Jianren ku 吳趼人哭
Wu Jingzeng 吳景曾
Wu Jizhi 吳繼之
Wu Song 武松
Wu Xinshe 吳莘畬 (1804–1863)
Wu Yunji 吳允吉 (1841–1882)
Xia 夏
Xia ding 夏鼎
Xia Zengyou 夏曾佑 (1863–1924)
xiandai 現代
xiandaihua 現代化
xiandaizhuyi 現代主義
"Xianggong" 襄公
Xianglin Sao 祥林嫂
xianshi zhuyi 現實主義
xiao 孝
xiao shimin 小市民
xiao you cai zhi ren 小有才之人
xiaoling 小令
xiaoshuo 小說
Xiaoshuo conghua 小說叢話
xiaoshuo geming 小說革命
Xiaoshuo lan 小說欄
Xiaoshuo lin 小說林
Xiaoshuo lin she 小說林社
Xiaoshuo xiaohua 小說小話
Xiaoshuo yuebao 小說月報

Xiaoxian bao 消閑報
xiehang 頡頏
xiezi 楔子
Xihe 羲和
Xijing fu 西京賦
xin 信
xin guo 信國
"Xin minzhu zhuyi lun" 新民主主義論
Xin qingnian 新青年
xin qu 新趣
Xin Shanghai 新上海
Xin Shenbao 新申報
xin tong 心痛
xin wenti 新文體
Xin xiaoshuo 新小說
xingling 性靈
xingzhi 性質
"Xinjiu wenti" 新舊問題
Xinmin tushuguan 新民圖書館
Xinwen bao 新聞報
xinxue 心血
xinxue 心學
xiushen 修身
Xiuxiang xiaoshuo 繡像小說
xixue 西學
Xu Guangping 許廣平 (1898–1968)
Xu Guangqi 徐光啓 (1562–1633)
Xu Jiyu 徐繼畬 (1795–1873)
Xu Qian 徐謙 (1871–1940)
Xu Renzhu 徐仁鑄 (1863–1900)
Xu Xilin 徐錫林
Xu Zhenya 徐枕亞 (1889–1937)
"Xu zhongxing" 序種姓
Xuanyuan 軒轅
Xue Fucheng 薛福成 (1838–1894)
Xue Pan 靴蟠
"Xue suan bitan" 學算筆談
Xuehai tang 學海堂
xueli 學理
"Xueshu zhi" 學術志
xueshuo goucheng 學說構成
xunli 循理

Xunzi 荀子
xuqie zheng 虛怯症
ya 雅
Yan Fu fanyi yanjiu wenzhang 嚴復繙譯研究文章
Yan Fu shengping ji wenxue huodong 嚴復生平及文學活動
Yan Shigu 顏師古 (581–645)
yanci 言詞
Yang Tingxi 楊廷熙
Yang Xiong 楊雄 (53 B.C.E.–18 C.E.)
yangchang 洋場
yanghua yangzi 洋話洋字
Yangwu 洋務
Yantai 煙台
yanyu 言語
Yanzi yiwen zhi 嚴子一文之
Yao 堯
Yao Nai 姚鼐 (1732–1815)
Ye Dehui 葉德輝 (1864–1927)
Ye Shaojun 葉紹鈞 (1894–1988)
yeji 野鷄
yeman 野蠻
yemande ren 野蠻的人
yi 艾
yi 義
yi 藝
yi fuyan pengyou de zhutuo 以敷衍朋友的囑託
Yi jing 易經
Yi Ya 易牙
"Yi yin zhengzhi xiaoshu xu" 譯印政治小說序
yin yiwei zhong 引以為重
Yinghuan zhilue 瀛寰志略
Yingyao siji 英軺私記
Yinzi 闉子
Yipin Xiang 一品香
yiqi 意氣
yisi 意思
yong 用
Youchao shi 有巢氏
Youxi bao 遊戲報

"Youxue, di'er" 游學, 第二
youya 優雅
Yu 虞
yu chao 于朝
Yu chu 虞初
Yu Huai 余懷 (1616–1696)
yu xizu zhouxuan zhi jiazhi 與晰族周旋之價值
yu ye 于野
Yu Yue 愈樾 (1821–1907)
Yuan shi buzheng 元史補正
Yuan Shikai 袁世凱 (1859–1916)
Yueyue xiaoshuo 月月小說
Yuli hun 玉梨魂
Yunsheng 雲生
Yuxi sheng 玉溪生
Yuyan bao 寓言報
Yuyuan 豫園
Zeng Guofan 曾國藩 (1811–1872)
Zeng Jing 曾靜 (1679–1736)
Zeng Xubai 曾虛白
Zha Siting 查嗣庭 (1664–1727)
Zhang Heng 張衡 (78–139)
Zhang Jingda 張靖達
Zhang Peilun 張佩綸 (1848–1903)
Zhang Shizhao 章士釗 (1882–1973)
Zhang Yinhuan 張蔭桓 (1837–1900)
Zhang yuan 張園
Zhang Zhunmai 張君勱 (1886–1969)
zhanghui xiaoshuo 章回小說
Zhao Boxuan 趙伯宣
zhen 真
Zhen Baoyu 甄寶玉
zhende ren 真的人
Zheng Suonan 鄭所南
zhengshi 政事
Zhengzhi weixin yaoyan 政治維新要言
zhezhong 折衷
zhi qi ye 治其業
zhi taiping 致太平
"Zhi yangqi yi" 製洋器議
zhi zhi ji sheng 至治極盛
Zhibao 直報

zhinan 指南
zhipei 支配
zhiqi 制器
zhishi fenzi 知識分子
zhiyi 制藝
zhong 忠
Zhong-dong zhanji benmo 中東戰紀本末
"Zhongguo wenxue shi" 中國文學史
Zhongguo zouxiang shijie, shijie zouxiang Zhongguo 中國走向世界, 世界走向中國
zhongxue 重學
Zhongxue wei ti, xixue wei yong 中學為體, 西學為用
Zhou 周
"Zhou benji" 周本紀
Zhou *dui* 周敦
Zhou Dunyi 周敦頤 (1017–1073)
Zhou guan 周官

Zhou Guisheng 周桂笙 (1873–1936)
Zhou Shoujuan 周瘦鵑 (1894–1968)
Zhu Xi 朱熹 (1130–1200)
Zhuang Renqiu 莊紉秋
zhuangyuan 狀元
Zhuangzi 莊子
Zhuoqu 琢渠
"Ziming zhong shuo" 自鳴鐘說
ziti 自體
zixing 自性
zixu 自序
ziyou 自由
zongfa 宗法
Zongli yamen 總理衙門
Zouxiang gonghe 走向共和
Zouxiang shijie congshu 走向世界叢書
zui 罪
Zuo zhuan 左傳
Zuo Zongtang 左宗棠 (1812–1885)

Works Cited

A Ying 阿英 (Qian Xingcun 錢杏邨). *Wan Qing xiaoshuo shi* 晚清小說史 (History of late Qing fiction). 1937. Reprint, Hong Kong: Zhonghua shuju, 1973.
——, ed. *Wan Qing wenxue congchao* 晚清文學叢鈔 (Compendium of late Qing literature). 4 vols. Beijing: Zhonghua shuju, 1980.
——, ed. *Wan Qing wenxue congchao: Xiaoshuo xiqu yanjiu juan* 小說戲曲研究卷 (Compendium of late Qing literature: Volume of studies on the novel and drama). Shanghai: Zhonghua shuju, 1960.
Adorno, Theodor W. "Extorted Reconciliation: On George Lukács' *Realism in Our Time*." In *Notes to Literature,* trans. Sherry Weber Nicholsen, vol. 1, pp. 216–240. New York: Columbia University Press, 1991.
Ahern, Emily. "The Power and Pollution of Chinese Women." In *Women in Chinese Society,* ed. Margery Wolf and Roxanne Witke, pp. 169–190. Stanford, CA: Stanford University Press, 1975.
Ahmad, Aijaz. "Jameson's Rhetoric of Otherness and the 'National Allegory.'" *Social Text* 17 (fall 1987): 3–25.
Alitto, Guy S. *The Last Confucian: Liang Shu-ming and the Chinese Dilemma of Modernity.* Berkeley and Los Angeles: University of California Press, 1979.
Allen, Young J. (Lin Lezhi 林樂知), and Ren Tingxu 任廷旭, trans. *Wenxue xingguo ce* 文學興國策 (Stratagems to revive the country through education). Shanghai: Shanghai shudian, 2002.
Altbach, Philip G. "Education and Neocolonialism." In *The Post-Colonial Studies Reader,* ed. B. Ashcroft, G. Griffiths, and H. Tiffin, pp. 452–456. London: Routledge, 1995.
Anderson, Marston. *The Limits of Realism: Chinese Fiction in the Revolutionary Period.* Berkeley and Los Angeles: University of California Press, 1990.
——. "The Scorpion in the Scholar's Cap: Ritual, Memory, and Desire in *Rulin waishi*." In Huters et al., *Culture and State,* pp. 259–276.
Anon. "Lun xiaoshuo zhi jiaoyu." In Chen Pingyuan and Xia, *Ershi shiji Zhongguo*

xiaoshuo lilun ziliao, 1.186–188. First published 1906, in *Xin shijie xiaoshuo she bao* 新世界小說社報 (Journal of the new world fiction society).

Ayers, William. *Chang Chih-tung and Educational Reform in China.* Cambridge, MA: Harvard University Press, 1971.

Bellamy, Edward. *Looking Backward.* 1888. Reprint, New York: Bantam Books, 1983.

Bennett, A. A. *John Fryer: The Introduction of Western Science and Technology into Nineteenth-Century China.* Cambridge, MA: East Asian Research Center, Harvard University, 1967.

Bergère, Marie-Claire. *The Golden Age of the Chinese Bourgeoisie, 1911–1937.* Trans. Janet Lloyd. Cambridge: Cambridge University Press, 1989.

———. "The Issue of Imperialism." In *The Chinese Revolution of 1911: New Perspectives,* ed. Chun-tu Hsueh. Hong Kong: Joint Publishing, 1986.

———. *Sun Yat-sen.* Trans. Janet Lloyd. Stanford, CA: Stanford University Press, 1998.

Berman, Marshall. *All That Is Solid Melts into Air: The Experience of Modernity.* New York: Penguin Books, 1988.

Bernal, Martin. "Liu Shih-p'ei and National Essence." In Furth, *The Limits of Change,* pp. 90–112.

Bhabha, Homi. *The Location of Culture.* London and New York: Routledge, 1994.

Birdwhistle, Anne. *Transition to Neo-Confucianism: Shao Yung on Knowledge and Symbols of Reality.* Stanford, CA: Stanford University Press, 1989.

Bland, J. O. P. *Recent Events and Present Policies in China.* London: William Heinemann, 1912.

Bol, Peter K. *"This Culture of Ours": Intellectual Transitions in T'ang and Sung China.* Stanford, CA: Stanford University Press, 1992.

Bonner, Joey. *Wang Kuo-wei: An Intellectual Biography.* Cambridge, MA: Harvard University Press, 1986.

Britton, Roswell S. *The Chinese Periodical Press 1800–1912.* Shanghai: Kelly and Walsh, 1933.

Brooks, Peter. *Reading for the Plot: Design and Invention in Narrative.* Cambridge, MA: Harvard University Press, 1992.

———. *Troubling Confessions: Speaking Guilt in Law and Literature.* Chicago: University of Chicago Press, 2000.

Butler, Judith. *Gender Trouble: Feminism and Subversion of Identity.* New York and London: Routledge, 1990.

Cai Jingkang 蔡景康. "Wan Qing xiaoshuo lilun chulun" 晚清小說理論初論 (Preliminary remarks on late Qing theory of fiction). In *Gudai wenxue lilun yanjiu* 古代文學理論研究 (Research on ancient Chinese literary theory), 1:403–421. Shanghai: Shanghai guji chubanshe, 1979.

Cangfu 傖父 (Du Yaquan 杜亞泉). "Da *Xin qingnian* zazhi jizhe zhi zhiwen" 答新青年雜誌記者之質問 (Responding to the questions posed by the correspondent of *New Youth* magazine). *Dongfang zazhi* 東方雜誌 15.12 (December 1918): 12–13.

———. "Jingde wenming yu dongde wenming" 靜的文明與動的文明 (The quiet civilization and the active civilization). *Dongfang zazhi* 13.10 (October 10, 1916): 1–8.

———. "Zai lun xinjiu sixiang zhi chongtu" 再論新舊思想之衝突 (More remarks on the clash between new and old thought). *Dongfang zazhi* 13.4 (April 10, 1916): 1–6.

———. "Zhanhou dongxi wenming zhi tiaohe" 戰後東西文明之調和 (The postwar reconciliation of Eastern and Western cultures). *Dongfang zazhi* 14.4 (April 15, 1917): 1–6.

———. *See also* Du Yaquan; Gao Lao.

Cao Xueqin 曹雪芹. *The Story of the Stone*. 5 vols. Trans. David Hawkes. Harmondsworth, England: Penguin Books, 1973–1986.

Cao Xueqin and Gao E 高鶚. *Hong lou meng* 紅樓夢 (Dream of the red chamber) [The story of the Stone]. Beijing: Renmin wenxue chubanshe, 1996.

Chang, Hao. *Chinese Intellectuals in Crisis: Search for Order and Meaning, 1890–1911*. Berkeley and Los Angeles: University of California Press, 1987.

———. *Liang Ch'i-ch'ao and Intellectual Transition in China, 1890–1907*. Cambridge, MA: Harvard University Press, 1971.

Chatterjee, Partha. *Nationalist Thought and the Colonial World: A Derivative Discourse?* Minneapolis: University of Minnesota Press, 1986.

———. *The Nation and Its Fragments: Colonial and Postcolonial Histories*. Princeton, NJ: Princeton University Press, 1993.

Chen Bohai 陳伯海 and Yuan Jin 袁進, eds. *Shanghai jindai wenxue shi* 上海近代文學史 (A literary history of modern Shanghai). Shanghai: Shanghai renmin chubanshe, 1993.

Chen Chi 陳熾. "*Shengshi weiyan* xu" 盛世危言序 (Preface to *Blunt words in a time of prosperity*). In *Chen Chi ji* 陳熾集 (Collected work of Chen Chi), pp. 303–306. Beijing: Zhonghua shuju, 1997.

Chen Diexian 陳蝶仙. *Huangjin sui* 黃金祟 (The money demon). In *Zhongguo jindai xiaoshuo shiliao huibian* 中國近代小說史料滙編 (Collected materials on modern Chinese fiction). Taipei: Guangwen shuju, 1980. *See also* Hanan, *The Money Demon*.

Chen Duxiu 陳獨秀. *Chen Duxiu zhuzuo xuan* 陳獨秀著作選 (Selected works of Chen Duxiu). 3 vols. Shanghai: Shanghai renmin chubanshe, 1993.

———. "Dong-xi minzu genben sixiang zhi chayi" 東西民族根本思想之差異 (The fundamental difference in the thought of the Eastern and Western nations). In *Chen Duxiu zhuzuo xuan*, pp. 165–171.

———. "Falanxi ren yu jinshi wenming" 法蘭西與近世文明 (The French and modern civilization). In *Chen Duxiu zhuzuo xuan*, pp. 136–139.

———. "Kongzi zhi dao yu xiandai shenghuo" 孔子之道與現代生活 (The way of Confucius and modern life). In *Chen Duxiu zhuzuo xuan*, pp. 230–237.

———. "Yijiuyiliu" 一九一六 ("1916"). In *Chen Duxiu zhuzuo xuan,* pp. 170–174.

———. "Zai zhiwen *Dongfang zazhi* jizhe" 再質問 東方雜誌 記者 (More questions addressed to the correspondents of the *Eastern Miscellany*). In *Chen Duxiu zhuzuo xuan,* pp. 478–491.

———. "Zhiwen *Dongfang zazhi* jizhe—*Dongfang zazhi* yu fubi wenti" 質問 東方雜誌 記者—東方雜誌 與復辟問題 (Questions addressed to the correspondent of *The Eastern Miscellany*—*The Eastern Miscellany* and the question of the restoration). In *Chen Duxiu zhuzuo xuan,* pp. 401–407.

Ch'en, Jerome. *China and the West: Society and Culture 1815–1937.* London: Hutchison, 1979.

Chen Pingyuan 陳平原. *Ershi shiji Zhongguo xiaoshuo shi: Diyi juan, yiba yiqi–yijiu yiliu* 二十世紀中國小說史第一卷: 一八九七, 一九一六 (The history of twentieth-century Chinese fiction: Volume 1, 1897–1916). Beijing: Beijing daxue chubanshe, 1989.

———. "Literature High and Low: 'Popular Fiction' in Twentieth-Century China." In Hockx, *The Literary Field,* pp. 113–133.

Chen Pingyuan and Xia Xiao-hong 夏曉虹, eds. *Ershi shiji Zhongguo xiaoshuo lilun ziliao: Diyi juan, 1897–1916* 二十世紀中國小說理論資料: 第一卷, 一八九七——一九一六 (Materials on the theory of twentieth-century Chinese fiction: Volume 1, 1897–1916). Beijing: Beijing daxue chubanshe, 1989.

Chen Sanli 陳三立. "Du Xunzi" 讀荀子 (Reading Xunzi). *Dongfang zazhi* 13.10 (October 10, 1916): 5.17–19.

Chen Song 陳崧, ed. *Wusi qianhou dongxi wenhua wenti lunzhan wenxuan* 五四前後東西文化問題論戰文選 (Selected essays from disputes over the issue of Eastern and Western cultures in the May Fourth period). Beijing: Zhongguo shehui kexue yuan chubanshe, 1989.

Chen, Xiaomei. *Occidentalism: A Theory of Counter-Discourse on Post-Mao China.* 2nd ed. Lanham, MD: Rowman and Littlefield, 2002.

Chen Xinghui 陳幸蕙. *"Ershi nian mudu zhi guai xianzhuang" yanjiu* 二十年目睹之怪現狀 研究 (A study of *Strange Events* . . .). History and Literature Series, no. 61. Taipei: National Taiwan University, 1983.

Chinnery, J. D. "The Influence of Western Literature on Lu Xun's 'Diary of a Madman.'" *Bulletin of Asian and African Studies* 23.2 (1960): 309–322.

Chou ban yi wu shimo 籌辦夷務始末 (Complete record of the management of barbarian affairs). Tongzhi 同治 46. Reprinted in *Yangwu yundong.*

Chow Tse-tsung 周策縱. *The May Fourth Movement: Intellectual Revolution in Modern China.* Cambridge, MA: Harvard University Press, 1960.

Choy, Howard Y. F., trans. "The Fate of 'Mr. Science' in China: The Concept of Science and Its Application in Modern Chinese Thought." *Positions: East Asia Cultures Critique* 3.1 (spring 1995): 1–68. *See also* Wang Hui, "Sai xiansheng zai Zhongguo."

Ci, Jiwei. *Dialectic of the Chinese Revolution: From Utopianism to Hedonism.* Stanford, CA: Stanford University Press, 1994.

Coble, Parks M., Jr. *The Shanghai Capitalists and the Nationalist Government, 1927–1937.* Cambridge, MA: Council on East Asian Studies, Harvard University, 1986.

Cohen, Dorrit. *Transparent Minds: Narrative Modes for Presenting Consciousness in Fiction.* Princeton, NJ: Princeton University Press, 1978.

Cohen, Paul A. *Between Tradition and Modernity: Wang T'ao and Reform in Late Ch'ing China.* Cambridge, MA: Harvard University Press, 1974.

———. "Christian Missions and Their Impact to 1900." In *The Cambridge History of China,* vol. 10, ed. John K. Fairbank, pp. 543–590. Cambridge: Cambridge University Press, 1978.

———. *Discovering History in China: American Historical Writing on the Recent Chinese Past.* New York: Columbia University Press, 1984.

———. *History in Three Keys: The Boxers as Event, Experience, and Myth.* New York: Columbia University Press, 1997.

Cohen, Paul A., and John E. Schrecker, eds. *Reform in Nineteenth-Century China.* Cambridge, MA: East Asian Research Center, Harvard University, 1976.

Conrad, Joseph. *Heart of Darkness.* New York: Norton, 1988.

Cui Wanqiu 崔萬秋. "Dongya bingfu fangwen ji" 東亞病夫訪問記 (Interview with the "Sickman of Asia"). In Wei Shaochang, *Nie hai hua ziliao,* pp. 139–142.

Dagenais, Ferdinand. *John Fryer's Calendar: Correspondence, Publications, and Miscellaneous Papers with Excerpts and Commentary.* Berkeley: Center for Chinese Studies, University of California, Berkeley, 1999.

Dai Yangben 戴揚本. "Feng Guifen yu *Jiaobinlu kangyi*" 馮桂芬與校邠盧抗議 (Feng Guifen and the *Jiaobinlu kangyi*). In Feng Guifen, *Jiaobinlu kangyi,* pp. 1–64.

de Bary, Brett. Introduction to *Origins of Modern Japanese Literature,* by Karatani Kojin, trans. and ed. Brett de Bary. Durham, N.C.: Duke University Press, 1993.

de Bary, Wm. Theodore, ed. *Sources of the Chinese Tradition.* New York: Columbia University Press, 1964.

de Lacouperie, Terrien. *The Languages of China before the Chinese: Researches on the Languages Spoken by the Pre-Chinese Races of China Proper Previously to the Chinese Occupation.* London: David Nutt, 1877.

de Man, Paul. *Blindness and Insight: Essays in the Rhetoric of Contemporary Criticism.* Minneapolis: University of Minnesota Press, 1983.

———. "Georg Lukács's *Theory of the Novel.*" In *Blindness and Insight,* pp. 51–59.

———. "Literary History and Literary Modernity." In *Blindness and Insight,* pp. 142–165.

Denton, Kirk, ed. *Modern Chinese Literary Thought: Writings on Literature, 1893–1945.* Stanford, CA: Stanford University Press, 1996.

des Forges, Alexander. "Manufacturing Shanghai, 1885–1935: From Vernacular Narratives to New Sensations." PhD diss., Princeton University, Princeton, NJ, 1998.

Di Baoxian 狄葆賢. "Lun wenxueshang xiaoshuo zhi weizhi" 論文學上小說之位置 (On the position of fiction in literature). *Xin xiaoshuo* (New fiction) 7 (1903). In Guo Shaoyu and Wang, *Zhongguo lidai wenlun xuan* 4.235–240.

Dickinson, G[oldsworthy] Lowes. "An Essay on the Civilizations of India, China, and Japan." In *Letters from John Chinaman and Other Essays*. London: George Allen and Unwin, 1946.

Ding Weizhi 丁偉志 and Chen Song 陳崧. *Zhongxi tiyong zhijian* 中西體用之間 (Between China and the West, essence and function). Beijing: Zhongguo shehui kexue yuan chubanshe, 1995.

Dirks, Nicholas B. *Castes of Mind: Colonialism and the Making of Modern India*. Princeton, NJ: Princeton University Press, 2001.

Dirlik, Arif. *Anarchism in the Chinese Revolution*. Berkeley and Los Angeles: University of California Press, 1991.

Doleželová-Velingerová, Milena. Introduction to *The Chinese Novel at the Turn of the Century,* ed. Milena Doleželová-Velingerová. Toronto: University of Toronto Press, 1980.

———. "Literary Historiography in Early Twentieth-Century China (1904–1928): Constructions of Cultural Memory." In Doleželová-Velingerová and Král, *Appropriation of Cultural Capital,* pp. 123–166.

———. "Typology of Plot Structures in Late Qing Novels." In Doleželová-Velingerová, *Chinese Novel*, pp. 38–56.

Doleželová-Velingerová, Milena, and Král, Oldrich, eds. *The Appropriation of Cultural Capital: China's May Fourth Project*. Cambridge, MA: Harvard University Asia Center, 2001.

Du Yaquan 杜亞泉. *Du Yaquan wenxuan* 杜亞泉文選 (Selected writings of Du Yaquan). Ed. Tian Jianye, Yao Mingyao, and Ren Yuanbiao. Shanghai: Huadong shifan daxue chubanshe, 1993.

———. *See also* Cangfu; Gao Lao.

Duara, Prasenjit. *Rescuing History from the Nation: Questioning Narratives of Modern China*. Chicago: University of Chicago Press, 1995.

Edkins, Joseph. *China's Place in Philology: An Attempt to Show That the Languages of Europe and Asia Have a Common Origin*. London: Trübner and Co., 1871.

Elman, Benjamin. *Classicism, Politics, and Kingship: The Ch'ang-chou School of New Text Confucianism in Late Imperial China*. Berkeley and Los Angeles: University of California Press, 1990.

———. "The Formation of 'Dao Learning' as Imperial Ideology during the Early Ming Dynasty." In Huters et al., *Culture and State,* pp. 58–82.

———. *From Philosophy to Philology: Intellectual and Social Aspects of Change in Late Imperial China*. Cambridge, MA: Council on East Asian Studies, Harvard University, 1984.

Elvin, Mark. "The Administration of Shanghai, 1905–1914." In *The Chinese City between Two Worlds,* ed. M. Elvin and G. William Skinner, pp. 239–262. Stanford, CA: Stanford University Press, 1974.

Esherick, Joseph W. *The Origins of the Boxer Uprising*. Berkeley and Los Angeles: University of California Press, 1987.

Fan Boqun 范伯群. "Guanyu Haishang shuomeng ren—Zhu Shouju" 關于海上說夢人—朱瘦菊 (On the Shanghai Teller of Dreams—Zhu Shouju). Unpublished manuscript, 2001.

Fang Hanqi 方漢奇. *Zhongguo jindai baokan shi* 中國近代報刊史 (A history of modern Chinese journalism). Taiyuan: Shaanxi jiaoyu chubanshe, 1991.

Feng Guifen 馮桂芬. *Jiaobinlu kangyi* 校邠盧抗議 (Words of remonstrance from a hut for the examination of the refined). Ed. Dai Yangben 戴揚本. Zhengzhou: Zhongzhou guji chubanshe, 1998.

Feuerwerker, Albert. "China's History in Marxian Dress." In *History in Communist China*, ed. A. Feuerwerker, pp. 14–44. Cambridge, MA: MIT Press, 1968.

Fu Lin 符霖. *Qinhai shi* 禽海石 (Stones in the sea). In *Zhongguo jindai wenxue daxi (1840–1919): Xiaoshuo ji 6* 中國近代文學大系: 小說集 6 (Comprehensive anthology of modern Chinese literature [1840–1919]: Collected novels, vol. 6). Shanghai: Shanghai shudian, 1991.

Fu Sinian 傅斯年. "Yishu ganyan" 譯書感言 (Thoughts on translation). *Xin chao* 新潮 1.3 (March 1919): 531–537.

Fuller, Michael. *The Road to Eastslope: The Development of Su Shi's Poetic Voice*. Stanford, CA: Stanford University Press, 1990.

Furth, Charlotte, ed. *The Limits of Change: Essays on Conservative Alternatives in Republican China*. Cambridge, MA: Harvard University Press, 1976.

———. "The Sage as Rebel." In Furth, *The Limits of Change*, pp. 113–150.

Galik, Marian. "Studies in Modern Chinese Intellectual History: 1. The World and China: Cultural Impact and Response in the Twentieth Century." *Asian and African Studies* (Bratislava) 11 (1975): 11–56.

Gao Lao 高勞 (Du Yaquan). "Da zhanzheng xuji shiyi" 大戰爭續記十一 (Continuing Notes on the Great War, #11) *Dongfang zazhi* 13.12 (December 10, 1916): 7–22.

———. *See also* Cangfu; Du Yaquan.

Gao Like 高力克. *Tiaoshi de zhihui: Du Yaquan sixiang yanjiu* 調適的智慧: 杜亞泉思想研究 (A suitable intelligence: A study of Du Yaquan's thought). Hangzhou: Zhejiang renmin chubanshe, 1998.

Gardner, Daniel K. *Chu Hsi and the* Ta-hsueh: *Neo-Confucian Reflection on the Confucian Canon*. Cambridge, MA: Council on East Asian Studies, Harvard University, 1986.

Genette, Gérard. *Figures of Literary Discourse*. Trans. Jane E. Lewin. New York: Columbia University Press, 1982.

Gernet, Jacques. *China and the Christian Impact: A Conflict of Cultures*. Trans. Janet Lloyd. Cambridge: Cambridge University Press, 1985.

Gimpel, Denise. *Lost Voices of Modernity: A Chinese Popular Fiction Magazine in Context*. Honolulu: University of Hawai'i Press, 2001.

———. "A Neglected Medium: The Literary Journal and the Case of *The Short*

Story Magazine (Xiaoshuo yuebao), 1910–1914." *Modern Chinese Literature and Culture* 11.2 (fall 1999): 53–106.

———. "Were They Really Reading Disraeli? The Translation and Reception of Foreign Literature in Early Chinese Newspapers and Magazines." Paper presented at the Transnational Dimensions of the Chinese Press conference, University of Oregon, Eugene, October 26, 2002.

Gogol, Nikolai. "The Diary of a Madman." In *The Diary of a Madman and Other Stories,* trans. Andrew R. MacAndrew, pp. 7–28. New York: New American Library, 1960.

Goodman, Bryna. *Native Place, City, and Nation: Regional Networks and Identities in Shanghai, 1853–1937.* Berkeley and Los Angeles: University of California Press, 1995.

Graham, A. C. *Disputers of the Tao.* La Salle, IL: Open Court, 1989.

Greider, Jerome. *Hu Shih and the Chinese Renaissance: Liberalism in the Chinese Revolution, 1917–1937.* Cambridge, MA: Harvard University Press, 1970.

Gunn, Edward M. *Rewriting Chinese: Style and Innovation in Twentieth-Century Chinese Prose.* Stanford, CA: Stanford University Press, 1991.

Guo Moruo 郭沫若. "Lun Zhong-De wenhua shu—zhi Zong Baihua" 論中德文化書—至宗白華 (On Chinese and German cultures—A letter to Zong Baihua). In Chen Song, *Wusi qianhou,* pp. 582–590.

Guo Shaoyu 郭紹虞 and Wang Wensheng 王文生, eds. *Zhongguo lidai wenlun xuan* 中國歷代文論選 (Selected Chinese essays on literature through the ages). Vols. 3–4. Shanghai: Shanghai guji chubanshe, 1980.

Haishang shuomeng ren 海上說夢人 (The Shanghai teller of dreams) (Zhu Shouju 朱瘦菊). *Xiepu chao* 歇浦潮 (Tides of the Huangpu) [The Shanghai tide]. Changsha: Hunan wenyi chubanshe, 1998.

———. See also Shouju; Zhu Shouju.

Han Bangqing 韓邦慶. *Haishang hua liezhuan* 海上花列傳 (Singsong girls of Shanghai). Beijing: Renmin wenxue chubanshe, 1982.

Han Fei 韓非. *Han Fei Tzu.* Trans. Burton Watson. New York: Columbia University Press, 1967.

Han Liangsheng 含涼生 (Fan Yanqiao 范煙橋). "Jin Songcen tan *Niehai hua*" 金菘岑談孽海花 (Jin Songcen discusses *Flower in a Sea of Retribution*). In Wei Shaochang, *Nie hai hua ziliao,* pp. 146–147.

Han shu 漢書 (History of the Han dynasty). Hong Kong: Zhonghua shuju, 1970.

Hanan, Patrick, trans. *The Carnal Prayer Mat.* Honolulu: University of Hawai'i Press, 1990.

———. *The Chinese Vernacular Story.* Cambridge, MA: Harvard University Press, 1981.

———. "The Missionary Novels of Nineteenth-Century China." *Harvard Journal of Asiatic Studies* 60.2 (December 2000): 413–443.

———, trans. *The Money Demon.* Honolulu: University of Hawai'i Press, 1999. See also Chen Diexian, *Huangjin sui.*

―― ["Anonymous"]. "The New Novel before the New Novel: John Fryer's Fiction Contest." In *Writing and Materiality in China: Essays in Honor of Patrick Hanan,* ed. Judith T. Zeitlin and Lydia H. Liu, pp. 317–340. Cambridge, MA: Harvard University Asia Center, 2003.

――, trans. *The Sea of Regret: Two Turn-of-the-Century Chinese Romantic Novels.* Honolulu: University of Hawai'i Press, 1995.

Hao, Yen-p'ing. *The Comprador in Nineteenth Century China: Bridge between East and West.* Cambridge, MA: Harvard University Press, 1971.

Hardt, Michael, and Antonio Negri. *Empire.* Cambridge, MA: Harvard University Press, 2000.

Hart, Roger. "The Jesuits as Missionaries of Science: The Dissemination of Euclid's *Elements* in Seventeenth-Century China." Paper delivered at the New Directions in the History of Chinese Science conference, University of California, Los Angeles, May 24, 1997.

Hartz, Louis. Introduction to *In Search of Wealth and Power: Yen Fu and the West,* by Benjamin I. Schwartz. Cambridge, MA: Harvard University Press, 1964.

Hay, Jonathan. "Painting and the Built Environment of Late-Nineteenth-Century Shanghai." In *Chinese Art: Modern Expressions,* ed. Maxwell K. Hearn and Judith G. Smith. New York: Metropolitan Museum of Art, 2001.

Hay, Stephan N. *Asian Ideas of East and West: Tagore and His Critics in Japan, China, and India.* Cambridge, MA: Harvard University Press, 1970.

He Lin 賀麟. "Yan Fu de fanyi" 嚴復的翻譯 (Yan Fu's translations). In Niu and Sun, *Yan Fu yanjiu ziliao,* pp. 233–247. Originally published in *Dongfang zazhi* 22.21 (1925).

Hegel, G. W. F. *Introduction to the Philosophy of History.* Trans. Leo Rauch. Indianapolis: Hackett, 1988.

Hershatter, Gail. *Dangerous Pleasures: Prostitution and Modernity in Twentieth-Century Shanghai.* Berkeley and Los Angeles: University of California Press, 1997.

Hockx, Michel. *Questions of Style: Literary Societies and Literary Journals in Modern China, 1911–1937.* Leiden: Brill, 2003.

――, ed. *The Literary Field of Twentieth-Century China.* London: Curzon Press, 1999.

Hockx, Michel, and Theodore Huters, trans. "A Journal and a 'Society.'" *Modern Chinese Literature and Culture* 11.2 (fall 1999): 1–39. *See also* Wang Xiaoming, "Yifen zazhi he yige 'shetuan.'"

Horkheimer, Max, and Theodor W. Adorno. *Dialectic of Enlightenment.* Trans. John Cumming. New York: Continuum, 1996.

Hsia, C. T. "Yen Fu and Liang Ch'i-ch'ao, as Advocates of New Fiction." In *Chinese Approaches to Literature from Confucius to Liang Ch'i-ch'ao,* ed. Adele Rickett, pp. 221–257. Princeton, NJ: Princeton University Press, 1978.

Hsia, Tsi-an. "Aspects of the Power of Darkness in Lu Hsün." In *The Gate of Darkness: Studies on the Leftist Literary Movement in China,* pp. 146–162. Seattle: University of Washington Press, 1968.

Hsiao Kung-chuan. *A Modern China and a New World: K'ang Yu-wei, Reformer and Utopian, 1858–1927.* Seattle: University of Washington Press, 1975.

Hsu, Tao-Ching. *The Chinese Conception of the Theatre.* Seattle: University of Washington Press, 1985.

Hu Guanying 胡冠瑩. "Zhongxi hebi pinpan—Wu Jianren zhengzhi sixiang chutan" 中西合璧拼盤—吳趼人思想初探 (An assorted combination of China and the West—a preliminary investigation of Wu Jianren's political thought). In Wu Jianren, *Wu Jianren quanji* 10.160–161.

Hu Shi 胡適. *Baihua wenxue shi* 白話文學史 (History of vernacular literature). Taipei: Hu Shi jinian guan, 1969.

———. "Dao yan" 導言 (Introduction). In Zhao Jiabi, *Zhongguo xin wenxue daxi* 1.1–39.

———. "Wenxue gailiang chuyi" 文學改良芻議 (Suggestions for literary reform). In Zhao Jiabi, *Zhongguo xin wenxue daxi* 1.62–71.

———. "Wushi nian lai zhi Zhongguo wenxue" 五十年來中國文學 (Chinese literature of the past fifty years). In *Xin wenxue luncong* 新文學論叢 (Discussions on the new literature), ed. Huang Zhaoxian 黃兆顯, pp. 10–91. Hong Kong: Lixing wenhua shiye, 1975.

Hu Ying. "Naming the First 'New Woman.'" In Karl and Zarrow, *Rethinking the 1898 Reform Period,* pp. 180–211.

———. *Tales of Translation: Composing the New Woman in China, 1899–1918.* Stanford, CA: Stanford University Press, 2000.

Huang, Martin W. *Desire and Fictional Narrative in Late Imperial China.* Cambridge, MA: Harvard University Asia Center, 2001.

———. *Literati and Self-Re/Presentation: Autobiographical Sensibility in the Eighteenth-Century Chinese Novel.* Stanford, CA: Stanford University Press, 1995.

Huang Ren. "Xiaoshuo xiao hua." In Jiang and Cao, *Huang Ren ji,* p. 302–322.

———. "Zhongguo wenxue shi" 中國文學史 (History of Chinese literature). In Jiang and Cao, *Huang Ren ji,* pp. 37–72.

Huang Yuanyong 黃遠庸. "Guoren zhi gongdu" 國人之公毒 (Our general malignancy). *Dongfang zazhi* 13.1 (January 10, 1916): 1–12.

———. "Xiangying lu" 想影錄 (Reflections). *Dongfang zazhi* 13.2 (February 10, 1916): 3.1–5.

———. "Xinjiu sixiang zhi chongtu" 新舊思想之衝突 (The clash between new and old thought). *Dongfang zazhi* 13.2 (February 10, 1916): 1–5.

———. *Yuansheng yizhu* 遠生遺著 (Writings left by [Mr.] Yuansheng). In *Minguo congshu* 民國叢書, ed. Lin Zhijun 林志鈞. 1919. Reprint, Shanghai: Shanghai shuju, n.d.

Huang Zunxian 黃遵憲. "Ribenguo zhi xueshu er: Wenxue" 日本國之學術二：文學 (Treatises on Japan, second treatise on scholarship: Letters). In Guo Shaoyu and Wang, *Zhongguo lidai wenlun xuan* 4.117–119.

Hummel, Arthur, ed. *Eminent Chinese of the Ch'ing Period.* 1943. Reprint, Taipei: Ch'eng-wen, 1967.

Huters, Theodore. "The Difficult Guest: May Fourth Revisits." *Chinese Literature: Essays, Articles, Reviews (CLEAR)* 6 (July 1984): 125–149.

———. "From Writing to Literature: The Development of Late Qing Theories of Prose." *Harvard Journal of Asiatic Studies* 47.1 (June 1987): 51–96.

———. *Qian Zhongshu*. Boston: G. K. Hall, 1982.

———. Review of *Translingual Practice*, by Lydia Liu. *Harvard Journal of Asiatic Studies* 58.2 (December 1998): 568–580.

Huters, Theodore, R. Bin Wong, and Pauline Yu, eds. *Culture and State in Chinese History: Conventions, Accomodations, and Critiques*. Stanford, CA: Stanford University Press, 1997.

Irigaray, Luce. "This Sex Which Is Not One." Trans. Claudia Reeder. In *New French Feminisms*, ed. Elaine Marks and Isabelle de Courtivron, pp. 99–106. Amherst: University of Massachusetts Press, 1980.

Jameson, Frederic. "Third-World Literature in the Era of Multinational Capitalism." *Social Text* 15 (fall 1986): 65–88.

Jiang Qingbo 蔣慶柏 and Cao Peigen 曹培根, eds. *Huang Ren ji* 黃人集 (Huang Ren's collected writings). Shanghai: Shanghai wenhua chubanshe, 2001.

Johnson, Linda. *Shanghai: From Market Town to Treaty Port, 1074–1858*. Stanford, CA: Stanford University Press, 1995.

Jones, Andrew. "The Violence of the Text: Reading Yu Hua and Shi Zhicun." *Positions: East Asia Cultures Critique* 2.3 (winter 1994): 570–602.

Judanis, Gregory. *Belated Modernity and Aesthetic Culture: Inventing National Literature*. Minneapolis: University of Minnesota Press, 1991.

Judge, Joan. *Print and Politics: "Shibao" and the Culture of Reform in Late Qing China*. Stanford, CA: Stanford University Press, 1996.

———. "Reforming the Feminine: Female Literacy and the Legacy of 1898." In Karl and Zarrow, *Rethinking the 1898 Reform Period*, pp. 158–179.

Kamachi, Noriko. *Reform in China: Huang Tsun-hsien and the Japanese Model*. Cambridge, MA: Council on East Asian Studies, Harvard University, 1981.

Kang Youwei 康有為. "*Riben shumu zhi zhiyu*" 日本書目誌識語 (A cognoscenti's notes on *A record of a bibliography of [books in] Japan*). In Chen Pingyuan and Xia, *Ershi shiji Zhongguo xiaoshuo lilun ziliao*, pp. 13–14.

Kao, Karl S. Y. "Self-reflexivity, Epistemology, and Rhetorical Figures." *Chinese Literature: Essays, Articles, Reviews (CLEAR)* 19 (December 1997): 59–83.

Karatani Kojin. *Origins of Modern Japanese Literature*. Trans. and ed. Brett de Bary. Durham, NC: Duke University Press, 1993.

Karl, Rebecca, and Peter Zarrow, eds. *Rethinking the 1898 Reform Period: Political and Cultural Change in Late Qing China*. Cambridge, MA: Harvard University Asian Center, 2002.

Kessler, Lawrence D. *K'ang-shi and the Consolidation of Ch'ing Rule, 1661–1684*. Chicago: University of Chicago Press, 1976.

Knechtges, David. Introduction to *Wen xuan, or Selections of Refined Literature*, by Xiao Tong, vol. 1. Princeton, NJ: Princeton University Press, 1982.

Ko, Dorothy. *Teachers of the Inner Chambers: Woman and Culture in Seventeenth-Century China*. Stanford, CA: Stanford University Press, 1994.

Kowallis, Jon. "Concerning Imbalanced Cultural Development." In "Warriors of the Spirit: 'On the Power of Mara Poetry' and Other Turn-of-the-Century *wenyan* Essays by Lu Xun." Unpublished manuscript, 1996.

Kuo Ting-yee and Liu Kwang-ching. "Self-strengthening: The pursuit of Western technology." In *The Cambridge History of China*, vol. 10, *Late Ch'ing 1800–1911*, pt. 1, ed. John K. Fairbank, pp. 491–542. Cambridge: Cambridge University Press, 1978.

Kwong, Luke S. *A Mosaic of the Hundred Days: Personalities, Politics, and Ideas of 1898*. Cambridge, MA: Council on East Asian Studies, Harvard University, 1984.

Lao, D. C., trans. *The Analects*. Harmondsworth, UK: Penguin Books, 1979.

Lee, Leo Ou-fan. "Incomplete Modernity: Rethinking the May Fourth Intellectual Project." In Doleželová and Král, *The Appropriation of Cultural Capital*, pp. 31–65.

———. *Shanghai Modern: The Flowering of a New Urban Culture in China, 1930–1945*. Cambridge, MA: Harvard University Press, 1999.

———. *Voices from the Iron House: A Study of Lu Xun*. Bloomington: Indiana University Press, 1987.

Lee, Leo Ou-fan, and Andrew Nathan. "The Beginnings of Mass Culture: Journalism and Fiction in the Late Ch'ing Period and Beyond." In *Popular Culture in Late Imperial China*, David Johnson, Evelyn S. Rawski, and Andrew Nathan, pp. 360–395. Berkeley and Los Angeles: University of California Press, 1985.

Levenson, Joseph R. *Confucian China and Its Modern Fate: A Trilogy*. Berkeley and Los Angeles: University of California Press, 1968.

———. *Liang Ch'i-ch'ao and the Mind of Modern China*. Berkeley and Los Angeles: University of California Press, 1959.

Lévi-Strauss, Claude. *The Savage Mind*. Chicago: University of Chicago Press, 1966.

Li Baojia 李寶嘉 (Li Boyuan 伯元). *Guanchang xianxing ji* 官場現形記 (Exposure of officialdom). 1957. Reprint, Beijing: Renmin wenxue chubanshe, 1979.

———. *Wenming xiaoshi* 文明小史 (Short history of civilization). Taipei: Shijie shuju, 1968.

Li Ruiteng 李瑞騰. *Wan Qing wenxue sixiang lun* 晚清文學思想論 (Literary thought in the late Qing). Taipei: Hanguang wenhua shiye, 1992.

Li Xiang 李詳. "Lun Tongcheng pai" 論桐城派 (On the Tongcheng school). *Guocui xuebao* 國粹學報 (National essence journal) 49 (1908).

Li Xizhu 李細朱. *Wanqing baoshou sixiang de yuanxing: Woren yanjiu* 晚清保守思想的原型: 倭仁研究 (The prototype of late Qing conservative thought: A study of Woren). Beijing: Shehui kexue wenxian chubanshe, 2000.

Li Zongying 李宗英 and Zhang Mengyang 張夢陽, eds. *Liushi nian lai Lu Xun yanjiu lunwen ji* 六十年來魯迅研究論文集 (Essays on Lu Xun from the last sixty years). Beijing: Zhongguo shehui kexue chubanshe, 1982.

Liang Qichao 梁啟超. "Bianfa tongyi" 變法通議 (Comprehensive discussion on reform). In *Yinbingshi wenji leibian* 1.1–99.

———. "Gao xiaoshuo jia" 告小說傢 (An indictment of the novelists). In Guo Shaoyu and Wang, *Zhongguo lidai wenlun xuan* 4.217–218.

———. *Intellectual Trends in the Ch'ing Period*. Trans. Immanuel C. Y. Hsü. Cambridge, MA: Harvard University Press, 1959. *See also* Liang Qichao, *Qingdai xueshu gailun*.

———. "Lun fojiao yu qunzhi zhi guanxi" 論佛教與群治之關系 (On the relationship between Buddhism and public governance). In *Yinbingshi wenji leibian* 1.658–665.

———. "Lun nüxue" 論女學 (On female education). In *Yinbingshi wenji leibian* 1.57–64.

———. "Lun xiaoshuo yu qunzhi zhi guanxi" 論小說與群治之關系 (On the relationship between fiction and public governance). In *Yinbingshi wenji leibian* 1.382–386.

———. "Lun youxue" 論幼學 (On the education of the young). In *Bianfa tongyi*. In *Yinbingshi wenji leibian* 1.40–56.

———. *Qingdai xueshu gailun* 清代學術概論 (Intellectual trends in the Ch'ing period). Shanghai: Shanghai guji chubanshe, 1998.

———. "Sanshi zishu" 三十自述 (Personal account at age thirty). In *Yinbingshi quanji* 飲冰室全集 (Complete works from the ice-drinker's studio), pp. 278–287. Yonghi shi: Zhiyang chubanshe, 1993.

———. "Shizhong dexing xiangfan xiangcheng yi" 十種德性相反相成義 (On the complementary and contradictory formulation of ten types of virtue). In *Yinbingshi wenji leibian* 1.247–248.

———. "Xin min shuo" 新民說 (On renewing the people). In *Yinbingshi wenji leibian* 1.101–225.

———. *Xin Zhongguo weilai ji* 新中國未來記 (The future of new China). Taipei: Guangya chuban gongsi, 1984.

———. "Xixue shumubiao houxu" 西學書目後序 (Postface to a bibliography of Western learning). In *Yinbingshi wenji leibian* 1.738–741.

———. "Xuyan" 緒言 (Preface) to *Xin Zhongguo weilai ji* 新中國未來記 (The future of new China). In A Ying, ed., *Wan Qing wenxue congchao*, vol. 1.1, pp. 1–2.

———. "Yi yin zhengzhi xiaoshu xu" (Preface to publishing translations of political novels). In *Yinbingshi wenji leibian* 1.742–743.

———. *Yinbingshi wenji* 飲冰室文集 (Writings from the ice-drinker's studio). Taipei: Xinxing shuju, 1959 (*Guoxue jiben congshu* 國學基本叢書).

———. *Yinbingshi wenji leibian* 飲冰室文集類編 (Categorical compendium of the collected writings from the ice-drinker's studio). 2 vols. Taipei: Huazheng shuju, 1974.

Lin Shu 林紓 "*Kuairou yusheng shu* xu" 塊肉餘生述序 (Preface to *David Copperfield*). In Guo Shaoyu and Wang, *Zhongguo lidai wenlun xuan* 4.164–165.

———. "*Sakexun jiehou yingxiong lue* xu" 撒克遜劫後英雄略序 (Preface to *Ivanhoe*). In Guo Shaoyu and Wang, *Zhongguo lidai wenlun xuan* 4.162–163.

———. "*Zeishi* xu" 賊史序 (Preface to *Oliver Twist*). In Guo Shaoyu and Wang, *Zhongguo lidai wenlun xuan* 4.165–166.

Lin, Shuen-fu. "Ritual and Narrative Structure in *Ju-lin wai-shih*." In *Chinese Narrative: Critical and Theoretical Essays*, ed. Andrew Plaks, pp. 244–265. Princeton, NJ: Princeton University Press, 1977.

Lin Yu-sheng 林毓生. *The Crisis of Chinese Consciousness: Radical Antitraditionalism in the May Fourth Era*. Madison: University of Wisconsin Press, 1979.

Lingnan yuyi nüshi 嶺南羽衣女士. *Dongou nü haojie* 東歐女豪傑 (Female heroes of eastern Europe). Taipei: Guangya chuban gongsi, 1984.

Link, Perry. *Mandarin Ducks and Butterflies: Popular Fiction in Early Twentieth-Century Chinese Cities*. Berkeley and Los Angeles: University of California Press, 1981.

Liu E 劉鶚 (Tieyun 鐵雲). *Lao Can youji* 老殘遊記 (The travels of Lou Can). 1903. Reprint, Beijing: Renmin wenxue chubanshe, 1957. *See also* Shadick, *The Travels of Lao Ts'an*.

Liu, Kwang-Ching. "Politics, Intellectual Outlook, and Reform: The T'ung-wen kuan Controversy of 1867." In *Reform in Nineteenth-Century China*, ed. Paul Cohen and John Schrecker, pp. 87–100. Cambridge, MA: East Asian Research Center, Harvard University, 1976.

Liu, Lydia. *Translingual Practice: Literature, National Culture, and Translated Modernity—China, 1900–1937*. Stanford, CA: Stanford University Press, 1995.

Liu Mengxi 劉夢溪, ed. *Zhongguo xiandai xueshu jingdian: Liu Shipei juan* 中國現代學術經典: 劉師培卷 (Classics of modern Chinese scholarship: Liu Shipei volume). Shijiazhuang: Hebei jiaoyu chubanshe, 1996.

Liu Na 劉納. *Shanbian: Xinhai geming shiqi zhi wusi shiqi de Zhongguo wenxue* 嬗變: 辛亥革命時期至五四時期的中國文學 (Transmutation: Chinese literature from the Xinhai revolution [1912] to the May Fourth period). Beijing: Zhongguo shehui kexue chubanshe, 1998.

Lu Shi'e 陸士諤. *Xin Shanghai* 新上海 (New Shanghai). Shanghai: Shanghai guji chubanshe, 1997.

Liu Shipei 劉師培. "Lun jinshi wenxue zhi bianqian" 論近世文學之變遷 (On the vicissitudes of recent Chinese literature). In Guo Shaoyu and Wang, *Zhongguo lidai wenlun xuan* 4.425–435.

———. *Lun wen zaji* 論文雜記 (Miscellaneous notes on literature). Beijing: Renmin wenxue chubanshe, 1984.

Liu Shih Shun, trans. *Vignettes from the Late Ch'ing*. Hong Kong: Chinese University of Hong Kong Press, 1975.

Lu Hanchao. *Beyond the Neon Lights: Everyday Shanghai in the Early Twentieth Century*. Berkeley and Los Angeles: University of California Press, 1999.

Lu Hsun. *A Brief History of Chinese Fiction*. Trans. Yang Hsien-yi and Gladys Yang. Peking: Foreign Languages Press, 1964.

Lu Xun 魯迅 (Zhou Shuren 周樹人). "Ah Q zhengzhuan" 阿Q正傳 (The true story of Ah Q). In *Lu Xun quanji* 1.487–532.

———. "'Ah Q zhengzhuan' de chengyin" 阿Q正傳的成因 (How "The True Story of Ah Q" was written). In *Lu Xun quanji* 3.376–384.

———. "Daoyan" 導言 (Introduction) to "Xiaoshuo erji" 小說二集 (The second anthology of fiction). In Zhao Jiabi, *Zhongguo xin wenxue daxi* 4.9.

———. "Gushu yu baihua" 故書與白話 (The classics and the vernacular). In *Lu Xun quanji* 3.213–216.

———. "Guxiang" 故鄉 (My old home). In *Lu Xun quanji* 1.476–486.

———. "Kuangren riji" 狂人日記 (Madman's diary). In *Lu Xun quanji* 1.422–433.

———. *Lu Xun quanji* 魯迅全集 (The complete works of Lu Xun). 16 vols. Beijing: Renmin wenxue chubanshe, 1981.

———. *Lu Xun: Selected Works.* 4 vols. Beijing: Foreign Languages Press, 1980.

———. "*Moluo* shi li shuo" 摩羅詩力說 (On the power of Mara poetry). In *Lu Xun quanji* 1:63–115.

———. *Nahan* 吶喊 (Call to arms). In *Lu Xun quanji* 1.415–570.

———. "*Nahan* zixu" 吶喊自序 (Personal preface to *Call to Arms*). In *Lu Xun quanji* 1.415–421.

———. "Shangshi" 傷逝 (Regret for the past). In *Lu Xun quanji* 2.110–131.

———. "Suigan lu ershiwu" 隨感錄二十五 (Random thoughts, no. 25). In *Lu Xun quanji* 1.295–297.

———. "Suigan lu sishisan" 隨感錄四十三 (Random thoughts, no. 43). In *Lu Xun quanji* 1.330–331.

———. "Suigan lu wushijiu" 隨感錄五十九 (Random thoughts, no. 59). In *Lu Xun quanji* 1.354–357.

———. "Wenhua pian zhi lun" 文化偏至論 (On the extremes of culture). In *Lu Xun quanji* 1.44–62.

———. "Zai jiulou shang" 在酒樓上 (In the wineshop). In *Lu Xun quanji* 2.24–34.

———. *Zhongguo xiaoshuo shilüe* 中國小說史略 (A brief history of Chinese fiction). In *Lu Xun quanji* 9.3–297.

———. "Zhufu" 祝福 (The new year's sacrifice). In *Lu Xun quanji* 2.5–23.

Lukács, Georg. *The Theory of the Novel.* Trans. Anna Bostock. Cambridge, MA: MIT Press, 1971.

Lunyu yinde 論語引得 (A concordance to the *Analects* of Confucius). Harvard–Yenching Institute Sinological Index Series. Beijing, 1940.

Luo Genzi 羅根澤 and Guo Shaoyu 郭紹虞, eds. *Zhongguo jindai wenlun xuan* 中國近代文論選 (Selection of modern Chinese essays on literature). Beijing: Renmin wenxue chubanshe, 1959.

Lutz, Jesse. *China and the Christian Colleges, 1850–1950.* Ithaca, NY: Cornell University Press, 1971.

Ma Guangren 馬光人, ed. *Shanghai xinwen shi* (1850–1949) 上海新聞史 (A history of journalism in Shanghai). Shanghai: Fudan daxue chubanshe, 1996.

Macartney, Lord George. *An Embassy to China, Being the Journal Kept by Lord Ma-*

cartney during His Embassy to the Emperor Ch'ien-lung, 1793–1794. Ed. J. L. Cranmer-Byng, London: Longmans, Green, 1962.

Mao Dun 茅盾 (Shen Yanbing 沈雁冰). "Du Nahan" 讀吶喊 (Reading Nahan). In Mao Dun quanji 18.398.

———. Mao Dun quanji 茅盾全集 (Complete works of Mao Dun). 22 vols. Beijing: Renmin wenxue chubanshe, 1989.

———. Wo zouguo de daolu, shang 我走過的道路, 上 (The path I traveled, volume 1). Hong Kong: Sanlian shudian, 1981.

Martin, W. A. P. The Awakening of China. New York: Doubleday, Page, and Co., 1910.

———. A Cycle of Cathay, or China, South and North. Chicago: Fleming H. Revell, 1896.

———. The Lore of Cathay, or the Intellect of China. Edinburgh and London: Oliphant, Anderson, and Ferrier, 1901.

Marx, Karl. "The Future Results of British Rule in India." In Tucker, The Marx-Engels Reader, pp. 659–664.

Marx, Karl, and Frederick Engels. The Manifesto of the Communist Party. In Tucker, The Marx-Engels Reader, pp. 469–500.

McDougall, Bonnie S. Fictional Authors, Imaginary Audiences: Modern Chinese Literature in the Twentieth Century. Hong Kong: Chinese University Press, 2003.

Mencius. Mencius. Trans. D. C. Lau. Harmondsworth. UK: Penguin Books, 1970.

Meng Yue 孟悅. "The Invention of Shanghai: Cultural Passages and Their Transformation, 1860–1920." PhD diss., University of California, Los Angeles, 2000.

———. "A Playful Discourse, Its Site, and Its Social Subject: Shen bao's 'Ziyoutan,' 1911–1917." MA thesis, University of California, Los Angeles, 1994.

———. "Re-envisioning the Great Interior: Gardens and the Upper Class between the Imperial and the 'Modern.'" MCLC 14.1 (spring 2002): 1–49.

Metzger, Thomas. Escape from Predicament: Neo-Confucianism and China's Evolving Political Culture. New York: Columbia University Press, 1977.

Michie, Alexander. Missionaries in China. 2nd ed. Shanghai: Kelly and Walsh, 1893.

Millard, Thomas F. China: Where It Is Today and Why. New York: Harcourt, Brace, 1928.

Min Tu-ki. National Polity and Local Power: The Transformation of Late Imperial China. Cambridge, MA: Council on East Asian Studies, Harvard University, 1989.

Ming, Feng-ying 明鳳英. In Search of a Position: The Paradox of Genre Typology in the Late Qing Polygeneric Novel-Romance, Political-Detective, and Science Fiction Novel, 1898–1911. PhD diss., University of California, Los Angeles, 1999.

Mittler, Barbara. A Newspaper for China? Power, Identity, and Change in the Shanghai News-Media. Cambridge, MA: Harvard University Asia Center, 2004.

Moretti, Franco. "Conjectures on World Literature." New Left Review, 2nd ser., 1 (January–February 2000): 54–68.

———. The Way of the World: The Bildungsroman in European Culture. London: Verso, 1987.

Morse, H. B. *The International Relations of the Chinese Empire.* Vol. 3, *The Period of Subjection, 1894–1911.* London, 1910–1918. Reprint, Taipei: Wenxing shudian, n.d.
Naipaul, V. S. *A Bend in the River.* New York: Vintage Books, 1989.
Nandy, Ashis. "Shamans, Savages, and the Wilderness: On the Audibility of Dissent and the Future of Civilizations." *Alternatives* 14 (1989): 263–277.
Needham, Joseph. *Science and Civilization in China.* Cambridge: Cambridge University Press, 1954–.
Newsinger, John. "Elgin in China." *New Left Review,* 2nd ser., 15 (May–June 2002): 126–139.
Niu Yangshan 牛仰山 and Sun Hongni 孫鴻霓, eds. *Yan Fu yanjiu ziliao* 嚴復研究資料 (Research materials on Yan Fu). Fuzhou: Haixia chubanshe, 1990.
Ouyang Jian 歐陽健. *Wan Qing xiaoshuo shi* 晚清小說史 (History of late Qing fiction). Hangzhou: Zhejiang guji chubanshe, 1997.
Owen, Stephen. "The End of the Past: Rewriting Chinese Literary History in the Early Republic." In *The Appropriation of Cultural Capital: China's May Fourth Project,* Doleželová-Velingerová and Král, pp. 167–192. Cambridge, MA: Harvard University Asia Center, 2001.
Polachek, James. *The Inner Opium War.* Cambridge, MA: Council on East Asian Studies, Harvard University, 1992.
Pong, David. *Shen Pao-chen and China's Modernization in the Nineteenth Century.* Cambridge: Cambridge University Press, 1994.
Pott, F. L., and D. D. Hawks. *A Short History of Shanghai: Being an Account of the Growth and Development of the International Settlement.* Shanghai: Kelly and Walsh, 1928.
Prusek, Jaroslav. *The Lyrical and the Epic: Studies of Modern Chinese Literature.* Ed. Leo Lee. Bloomington: Indiana University Press, 1980.
Pusey, James Reeve. *China and Charles Darwin.* Cambridge, MA: Council on East Asian Studies, Harvard University, 1983.
Qian Jibo 錢基博. *Xiandai Zhongguo wenxue shi* 現代中國文學史 (Literary history of modern China). Hong Kong: Longmen shudian, 1965.
Qian Zhixiu 錢智修. "Gongli zhuyi yu xueshu" 功利主義與學術 (Utilitarianism and scholarship). *Dongfang zazhi* 15.6 (June 1918): 1–5. Reprinted in Chen Song, *Wusi qianhou,* pp. 56–63.
Qian Zhongshu 錢鍾書. "Lin Shu de fanyi" 林紓的翻譯 (The translations of Lin Shu). In *Jiu wen si pian* 舊文四篇 (Four old pieces), pp. 62–94. Shanghai: Shanghai guji chubanshe, 1979.
———. *Tan yi lu* 談藝錄 (On the art of poetry). Hong Kong: Zhonghua shuju, 1986.
———. *Weicheng* 圍城 (Fortress besieged). Shanghai: Chenguang chuban gongsi, 1949.
——— [Zhongshu jun 鍾書君]. [Review of] Zhou Zuoren 周作人 *Zhongguo xin wenxue de yuanliu* 中國新文學的源流 (The sources of the new Chinese litera-

ture). In "Shubao qunqiu" 書報春秋 (Annals of publishing). *Xinyue yuekan* 新月月刊 (Crescent moon) 4.4 (November 1932): 9–15.

Quan Hansheng 全漢昇. "Qing mo de 'xixue yuan chu Zhongguo' shuo" 清末的西學源出中國說 (The notion of "Western learning having its origins in China" in the late Qing). In *Zhongguo jindai shi luncong* 中國近代史論叢, ed. Bao Zunpeng 包遵彭, Li Dingyi 李定一, and Wu Xiangxiang 吳相湘, collection 1, vol., 5, pp. 216–258. Taipei: Zhongzheng shuju, 1956.

Rankin, Mary Backus. *Early Chinese Revolutionaries: Radical Intellectuals in Shanghai and Chekiang, 1902–1911.* Cambridge, MA: Harvard University Press, 1971.

Readings, Bill. *The University in Ruins.* Cambridge, MA: Harvard University Press, 1996.

Reischauer, E. O., and J. K. Fairbank. *East Asia: The Great Tradition.* Cambridge, MA: Harvard University Press: 1960.

Reynolds, Douglas R. *China, 1898–1912: The Xinzheng Revolution and Japan.* Cambridge, MA: Council on East Asian Studies, Harvard University, 1993.

Rolston, David L., ed. *How to Read the Chinese Novel.* Princeton, NJ: Princeton University Press, 1990.

Ropp, Paul. *Dissent in Early Modern China: Ju-lin wai-shih and Ch'ing Social Criticism.* Ann Arbor: University of Michigan Press, 1981.

Ruan Yuan 阮元. *Yanjingshi ji* 揅經室集 (Collection from the classical research studio). Beijing: Zhonghua shuju, 1993.

Said, Edward. *Orientalism.* New York: Random House, 1978.

Sakai, Naoki. "Modernity and Its Critique: The Problem of Universalism and Particularism." *South Atlantic Quarterly* 87.3 (summer 1988): 475–504.

Sang Bing 桑兵. *Qingmo xin zhishijie de shetuan yu huodong* 清末新知識界的社團與活動 (The activities and associations of the intellectual world at the end of the Qing). Beijing: Sanlian shudian, 1995.

Schmidt, J. D. *Within the Human Realm: The Poetry of Huang Zunxian, 1848–1905.* Cambridge: Cambridge University Press, 1994.

Schneider, Laurence. "National Essence and the New Intelligentsia." In Furth, *The Limits of Change,* pp. 57–89.

Schwartz, Benjamin I. *In Search of Wealth and Power: Yen Fu and the West.* Cambridge, MA: Harvard University Press, 1964.

———. "The Limits of 'Tradition versus Modernity': The Case of the Chinese Intellectuals." In *China and Other Matters,* pp. 45–64. Cambridge, MA: Harvard University Press, 1996. Originally published in 1972.

Schwarz, Vera. *The Chinese Enlightenment: Intellectuals and the Legacy of the May Fourth Movement of 1919.* Berkeley and Los Angeles: University of California Press, 1986.

Shadick, Harold, trans. *The Travels of Lao Ts'an.* New York: Columbia University Press, 1990. *See also* Liu E, *Lao Can youji.*

Shang Hongkui 商鴻逵 and Liu Bannong 劉半農. "Sai Jinhua benshi" 賽金花本事

(The original story of Sai Jinhua). Appended to Zeng Mengpu, *Niehai hua* (1990), pp. 493–535.
Shanghai Tushuguan 上海圖書館, ed. *Lao Shanghai fengqing lu* 老上海風情錄 (Customs of old Shanghai). Shanghai: Shanghai wenhua chubanshe, 1998.
Shimada Kenji. *Pioneer of the Chinese Revolution: Zhang Binglin and Confucianism.* Trans. Joshua Fogel. Stanford, CA: Stanford University Press, 1990.
Shisan jing zhushu 十三經注疏 (The annotated Thirteen Classics, with commentaries). Beijing: Zhonghua shuju, 1980.
Shouju 瘦菊 (Zhu Shouju 朱瘦菊). *Cizhong renyu* 此中人語 (The talk of the town). Shanghai: Xinmin tushuguan, 1918.
———. *See also* Haishang shuomeng ren; Zhu Shouju.
Sima Qian 司馬遷. *Shiki kaichu kosho* 史記會注攷證 (Authenticated collation of commentaries on the Records of the Historian), ed. Takigawa Kametaro 瀧川龜太郎. 1934. Reprint, Taipei: Hongye chubanshe, 1973.
———. "Sima Xiangru liezhuan" 司馬相如列傳 (Biography of Sima Xiangru). In Sima, *Shiki kaichu kosho* 117.104.
Smith, Arthur H. *Chinese Characteristics.* New York: Fleming H. Revell, 1894.
Spence, Jonathan. *The Search for Modern China.* New York: W. W. Norton, 1990.
———. *To Change China: Western Advisers in China, 1620–1960.* Boston: Little, Brown, 1968.
Strand, David. *Rickshaw Beijing: City People and Politics in the 1920s.* Berkeley and Los Angeles: University of California Press, 1989.
Sun, Lung-kee. "Lu Xun: China's First Proto-modernist." Paper presented at the fifty-fourth annual meeting of the Association for Asian Studies, Washington, DC, April 5, 2002.
Tan Sitong 譚嗣同. "Sanshi ziji" 三十自記. In *Tan Sitong quanji* 譚嗣同全集 (Complete works of Tan Sitong), pp. 55–57. Beijing: Sanlian shudian, 1954.
Tanaka, Stefan. *Japan's Orient: Rendering Pasts in History.* Berkeley and Los Angeles: University of California Press, 1993.
Tang, Xiaobing. *Global Space and the Nationalist Discourse of Modernity: The Historical Thinking of Liang Qichao.* Stanford, CA: Stanford University Press, 1996.
———. "'Poetic Revolution,' Colonization, and Form at the Beginning of Modern Chinese Literature." In Karl and Zarrow, *Rethinking the 1898 Reform Period*, pp. 245–265.
Tang Zhen 湯震. *Weiyan* 危言 (Blunt words). *Zhixue congshu chuji* 質學叢書初集. N.p., 1897.
Tang Zhenchang 唐振常. *Tang Zhenchang sanwen* 唐振常散文 (Essays of Tang Zhenchang). Hangzhou: Zhejiang wenyi chubanshe, 2000.
Tang Zhesheng 湯哲聲 and Tu Xiaoma 塗小馬, eds. *Huang Ren* 黃人. Beijing: Zhongguo wenshi chubanshe, 1998.
Tao Zengyou 陶曾佑. "Lun xiaoshuo zhi shili jiqi guanxi" 論小說之勢力及其關系 (On the power and significance of literature). In Luo and Guo, *Zhongguo jindai wenlun xuan*, pp. 246–250.

———. "Zhongguo wenxue zhi gaiguan" 中國文學之概觀 (A general survey of Chinese literature). In Luo and Guo, *Zhongguo jindai wenlun xuan,* pp. 241–245.

———. "Lun xiaoshuo zhi shili jiqi yingxiang" 論文學之勢力及其影響 (On the power and influence of fiction). In Chen Pingyuan and Xia, *Ershi shiji Zhongguo xiaoshuo lilun ziliao,* pp. 226–228. First published in *Youxi shijie,* 遊戲世界 (World of play) 10 (1907).

Teng, Ssu-yu, and Fairbank, John K. *China's Response to the West: A Documentary Survey.* Cambridge, MA: Harvard University Press, 1954.

Trevor-Roper, Hugh. *The Hermit of Peking: The Hidden Life of Sir Edmund Backhouse.* New York: Knopf, 1977.

Tucker, Robert C., ed. *The Marx-Engels Reader.* 2nd ed. New York: W. W. Norton, 1978.

Wang Anyi 王安憶. "Shanghai de gushi: Du *Xiepu chao*" 上海的故事: 讀歇浦潮 (A story of Shanghai: Reading *Xiepu chao*). In *Wo du Wo kan* 我讀我看 (I read, I see), pp. 33–43. Shanghai: Renmin wenxue chubanshe, 2001.

Wang, David Der-wei. *Fin-de-siècle Splendor: Repressed Modernities of Late Qing Fiction, 1849–1911.* Stanford, CA: Stanford University Press, 1997.

Wang, Guanhua. *In Search of Justice: The 1905–1906 Chinese Anti-American Boycott.* Cambridge, MA: Harvard University Asia Center, 2001.

Wang Guowei 王国维. "Wenxue xiaoyan" 文學小言 (Remarks on literature). In Guo Shaoyu and Wang, *Zhongguo lidai wenlun xuan* 4.378–382.

Wang Hui. 汪暉. "Contemporary Chinese Thought and the Question of Modernity." Trans. Rebecca Karl. In *China's New Order: Society, Politics, and Economy in Transition,* ed. Theodore Huters, pp. 141–187. Cambridge, MA: Harvard University Press, 2003.

———. "Lu Xun (shang): Geren, ziwo jiqi dui qimeng zhuyi lishiguan de fouding yu queren (1903 nian–1924 nianjian de sixiang)" 魯迅上: 各人, 自我及其啓蒙主義歷史觀的否定與確認 1903年–1924年間的思想 (Lu Xun [I]: Individualism, the self, and their negative and positive contributions to the Enlightenment view of history [his thought between 1903 and 1924]). In *Wang Hui zixuan ji,* pp. 117–159.

———. "'Sai xiansheng' zai Zhongguo de mingyun: Zhongguo jindai sixiangzhong de kexue gainian jiqi shiyong" 賽先生在中國的命運: 中國近代思想中的科學概念及其使用 (The fate of "Mr. Science" in China: The concept of science and its application in modern Chinese thought). *Xueren* 學人 (The scholar) 1 (November 1991): 49–123. *See also* Choy, "The Fate of 'Mr. Science' in China."

———. *Wang Hui zixuan ji* 汪暉自選集 (Self-selected collection of Wang Hui). Guilin: Guangxi shifan daxue chubanshe, 1997.

———. "Yan Fu de sange shijie" 嚴復的三個世界 (The three worlds of Yan Fu). *Xueren* 12 (October 1997): 29–130.

———. "Zhang Taiyan's Concept of the Individual and Modern Chinese Identity." In Wen-hsin Yeh, *Becoming Chinese,* pp. 231–259.

———. "Zhongguo jin-xiandai sixiangzhong de 'kexue' gainian jiqi shiyong" 中國近現代思想的科學概念 (The conception of science and its applications in modern Chinese thought). In *Wang Hui zixuan ji,* pp. 208–269.

Wang Junnian 王俊年. "*Wo Foshan ren* nianpu" 我佛山人年普 (Chronological biography of "I, a person of Foshan"). In Wu Jianren, *Wo Foshan ren wenji* 8.345–350.

Wang Lixing 王立興. "Zeng Pu jiqi *Niehai hua* de zai pingjia" 曾樸及其孽海花的再評價 (Reevaluating Zeng Pu and his *Niehai hua*). In *Zhongguo jindai wenxue kaolun* 中國近代文學攷論 (Essays on the study of modern Chinese literature), pp. 126–129. Nanjing: Nanjing daxue chubanshe, 1992.

Wang Shuo. *Playing for Thrills.* Trans. Howard Goldblatt. New York: William Morrow, 1997.

Wang Shuqian 汪淑潛. "Xinjiu wenti" 新舊問題 (The question of the new and the old). In Chen Song, *Wusi qianhou,* pp. 7–11.

Wang Tao 王韜. "Yuan xue" 原學 (On the origins of learning). In *Taoyuan wen xinbian* 弢園文新編 (New collection of writing from Tao's garden), ed. Zhu Weizheng 朱維錚 and Qian Zhongshu 錢鍾書, pp. 3–4. Beijing: Sanlian shudian, 1998.

Wang Xiaoming 王曉明. *Wufa zhimian de rensheng: Lu Xun zhuan* 無法直面的人生: 魯迅傳 (The life that cannot be faced: A biography of Lu Xun). Shanghai: Shanghai wenyi chubanshe, 1993.

———. "Yifen zazhi he yige 'shetuan': Chong ping 'wusi' wenxue chuantong" 一份雜誌和一個社團: 重評五四文學傳統 (A journal and a "society": Reevaluating the "May Fourth" literary tradition). In *Piping kongjian de kaichuang: Ershi shiji Zhongguo wenxue yanjiu* 批評空間的開創: 二十世紀中國文學研究 (The opening of critical space: Studies on twentieth-century Chinese literature), ed. Wang Xiaoming, pp. 186–209. Shanghai: Dongfang chuban zhongxin, 1998. *See also* Hockx and Huters, "A Journal and a 'Society.'"

Wang Yangzong 王揚宗. *Fu Lanya yu jindai Zhongguo de kexue qimeng* 傅蘭雅與近代中國科學啓蒙. Beijing: Kexue chubanshe, 2000.

Wang Yiliang 王貽梁. "Qichi shenqu da zhangfu, bainian shishi jing ruhe" 七尺身軀大丈夫百年世事竟如何 (A man of stature and his long employment in the world of affairs). In Zheng Guanying, *Shengshi weiyan,* pp. 2–3.

Wang Yuanhua 王元化. "Du Yaquan yu dong-xi wenhua wenti lunzhan" 杜亞泉與東西文化問題論戰 (Du Yaquan and the debate on Eastern and Western cultures). *Xueren* 5 (February 1994): 1–23.

Wang Yusheng. "Hua Hengfang: Forerunner and Disseminator of Modern science in China." In *Chinese Studies in the History and Philosophy of Science and Technology,* ed. Dainian Fan and Robert Cohen. Netherlands: Kulwer Academic Publishers, 1996.

Wang Zhichun 王之春. "Guang xuexiao" 廣學校 (On extending the educational system). In *Guochao rou yuan ji* 國朝柔遠記 (Records from our dynasty concerning accommodating strangers), ed. Wang Zhichun. Reprint, Taipei: Guangwen shuju, 1978.

Wang Zhongqi 王鐘麒. "Zhongguo lidai xiaoshuo shi lun" 中國歷代小說史論 (On the history of the Chinese novel through the ages). In Guo Shaoyu and Wang, *Zhongguo lidai wenlun xuan* 4.259–265.

Wei Shaochang 魏紹昌. "Guanyu Sai-Wa gongan de zhenxiang: Cong Zeng Pu *Niehai hua* shuo dao Xia Yan de *Sai Jinhua*" 關于賽瓦公案的真相從曾樸孽海華說到夏衍的賽金花 (On the truth of the Sai [Jinhua] Wa[ldersee] case: From Zeng Pu's *Niehai hua* to Xia Yan's *Sai Jinhua*). In Wei Shaochang, *Wan Qing si da xiaoshuojia*, pp. 217–238.

———, ed. *Niehai hua ziliao* 孽海華資料 (Materials on *Niehai hua*). Shanghai: Shanghai guji chubanshe, 1982.

———. *Wan Qing si da xiaoshuojia* 晚清四大小說家 (Four great novelists of the late Qing period). Taipei: Shangwu yinshuguan, 1993.

———, ed. *Yuanyang hudie pai yanjiu ziliao* 鴛鴦蝴蝶派研究資料 (Research materials on the butterfly and mandarin duck school). Shanghai: Shanghai wenyi chubanshe, 1962.

Widmer, Ellen, and Kang-i Sun Chang, eds. *Writing Women in Late Imperial China*. Stanford, CA: Stanford University Press, 1997.

Williams, Raymond. *Culture and Society*. New York: Harper and Row, 1958.

———. *Keywords: A Vocabulary of Culture and Society*. New York: Oxford University Press, 1976.

———. *The Long Revolution: An Analysis of the Democratic, Industrial, and Cultural Changes Transforming Our Society*. New York: Columbia University Press, 1961.

Wong, Timothy C. "Notes on the Textual History of *Lao Ts'an yu-chi*." *T'uong Pao* 69.1–3 (1983): 23–32.

Wright, Mary C, ed. *China in Revolution: The First Phase, 1900–1913*. New Haven, CT: Yale University Press, 1968.

———. *The Last Stand of Chinese Conservatism: The T'ung-chih Restoration, 1862–1874*. Stanford, CA: Stanford University Press, 1962.

Wu Fang 吳方. "Liu Shenshu xiansheng xiaozhuan" 劉申叔先生小傳 (Short biography of Mr. Liu Shenshu [Shipei]). In Liu Mengxi, *Zhongguo xiandai xueshu jingdian*, p. 404.

Wu Jianren 吳趼人. *Ershi nian mudu zhi guai xianzhuang* 二十年目睹之怪現狀 (Strange events eyewitnessed in the past twenty years). 1959. Reprint, Beijing: Renmin wenxue chubanshe, 1978.

———. *Henhai* (Sea of regret). In *Wu Jianren quanji*, 5.1–78.

———. *Jianyi waibian* 趼囈外編 (Jianren's somniloquy: The outer chapters). In *Wu Jianren quanji* 8.1–121.

———. "*Jin shinian zhi guai xianzhuang* zixu" 近十年之怪現狀自序 (Author's preface to *Strange Events of the Past Ten Years*). In *Wu Jianren quanji* 3.299–300.

———. *Wo Foshan ren wenji* 我佛山人文集 (Collected writings of "I, a person of Foshan"). Ed. Lu Shudu 盧叔度. 8 vols. Guangzhou: Huacheng chubanshe, 1988.
———. *Wu Jianren ku* 吳趼人哭 (Wu Jianren laments). In *Wu Jianren quanji* 8.227–237.
———. *Wu Jianren quanji* 吳趼人全集 (Complete works of Wu Jianren). Ed. Hai Feng 海風. 8 vols. Harbin: Beifang wenyi chubanshe, 1998.
———. *Xin shitou ji* 新石頭記 (The new story of the Stone). Zhengzhou: Zhongzhou guji chubanshe, 1986.
———. "*Yueyue xiaoshuo* xu" 月月小說序 (Preface to *Monthly Fiction*). In *Wu Jianren quanji* 8.198.
Wu Jingzi 吳敬梓. *Rulin waishi* 儒林外史 (The scholars). 1958. Reprint, Hong Kong: Taiping shuju, 1969.
———. *The Scholars*. Trans. Yang Hsien-yi and Gladys Yang. Beijing: Foreign Languages Press, 1957.
Wu Rulun 吳汝綸. "Da Yan Jidao" 答嚴幾道 (In reply to Yan Jidao [Fu]). In Guo Shaoyu and Wang, *Zhongguo lidai wenlun xuan* 4.150–151.
———. "*Tianyan lun* xu" 天演論序 (Preface to *Evolution and Rthics*). In Guo Shaoyu and Wang, *Zhongguo lidai wenlun xuan* 4.144–148.
Wu Wenqi 吳文祺. *Jin bai nian lai de Zhongguo wenyi sichao* 近百年來的中國文藝思潮 (Trends in Chinese literary thought over the last century). Hong Kong: Longmen shudian, 1969.
Wu Yu 吳虞. "Du Xunzi shu hou" 讀荀子後 (After having read Xunzi). *Xin qingnian* 3.1 (April 1917).
Wue, Roberta. "Making the Artist: Ren Bonian (1840–1895) and Portraits of the Shanghai Art World." PhD diss., Institute of Fine Arts, New York University, 2001.
Xia Xiaohong 夏曉虹. *Wan Qing shehui yu wenhua* 晚清社會與文化 (Late Qing culture and society). Wuhan: Hubei jiaoyu chubanshe, 2000.
Xiao Tong 蕭統. *Zengbu liu chen zhu wenxuan* 增補六臣注文選 (*Wenxuan* with six commentaries and supplements). Taipei: Huazheng shuju, 1974.
Xie Junmei 謝俊美. "*Xing shi congshu* zongshu" 醒獅叢書總述 (General introduction to the *Awakened Lion series*). In Zhang Zhidong, *Quanxue pian*, pp. 1–5.
Xiong Yuezhi 熊月之. "Lishi shang de Shanghai xingxiang sanlun" 歷史上的上海形象散論 (Random remarks on the image of Shanghai in history). *Wenlin* 文林 43.3 (1996): 139–153.
———. "Lue lun wanQing Shanghai xin xing wenhuaren de chansheng yu juhui" 略論晚清上海新型文化人的産生與聚滙 (Notes on the concentration and creation of the new form of cultural figure in late Qing Shanghai). *Jindaishi yanjiu* 近代史研究 4 (1997): 257–272.
———. *Xixue dongjian yu wanqing shehui* 西學東漸與晚清社會 (The movement east of Western learning and late Qing society). Shanghai: Shanghai renmin chubanshe, 1994.

Xu Jilin 許己霖 and Tian Jianye 田建業, eds. *Yixi ji* 一溪集 (One creek collection). Beijing: Sanlian shudian, 1999.

Xu Zhenya 徐枕亞. *Yuli hun* 玉梨魂 (Jade pear spirit). Taipei: Wenhua tushu gongsi, 1991.

Yan Fu 嚴復. "Jiuwang juelun" 救亡決論 (Decisive words on our salvation). In *Yan Fu ji* 1.40–54.

———. "Lun shi bian zhi ji" 論世變之亟 (On the urgency of change in the world). In *Yan Fu ji* 1.1–5.

———. "Pi Han" 辟韓 (Refuting Han [Yu]). In *Yan Fu ji* 1.32–36.

———. "*Tianyan lun* yi liyan" 天演論譯例言 (Introductory remarks to the translation of *Evolution and Ethics*). In *Yan Fu ji* 5.1321–1323.

———. *Yan Fu ji* 嚴復集 (Collected works of Yan Fu). Ed. Wang Shi 王栻. 5 vols. Beijing: Zhonghua shuju, 1986.

———. *Yan Fu shi wen xuan* 嚴復詩文選 (Poetry and prose of Yan Fu). Ed. Zhou Zhenfu 周振甫. Beijing: Renmin wenxue chubanshe, 1959.

———. "Yi *Tianyan lun* zixu" 譯天演論自序 (Preface to the translation of *Evolution and Ethics*). In *Yan Fu ji* 3.1319–1321.

———. "You ru sanbao" 有如三保 (Preserving the triad [of race, nations, and teachings]). In *Yan Fu ji* 1.79–83.

———. "Yu Liang Qichao shu" 與梁啓超書 (Letter to Liang Qichao). In *Yan Fu ji* 3.513–515.

———. "Yu Liang Rengong lun suo yi 'Yuan fu' shu" 與梁任公論所譯原富書 (Letter to Liang Qichao concerning the translation of *The Wealth of Nations*). In *Yan Fu ji* 3.515–518.

———. "Yu *Waijiao bao* zhuren lun jiaoyu shu" 與外交報主人論教育書 (Letter to the proprietors of *Waijiao bao* concerning education). In *Yan Fu ji* 3.557–565.

———. "Yuan qiang" 原強 (On the origins of [national] strength). In *Yan Fu ji* 1.5–32.

———. "*Zhina jiaoan lun* tiyao" 支那教案論 提要 (Summary of *Missionaries in China*). In *Yan fu ji* 1.54–55.

Yan Fu and Xia Zengyou 夏曾佑. "Guowen bao fuyin shuobu yuanqi" 國聞報附印說部緣起 (The reasons behind our decision to publish a fiction supplement). In Guo Shaoyu and Wang, *Zhongguo lidai lunwen xuan* 4.196–205.

Yan Fusun 嚴芙孫. "Haishang shuomeng ren" 海上說夢人. In Wei Shaochang, *Yuanyang hudie*, p. 463.

Yang Nianqun 楊念群. *Ruxue diyuhuade jindai xingtai: San da zhishi qunti hudongde bijiao yanjiu* 儒學地域化的近代形態：三大知識群體互動的比較研究 (The modern form of regional Confucianism: A comparative study of three intellectual groups). Beijing: Sanlian shudian, 1997.

Yang Zhijun 楊志鈞. *Wuxu bianfa shi* 戊戌變法史 (History of the 1898 reform). Beijing: Beijing renmin wenxue chubanshe, 1984.

Yangwu yundong 洋務運動 (The foreign affairs movement). Ed. Zhongguo shixue hui 中國史學會 (Chinese historical association). 8 vols. Shanghai: Shanghai renmin chubanshe, 1961.

Ye Dehui 葉德輝. "*Youxuan jinyu* ping" 輶軒今語 評 (Critique of *Words for the Present from a Light Carriage*). In *Yijiao congbian* 翼教叢編 (Compendium to promote the doctrine), ed. Su Yu 蘇輿, pp. 70–88. 1898. Reprint, Shanghai: Shanghai shudian, 2002.

Yeh, Catherine Vance. "The Life-style of Four *Wenren* in Late Qing Shanghai." *Harvard Journal of Asiatic Studies* 57.2 (December 1997): 419–470.

———. "Zeng Pu's 'Niehai hua' as a Political Novel—A World Genre in Chinese Form." PhD diss., Harvard University, Cambridge, MA, 1990.

Yeh Sheng-tao [Ye Shaojun]. *Schoolmaster Ni Huan-chih*. Trans. A. C. Barnes. Peking: Foreign Languages Press, 1958.

Yeh, Wen-hsin, ed. *Becoming Chinese: Passages to Modernity and Beyond*. Berkeley and Los Angeles: University of California Press, 2000.

Young, Ernest P. "The Hung-hsien [Hongxian] Emperor as a Modernizing Conservative." In Furth, *The Limits of Change,* pp. 171–190.

———. *The Presidency of Yuan Shih-k'ai: Liberalism and Dictatorship in Early Republican China*. Ann Arbor: University of Michigan Press, 1977.

Young, Robert. *White Mythologies*. London and New York: Routledge, 1990.

Yuan Jin 袁進. *Jindai wenxue de tuwei* 近代文學的突破 (The breaking forth of modern literature). Shanghai: Shanghai renmin chubanshe, 2001.

———. "*Minquan su* yanjiu" 民權素 研究 (A study of *Minquan su*). Paper presented at the conference "Subscribing to a New Culture: Chinese Literary Journals of the 1910s," Philipps University, Marburg, Germany, June 19–24, 2001.

———. "Wenhua yu xinli de bianyi" 文化與心理的變異 (Changes in culture and mentality). In Chen Bohai and Yuan, *Shanghai jindai wenxue shi*, pp. 29–58.

———. *Yuanyang hudie pai* 鴛鴦蝴蝶派 (The mandarin duck and butterfly school). Shanghai: Shanghai shudian, 1994.

———. *Zhongguo wenxue guannian de jindai bianghe* 中國文學觀念的近代變革 (The modern transformation of Chinese notions of literature). Shanghai: Shanghai shehui kexueyuan chubanshe, 1996.

Zamperini, Paola. "Fu Caiyun: A Chinese Harlot's Journey in the Sea of Retribution." MA thesis, University of California, Berkeley, 1994.

Zarrow, Peter. *Anarchism and Chinese Political Culture*. New York: Columbia University Press, 1990.

Zeng Mengpu. *See* Zeng Pu.

Zeng Pu 曾樸 (Zeng Mengpu 曾夢樸). *Niehai hua* 孽海華 (Flower in a sea of retribution). Shanghai: Shanghai guji chubanshe, 1980.

———. *Niehai hua*. Taipei: Wenhua tushu gongsi, 1990.

———. "Xiugai hou yao shuo de jiju hua" 修改後要說的幾句話 (A few remarks after having revised), dated 1928. Appended to Zeng Mengpu, *Niehai hua* (1990), pp. 407–411.

———. "Zeng Mengpu xiansheng fu Hu Shizhi xiansheng de xin" 曾孟樸先生復胡適之先生的信 (Mr. Zeng Mengpu's response to Mr. Hu Shizhi's letter). Appended to Zeng Mengpu, *Niehai hua* (1990), pp. 413–423.

Zeng Xubai 曾虛白. "Zeng Mengpu nianpu" 曾孟樸年谱 (Chronological biography of Zeng Mengpu). In Wei Shaochang, *Niehai hua ziliao,* pp. 152–197.

Zhang Bilai 張畢來. "*Niehai hua* de sixiang he yishu" 孽海華的思想和藝術 (The art and thinking in *Flower in a Sea of Retribution*). Appended to Zeng Mengpu, *Niehai hua* (1990), pp. 537–547.

Zhang Binglin 章柄麟 (Taiyan 太炎). "Dongjing liuxuesheng huanying hui yanshuo ci" 東京留學生歡迎會演說詞 (Speech at the welcome meeting of [Chinese] students studying in Tokyo). In Zhang Bingling, *Zhang Taiyan zhenglun* 1.269–280.

———. "Guojia lun" 國家論 (On the nation). In Zhang Bingling, *Zhang Taiyan zhenglun* 1.359–369.

———. "Xu zhongxing" 序種姓 (The origin of caste). In Zhang Binglin, *Zhang Taiyan xuanji,* pp. 194–263.

———. *Zhang Taiyan xuanji* 章太炎選集 (Selected works of Zhang Taiyan). Ed. Zhu Weizheng 朱維錚 and Jiang Yihua 姜義華. Shanghai: Shanghai renmin chubanshe, 1981.

———. *Zhang Taiyan zhenglun xuanji* 章太炎政論選集 (Selected political writings of Zhang Taiyan). Ed. Tang Zhijun 湯志鈞. 2 vols. Beijing: Zhonghua shuju, 1977.

Zhang Yuanji 張元濟. *Zhang Yuanji riji* 張元濟日記 (Diary of Zhang Yuanji). Shijiazhuang: Hebei jiaoyu chubanshe, 2001.

Zhang Zhidong 張之洞. *Quanxue pian* 勸學篇 (Exhortation to learning). Zhengzhou: Zhongzhou guji chubanshe, 1998.

Zhao Jiabi 趙家璧, ed. *Zhongguo xin wenxue daxi* 中國新文學大系 (Compendium of the new Chinese literature). 10 vols. Shanghai: Liangyou tushu gongsi, 1935–1936.

Zhao Jinyu 趙金鈺. "Minbao" 民報. In *Xinhai geming shiqi qikan jieshao* 辛亥革命期刊介紹 (Introduction to the periodicals of the Xinhai [1911] revolution period), ed. Ding Shouhe 丁守和, 1.504–536. Beijing: Renmin chubanshe, 1982.

Zheng Guanying 鄭觀應. "Huaren yi tong xiwen shuo" 華人宜通西文說 (On the theory that Chinese ought to learn Western languages). Appended to "Xixue" 西學 (Western learning), in *Zheng Guanying ji,* p. 284.

———. *Shengshi weiyan* 盛世危言 (Blunt words in a time of prosperity). Ed. Wang Yiliang 王貽梁. Zhengzhou: Zhongzhou guji chubanshe, 1998.

———. "*Shengshi weiyan* zixu" 盛世危言自序 (Personal preface to *Blunt Words in a Time of Prosperity*). In Zheng Guanying, *Shengshi weiyan,* pp. 50–52.

———. *Zheng Guanying ji* 鄭觀應集 (Works of Zheng Guanying). Shanghai: Shanghai renmin chubanshe, 1982.

Zheng Yimei 鄭逸梅. "Huang Moxi" 黃摩西. In Jiang and Cao, *Huang Ren ji*, pp. 372–373.

Zheng Zhenduo 鄭振鐸. "Lin Qinnan xiansheng" 林琴南先生 (Mr. Lin [Shu]). In *Zhongguo wenxue yanjiu* 中文學研究 (Studies of Chinese literature), 3.1214–1229. Hong Kong: Guwen shuju, 1970.

Zhong Birong 鐘碧容. "Huang Yuanyong" 黃遠庸. In *Minguo renwu zhuan* 民國人物傳 (Biographies of Republican figures), ed. Yan Ruping 嚴如平 and Zong Zhiwen 宗志文, 5.282. Beijing: Zhonghua shuju, 1986.

Zhou Wu 周武. *Zhang Yuanji: Shujuan rensheng* 張元濟：書卷人生 (Zhang Yuanji: A life of books). Shanghai: Shanghai jiaoyu chubanshe, 1999.

Zhou Zhenfu 周振甫. *Yan Fu sixiang shuping* 嚴復思想述評 (A critical account of Yan Fu's thought). Kunming: Zhonghua shuju, 1940.

Zhou Zuoren 周作人. "Ren de wenxue" 人的文學 (Humane literature). In Zhao Jiabi, *Zhongguo xin wenxue daxi* 1.219–225.

———. *Zhongguo xin wenxue de yuanliu* 中國新文學的源流 (On the origins of China's new literature). Beijing: Renwen shudian, 1934.

Zhu Shouju. *See* Haishang shuomeng ren; Shouju.

Zhu Weizheng 朱維錚. "*Qingdai xueshu gailun* daodu" 清代學術概論導讀 (Reading *Intellectual Trends in the Qing Period*). In Liang Qichao, *Qingdai xueshu gailun*, pp. 1–43.

———. *Qiusuo zhen wenming: Wan Qing xueshu shi lun* 求索真文明：晚清學術史論 (In search of the true civilization: On the history of late Qing learning). Shanghai: Guji chubanshe, 1996.

Zhuang Zhou 莊周. *Chuang tzu*. Trans. Burton Watson. New York: Columbia University Press, 1968.

———. *Chuang-tzu: The Inner Chapters*. Trans. A. C. Graham. London: George Allen and Unwin, 1981.

Zuo zhuan 左傳 (Zuo commentary). In *The Ch'un ts'ew with the Tso chuen*, vol. 5 of *The Chinese Classics*, trans. James Legge. 1872. Reprint, Taipei: Wenxing shudian, 1966.

Index

Adorno, Theodor, 123, 173, 203
Allen, Young J. (Lin Lezhi), 77–78, 95
Analects, 51
Anderson, Marston, 259, 261
anxiety, discourse of, 2, 8, 10, 13, 19, 28, 44, 55, 174, 214, 271; defined, 58

baihua (the vernacular language), 92, 227, 317 n. 52, 318 n. 57
Bellamy, Edward, *Looking Backward,* 107, 151
Benjamin, Walter, 261
Bentham, Jeremy, 223
Bergère, Marie-Claire, 75, 230
Berman, Marshall, 11–12
Bhabha, Homi, 17, 247–248
bi (plain style), 87, 89
bildungsroman, 131–132
Bismarck, Otto von, 38
Bland, J. O. P., 61–62
Bonner, Joey, 98
Boxer Rebellion, 2, 130, 153, 160, 165, 175, 200, 214, 284 n. 25, 304 n. 53
boycott of American goods, 129, 159
Brooks, Peter, 252, 261–262, 268
Buddhist canon, translation of, 83
Buddhist ideas, 256–257, 260
Buddhist terminology, 113–114

Bungaku, 78
Butler, Judith, 17

Cai Yuanpei, 59, 88
Caifeng bao, 126
Cao Xueqin: *Hong lou meng* (Dream of the red chamber), 97, 110; *Shitou ji* (Story of the Stone), 63, 97–98, 102, 110, 111, 133, 137, 151–152, 156–157, 165, 170, 244
Central China Post, 129
Chang, Eileen (Zhang Ailing), 233
Chang, Hao, 113–114
Changes (Yijing), 57
Chatterjee, Partha, 16, 23, 63, 164, 178, 193–194
Chen Chi, 35–37, 49, 197
Chen Diexian, 260
Chen Duxiu, 14, 207, 209–212, 218–220, 223–227, 232, 250, 258–259; "1916," 219–220; "Dong-xi minzu genben sixiang zhi chayi," 210; "Falanxi ren yu jinshi wenming," 209–210
Chen Jitong, 174
Chen Li, 35
Chen Qianqiu, 95
China Merchants' Steam Navigation, 162

China/West binary, 18, 68, 209–210, 216–222, 226–227, 264, 314 n. 18; spirit vs. materialism, 177–178, 213, 221–222, 310 n. 15
Chinese exclusion acts, 129, 156
Chinese Recorder, 106
Chinnery, J. D., 271
Chubao, 129, 159
Church Missionary Society (CMS), 103–105
Ci Jiwei, 1
Cian, 29
Cixi, 29–30, 34, 284 n. 25
Cizhang (belles letters), 94
Coetzee, J. M., 268
Cohen, Paul, 2, 24
"colonial subject," 176, 248
Commercial Press, 210, 229, 250, 318 n. 57
Confucian classics, 183
Confucian propriety, 200, 313 n. 64
Confucianism, 50, 53, 55, 64, 132, 136, 143–144, 152, 196, 217, 289 n. 22
Confucius, 57, 88, 244
Conrad, Joseph, 261–262, 266, 271
Cultural Revolution, 77, 227, 277–278

dao, 82, 83, 90; vs. *qi*, 36–37, 197, 285–286 n. 42
Daoism, 55
Daoxue, 132, 134
Darwin, Charles, 69, 70
Darwinism, social, 67–68, 71, 115, 193
de Lacouperie, Terrien, 28, 41
de Man, Paul, 268–269
Deng Shi, 89
Di Baoxian, 115
Dickens, Charles, 71, 86
Dickinson, G. Lowes, 19–20
Ding Weizhi and Chen Song, 35
Dongfang zazhi, 66, 210–211, 213–214, 216–217, 218–219, 222–224, 227, 250, 318 n. 57

Dostoyevsky, Fyodor, 268
Dream of the Red Chamber. *See* Cao Xueqin
Du Yaquan, 14, 35, 216–227, 250, 318 n. 57; "Jingde wenming yu dongde wenming," 217–219; "Zhanhou dongxi wenming zhi tiaohe," 220–221
Duan Fang, 89
Duan Yucai, 94
Duara, Prasenjit, 6, 9, 11

Edkins, Joseph, 28
Elvin, Mark, 230
"examination style" prose, 37, 39, 83, 94, 96, 119, 134, 296 n. 61

Fan Boqun, 231
Fang Dongshu, 27
Feng Guifen, 28–29, 35
first-person narration, 131, 301 n. 17
Foshan shuyuan, 125
Fryer, John (Fu Lanya), 14, 103–108, 111, 125–126
Fu Lin, 260
Fu Sinian, 68, 71
Fugu (restoring tradition), 214
Fuzhou Shipyard School of Navigation, 46, 174

Gandhi, 177
Gao Qi, 135
Gezhi, 127, 222
Gezhi huibian, 105
Gezhi shuyuan, 105
Gimpel, Denise, 152
Gogol, Nikolai, 273
Gong Chen, 197
Gong Zizhen, 197
gong/si binary, 49–52, 240, 276, 288 n. 21, 289 n. 25
Goodman, Bryna, 243
guanchang (the official realm), 154

Guangxue hui, 77
Guangzhi book company, 130
Gujing jingshe Academy, 27
Guo Songtao, 33
Guocui xuebao, 89
Guomindang, 245
Guowen bao, 63, 108
guwen (archaic prose), 79, 82, 84, 85–87, 90–91, 94, 117

Han Banqing, 240
Hankou ribao, 128
Hanlin Academy, 34
Hao, Yen-p'ing, 191–192
Hardt, Michael, and Antonio Negri, *Empire,* 248
Hawks Pott, F. L., *Short History of Shanghai,* 159
He Jingming, 156
He Zhen (Ban), 88
Hegel, G. W. F., 6, 14–15, 61; on Asia, 14, 60
Hershatter, Gail, 238
Hong Jun (Wenqing), 44, 178
Hong lou meng. See Cao Xueqin
House of Mirth, The, 249
Hsia, Tsi-an, 263
Hsu Tao-ching, 236
Hu bao, 105
Hu Shi, 68, 94, 96, 116
Hu Ying, 193
Hua Hengfang, 84–85
Huang Jie, 89
Huang Ren, 91, 118, 127
Huang Yuanyong (Yuansheng), 211–219, 224, 226
Huang Zunxian, 35, 101–102
"Hundred Days Reform" of 1898, 130, 175, 214
Huxley, Thomas Henry, 57, 68–69, 70, 71, 83, 115; *Evolution and Ethics,* 82
Hybridity, 8, 71, 93, 131, 165, 206, 216, 250

Ibsen, Henrik, 255, 257
imperialism, 13, 59–60
India, 60–62, 164, 176–177
Irigaragy, Luce, 16–17

Jameson, Frederic, 16, 273
Japan, as model, 18–19
Jesuits, 25
Jiang Biao, 35
Jiangnan Arsenal (Jiangnan zhizaoju), 84, 95, 105, 125–126, 183, 245, 311 n. 25
Jin Ping Mei (The golden lotus), 180
Jin Songcen, 43
jindai (period), 3, 8, 11, 253, 278
Jingbao, 162
Jingzhong ribao, 88

Kang Youwei, 37–38, 78, 94, 107, 109–110, 112, 124
Kangxi Emperor, 25–26
Kantian aesthetics, 97–98
Kao, Karl, 262
Kierkegaard, Søren, 255

learning, Western *(xixue),* 34, 37, 44–46, 57, 178–183; vs. domestic, 23, 179, 186
Lee, Leo, 120
Levenson, Joseph, viii, 4, 10–11, 58–59, 66, 70–71, 277
Li Baojia (Boyuan), 126, 174, 191, 204, 229
Li Hongzhang, 30, 105
Li Shanlan, 28
Li Shizhen, 271
Li Shuchang, 44
Li Xiang, 87
Li Yu, 100
Liang Qichao, 35, 74, 174, 205, 207; on Chinese spirituality vs. Western materialism, 8, 177, 214, 221; on *gong/si* binary, 51–52, 191,

Liang Qichao *(continued)*
243; "Lun xiaoshuo yu qunzhi zhi guanxi," 112–114; and nationalism, 62; "New Prose Style" of, 81, 93–97, 112; on the novel, 107–115, 119, 123, 137–138, 149, 153, 250, 254, 260, 277; revolution in the realm of fiction, 103; revolution in the realm of poetry, 101; "Sanshi zishu," 90, 94; "Xin min shuo," 51–52, 62, 114, 240; *Xin Zhongguo weilai ji,* 107, 114, 169; and Yan Fu, 47, 67–68, 71

Liang Shuming, 8, 213, 222

Lin Shu, 71, 85–87

Lin Yu-sheng, 181, 206, 259; "Totalistic iconoclasm," 55, 206

Link, Perry, 229

Liu E, *Lao Can youji* (The travels of Lao Can), 1–2, 50, 147, 174, 204, 229

Liu, Lydia, 11

Liu Shipei, 41, 88–93, 96–97, 116, 117–119, 193, 205; *Lunwen zaji,* 92–93

Liu Xihong, 33

London Times, 64

Lu Hanchao, 238

Lu Jiuyuan, 95

Lu Runxiang, 197

Lu Xun, 17, 18, 19, 35, 43–44, 53, 67, 81, 229–230, 276–277; "Guxiang" (My old home), 263, 267–268, 271, 277; "Kuangren riji" (Diary of a madman), 171, 185, 264–265, 271–274, 276–277; on the late Qing novel, 136–137, 149–150; "Moluo shili shuo" (On the power of Mara poetry), 254–255; *Nahan* (Call to arms), 255, 259, 302 n. 32; *Panghuang* (Hesitation), 261; "Shangshi" (Regret for the past), 263; "Wenhua pianzhi lun" (On cultural extremes), 255–258, 263, 265, 299 n. 57; "Zai jiulou shang" (In the wineshop), 265, 270–271; "Zhufu" (The new year's sacrifice), 261, 265–266, 313 n. 64

Lukács, Georg, 123, 268–269

Ma Jianzhong, 44

"Mandarin ducks and butterflies," 229

Mao Dun, 222, 253

Mao Zedong, 2, 31, 111

Martin, W. A. P. (Ding Weiliang), 1, 61–62, 104

Marx, Karl, 60, 229

Marxism, 277–278

May Fourth discourse, 103, 232–233

May Fourth generation, 67–68

May Fourth movement (period), vii, 3, 4, 7, 8, 82, 207, 258, 264

McDougall, Bonnie, viii, 20

Mei Gucheng, 25–26

Mencius, 51

Meng Yue, 247

Michie, Alexander, 64

Mill, John Stuart, 70, 223

Millard, Thomas, 151

Min Tu-ki, 203

Minbao, 88, 256

Minquan bao, 204

modernity, vii, 4, 5, 11–12, 13, 127, 164, 170, 173, 176–177, 194, 213–214, 264, 269, 274

modernization, 3, 5, 15, 19, 102, 176, 183, 248, 269

Montesquieu, 61, 68, 70

Moretti, Franco, 16

Mori Arinori, 77

Munz, Peter, 62

Naipaul, V. S., 43–44, 60, 269–271

Nandy, Ashis, 23

Nanfang bao, 129, 159

Nanshe, 118, 205

Nanyang gongxue, 64
Nathan, Andrew, 120
national essence *(guocui)*, 78–79, 89
nationalism, 8, 10–11, 14, 45, 62, 177, 264, 276; vs. culturalism, 4, 17–19, 314–315 n. 18; and literature, 15–16; paradox of, 15–16, 163
"neocolonial," 3
New Culture movement, 8, 9, 11, 68, 213, 222, 227, 232
New Literature, viii, 260
New Novel, 101, 103, 112–118, 124, 129, 132, 204, 205, 232
"new" vs. "old," 208–209, 214–216
Nietzsche, 98, 255
North China Daily News, 64, 284 n. 23, 291 n. 59
North China Herald, 104, 284 n. 23, 291 n. 59

Occidentalism, 13–14
Opium War (first), 3
Opium War, second, 24, 27, 198
Orientalism, 14
Ouyang Jian, 112

Peking University (Beijing daxue), 20, 59, 68, 89, 207
pianti (parallel prose), 90, 205
"postcolonial," 17, 248
Pusey, James, 69

Qian Jibo, 94
Qian Zhixiu, 65–66, 222–223, 226, 230
Qian Zhongshu, 71
Qiu Tingliang, 102
Qixin bao, 126
Qu Qiubai, 111, 228
Qu Yuan, 254

Ramakrisna, 193
Readings, Bill, 15

Ren Tingxu, 77–78
renge (human character), 215, 218
renyu (human desire), 217–218
Reynolds, Douglas, 5, 18
Ricci, Matteo, 25
Richard, Timothy (Li Timotai), 95, 107
Ruan Lingyu, 231
Ruan Yuan, 26–27, 35, 81, 87–88, 90, 94
Rulin waishi. See Wu Jingzi

Sai Jinhua, 174, 178, 200
Saint-Simon, 192–193
Sakai, Naoki, 3, 40–41, 258
Schneider, Laurence, 78
Scholars, The. See Wu Jingzi
Schopenhauer, Arthur, 97–98
Schwartz, Benjamin, viii, 4, 5, 65–66, 69–71
science, 56–57, 66, 182–183, 213
scientific education, 216
"semicolonial," 2, 3, 14, 17, 164
Shanghai: courtesans, 238; foreign settlement and Chinese city compared, 244–245, 247; newspapers, 126, 129, 206; public space in, 128; public vs. private, 233–240; publishing, 88, 100–101, 112, 124, 153, 174, 207; *shikumen* townhouse, 238–241; *xiaoshimin,* 239; *Yuyuan,* 246; *Zhang yuan* (Zhang garden), 128, 244
Shanghai Translation Bureau (Shanghai fanyi guan), 181
Shanghai xin bao, 104–105
Shanshu, 137
Shen bao, 105, 211, 244–245
Shen Fu, 131
Shibao, 115
Shijie shuju, 232
Shitou ji. See Cao Xueqin

Shuihu zhuan (The water margin), 86, 110, 180
Siku quanshu zongmu tiyao, 26
Sima Qian, *Shiji,* 57, 60, 83, 86, 94
Sino-Japanese War, 24, 46–47, 174, 275
Sister Carrie, 249
sixiang (thought, ideology), 211, 213, 214
Smith, Adam, 47
Soochow University (Dongwu daxue), 118
Spencer, Herbert, 65, 69–71, 76
Story of the Stone, The. See Cao Xueqin
Su Shi, 134, 156
Subao, 75
subjectivity, 255, 258
Sun Lung-kee, 255
Sun Yat-sen, 88–89, 205

Tagore, Rabindranath, 177
Tan Sitong, 90–91, 107
Tang Caichang, 35
Tang Zhen, 35, 39
Tang Zhenchang, 211
Tao Zengyou, 117–118
teleology, Hegelian, 5, 6, 7, 8, 11, 14–15
ti/yong, 4, 49, 120, 128, 167, 177, 285 n. 42, 287 nn. 13, 14
Tianxia, 51, 57, 166, 314 n. 18
Tianyi bao, 88
Tongcheng school, 27, 68, 80–82, 85, 87, 90, 91, 93, 96
Tongmeng hui, 88–89, 205
Tongwen guan, 30, 46, 52, 61, 103–104, 181, 308 n. 2
Tongzhi Restoration, 125
traditional/modern binary, 3, 5

Übermensch (chaoren), 257
universality, 40–41, 45, 59, 175, 177, 206, 216

utilitarianism, 65–66, 120, 222–227, 230, 255, 299 n. 57

Waldersee, Count, 200
Wang Anyi, 233
Wang Dungen, 232
Wang Guowei, 81, 97–99
Wang Hui, 54–55, 66–67, 173, 181, 255–256, 278
Wang Kaiyun, 35
Wang Niansun, 94
Wang Shuo, 252
Wang Shuqian, 208–211
Wang Tao, 29, 35, 44, 285 n. 37
Wang Xiaoming, 20, 224–225, 272
Wang Yangming, 95
Wang Yuanhua, 227
Wang Zhichun, 35, 37
Wang, David Der-wei, 4, 170, 280 n. 15
Wanguo gongbao, 77, 105–106, 107
"wealth and power" *(fuguo qiangbing),* 63, 222
wen (writing), 78–80, 84, 87–90, 97, 115
wen yi zai dao, 96, 134
wenhua ren, 153, 160, 307 n. 28
wenming ("civilization," "civilized"), 167, 210, 214, 217–218, 307 n. 28
wenren, 117, 134–135, 153–156, 159–160
Wenxuan school, 87, 91, 93, 96, 205
wenxue (defined), 76–80, 87, 91, 109, 294 n. 14
wenzhang (literature), 97
Westernization, wholesale, 55, 63
Williams, Raymond, 15, 74, 90, 203
Wo Ren, 31–32, 34, 52–53, 100
women's education, 179–180, 310 n. 21
Wright, Mary, 1, 4, 5, 126
Wu Jianren, 174–175, 204, 229, 233, 243, 253; *Ershi nian mudu zhi guai xianzhuang* (Strange events), 151–

156, 160, 165, 166, 171, 187, 191, 198, 240; *Henhai* (Sea of regret), 130, 157, 307 n. 45; *Jianyi waibian* (Jianren's somniloquy: The outer chapters), 126–127; on the novel, 115, 123, 127–128; on Shanghai, 128, 131, 153–165, 171, 230; *Wu Jianren ku* (Wu Jianren laments), 128; *Xin shitou ji* (New story of the Stone), 63, 107, 129, 214, 230
Wu Jingzi, *Rulin waishi* (The scholars), 102, 133–135, 136, 155–156, 191, 240
Wu Rulun, 82–85, 98
Wu Xinshe, 124–125
Wu Yunji, 125
Wue, Roberta, 234

Xia Xiaohong, 113
Xia Zengyou, 63, 108–109, 111, 116
xiaoshuo, viii, 80, 87, 180, 205; *qianze xiaoshuo* (novel of censure), 136; *shehui xiaoshuo* (social novel), 124, 240
Xiaoshuo lin, 118, 174
Xiaoxian bao, 126
Xie Junmei, 7, 10
Xin qingnian (Qingnian zazhi), 14, 20, 207, 210, 212, 214, 218–219, 223–226, 230, 232, 252, 258–259, 271, 314 n. 13, 315 n. 24
Xin Shenbao, 232
Xin xiaoshuo, 112, 114, 115, 118, 129, 156, 160
Xinmin tushuguan, 232
Xinwen bao, 161
Xiong Yuezhi, 41
Xiuxiang xiaoshuo, 156
Xu Guangping, 262
Xu Jiyu, *Yinghuan zhilue*, 95
Xu Renzhu, 39
Xu Xilin, 271
Xu Zhenya, 204

Xue Fucheng, 35
Xuehai tang Academy, 27, 94–95
Xunzi, 69, 70, 212, 316 n. 30

Yan Fu, 6–7, 12, 19, 74, 76, 78, 95, 98, 176–177, 193, 205, 253, 258; awareness of Western judgment, 63–64; on east/west binary, 48–59, 71–72, 206–207, 209, 276; on fiction, 103, 108–109, 116; on *gong/si* binary, 49–52, 191, 243; "Jiuwang juelun," 47–48, 55–56; and liberalism, 13, 65–66; and Lu Xun, 67, 276; "Lun shibian zhiji," 47–50, 53–54, 59–60, 72; and national identity, 35, 48–49, 54–55, 57–60, 63, 119–120, 264; "Pi Han," 47; and prose style, 68, 82–85, 93; and science (*gezhi*), 53, 56, 66–67; on *ti/yong*, 287 n. 14; on translation, 60, 82–83; translation of T. H. Huxley, 57, 115; on Yangwu ideology, 39, 42, 48, 53–54, 56, 58, 72; "Yuan qiang," 47–48, 50–51, 63–64, 69
Yang Nianqun, 8–9, 10
Yang Tingxi, 32–33
Yang Xiong, 83
Yangwu movement, 6–7, 37, 40–41, 53, 57, 175, 206–207; ideology of, 6, 24–25, 34–35, 41, 44–45, 48, 56, 58, 72, 108
Yao Nai, 81, 85, 94
Ye Dehui, 35
Ye Shaojun, 204
Yipin xiang, 44
Yixin (Prince Gong), 29–35, 52
Young, Ernest, 204
Youxi bao, 126
Yu Yue, 35
Yuan Jin, 101, 106
Yuan Shikai, 205–208, 211, 242, 245, 282 n. 49

Yueyue xiaoshuo, 129–130
Yuyan bao, 126, 128

Zeng Guofan, 79, 84, 105
Zeng Pu, 43, 204, 229
Zeno's Racecourse, 5
Zhang Binglin (Taiyan), 41, 75–76, 81, 88, 97, 118, 174, 193, 256–257, 258
Zhang Junmai, 68–69, 71
Zhang Yuanji, 64
Zhang Zhidong, 18, 25, 49
Zhang Zhizhao, 68

Zheng Guanying, 35–40, 125, 127, 180–183; on *ti/yong,* 288 n. 14
Zhibao, 47–48
Zhou Dunyi, 96, 134
Zhou Guisheng, 129–130, 137
Zhou Shoujuan, 232
Zhou Zhenfu, 47, 69, 71, 72
Zhu Xi, 96
Zhuangyuan, 44, 179, 186–187, 197
Zhuangzi, 214
Zongli yamen, 30–33, 173
Zuo Zongtang, 30

About the Author

THEODORE HUTERS is professor of Chinese in the Department of Asian Languages and Cultures at UCLA. Interested primarily in the literary and intellectual history of late nineteenth and early twentieth century China, he has written and edited a number of books and articles on literary and intellectual figures and trends from this period. His books include *Qian Zhongshu* (1982), *Reading the Modern Chinese Short Story* (1990), and *Culture and State in Chinese History* (1997). In 2004–2005 he served as Study Center Director of the University of California Education Abroad Program in Beijing.

Production Notes for Huters/*Bringing the World Home*
Cover design by Santos Barbasa Jr.
Text design and composition by Tseng Information Systems, Inc. using BiotT display type and ITC New Baskerville text type
Printed by The Maple-Vail Book Manufacturing Group
Printed on 60# Sebago Eggshell, 420 ppi

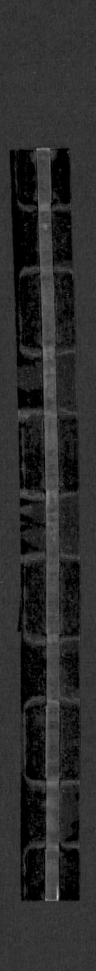